Odd
Men
Out

To Daniel
with best
regards
from
John-Pierre

Odd Men Out

MALE HOMOSEXUALITY IN BRITAIN
FROM WOLFENDEN TO GAY LIBERATION,
1954-1970

JOHN-PIERRE JOYCE

The Book Guild Ltd

First published in Great Britain in 2019 by
The Book Guild Ltd
9 Priory Business Park
Wistow Road, Kibworth
Leicestershire, LE8 0RX
Freephone: 0800 999 2982
www.bookguild.co.uk
Email: info@bookguild.co.uk
Twitter: @bookguild

Copyright © 2019 John-Pierre Joyce

The right of John-Pierre Joyce to be identified as the author of this
work has been asserted by him in accordance with the
Copyright, Design and Patents Act 1988.

All rights reserved. No part of this publication may be
reproduced, transmitted, or stored in a retrieval system, in any form or by any means,
without permission in writing from the publisher, nor be otherwise circulated in
any form of binding or cover other than that in which it is published and without
a similar condition being imposed on the subsequent purchaser.

Typeset in 12pt Adobe Garamond Pro

Printed on FSC accredited paper
Printed and bound in Great Britain by 4edge Limited

ISBN 978 1912881 673

British Library Cataloguing in Publication Data.
A catalogue record for this book is available from the British Library.

For Dad, Johnnie and Paola

Contents

INTRODUCTION

In the days of single and LP records, when an electric turntable and diamond-sharp needle could produce a resonant quality of sound unsurpassed today, my parents would occasionally unsleeve, dust and play a vinyl disc, reminiscing about 'the good old days' of the 1960s, when music (Beatles, Stones, Dusty etc.) was 'proper music' and life really was good. I was born in late 1969 – at the very end of the decade and too late to have experienced it. But sometimes, if I tried hard enough, I could almost feel a time glimpsed in family photos and in the shaky cinefilms my parents reeled out from time to time. Many years later, when considering issues of sex, sexuality and the place of homosexual men in history, my thoughts turned back to that period, and the question formed in my mind: What was it like for gay men in the so-called "swinging 60s"? Of course, I knew and had read about the 1957 Wolfenden Report and the 1967 Sexual Offences Act. But there was scant information about ordinary gay men's lives in between and beyond those dates. The years 1957 to 1970 were largely glossed over as a time of slow but inevitable legal change, accompanied by a gradual tolerance of and freedom for gay men. Despite a crop of books on gay history published in the 1990s and early 2000s, there was a dearth of recent publications on the subject, except for a few narrowly focused, theory-driven academic studies. This prompted me to find out more about the British gay male experience in the late 1950s and 1960s.

Odd Men Out covers the years 1954 to 1970, from the circumstances leading up to the publication of the Wolfenden Report in 1957 to the years immediately following the 1967 Sexual Offences Act. The book is a chronological narrative, with individual chapters focusing on particular themes. Chapter 1 reveals something of the lives of gay men in the early to mid-1950s through the eyes of contemporary observers, including Wolfenden Committee members and witnesses. Chapter 2 delves deep into the Wolfenden Report, analysing its main recommendations and casting a critical eye over some of its lesser-known points. Chapter 3 looks at the medical treatments meted out to gay men in the 1950s and 1960s. Chapter 4 examines the everyday lives of gay men in the early to mid-1960s. Chapter 5 pays attention to representations of gay men on radio and television, and in films, literature, the theatre and the press. Chapter 6 traces the homosexual law reform process from 1960 to 1967 and the corresponding shift in public attitudes towards gay men. Chapter 7 takes the story forward to 1970, examining the failings of the 1967 Act and asking to what extent gay men's lives had improved.

There are no new interpretations of the past. But there are some interesting discoveries. The first ever mention of the word 'homosexuality' in the broadcast media, for example, was not, as some historians have claimed, on BBC Radio's *Woman's Hour* in 1955 but on *Behind the News* in 1953. Far from being hostile towards homosexual law reform, the British establishment was surprisingly favourable towards it, at least until the liberal window of opportunity was slammed shut by the exigencies of party politics. The Lord Chamberlain's lifting of the ban on depictions of homosexuality on stage in 1958 was not prompted by the Wolfenden Report. Rather, a change in the rules had already been under consideration and was finally hastened by the dilemma of what to do about drag queens in a comic revue called *We're No Ladies*. An in-depth analysis of medical cures for homosexuality reveals that hundreds of men were the victims of appalling treatments which doctors knew were ineffective and, in some cases, lethal. This remains a scandal that has never been fully acknowledged or investigated. A close examination of public attitudes shows that beyond opinion polls and surveys (never reliable indicators of people's true thoughts and beliefs anyway), the British public did not have a problem with homosexuality. Women and the young in particular expressed sympathetic *laissez faire* views on the subject, particularly after the *annus mutabilis* of 1963. The Sexual Offences Act, far from being a landmark of permissive legislation, was rather a grudging and anachronistic tidying up of the legal anomalies highlighted by the Wolfenden Report. Instead of freeing up gay men's lives, it opened the door to a new era of oppression, injustice and hostility.

Odd Men Out is about male homosexuality. The history of gay women is not explored. This was a deliberate decision on my part, due to reasons of time and capacity. I was unable to undertake the research and the writing of both male and female homosexuality. The male experience was also markedly different to that of the female. Lesbian behaviour, for example, was never specifically outlawed by the state. Gay women, of course, had their own issues to deal with, and theirs is a history that deserves to be told. But not by me.

As the title indicates, the book covers 'Britain'. From the outset, I was conscious of the London-centric nature of many gay histories – inevitable, given the large volume of records and documentary evidence available in the capital. To redress the balance I have tried to include information about people and places in other parts of England, Scotland and Wales. Northern Ireland is not well represented in gay history archives. So instead of forcing tokenistic references to that part of the United Kingdom, I have left it out. Like the women's history, the experiences of gay men in Northern Ireland deserve to be told. But again, I must leave that to others.

Odd Men Out does not conform to a particular historical theory. It simply sets out the facts without a pre-determined agenda or judgements. I would like readers to make up their own minds about what to think and how to react. Along the way, I hope they will encounter moments of humour and compassion, as well as shock and even outrage. I have tried to preserve the voices of a generation of gay men and others who are beginning to disappear from our lives and our collective memory.

Keeping a record of their words and deeds is vital in order to educate younger generations, who are often woefully ignorant of the not-so-very-distant past. They need to know their history if they are to preserve their liberty and guard against old and new forms of prejudice, discrimination and persecution. It was Antony Grey, the long-serving secretary of the Homosexual Law Reform Society, who pointed out in 2008 (at about the time I started my research): 'I think it's very important that people should remember how it was and how it could be again in the future, because I think things can go backwards as well as forward. The price of liberty is eternal vigilance.'*

---

* *The BBC and the Closet*, BBC Radio 4, 29 January 2008

NOTE ON LANGUAGE

Odd Men Out does not align itself with models of 'queer theory'. Nor does it seek to form part of current discourses on lesbian, gay, bisexual, transgender and queer/questioning plus (LGBTQ+) rights. I have therefore eschewed use of the word 'queer' to denote homosexual men. During the period with which *Odd Men Out* is concerned the word was (and still is to many) a form of insult and abuse rather than a badge of identity, difference and pride. I only use it in direct quotations from contemporary historical sources. The word 'gay', on the other hand, was used by homosexual men to refer to themselves from at least the mid-1950s,* although it was not well known among the general public or referred to in the media until the mid-1960s. I have therefore chosen to use the word 'homosexual' in chapters one, two and three, and 'gay' in chapters four, five, six and seven.

---

* See Rupert Croft-Cooke, *The Verdict of You All*, Secker & Warburg, 1955; Donald West, *Homosexuality*, Duckworth, 1955; Peter Wildeblood, *Against the Law*, Weidenfeld & Nicolson, 1955

If we try to imagine what it would be like for a midget to be regarded as a criminal we can form some idea of the appalling strain to which so many homosexuals are subjected.

Eustace Chesser,
Odd Man Out: Homosexuality in Men and Women, Gollancz, 1959

'I'm a born odd man out Farr, but I've never corrupted the normal.'
Victim, Allied Film Makers, 1960

'We shall always, I fear, resent the odd man out. That is their burden for all time, and they must shoulder it like men – for men they are.'
Lord Arran, House of Lords, 21 July 1967

Chapter 1

HUNTLEYS

Most ordinary people had never heard of homosexuality; and of those who had, the great majority regarded it with something nearer to disgust than to understanding.

Turning Points: The Memoirs of Lord Wolfenden [1]

When the Home Office and Scottish Home Office Departmental Committee on Homosexual Offences and Prostitution sat down on 15 September 1954 to consider 'the law and practice relating to homosexual offences and the treatment of persons convicted of such offences' it was, quite literally, lost for words. As the committee's chairman John Wolfenden later pointed out, the word 'homosexual' either had no meaning to most people or else evoked feelings of horror and revulsion. In order to spare the supposed embarrassment of the committee's secretaries, Wolfenden even suggested adopting the terms 'Huntleys' and 'Palmers' to refer to the homosexuals and prostitutes of the committee's joint enquiry[*2] – after the biscuit manufacturer in Reading, where he was university vice-chancellor.

Part Two[**] of the Wolfenden Committee's final report had little to say about homosexual men as individuals. This was due to the committee's

---

[*]   The committee also examined 'the law and practice relating to offences against the criminal law in connection with prostitution and solicitation for immoral purposes'.

[**] Part One was a general introduction. Part Two dealt with homosexual offences. Part Three dealt with prostitution.

specific remit to only examine the operation of the law against them and to suggest any legislative changes they thought necessary. But after 62 days of meetings, 32 days spent interviewing 31 witnesses, the assessment of evidence from 35 professional and public bodies and six government departments and the examination of memoranda from 11 other organisations and 18 individuals, the committee learned much about the lives of male homosexuals in Britain.

They began their investigation with a 'dictionary definition' of homosexuality as 'a sexual propensity for persons of one's own sex'. It was, the committee said, a 'state' or 'condition' that could not, in of itself, be criminal. When considering how best to define a homosexual man, they decided to adopt the seven-point 'heterosexual-homosexual rating scale' devised by sexologist and biologist Alfred Kinsey in the United States in the 1940s: [3]

0. Exclusively heterosexual
1. Predominantly heterosexual, only incidentally homosexual
2. Predominantly heterosexual, but more than incidentally homosexual
3. Equally heterosexual and homosexual
4. Predominantly homosexual, but more than incidentally heterosexual
5. Predominantly homosexual, but incidentally heterosexual
6. Exclusively homosexual. [4,5]

Kinsey himself met some of the committee members during a trip to London in October 1955, and his rating scale continued to be used as a measure of homosexuality until at least the late 1960s.

Other doctors went further in their definitions of homosexual men. The psychiatrist Peter Scott sent a memorandum to the Wolfenden Committee in which he listed five specific 'groups' he had observed in hospitals, prisons and remand homes:

1. 'Adolescents and mentally immature adults' who were 'uncomfortably aware of their attraction to both sexes' but did not know 'how to resolve their quandary'
2. 'Severely damaged personalities' (such as 'the very effeminate, self-advertising, female-impersonating individual who talks in an affected manner, walks with a mincing gait [and] wears make-up and frilly underclothes'), 'inadequate, downtrodden, dull' personalities and 'deeply resentful, antisocially inclined' individuals
3. 'Relatively intact personalities' who were content with their sexuality and had adjusted to it. These included 'youths who have digested scruples and are living pleasurably, often under the patronage of older homosexuals of the same sort'.
4. 'Latent and well-compensated homosexuals' who were either unaware of their homosexuality or had suppressed it. They were often 'men of considerable strength of character' who might also be 'intelligent, perhaps married with healthy children'.
5. Homosexual men with a 'serious mental disability', including 'organic brain damage and the extremes of personality defects'. [6]

In April 1954 the family doctors' journal *The Practitioner* issued its own guide. C.G. Learoyd divided homosexual men into three types:

1. 'Puppy prurients', who were in an 'adolescent, exploratory phase'
2. 'Emotionally immature' men 'on the fringes', who were living 'some strange fantasy life of their own' caused by 'an inability to develop emotionally beyond the adolescent'. For them, homosexuality was 'an addiction'. Because of 'lack of mental control', they might also exhibit 'other sexual abnormalities', such as masochism, sadism, exhibitionism, transvestism and all the doglike interests in excretion and excretory products'.
3. 'Regressors' – men 'of weak will', who may have had homosexual experiences in their youth and occasionally returned to them after drinking 'too much alcohol'. Senility was also a 'cause of

regression', particularly when 'accompanied by the unremitting sexual desire from an enlarged prostate'. [7]

In the same journal, psychiatrist W. Lindesay Neustatter wrote that homosexual men were either bisexuals or 'complete inverts who have never had any normal impulses'. He pointed out that 'the most masculine-looking men' could be homosexual, although 'the "nancy-boy" type' was also common. He also noted that homosexual men were 'unable to whistle, and have a strong preference for the colour green – a favourite colour in children'. [8]

The British Medical Association submitted evidence to the Wolfenden Committee in which it claimed that some homosexual men had 'a tendency to self-display in dress and hair styles and in the use of scent and make-up'. In 'effeminate' types there was a 'certain softness which is difficult to describe but easy to sense. The voice may be high-pitched and facial hair scanty'. Others, the BMA added, were 'virile and masculine'. Homosexual men were also 'often charming and friendly people' and 'well known to be of artistic temperament'. [9]

Some doctors believed that homosexuality could be scientifically diagnosed. T.G. Grygier, a psychologist at Banstead Hospital in Surrey, claimed that psychometric testing could be used to tell homosexual men apart from other patients. In a paper published in *The Journal of Mental Science* in July 1957 he compared various methods for 'measuring the psychological characteristics of the homosexual and the direction and intensity of his impulses'. These included the 'selective vocabulary test', in which patients were asked to define a list of words. Homosexual men, Grygier noted, tended to use words less familiar to 'normal' men and more commonly used by women. In the 'Szondi test' photographs of 'a homosexual, a sadist, an epileptic, a hysteric, a catatonic schizophrenic, a paranoid schizophrenic, a manic-depressive depressive and a manic-depressive manic' were shown to patients, who then had to choose the images they liked and disliked the most. In the 'thematic apperception test' homosexuality could be detected from the stories patients made up using a series of pictures. The 'Rorschach' and 'draw-a-person' tests were, Grygier thought, the most useful in diagnosing homosexuality. In the former, patients interpreted inkblot patterns on cards. In the latter, patients drew pictures of males and females. According to Grygier, homosexual men showed 'particular emphasis in their drawings on ears, hips and buttocks'. They also drew 'large eyes and eye-lashes', 'put heels on the shoes of male figures', twisted perspectives 'so that one cannot tell whether it is the front or the rear of the figure' and revealed 'homosexual panic in their shading of the legs or trousers or delineation of legs through transparent trousers'. Grygier also favoured his own 'dynamic personality inventory', which could both 'differentiate between homosexuals and well-adjusted individuals' and 'distinguish between different types of homosexuals'. The inventory was comprised of a list of more than 300 items which patients could rate according to their preferences, resulting in a scaled measure of masculinity or femininity. [10]

The association in the professional and popular mind between homosexuality and effeminacy, mental illness, crime and anti-social behaviour was already well-established. In 1958 doctors R.E. Hemphill, A. Leitch and J.R. Stuart published a report in the *British Medical Journal* based on their analysis of 64 homosexual inmates at Leyhill and Horfield prisons near Bristol. Most of the men, they found, were 'of good intelligence, whose only connexion with the world of crime has been through homosexual practices'. Twenty-four were or had been married. Fifteen had children. Ten (16%) had experienced 'psychiatric illness', and three of these (5% of the total) had been admitted to hospital for treatment. This compared with 8% and 3% respectively of the general population. In three cases the doctors found 'deviations other than homosexuality'. One prisoner was attracted to boys' noses, 'and if he grabbed a boy's nose he had an orgasm'. Another was 'stimulated by the sight and touch of breasts, male or female; even his own'. The third prisoner 'desired to be a woman in every possible way'. He even 'kept house' for women and 'indulged in sex play with them to the point of orgasm, but "only as a fellow lesbian". He eagerly wanted to be a man's mistress or wife, bear children, breast-feed them, and rear them.' Only 12 of the 64 prisoners felt ashamed or guilty about their homosexuality.

'The majority of the remainder were indifferent to the social and legal sanctions, but were anxious to avoid being caught again or punished.' [11]

It was unclear exactly how many homosexual men there were in Britain. The only large-scale survey available to the Wolfenden Committee was Kinsey's *Sexual Behavior in the Human Male*, published in 1948. It revealed that 'homosexual activity in the human male' was 'much more frequent than is ordinarily realised'. Information from 12,000 case histories and data from 5,300 men showed that 37% of the male population in the US had indulged in some kind of homosexual activity 'to the point of orgasm' at least once in their lives between adolescence and old age. Four per cent were 'exclusively homosexual'. Some Wolfenden Committee witnesses thought that 'something very like these figures would be established in this country if similar enquiries were made', although most thought that Kinsey's figures 'would be on the high side for Britain'. The committee also looked at the results of an enquiry in Sweden which suggested that 1% of men there were exclusively homosexual and that 4% of males had both homosexual and heterosexual 'impulses'. What the committee did not know was that in 1949 the social research organisation Mass Observation had conducted its own sex survey in Britain and had found that a quarter of adult men had taken part in homosexual acts. The so-called 'Little Kinsey' survey questioned 2,052 people about their sexual behaviour, and some of the results were published in limited instalments in the *Sunday Pictorial* in July 1949. But because most of its findings were considered so shocking, the full report was suppressed and later consigned to the University of Sussex archives, where it remained largely forgotten. [12, 13]

The only other data available to the Wolfenden Committee came from two recent studies – one of young criminals; the other of university students. T.C.N. Gibbens (who appeared before the committee on behalf of the Institute of Psychiatry and the Howard League for Penal Reform) looked at a sample of 200 'borstal lads' aged between 16 and 21. He found that 5% were 'real' homosexuals with 'major and persistent tendencies'. Psychologist S.J.C. Spencer, meanwhile, sampled

100 'normal' male Oxford University undergraduates. Of these, 35% admitted to 'some sort of homosexual interest'. [14, 15]

In a later study, Wolfenden Committee member Desmond Curran and fellow psychiatrist Denis Parr claimed that 5% of 5,000 male psychiatric cases they had seen in private practice were homosexual. Parr also found that 5% of 200 psychiatric in-patients treated at St George's Hospital and the Wimbledon and Belmont Neurosis Unit in south London were homosexual. In 1957 the *Daily Express* carried a story in which a doctor, Rodney Long, claimed that there were 'nearly 1,000,000' homosexual men who might need the sort of clinic he was planning to open near Harley Street in London. In 1959 an anonymous GP told the medical journal *The Lancet*: 'My experience as a homosexual over the past thirty years has convinced me that at least 10% of adult men fall into the Kinsey ratings 4, 5 and 6.' Most commentators, however, agreed that the proportion of mature males in Britain who were homosexual was about 5%, or one in twenty. Since there were around 18 million males over the age of 15 in 1957, it followed that approximately 900,000 of them were homosexual. [16, 17, 18, 19]

If the precise number of homosexual men was unclear, there was less doubt about what they got up to. The Wolfenden Committee and their witnesses discussed in depth and with surprising frankness the various 'practices' of homosexual men. As well as 'buggery' (or 'sodomy' as it was legally termed in Scotland), the committee learned about 'mutual masturbation', 'intercrural contact' and 'oral-genital contact (with or without emission)'. They concluded that 'the majority of practising homosexuals indulged at some time or other in all types of homosexual acts', although some activities might 'take on a recondite form' and 'techniques' could 'vary considerably'.[20]

When sociologist Michael Schofield (writing under the pseudonym Gordon Westwood) researched the subject for his 1952 book *Society and the Homosexual*, he too found wide differences in 'the frequency of overt sexual activity'. He wrote: 'There are some men who are very definitely homosexual and yet have never had an overt experience; there are others who have seven or more experiences each week. Many of the virile types are promiscuous; many of the effeminate types are inexperienced. There seems to be no correlation between their appearance and the frequency of sexual intercourse.' Desmond Curran and Denis Parr thought that 'practising' homosexuals probably committed 'at a conservative estimate an average of at least ten (criminal) acts annually'. Parr also found that in his sample of 200 homosexual psychiatric patients 177 were 'practising', committing an average of 15 'criminal acts' a year. Buggery was noted in 42% and fellatio in 24%. 'The more we see of these cases,' Parr noted, 'the more we incline to the view that there are few regularly practising homosexuals who do not try a variety of acts at one time or another.' Most homosexual men, he added, practised both 'active' and 'passive' roles in buggery: 'Some were predominantly passive at one time in their lives and predominantly active at another. The exclusive passivity of one man who could masturbate only by means of a candle inserted per rectum was, in our experience, unique.' T.C.N. Gibbens, meanwhile, discovered that 17 of his 200 borstal lads had witnessed mutual masturbation and 'other homosexual incidents' at various institutions, including the armed forces. Many had also been the subject of 'homosexual approaches in the general community'. Thirty-four out of 100 boys interviewed by Gibbens in 1955 claimed that adult men had 'tried to make a pass' or else 'interfere' with them. Sometimes 'money was offered in some quiet place'. But all 34 'usually looked upon the incident as quite trivial and not worth mentioning' and the experience 'usually had no ill-effect'. [21, 22, 23, 24]

Homosexuality, it seemed, was everywhere. Cruising in public toilets was believed to be particularly widespread. Thirty-five of Denis Parr's 200 psychiatric patients 'specifically admitted to acts in public lavatories, affectionately known as "cottages" in the parlance of the queer world'. London's chief metropolitan magistrate Lawrence Dunne told the Wolfenden Committee about popular conveniences in and around Soho, Piccadilly Circus and Leicester Square. John Nott-Bower, commissioner of the Metropolitan Police, explained that activities in Westminster toilets usually took place where there were no attendants. 'Perverts', he said, cut holes in partitions between cubicles so that they could pass notes to each other and have sex through them. When the council put metal plates over the partitions more holes appeared and the offences continued. Police constable Butcher, who worked in C Division (Mayfair and Soho), told the committee that homosexual activity around Mayfair was mostly visible at lunchtimes, when office workers moved between three urinals 'famous throughout the world' – at Providence Court, George Yard and Three Kings Yard. PC Darlington, whose beat covered B Division (Victoria, Chelsea and South Kensington), said that most arrests in his area took place at night. [25, 26]

Lawrence Dunne listed other sites in the West End where pick-ups could be had: Ramillies Place, Falconberg Mews, the area next to the Adelphi Hotel, in front of the County Fire Offices at Piccadilly Circus and in the royal parks – where at night soldiers from the Guards and Household Cavalry became 'professional importuners'. He also described 'nests' of homosexuals in Mayfair and Paddington, and pubs and flats where 'male harpies' gathered. The Scottish Association of Sheriffs-Substitute and Glasgow's assistant chief constable James Robertson also referred in their evidence to 'habitual loci' for homosexual activity, including Glasgow Green and Carlton Hill in Edinburgh. In its submission of evidence, the BMA observed that homosexual men gathered in 'special clubs and certain houses, both in town and country, where their activities are unlikely to be detected, and where they introduce individuals who may adopt similar practices'. [27, 28, 29]

Cruising for sex was certainly common. In his 1952 novel *Hemlock and After* Angus Wilson describes an encounter between bookshop assistant Eric Craddock and rent boy Ron Wrigley outside St Albans cathedral.

Ron Wrigley was leaning against the railings of the abbey lawn when he saw a young chap go by who gave him a quick but searching stare. He turned at his leisure and watched Eric walk up to the West Door. Oh yeah! he thought. I thought so. Not with all those beyootiful waves and that walk, you can't tell me. Not that the old sweatshirt and flannels looked very promising, but he had finished his little business for the day and there was an hour before the pubs opened. In any case

Ron, like Eric, was given to casual acquaintance when he'd nothing better on. He took out a cigarette and strolled over to Eric, who was trying vainly to study the details of the porch. 'Got a light?' he asked in glottal Cockney. [30]

Art critic and auctioneer Brian Sewell remembered a similar pick-up in 1957: 'Waiting near Paddington station for a bus to take me home, a Teddy boy asked me for a light. It was my own fault, for I had been covertly looking at him and his codpiece prominence in skin-tight jeans. "I don't smoke," I said. "I don't want to," he replied. "I was just asking."' [31]

Men in search of sex could also count on the services of the armed forces, and of sailors in particular. In Gillian Freeman's 1955 novel *The Liberty Man* Derek Smith explains the attractions of mariners for homosexual men.

'Men like that like to be with matelots, even if we don't give 'em what they're after. Our uniforms do for us what a sexy dress does for a girl. And we're light-hearted, and don't mind a joke or two, and we get free cigarettes and drinks.' [32]

Freeman and her husband, the writer and ballet critic Edward Thorpe, observed at close hand the friendships between sailors and homosexual men. Freeman began her writing career while working as a literary secretary for the novelist Louis Golding. At the same time, drama student Thorpe boarded at Golding's house in London. 'Louis was one of those people who had a thing for sailors,' recalled Thorpe, 'and he used to have big parties in his house with sailors there. Through that we came into contact with other gay people. The house was full of matelots. They weren't gay men. They were straight, you see, but they were prepared to be friendly to fairly wealthy gay men.' [33]

Such anecdotes challenged the theory that homosexuality was the result of the 'seduction' of youths by older men. Early on, the Wolfenden Committee questioned the validity of the seduction theory, calling it 'unrealistic', and noting that many young men tempted into homosexual acts subsequently became 'entirely heterosexual in their disposition'. The committee acknowledged that some men might indulge in homosexual behaviour under 'special circumstances' where there was no contact with women, such as in prison, but they concluded that most men reverted to heterosexual behaviour 'when opportunity affords'. Medical witnesses also agreed that seduction had 'little effect in inducing a settled pattern of homosexual behaviour'. S.J.C. Spencer backed up this view in his survey of 100 students at Oxford, and in a related study of 100 'psychiatric cases' at the university. The existence of 'homosexual coteries' was, he thought, most likely a consequence of students living in a 'residential and predominantly male university like Oxford'. Denis Parr, however, was unconvinced even by this argument. He wrote: 'The significance of segregated or boarding school education as a contributory factor in homosexuality has been greatly exaggerated.' [34, 35, 36]

Whatever the origins and extent of homosexual behaviour, the fact remained that it was completely illegal. In 1956 the Conservative government passed the Sexual Offences Act, which consolidated previous legislation on sex crimes – including the notorious section 11 ('Labouchère amendment') of the Criminal Law Amendment Act 1885, which outlawed 'any act of gross indecency' between males. The new Act covered England and Wales but not Scotland, where homosexual offences were still dealt with under the 1885 Act and various other laws. [37]

Homosexual Offences in England and Wales, 1956-1967

Offence	Statute	Triable at	Maximum penalty
Buggery*	Sexual Offences Act 1956	Assizes**	Life imprisonment
Attempted buggery	Common law	Assizes or Quarter Sessions***	Ten years' imprisonment
Indecent assault on a male by a male	Sexual Offences Act 1956	Assizes or Quarter Sessions	Ten years' imprisonment
Gross indecency between males	Sexual Offences Act 1956	Assizes or Quarter Sessions	Two years' imprisonment
Procuring acts of gross indecency between males	Sexual Offences Act 1956	Assizes or Quarter Sessions	Two years' imprisonment
Attempting to procure acts of gross indecency between males	Common law	Assizes or Quarter Sessions	Two years' imprisonment
Assault with intent to commit buggery	Sexual Offences Act 1956	Assizes or Quarter Sessions	Ten years' imprisonment
Persistent soliciting or importuning of males by males for immoral purposes	Sexual Offences Act 1956	Magistrates' Court / Assizes or Quarter Sessions	Six months' imprisonment / Two years' imprisonment
Indecency between males	Local bye-laws	Magistrates' Court	£5 fine

Source: Wolfenden Report

*   Defined as sexual intercourse 'per anum' between a man and a man, woman or beast

**   Courts sitting at intervals in each county of England and Wales to administer civil and criminal law. In 1972 the civil jurisdiction of assizes was transferred to the High Court and criminal jurisdiction to the Crown Court.

***   County court sessions held four times a year by a justice of the peace to hear criminal charges and civil and criminal appeals. In 1972 quarter session courts were replaced by permanent Crown Courts.

Homosexual Offences in Scotland, 1956-1980

Offence	Statute	Triable at	Maximum penalty
Sodomy	Common law	High Court of Justiciary*	Life imprisonment
Attempted sodomy	Common law	High Court of Justiciary / Sheriff Court** (with jury) / Sheriff Court (without jury)	Life imprisonment / Two years' imprisonment / Three months' imprisonment
Indecent assault on a male by a male	Common law	High Court of Justiciary / Sheriff Court (with jury) / Sheriff Court (without jury)	Life imprisonment / Two years' imprisonment / Three months' imprisonment
Lewd and libidinous practices and behaviour between male persons	Common law	High Court of Justiciary / Sheriff Court (with jury) / Sheriff Court (without jury)	Life imprisonment / Two years' imprisonment / Three months' imprisonment
Gross indecency between males	Criminal Law Amendment Act 1885	Sheriff Court (with jury) / Sheriff Court (without jury)	Two years' imprisonment / Three months' imprisonment
Procuring acts of gross indecency between males	Criminal Law Amendment Act 1885	Sheriff Court (with jury) / Sheriff Court (without jury)	Two years' imprisonment / Three months' imprisonment
Attempting to procure acts of gross indecency between males	Criminal Law Amendment Act 1885	Sheriff Court (with jury) / Sheriff Court (without jury)	Two years' imprisonment / Three months' imprisonment
Persistent soliciting or importuning of males by males for immoral purposes	Immoral Traffic (Scotland) Act 1902 / Criminal Law Amendment Act 1912	Sheriff Court (with jury) or any court of summary jurisdiction / As above	Two years' imprisonment / Six months' imprisonment
Indecency between males	Local bye-laws	Any court of summary jurisdiction	£5 fine

Source: Wolfenden Report

*   Scotland's supreme criminal court
** Equivalent to a county court in England and Wales

The disparities between the different laws against homosexual behaviour quickly became apparent to the Wolfenden Committee. They noted, for example, that in England and Wales section 32 of the Sexual Offences Act (which replaced section one of the Vagrancy Act 1898) was used almost exclusively to prosecute male importuning. In Scotland, on the other hand, the equivalent Immoral Traffic (Scotland) Act 1902 was not used at all against homosexual men. The authorities there took the view that it was 'not intended to deal with this type of offence'. [38]

The Wolfenden Committee also noticed the 'curious situation' in England and Wales whereby local bye-laws were used to punish homosexual behaviour. Such bye-laws were regulations passed by local authorities, subject to ministerial confirmation, which covered various forms of indecency. They often included homosexual offences which might also fall within the gross indecency provisions of the Sexual Offences Act. Byelaws made under the Municipal Corporations Act 1882, for example, ordered that 'no person shall in any street or public place commit, or solicit, incite or provoke any other person to commit any indecent act to the annoyance of residents or passengers'. A London County Council byelaw of 1900 prohibited 'any act of gross indecency in any street or any open space to which the public have access'. The 1932 byelaws for parks, gardens and open public spaces ordered that 'no person shall in any open space do any act which outrages public decency'. The (London) Hyde Park Regulations of 1932 additionally required that 'no person shall sit, lie, rest or sleep on any seat or any part of the park in any indecent posture or behave in any manner reasonably likely to offend against public decency'. In Scotland municipalities (or burghs) also had the power to make byelaws to prevent 'nuisances'. In Edinburgh, for example, the Cleansing Byelaws ruled that 'no person shall loiter in a public convenience or use the same for any purpose other than as a lavatory or toilet apartment'. [39]

The plethora of national and local laws administered by different courts dispensing different punishments for different types of homosexual offences resulted in a lottery of justice. A man caught in an indecent act in England or Wales, for example, could either be charged under a local bye-law and receive a £5 fine at a magistrates' court or be sent to an assize or quarter sessions court and face a prison sentence of up to two years. By the same token, a man arrested for the lesser crime of importuning could be sent to a magistrates' court and receive the comparatively harsher sentence of six months' imprisonment. 'It seems to us anomalous,' the Wolfenden Committee noted, 'that a man who actually commits an indecent act in a public place should be liable only to a fine of five pounds if dealt with summarily, while a man who searches unsuccessfully for a partner is liable on summary conviction to six months' imprisonment for importuning.' Such inconsistencies led many men who were arrested for gross indecency to instead accept a charge of importuning because it carried a shorter maximum sentence if tried by a magistrate. But because importuning could also be tried by juries at assize or quarter sessions, the penalty could equally end up being two years in prison. [40]

The police were aware of these discrepancies and often exploited them. Several Wolfenden witnesses attested that men were frequently charged with offences that did not match the behaviour they were arrested for. 'It has been suggested,' the committee remarked, 'that the police sometimes advise persons found committing acts of gross indecency in public lavatories to plead guilty at the magistrates' court to importuning in order to avoid going to trial before a jury on a charge of gross indecency.' The reason for this was that the police were better able to secure convictions on lesser charges at lower courts without the need to build complex cases based on secure evidence. During a radio interview in 1954 former London magistrate Claude Mullins recalled: 'Many of the cases that I dealt with were charged by the police under a London County Council byelaw dealing merely with indecent conduct in a public place. The penalty for offences under this byelaw was a maximum of £5. Sometimes quite serious cases were so charged for the simple reason that the police had insufficient evidence to prove a more serious offence.' [41, 42]

The Wolfenden Committee also found significant variations in the way prosecutions were handled. In Scotland proceedings against homosexual offences were instigated not by the police but by a public prosecutor, the procurator fiscal, who also determined the court at which a hearing should be held. Offences were prosecuted 'in the public interest', and not all cases brought before him had to be acted on. Because proceedings could only be initiated for an offence less than six months old, and because older cases had first to be reported to the Crown Office, there were virtually no prosecutions of 'stale' offences in Scotland. The opposite occurred in England and Wales, where instances of the police pursuing homosexual offences committed many years earlier were not unknown. In Scotland a higher standard of proof was also required. No one could be convicted of a homosexual offence unless there was evidence from at least two witnesses, or unless the corroboration of one witness was supported by irrefutable evidence. It was therefore rare to secure evidence against consenting adults committing homosexual acts in private. And although written statements of guilt counted as corroboration, they were rarely obtained because the police were not allowed to question a suspect with the aim of making him incriminate himself. Nor were the police allowed to question suspects after they had been cautioned. If a man in custody did wish to make a statement, he had the right to have a solicitor present, and the statement had to be taken by a magistrate or a police officer not directly involved in the investigation. In England and Wales the police could question a suspect up to the moment of taking him into custody. They could also take written admissions of guilt. Of the 480 men convicted of homosexual offences in private in England and Wales between March 1953 and March 1956 449 (94%) made written statements admitting their guilt. Of the nine similar convictions in Scotland in the same period only one (11%) made a written admission. [43, 44, 45]

There were also variations in the way different police forces administered the law. In some parts of the country this was done with 'discretion', and no action was taken unless there were complaints from the public, or unless the police themselves came across illegal behaviour. In other regions the Wolfenden Committee detected 'a firm effort to apply the full rigour of the law'. Referring to the arrest in January 1954 of Lord Montagu of Beaulieu, his cousin Michael Pitt-Rivers and the journalist Peter Wildeblood for 'conspiracy to incite certain male persons to commit serious offences with male persons', the committee recognised that 'wide currency has been given to a suggestion that a prosecution which took place not long before we were appointed was part of a nation-wide "witch-hunt" against homosexuals'. On balance, however, they concluded that there was 'no evidence of any "drive" on a national scale' by the police – although they did concede that 'there may from time to time arise particular local campaigns against this kind of offence, either as the result of a deliberate drive by the police or by reason of local public indignation'. [46]

The role of plain-clothes police officers in detecting homosexual crime was also examined by the committee. Such officers worked in teams of two or three and often encouraged men to importune or commit indecent acts. Arrests were swift and brutal, and could be made on the flimsiest of pretexts – a gesture, a nod or a smile. In *Hemlock and After* a man is arrested moments after propositioning writer Bernard Sands in London's Leicester Square.

> Bernard was startled by a firmly enunciating, slightly Cockney voice. 'Excuse me, sir, I'm a police officer. We are charging this man with importuning. I have had occasion to notice that he approached you a few minutes ago. I should be glad to know if you wish to offer further evidence against him.' Bernard's eyes were riveted upon the face of the young man with the long dark hair. His underlip was trembling, his eyes, overlarge with terror, were on the point of tears. His arms were held tightly by the speaker. 'Certainly not,' he said, 'he only asked me for a match.' Two figures hovered vaguely in the background – another detective, no doubt, and the man who was charging him. 'Very good, sir.' The detective's tone was angry. As they moved away the young man's terror woke into struggle and protest. Bernard stood, cold with horror. [47]

In April 1957 another young man, 22-year-old drama student Brian Epstein, was ensnared by a plain clothes police officer for 'persistently importuning' in a public lavatory at Swiss Cottage underground station in London. On the advice of a detective, the future Beatles manager pleaded guilty at Marylebone magistrates' court and was fined. He later wrote to his solicitor, 'The damage, the lying criminal methods of the police in importuning *me* and consequently capturing me, leaves me cold, stunned and finished.'[48]

The Wolfenden Committee generally supported undercover police surveillance as a means of preventing and detecting 'this particular offence', even though some witnesses claimed that police officers acted as *agents provocateurs* by deliberately enticing homosexual men into committing illegal acts. But the committee were assured by John Nott-Bower and 'other senior police officers' that the police 'do everything they can do to ensure that their officers do not act in a deliberately provocative manner'. They were also 'favourably impressed' by PCs Butcher and Darlington, and by 'the way in which they carried out their unpleasant task'. They accepted that 'a police officer legitimately resorts to a degree of subterfuge in the course of his duty', but they also maintained that 'the police should be above suspicion'. If they were not, 'it would be better that a case of this comparatively trivial crime should occasionally escape the courts'. [49]

The committee were more concerned about police interrogation methods, and in particular about so-called 'chain' prosecutions in which large numbers of men were rounded up and charged with sexual offences. 'The following,' they said, 'is a pattern which we encountered frequently': [50]

A man is questioned by the police about an offence under enquiry, and in the course of the interrogation admits having indulged in homosexual behaviour with men whom he names. These men are then confronted with the statement made by the first man, and, in turn, make statements inculpating further men. This process repeats itself until eventually a large number of men may be involved. The police sometimes take considerable trouble in following up alleged offences revealed in this way, and their enquiries often bring to light offences committed some years earlier. [51]

The police often persuaded suspects to reveal the identities of other homosexual men by promising to 'go easy' on them by securing a discharge, a lesser charge or a light sentence. In Compton Mackenzie's 1956 novel *Thin Ice* Detective Inspector Brackenbury tries to tempt Arthur Weeks in this way in order to incriminate the homosexual MP Henry Fortescue.

> 'Now, look here, Weeks, you haven't got to worry about yourself or anything that might happen to you. All you've got to do is to help the police, and the police will help you. If you were asked if anything took place between you and Mr Fortescue, and you told us just what did take place, nothing at all would happen to you, whatever it was, because you'd have been so helpful, which is very important when you're dealing with the police.' [52]

The apparent rise in homosexual crime worried many Wolfenden witnesses. In 1945 there were 2,000 cases of buggery, indecent assault and gross indecency 'known to the police' in England and Wales – either through complaint, arrest or charge. By 1952 that number had risen to 5,443. In 1953 there were 5,680 incidences. In 1954 there were 6,327. In 1955 the number increased to 6,644 – more than treble the figure of ten years earlier. In 1956 196 offences were reported. But the statistics should be treated with some caution. There had already been a steady rise in reported homosexual crime since 1936, when 1,167 cases were recorded – compared to just 840 the year before. The increases should also be seen in the context of a sharp rise in the number of all sexual offences – from 8,546 in 1945 to 17,078 in 1955. This was partly a consequence of new child protection measures, and of attempts to clamp down on 'vice' generally. [53, 54]

Nevertheless, there was a common perception that homosexuality was on the rise. In its evidence to the Wolfenden Committee, the British Medical Association blamed the 'apparent increase in homosexual practices' on 'the weakening, in a significant proportion of the population, of the sense of personal responsibility with regard to social and national welfare'. The BMA also felt that contemporary social conditions were 'favourable to sexual indulgence. Widespread irresponsibility and selfishness have a demoralising effect. Responsible citizenship is needed.' [55]

The Wolfenden Committee suggested that the rise in the homosexual crime figures was due to more 'efficient' police methods: 'It was to be expected that the more intensive training given to police officers in recent years would result in the discovery of a higher proportion of offences; but this does not necessarily indicate that more offences have occurred. We understand, too, that efforts have been made in recent years to improve the methods by which offences known to the police are recorded, and these may have been reflected in higher figures.' [56]

The number of prosecutions for homosexual offences – as opposed to reported incidences – also showed a noticeable increase. In 1945 proceedings were taken against 782 men in England and Wales. By 1952 that number had risen to 2,109. In 1953 there were 2,267 prosecutions. In 1954 there were 2,442. In 1955 there were 2,504. But measured against the number of known offences, prosecution rates were relatively low. In 1955, for example, just 38% of all reported offences (2,504) were prosecuted. Conviction rates, however, were high. Eighty-nine per cent of men prosecuted between 1952 and 1955 were convicted. In the peak year of 1955 91% of prosecuted men were convicted. For those prosecuted for importuning, conviction rates were even higher. In 1954 93% of the 481 men prosecuted for this offence were convicted. In 1955 95% of the 521 men prosecuted were convicted. There were, however, few convictions of consenting adult males who had sex in private. The Wolfenden Committee found only 300 in England and Wales between March 1953 and March 1956 – just 5% of all homosexual convictions. Of these, 119 men (40%) were imprisoned. In Scotland in the same period just seven out of 350 consenting adults (2%) were convicted. Four of them went to prison. [57, 58]

The way the courts dealt with offenders varied widely. At the lower end of the punishment scale offenders in England and Wales might receive a discharge (absolute or conditional), a binding over, probation or a fine. Imprisonment could last from a few days to ten years. Young offenders under the age of 21 could be sent to a borstal institution, detention centre or approved school, or else committed to 'the care of a fit person' or compelled to visit an attendance centre for up to 12 hours over a fixed period. In Scotland offenders might incur an 'admonition', a 'deferred sentence' (similar to a conditional discharge) or a 'caution for good behaviour' (similar to binding over), or be sent for 'preventative detention'. In 1955 771 (28%) of the 2,782 men in England and Wales found guilty of buggery, indecent assault, gross indecency and importuning were sent to prison for varying periods. In Scotland in the same year 30 (38%) of the 80 men convicted of sodomy or gross indecency went to gaol.[59]

The Wolfenden Committee thought that variations in sentences imposed by different courts for different offences led to 'a feeling of arbitrariness and injustice' in the way the law was administered. This was often compounded by a perception that judges and magistrates allowed their personal prejudices to influence judicial decisions. The committee observed that the 'disgust and indignation' felt by law enforcers for homosexual offences could find 'expression in the sentences imposed'. Writing in 1955, John Tudor Rees, a former chairman of Surrey quarter sessions, remembered how at one assize 'a man pleaded guilty to a charge involving homosexuality. The judge told him that he was "a pestilential person" and sent him to prison for ten years. A little later, at another assize, the judge said, "This seems to be a pathological case", and put the man on probation for three years.' Michael Schofield also thought that the severity of punishments varied according to 'the understanding of the magistrate or judge'. [60, 61]

Prison, it was generally agreed, did little to change homosexual men's ways. Peter Wildeblood was scathing about his time in gaol for conspiracy to incite homosexual offences with two Royal Air Force servicemen. After his release in March 1955 he wrote a book about his experiences in which he claimed that imprisonment did not 'deter a single person from committing acts'. He added, 'I have never met a homosexual who has resolved to mend his ways as a result of being imprisoned.'

According to Wildeblood, prisoners felt no 'remorse or shame' for their crimes, and their indifference and defiance was often 'strengthened by the fact that no moral stigma attaches to adult homosexuality in the prison community'. Indeed, many offenders found that prison fostered rather than deterred homosexuality. The writer Rupert Croft-Cooke was imprisoned for six months for indecency in 1953. In his 1955 book *The Verdict of You All* he gave a startling account of homosexual life in Brixton and Wormwood Scrubs prisons in London. [62]

> At Brixton there is more homosexuality than at the Scrubs, owing partly to its overcrowded state and the necessity there to keep three men in a cell. It is the merest wishful thinking to suppose that this is any serious discouragement to homosexuality, for it frequently promotes it. Far from feeling embarrassment, three men learn to adapt themselves to the situation in various ways, the least noxious of which, perhaps, is that one of them remains on guard with his back to the spy-hole in the door. Men convicted of homosexual offences are given cells to themselves, but this, again, has little influence since these practices in prison are rarely theirs, and in any case most of the more abandoned inverts have been imprisoned for quite different reasons, theft or blackmail, and hence do not qualify for a single cell.
>
> At the Scrubs there were other opportunities which were awaited and taken. There were places and occasions in the Old Rec[reation room] which lent themselves to a certain amount of surreptitious contact, and there was one workshop in which it was almost encouraged. The CTs* were more rabid and more shameless about it, but they were young vigorous animals who were being forced to live together for years in unnatural conditions and without any guidance or leadership. It was inevitable that they should seek some assuagement. They made no bones about it. [63]

Nevertheless, the Wolfenden Committee thought that prison was 'an expression of society's disapproval' of homosexual behaviour, and that

---

*   Corrective Training inmates

it could provide a 'salutary shock' for offenders. The committee agreed that 'there doubtless are some homosexual offenders to whom prison does more harm than good', but they believed that 'there undeniably are others to whom it teaches an important lesson'. Prison was also essential 'for the protection of the community' and would 'always have its place as a method of dealing with the homosexual offender'. [64]

Not all the estimated 900,000 homosexual men in Britain came into conflict with the law. The Wolfenden committee recognised that 'the number of those prosecuted in respect of homosexual acts constitutes but a fraction of those who from time to time commit such acts'. It noted that 'there are many homosexuals whose behaviour never comes to the notice of the police or the courts', and that the law 'probably makes little difference to the amount of homosexual behaviour which actually occurs'. Denis Parr reckoned that the ratio of criminal acts to known offences was somewhere in the region of 2,500:1. In other words, for every homosexual crime reported another two-and-a-half thousand others were taking place. Parr thought that 'legal considerations were of minimal significance' in preventing homosexual acts. John Tudor Rees agreed that 'the number of prosecutions bears no indication at all to the volume of cases that go undetected, or to the extent to which unnatural practices are carried on in private'. [65, 66, 67, 68]

The illegality of homosexuality inevitably coloured public attitudes towards the subject. These ranged from ridicule and disgust to outright hostility. 'The British view homosexuality with the same moral horror today as they always have,' wrote psychologist Edward Glover in his introduction to Michael Schofield's *Society and the Homosexual* in 1952. 'It is considered to be something so degraded that even its existence is only acknowledged in the form of pornographic humour or disgusted scorn. The amount of prejudice and extreme emotional reaction engendered by the very word is remarkable.' According to Psychologist Donald West, most people saw homosexual men as 'degenerate personalities, moral pariahs who obstinately persist in tasting forbidden fruit, effete "pansy" types incapable of natural manliness, dangerous seducers of the young, victims of circumstance, sufferers from psychological disorder, cases of glandular disease, or even the forerunners of a new biological type – the third sex.' The BMA told the Wolfenden Committee that 'ways in which male homosexuals arouse the hostility of the public include their alleged tendency to place their loyalty to one another above their loyalty to the institution or government they serve, and, on the part of homosexuals in positions of authority, to give preferential treatment to homosexuals, or to require homosexual subjection as expedient for promotion'. [69, 70, 71]

The belief that older homosexual men preyed on youths was also explicit in the BMA's evidence. It warned that 'school teachers and others concerned with youth should be able to recognise the type of boy who appears to be liable to develop homosexual tendencies' in order to protect them from predatory older men and to keep them apart from other boys. It also thought that schools and youth organisations should nurture 'a high level of national morale' among young males, and that 'provisions for athletic activities and competition in work and games' would help promote 'a healthy atmosphere in which homosexual practices have no place'. To this end, the BMA recommended that 'those associated with the education, training, and activities of youth should be carefully selected'. In addition, 'more care on the part of those responsible for such appointments would eliminate the risk of presenting excellent opportunities for indulgence to those homosexuals who, consciously or unconsciously, are attracted to work amongst youth just because of its opportunities'. [72]

Even public discussion of homosexuality was considered taboo. When a radio documentary on the subject was first mooted in 1953 the BBC rejected the idea. Chief assistant of talks at the Home Service Donald Boyd wrote to producer Isa Benzie, 'As I understand it, [homosexuality] is a distortion of the natural appetite, which is incurable and unpredictable. The majority of homosexuals are actively predatory and insatiable for their own sex.' He later told assistant controller of talks Jim Thornton, 'It is a subject full of fear, particularly at the moment when it is obvious that the police are hunting perverts insatiably.' Approved school headmaster and former prison governor Cyril Joyce (whose charges at the Hollesley Bay borstal centre in the 1940s included the writer Brendhan Behan) told BBC Radio's *Woman's Hour* in 1955, 'I don't think we can possibly lose sight of the dangers that are inherent in the suggestion that we should become more tolerant about [homosexuality]. I expect you will be horrified to know that one result of the publicity given to the suggestion that homosexuality should no longer be treated as a criminal offence is that some boys that I know well have already started to say to me, "Yes, sir, but this isn't wrong any more, is it?"' [73, 74, 75]

Mentions of homosexuality in plays and films were tightly censored. Plays were controlled by the Theatres Act 1843, which gave the Lord Chamberlain the power to grant licences for public performances. From 1952 to 1963 the post was held by the Earl of Scarborough, Roger Lumley, a former Conservative MP and ex-governor of Bombay. He held his office as a member of the royal household rather than as a government minister and was assisted by a team of ex-army officers from elite regiments whose job it was to examine new playscripts in order to determine whether or not they were fit for public performance. In the interests of 'good manners', 'decorum' and 'public peace', certain language, references and themes were forbidden. Homosexuality was one of them. In 1953 Julien Green's play *South* was refused a licence because it alluded to 'the perversion of homosexuality'. Set on the eve of the American Civil War, it focuses on Polish-born army officer Jan Wicziewsky, who falls in love with the son of a Southern plantation-owning family. Despite its 'platonic' homosexuality and the fact that the script was 'not exactly scabrous in the manner of other plays', *South* was rejected outright. [76, 77]

Between 1953 and 1957 similar fates befell Maurice Rostand's *The Trial of Oscar Wilde* (a 'general atmosphere of sodomy'), Ruth and Augustus Goetz's adaptation of André Gide's *The Immoralist* ('riddled with its subject'), Robert Anderson's *Tea and Sympathy* ('the Lord Chamberlain does not allow any plays about perversion'), Philip King's and Robin Maugham's *The Lonesome Road* ('homosexuality is a forbidden topic'), Ronald Duncan's *The Catalyst* ('it would be disastrous to pass') and Reginald Beckwith's *No Retreat* ('a justification for homosexual tendencies'). With the exception of *No Retreat*, all of these plays were instead given performances at club theatres – small, private societies whose members paid a subscription and which were outside the Lord Chamberlain's jurisdiction. [78, 79, 80, 81, 82, 83]

Philip King's play *Serious Charge*, which opened at London's Adelphi Theatre in November 1953, was unusual in not being banned, despite having a homosexual theme. The title alludes to the euphemism used by newspapers to refer to homosexual offences, and the plot concerns a vicar, Howard Philips, who is falsely accused of molesting local tearaway Larry Thompson. The Lord Chamberlain's script reader C.D. Heriot detected 'the forbidden topic of homosexuality' in the play, but he conceded that there was 'no doubt at any time that the vicar is innocent of the "serious charge"'. The Lord Chamberlain himself was not wholly convinced that 'the question of propriety' did not arise, but because it was 'a straight play' he gave it a licence. [84]

The accusation against Philips is clearly false. But King drops in enough stereotypical hints to make the vicar's parishioners as well as the audience at least suspect him of being homosexual. In addition to being a clergyman, Philips is a bachelor who lives with his mother. Twice in the play attention is also drawn to his creative talents. In the first instance a neighbour, Hester Byfield, pays Philips' mother a visit.

> Hester: I do love this room. You've made it so cosy, and yet so – artistic – if you know what I mean. What you might call a real woman's room.
> Mrs Philips: (laughing) Oh dear!
> Hester: Why – what?
> Mrs Philips: You mustn't let my son hear you say that. You see the décor is his entirely. He really has quite a flair for interior decorations.
> Hester: Oh, I can see he has quite a flair. One would never think it – meeting him. One usually thinks of artistic men as being rather – well, you know what I mean. [85]

Representations of homosexual men in the cinema were also tightly controlled. Films were overseen by the British Board of Film Censors, a self-regulating industry body set up in 1913 to judge the acceptability of films for public viewing. The BBFC gave films certificates with advisory ratings and could request changes or cuts before issuing one. Without a certificate local authorities might not permit the screening of a film in their area. Homosexuality was not specifically banned, but it was not considered a suitable subject for cinematic treatment. In 1954 the producer and director John Woolf put forward a proposal for a film version of Robert Anderson's play *Tea and Sympathy*, which deals with homosexual bullying at an American boys' school (and which was banned by the Lord Chamberlain that same year). A BBFC script reader wrote: 'I hope that our present standards in regard to the discussion of homosexuality in the cinemas of this country will not be relaxed. It is a subject which ought now to be debated and further ventilated, but not in the cinema. The atmosphere is all wrong. Who can doubt that a theatre provides the safer and cooler climate for the analysis of this sort of inflammable stuff? The audience, also, is largely wrong, except in a few "specialised houses" in the West End of London. Millions of boys and girls of the "working" classes, educated side by side, working side by side, married in their late teens and early twenties, do not need to consider this problem at all, and if they need not, it is a pity to thrust it upon them in the guise of entertainment. There is no need to make out to the rest of the world, and particularly to what is left of the empire, that "le vice anglais" is our sole preoccupation.' [86]

Not everyone, however, was pleased to see the film idea rejected. Another reader, John Trevelyan (later secretary of the BBFC), defended *Tea and Sympathy* and its treatment of a controversial subject.

Adolescent homosexuality is a normal feature of school life. It is not, of course, practised by every boy, but those who do practise it are not regarded as outcasts. In most cases it is merely a temporary substitute for heterosexual relations, and those who practice adolescent homosexuality do not necessarily continue the practice in adult life. Naturally one wonders whether things have changed very much since one was at public school oneself a good many years ago. I had the opportunity of asking the headmaster of one of the best known schools, and he told me that things were much the same as they used to be in our time: they do what they can to stop it but have little success. He had a reasonable attitude to it, I thought, in saying that adolescent boys are normally very much interested in sex and, in many cases, strongly sexed, and that this was the easiest outlet for them. I would like to see the play, and I would like to see a really well-made film of it, in the 'X' category of course, but I suppose that we would be open to criticism if we allowed it. It is a pity, but there it is. [87]

Two years later *Tea and Sympathy* was filmed by Metro-Goldwyn-Mayer with all of its homosexual references removed, and it was passed by the BBFC. Only a few allusions to homosexuality remained, as when schoolboy Al explains to housemaster's wife Laura Reynolds why other boys at their New England school call Tom Lee (John Kerr) 'sister boy'.

> Al: Mrs Reynolds, he does kind of… Well, why does he have to walk so, so…?
> Laura: Oh, Al!
> Al: Long hair and music all the time. [88]

The only other cinematic suggestion of homosexuality was in *The Strange One*, released in July 1957. Based on Calder Willingham's novel and stage play *End as a Man*, the film follows the bullying antics of army sergeant Jocko De Paris (Ben Gazzara) at a US military college. The film hints at a homoerotic attraction between De Paris and cadet Perrin McKee, nicknamed 'Cockroach' (Paul E. Richards). 'I'm a creative writer,' Cockroach tells De Paris. 'I have the fire of genius in me. An artist just isn't appreciated in this country. Why, in Europe, with my talents, I'd already be famous. Now, you may not believe this, but most of the cadets around here regard me as a creep.' Later he tells De Paris that he is writing a novel about him. 'You're the hero of it, Jock. I call you Nightboy. All I want to have is your confidence and your friendship.' The film was given an X certificate after the BBFC ruled that 'there should be no suggestion that Perrin (the Cockroach) is a homosexual'. Film critics, however, saw through the subtleties. Anthony Carthew of the *Daily Herald* called *The Strange One* 'the first English language film ever to portray a homosexual'. The *Daily Mail* pointed to 'the perversions which flourish amid such militant montasticism'. The London *Evening Standard* called Paul E. Richards' performance 'the most honestly observed homosexual in any film I can recall'. Others saw Cockroach as 'alarmingly overt', 'fawning', 'grotesque' and 'the homosexual who wears a repulsive rubber cap under the shower'. [89, 90, 91, 92, 93, 94, 95, 96]

Films and plays reflected the popular assumption that homosexual men tended to work in certain professions, such as the arts, the church, teaching, nursing, youth work and the armed forces. The Wolfenden Committee agreed that there were instances where 'latent homosexuality' might motivate some men to engage in 'activities of the greatest value to society', but they rejected the idea that homosexuality was 'peculiar to members of particular professions or social classes'. Evidence put before them convinced the committee that homosexuality existed 'among all callings and at all levels of society; and that among homosexuals will be found not only those possessing a high degree of intelligence, but also the dullest oafs'. Michael Schofield similarly pointed out that homosexual men could be found 'throughout the entire physical range of the population, from the virile, manly sportsman to the mincing, lisping butterfly. On one end of this scale are footballers, boxers, strong, muscular labourers and tough, energetic businessmen. On the other end are slim, soft-skinned, high-voiced pansies who are indistinguishable from women when wearing female clothes.' [97, 98]

In contrast to the popular stereotype, most homosexual men led quiet and discreet lives, avoiding situations that might lead to the exposure of their sexuality. In Martyn Goff's 1957 novel *The Plaster Fabric* Laurie Kingston is constantly on his guard at the bookshop where he works with fellow sales assistant Ron Eccles.

> He felt awkward when people asked him if he was going to get married.
> He liked to conclude such conversations as quickly and discreetly as

possible. Sometimes, though, he felt that it sounded more natural if he made some jovial or casual comment. Either way he was awkward and afraid. A hundred times he had heard Eccles' surprised, 'Aren't you interested in women or something?' in the split second that he changed a conversation or avoided a question. [99]

Donald West remembered hiding his own sexuality while researching and writing his book *Homosexuality* (1955) by using his professional status as a psychologist and the fact that it was 'a terrible thing' to suggest that somebody might be homosexual: 'I was protected by the hypocritical medical label, the flattering foreword by a leading criminologist, the culture of avoiding personal questions about sexuality and the fact that to accuse a hospital doctor of sexual perversion could have been serious defamation. This enabled me to publish my book, but it had to be written under the cloak of detached psychological analysis and in language suggesting the author was one of "us" talking about "them".'
[100, 101]

Such deceit occasionally took a humorous turn. Peter Wildeblood remembered overhearing a conversation at a party.

'My mother said something rather good the other day. She was buying curtain material at a department store with an aunt of mine, and suddenly for no reason at all this aunt started talking about homosexuality, and how everyone who was that way should be strangled at birth. So my mother looked her straight in the eye and said: "Sybil, don't be so silly. If that was done, we should have no plays to go to, no books to read, no television to watch, and what is more, this place would be self-service!"'
'Good for her. Does she know about you?'
'Heavens, no. She'd probably have a fit if she did.' [102]

The consequences of family and friends finding out about someone's homosexuality could be disastrous. In Fritz Peters' 1951 novel *Finistère* Scott Fletcher, a friend of 16-year-old Matthew Cameron's father, finds out that Matthew has been having a relationship with his athletics teacher. Fletcher's reaction is immediate and damning.

> 'I know this kind of thing goes on but to have it happen to someone you know! I don't care about the rest of the people. But this… it's horrible! It's… well, I can't believe it. Everyone knows it's wrong.' [103]

Gerald Middleton, a history professor in Angus Wilson's 1956 novel *Anglo-Saxon Attitudes*, is less hostile but nonetheless deeply disturbed when he finds out about his son's homosexuality.

> 'I didn't know that John was a homosexual. I know very little about him really, and even less about the subject we're discussing. I've only come across it three or four times in my life, among people I actually knew, that is. It revolts me rather, I think.' [104]

John's mother Inge appears to be more accepting. But when his boyfriend Larry steals Inge's jewellery and threatens to tell the police about John if she reports him, her reaction is one of denial and revulsion.

> Inge turned towards him a doll's face of horror. Then she put her hands over her ears. 'Don't speak such things. Go away! Go away! It's terrible.' The thing that she feared most was happening to her, that she dreaded most. Someone was telling her things that she could not bear to hear and she could not stop them. [105]

Younger people's attitudes were often little different to those of their parents. In *The Liberty Man* a group of middle class students visit the fictional Rob Roy pub near London's Shaftesbury Avenue. Despite their outward liberalism, they are embarrassed and uncomfortable with what they see.

> 'This is a queer pub, isn't it?' said Bob, who had been watching a pale-faced American eyeing a pink young guardsman for some moments. He said it bravely, as an intellectual should, knowing no boundaries.

'Students come here as well,' said Matthew, arriving back with the sandwiches and overhearing. 'And theatre people. It's got an historical reputation. Anyone who's anyone's been here. Bit of both, I'd say.'

'How hateful,' said Eleanor, drawing into herself almost visibly. [106]

In Audrey Erskine Lindop's 1955 novel *Details of Jeremy Stretton* Jeremy professes to hate 'queers'.

He knew that it 'went on', but where, when and how it went on was a matter for the authorities or the occasional salacious story. It occurred only in that curious outer ring of human life. It lay with disaster, disablement, lunacy and close bereavement. It was reserved with misfortune for other people. It was something which could not happen to oneself. A pervert was a complication on a higher plane of which he had only the flimsiest conception. He believed it to be vaguely connected with the activities of Oscar Wilde and therefore possibly one of the lopsided facets of genius. A queer, a queen, a pouf, a pansy, a nancy-boy and a fairy were variations upon the description of 'one of those'. To his mind, perversion was a crime and its adherents were criminals. [107]

For homosexual men who lived together, life could be especially difficult. 'Two men cannot share accommodation or associate too closely without suspicion of law-breaking and fear of denunciation', wrote Donald West in *Homosexuality*. John Fraser, a young actor under contract to Rank Organisation in the 1950s, recalled how he and his partner George 'had disagreements, principally over my fear of journalists or anyone in the business discovering that I was sharing my life with a man. It seems mad now, but I wouldn't allow him to answer the phone. And we were never seen together on the sort of occasions where the press might be in attendance. Going to the airport, we used to go separately and meet up on the plane because there were people taking photographs. We just had to be surreptitious.' [108, 109, 110]

Men who were not in the public eye also risked having their careers ruined if their homosexuality was revealed. Employees could be sacked without reason and then find it difficult to get another job. In *The Plaster Fabric* Laurie is forced to leave the bookshop after Ron finds out about his relationship with a guardsman and threatens to tell their manager: 'Keep away from me – and the shop. We don't want your type polluting the atmosphere, dragging every schoolboy into a corner to show him filthy sex books. If you ever set foot in that shop or cross my path again, I'll mash you within an inch of your life.' [111]

Not all homosexual men lived fearful, furtive lives, however. Many had long-term relationships and enjoyed extensive social networks. Carl Winter, director of the Fitzwilliam Museum in Cambridge and a fellow of Trinity College, told the Wolfenden Committee about his circle of friends, both homosexual and heterosexual.

> We are all completely at ease in one another's company and the world in which we live, which is a much more extensive world, I think, than many people would suppose. We visit each other's houses, go abroad, travel, look at the sort of things that interest us – art, exhibitions, ballet – and have a satisfactory life within that sphere. Somebody from outside is every now and then caught up in it. Somebody presents himself at one's door, and if he is in character a sympathetic person he is admitted, if not, he is excluded. [112]

House parties were the usual means for homosexual men to meet and socialise with each other. David George remembered hosting two kinds at his home in Hampstead, north London: 'One was "hair up" and one was "hair down". Or sometimes we changed it to "earrings in" or "earrings out". At one, men could dance together, but at the other they couldn't because it was a "normal" party.' Entering a circle of friends was, as Donald West explained, 'a matter of visiting the right places in the right clothes and knowing the right conversational gambits and double entendres'. A newcomer, he noted, 'puts on just the shadow of a meaningful look, remarks with just a tinge of the accepted inflexion, "Isn't it gay in here?" and, if he is a presentable young man, he is lonely no more. An uninformed bystander would notice nothing untoward. Among these circles the initiated make themselves understood by the use of a slang that is almost a Masonic code.' West's mention of the word 'gay' is an early example of its use in Britain. Rupert Croft-Cooke also used it in *The Verdict of You All*, and in his 1955 book *Against the Law* Peter Wildeblood recounted first hearing it in 1946. The word's subcultural meaning was further explained in Gore Vidal's 1948 novel *The City and the Pillar*, published in Britain in 1949. In the course of the book its hero, Jim Willard, navigates Hollywood's homosexual scene and learns its secret slang. [113, 114]

> Like jazz musicians and dope addicts, they spoke in code. The words 'fairy' and 'pansy' were considered to be in bad taste. They preferred to say that a man was 'gay', while someone quite effeminate was a 'queen'. As for those manly youths who offered themselves for seduction while proclaiming their heterosexuality, they were known as 'trade', since they usually wanted money.' [115]

Most large towns and cities in Britain hosted 'gay' venues. Edwin Morgan remembered visiting pubs and bars in Glasgow in the 1950s: 'There were no clubs in the modern sense of the term. It was a very unorganised, scattered and spontaneous kind of scene. There were certain pubs you could go to. The best known was in West Nile Street, called the Royal. Some of the hotels had either a bar or a lounge. The Central Hotel at the Central Station was a place that people would often go to. They might meet in a pub and go to the Central Hotel for a coffee afterwards.' Allan Horsfall, a Labour councillor from Nelson in Lancashire, remembered 'little corners of places where gay men would meet and talk in code. It was often in the better hotels, or what would pass in a small town as the better hotel, because there was less hassle there.' [116, 117]

In smaller towns and villages there were few, if any, places to go to. In *Details of Jeremy Stretton* Eddie Baines is a wine and spirits merchant who moves from London to Berkhamstead in Hertfordshire after serving a six month prison sentence for importuning in Hyde Park. 'It's close in a town like that,' he tells Jeremy during a trip back to London. 'There's nowhere to go and you've got to be careful. That's why I come up to town now and then.'[118]

Loneliness, isolation and frustration sometimes led men to seek sex in public places, such as toilets and parks, where there was a greater risk of arrest. 'All these unfortunate people who went to prison for cottaging and that sort of thing were mostly out in the provinces and suburban people who didn't know how to protect themselves or didn't know what to do if they were caught,' recalled theatre director Adrian Brown. 'They were the ones who got sent to prison for several years for smiling at someone in a public place.'[119, 120]

The illegality of homosexuality had other consequences. As Donald West explained in *Homosexuality*, English law classified buggery as a felony rather than a misdemeanour, and a citizen who knew that such an offence had been committed – or was likely to take place – had a legal duty to report it to the police. Failure to do so would itself be a criminal offence – a 'misprision of felony'. This obligation compelled doctors and medical staff to tell the police about patients' homosexuality, or else themselves risk arrest and prosecution. As a result, many men were discouraged from seeking medical help or advice. As Denis Parr explained, 'It is regrettable that none of us can guarantee a patient permanent and unconditional secrecy in respect of case notes. There is no knowing, for example, whether at some future date somebody may be subpoenaed to reveal every detail of a case history in a court of law. For this reason, some doctors feel that it is wrong to leave written records of criminal sexual practices in hospital files.' The Wolfenden Committee received a copy of Donald West's book and seriously considered the implications of this aspect of the law: 'We think that anything which tends to discourage a homosexual from seeking medical advice is to be deprecated. Further, it is important that doctors called upon to furnish medical reports for the courts should enjoy the full confidence of the person under examination. This is not likely to be the case if the person being examined feels that the doctor is under an obligation to reveal to the court every act of buggery disclosed in the course of the examination.'[121, 122, 123]

The Wolfenden Committee was also concerned about blackmail. They heard and read a great deal about the subject (which they described as 'a pernicious social evil') and its various forms – from major criminal rackets and long-term extortion to 'small demands for money or other benefits' and 'the threat of disclosure' to family, friends and employers. The committee probably knew about the criminal career of blackmail king Harry Raymond, who was profiled by the Sunday *Empire News* in July 1955. In a two-part series, former Scotland Yard detective Robert Fabian described how, during the 1930s and 1940s, Raymond had run a network of young male 'decoys' from a café and an eight-bedroom house in London's Soho. Their job was to attract homosexual 'mugs', who were then blackmailed by Raymond. The swindle earned the gang £100 or more a night. Some victims ended up paying thousands of pounds in hush money. Raymond took 60% of the profits and the 'boys' shared the rest. Raymond went on to set up The Kama Society of Happiness, a male escort service aimed at blackmailing wealthy older men. But the venture collapsed and Raymond was eventually tracked down and imprisoned for eight years. He was released in October 1954. [124, 125, 126]

Homosexual men did have some protection from blackmail under the Larceny Act 1916, which outlawed (with a maximum penalty of life imprisonment) the making of threats or demands related to an accusation of buggery. But the Wolfenden Committee recognised that 'the fear of exposure' was usually enough to make homosexual men comply with blackmailers' demands, and that most victims were 'naturally hesitant about reporting their misfortunes to the police'. The committee even heard about one case in which a 49-year-old man was blackmailed by his 35-year-old former lover, and when the older man complained to the police both of them were charged with buggery and sentenced to nine months in prison. [127]

The extent of blackmail was, however, disputed. The Wolfenden Committee found a total of just 71 cases in England and Wales between 1950 and 1953. Of these, 32 (45%) were 'connected with homosexual activities'. As these represented an average of just eight cases a year, the committee suggested that 'the amount of blackmail which takes place has been considerably exaggerated'. In Scotland there were a total of 125 blackmail cases between 1946 and 1953, of which only one (less than 1%) was homosexual-related. The committee did not think that the problem of blackmail alone was 'sufficient ground' for changing the law, but they conceded that the threat of exposure would 'lose much of its edge' if homosexual behaviour were no longer a criminal offence. 'The present law', they noted, 'does afford to the blackmailer opportunities which the law might well be expected to diminish'. Blackmail was also a useful issue for law reformers to rally around. It evoked sympathy for homosexual men as victims rather than perpetrators of crime, and it highlighted the defects in an aspect of the law which, the committee concluded, did not 'command the universal respect of those who are charged with enforcing it'. This in turn reflected a growing concern among lawyers and politicians that public perception of the 'unfairness' and 'injustice' of legislation against homosexual men was beginning to bring the justice system generally into disrepute. [128]

The catalyst for change came on 4 November 1953 when the former Conservative home secretary Samuel Hoare, Lord Templewood, made a speech in the House of Lords in which he blamed the country's moral decline on violent crime, homosexuality and other forms of 'vice'. A week later, on 11 November, the subject of homosexuality was broached for the first time on broadcast media on BBC Radio's fortnightly current affairs programme *Behind the News*. Speakers included scientist, poet and director of the National Coal Board Research Establishment Jacob Bronowski, history professor Alan Bullock and Reading University vice chancellor John Wolfenden. Bronowski was quick to explain that 'this subject springs to mind, not because I'm remotely interested in homosexuality – that is, the sexual relations between men – but because it was spoken about in the House of Lords by Lord Samuel just a week ago, and my simple view is that what is good enough for the House of Lords is good enough for the BBC.' Bullock thought that homosexuality was 'very much on the increase', and he wanted a royal commission to investigate the issue and gather evidence 'which doctors, psychologists, chief constables and all those people who are one way and another concerned with this side of life could give us upon the prevalence of these practices'. Wolfenden 'entirely agreed' and also wanted to know 'a great deal more about the facts'. He added: 'I would like to know, as a result of an enquiry, the precise distinction there is either in people's minds or in practice between what we commonly talk about as vice in this context on the one hand and crime on the other. There are lots of vices that aren't crimes, and there are lots of crimes that aren't vices.' [129]

On 27 November the issue was again discussed (although the word 'homosexuality' was not specifically used) on BBC Television's *In The News*. Three weeks later, on 3 December, homosexuality was raised in the House of Commons when Conservative MP William Shepherd asked the home secretary David Maxwell Fyfe how many homosexual offences had been committed in 1953. Fellow Conservative MP Robert Boothby and the Labour MP Desmond Donnelly then called on the government to set up a royal commission to examine sexual offences legislation, and the laws on homosexuality in particular. On 7 December Boothby sent Maxwell Fyfe a letter in which he stated that it was 'the duty of the state to protect youth from corruption, and the public from indecency or nuisance', but that what consenting adults did in private, 'though it might be an issue between them and their maker, was not an issue between them and the state'. He thought that the matter should be considered 'either by a royal commission or an expert departmental committee, so that parliament may have the necessary knowledge and authority for legislative action'. [130, 131]

Boothby never fully explained why he took up the issue of homosexual law reform, although it was common knowledge that he had had homosexual relationships while a student at Oxford University. In his memoirs, published in 1978, Boothby wrote: 'Before I left Oxford I made up my mind that, if ever I went into public life, I would stop talking about it, and instead do something practical to remove the fear and misery in which many of our most gifted citizens were then compelled to live.' He added that he had 'done and written so much' about homosexual men because 'they have played an important part in shaping all our lives. My trouble is that, to a considerable extent, and much against my will, I share their general outlook on life.' [132]

On 17 February 1954 – six weeks after the arrest of Lord Montagu, Michael Pitt-Rivers and Peter Wildeblood – David Maxwell Fyfe issued a cabinet memorandum on sexual offences. He acknowledged that there was 'a considerable body of opinion which regards the existing law as antiquated and out of harmony with modern knowledge and ideas and, in particular, represents that the criminal law, in dealing with unnatural, and with normal, sexual relations, should confine itself to the protection of the young and the preservation of public order and decency'. He suggested that ministers consider the case for 'setting in train some inquiry into homosexual offences', and that 'a dispassionate survey by a competent and unprejudiced body might be of value in educating public opinion, which at present is ill-informed and apt to be misled by sensational articles in the press'. [133]

On 20 February Robert Boothby spoke in favour of a motion (eventually carried by 27 votes to 11) at the Hardwicke Society – a debating club for barristers – to change 'the penal laws relating to homosexual offences'. He also called for 'the appointment of a royal commission' to investigate the issue. Four days later, on 24 February, the cabinet discussed Fyfe's memorandum and agreed to 'resume at a later meeting their discussion of the question whether a formal enquiry should be instituted into the law relating to prostitution and to homosexual offences'. On 17 March the matter was again discussed in cabinet. Housing and local government minister Harold Macmillan noted in his diary: 'A very long cabinet – lasting till 1:45, and ranging from homosexuality to the price of milk.' Maxwell Fyfe told his colleagues that 'the unexplained increase in homosexual offences constituted a serious social problem which the government could not ignore; and in these circumstances the only course open to them was to appoint a royal commission or other appropriate form of enquiry to examine the problem and to suggest appropriate remedies'. [134, 135, 136]

On 24 March Montagu, Pitt-Rivers and Wildeblood were found guilty of homosexual offences. Montagu was sentenced to six months in prison; Pitt-Rivers and Wildeblood to 18 months each. On 28 March *The Sunday Times* carried an editorial called 'Law and Hypocrisy' in which it protested: 'The law, it would seem, is not in accord with a large mass of public opinion. Let it be admitted that the offences are to most of us disgusting; so too are other practices which are not punishable at law. The case for a reform of the law as to acts committed in private between adults is very strong. The case for authoritative inquiry into it is overwhelming.' On 15 April the cabinet again discussed sexual offences. Maxwell Fyfe 'felt obliged to press his earlier proposal for the holding of an independent enquiry into the law relating to prostitution and homosexual offences'. Because the cabinet was reluctant to set up another royal commission, such as those already sitting on mental illness and the civil service, Maxwell Fyfe was 'ready to agree that this enquiry should be made by a departmental committee'. For a sensitive subject like homosexuality, a departmental committee also had the advantage of being allowed to keep evidence secret and anonymous. [137, 138]

The cabinet approved Maxwell Fyfe's proposal and their decision was announced in parliament on 28 April during an adjournment debate initiated by Robert Boothby and Desmond Donnelly. Home Office minister Hugh Lucas-Tooth told MPs that the home secretary was 'anxious to secure the services of able and experienced men and women to serve upon this committee and, therefore, it may be some little time before he is in a position to announce its membership and terms of reference'. On 8 July, in response to a question from Boothby, Maxwell Fyfe announced that the committee would look into 'the law and practice relating to homosexual offences and the treatment of persons convicted of such offences by the courts' and report on 'what changes, if any, are in their opinion desirable'. He also told the Commons: 'Mr J.F. Wolfenden, CBE, vice-chancellor of Reading University, has agreed to serve as chairman'. Maxwell Fyfe had already talked to Wolfenden about taking on the chairmanship of the committee while the two of them had travelled on a sleeper train from Liverpool to London earlier that summer. Wolfenden had then discussed the proposal with his family and with the chancellor of Reading University, Samuel Hoare. It was Hoare who had spoken out against homosexuality and other forms of 'vice' in the House of Lords in November 1953. But he advised Wolfenden to accept the appointment.[137]

In August 1954 the names of the 14 other committee members were released:

1. James Adair, a solicitor, former procurator-fiscal for Glasgow and chairman of the Scottish Council of the YMCA
2. Mary Cohen, chairwoman of the Scottish Association of Mixed Clubs and Girls' Clubs and vice-president of the City of Glasgow Girl Guides
3. Desmond Curran, a consultant psychiatrist at St George's Hospital in London
4. Vigo Auguste Demant, canon of Christ Church, Oxford and regius professor of moral and pastoral theology at Oxford University
5. Kenneth Diplock, recorder of Oxford and a high court judge from 1956
6. Hugh Linstead, a barrister, pharmaceutical chemist and Conservative MP for Putney
7. Peter Kerr, Marquess of Lothian and a foreign office minister
8. Kathleen Lovibond, chairwoman of Uxbridge juvenile magistrates' court and mayor of Uxbridge from 1956
9. Victor Mishcon, a solicitor and chairman of London County Council
10. Goronwy Rees, principal of University College of Wales, Aberystwyth
11. R.F.V. Scott, Church of Scotland minister at St Columba's Church in London
12. Lily Stopford, an ophthalmologist and magistrate
13. William Wells, a barrister and Labour MP for Walsall
14. Joseph Whitby, a general practitioner in London.

Not all the committee members lasted the full three years of the enquiry. R.V.F. Scott resigned in March 1956 after he was appointed moderator of the general assembly of the Church of Scotland and could no longer spend much time in London. Goronwy Rees left in April 1956 after compromising his neutrality by giving information to the *People* newspaper about the homosexual spy Guy Burgess.

Committee meetings were mostly held at the Home Office in London, with some sittings at the Scottish Home Department in Edinburgh. In his memoirs John Wolfenden recounted the committee's first meeting.

> 'Vice, sir? Room 101,' said the door-keeper at the Home Office entrance. From the start it was clear, or ought to have been, that we were concerned with the law. We were not concerned with homosexuality as a state or condition, except in so far as that was relevant to the treatment of those who had already been convicted by the courts. We were not there to write a sociological treatise or a handbook of moral theology or a textbook for medical students. We read mountains of memoranda submitted as written evidence; and we interviewed dozens of oral witnesses. From time to time facetious gossip column writers asked if we were undertaking first-hand experience in the relevant fields. For my part I thought it prudent to avoid public lavatories in the West End. [140]

Wolfenden also told the committee, 'I have not the faintest idea at this moment what we shall ultimately recommend; but, whatever it turns out to be, my guess is that it will be unwelcome to approximately 50% of Her Majesty's subjects. In short, we can't win.' Wolfenden gave the impression that he knew little about homosexuality. This was somewhat disingenuous, given that he had known for some time that his son Jeremy was homosexual. Aged 20 at the time of his father's appointment and studying politics, philosophy and economics at Oxford University, Jeremy Wolfenden was open about his sexuality. Theatre director Anthony Page knew him at university and remembered him well: 'He had no guilt about it at all. He was quite a sweet, sentimental character. He was very refreshing to meet.' There was also Jeremy Wolfenden's story (possibly apocryphal) that after his father was appointed chairman of the committee he wrote his son a letter: 'Dear Jeremy, you will probably have seen from the newspapers that I am to chair a committee on homosexual offences and prostitution. I have only two requests to make of you at the moment: 1) That we stay out of each other's way for the time being; 2) that you wear rather less make-up.' [141, 142, 143]

Among the mass of written evidence submitted to the Wolfenden Committee were anonymous memoranda from two homosexual men. One was a 'professional man'; the other a 'homosexual medical practitioner', aged 46. Three other homosexual men met the committee in person: Peter Wildeblood, Patrick Trevor-Roper and Carl Winter. Wildeblood effectively invited himself in May 1955 – somewhat to the committee's dismay, since he was a convicted criminal only recently out of gaol. Trevor-Roper (an ophthalmic surgeon and the younger brother of the historian Hugh Trevor-Roper) and Winter received more formal invitations.

Originally Trevor-Roper and the writer Angus Wilson had approached Goronwy Rees about appearing before the committee because, as Trevor-Roper later explained, 'Several of us felt that the only homosexuals they'd have to give evidence would be the ones they could lay their hands on – people who'd been caught and who'd been in prison, or were occasionally exhibitionists from the sort of ballet-ish, transvestite world. They might not get a more considered view of people who were in fairly established jobs.' Through Rees, a dinner was arranged with Wolfenden and fellow committee member William Wells at the Oxford and Cambridge Club in London. Trevor-Roper remembered Wells as 'very sympathetic' and Wolfenden as 'mildly sympathetic, but slightly holding his nose in the air'. Both Trevor-Roper and Wilson were then asked to speak to the committee 'because the people they'd had hadn't been very articulate or at all balanced'. In the event, Wilson was unable to attend because he was on a literary tour abroad, so Winter was asked to replace him. The pair first sent in memoranda and then met with the committee under the protective aliases of 'Doctor' (Trevor-Roper) and 'Mr White' (Winter). Trevor-Roper recalled their meeting at the Home Office in July 1955. [144, 145]

We came in the door and the old porter said, 'What are you [here] for? Oh, the Wolfenden Committee. Ah, two more for vice!' echoed down these great halls. Goronwy spoke up rather splendidly, and gave us a very warm and encouraging entrance, saying in effect he was entirely on our side. Questions were polite, and details asked. Did homosexuality exist among consultants at my hospitals? I said, 'Oh yes', I knew personally that four out of twenty-odd consultants at Westminster [Hospital] were homosexual. I didn't add that two of them I'd had sex with. The only enemy was the procurator fiscal for Glasgow, Adair, who started all his remarks with, 'So you mean to say that...?' with a sneer and a dismissal and so on. We came out after an hour, shaken, but I dare say we'd achieved something. [146]

Chapter 1 references

1. The Bodley Head, 1976
2. *Report of the Committee on Homosexual Offences and Prostitution*, Her Majesty's Stationery Office, 1957 [Wolfenden Report]
3. Ibid.
4. Ibid.
5. Alfred C. Kinsey, Wardell B. Pomeroy, Clyde E. Martin, *Sexual Behavior in the Human Male*, W.B. Saunders, 1948
6. P.D. Scott, 'Homosexuality with Special Reference to Classification', *Proceedings of the Royal Society of Medicine*, September 1957
7. C.G. Learoyd, 'The Problem of Homosexuality', *The Practitioner*, April 1954
8. W. Lindesay Neustatter, 'Homosexuality: The Medical Aspect', op. cit.
9. *Homosexuality and Prostitution, A Memorandum of Evidence Prepared by a Special Committee of the Council of the British Medical Association for Submission to the Departmental Committee on Homosexuality and Prostitution*, British Medical Association, 1955
10. T.G. Grygier, 'Psychometric Aspects of Homosexuality', *The Journal of Mental Science*, July 1957
11. R.E. Hemphill, A. Leitch, J.R. Stuart, 'A Factual Study of Male Homosexuality', *British Medical Journal*, 7 June 1958
12. Wolfenden Report
13. Liz Stanley, *Sex Surveyed, 1949 to 1994: From Mass-Observation's 'Little Kinsey' to the National Survey and the Hite Reports*, Taylor & Francis, 1995
14. T.C.N. Gibbens, 'The Sexual Behaviour of Young Criminals', *The Journal of Mental Science*, July 1957
15. S.J.C. Spencer, 'Homosexuality Among Oxford Undergraduates', *The Journal of Mental Science*, April 1959

16. Desmond Curran, Denis Parr, 'Homosexuality: An Analysis of 100 Male Cases Seen in Private Practice', *British Medical Journal*, 6 April 1957

17. Denis Parr, 'Homosexuality in Clinical Practice', *Proceedings of the Royal Society of Medicine*, September 1957

18. 'One Million Need This New Clinic', *Daily Express*, 23 August 1957

19. 'Male Homosexuality', *The Lancet*, 12 December 1959

20. Wolfenden Report

21. Gordon Westwood, *Society and the Homosexual*, Gollancz, 1952

22. Desmond Curran, Denis Parr, 'Homosexuality: An Analysis of 100 Male Cases Seen in Private Practice', op. cit.

23. Denis Parr, 'Homosexuality in Clinical Practice', op. cit.

24. T.C.N. Gibbens, 'The Sexual Behaviour of Young Criminals', op. cit.

25. Denis Parr, 'Homosexuality in Clinical Practice', op. cit.

26. Frank Mort, 'Mapping Sexual London: The Wolfenden Committee on Homosexual Offences and Prostitution, 1954-57', *New Formations*, Spring 1999

27. Frank Mort, 'Mapping Sexual London', op.cit.

28. Roger Davidson, Gayle Davis, '"A Field for Private Members": The Wolfenden Committee and Scottish Homosexual Law Reform, 1950-67', *Twentieth Century British History*, Vol. 15, No. 2, 2004

29. *Homosexuality and Prostitution, A Memorandum of Evidence*, op. cit.

30. Angus Wilson, *Hemlock and After*, Secker & Warburg, 1952

31. Brian Sewell, *Outsider: Always Almost; Never Quite*, Quartet Books, 2011

32. Gillian Freeman, *The Liberty Man*, Longmans, 1955

33. Gillian Freeman, Edward Thorpe, personal interview with author, 31 November 2012

34. Wolfenden Report

35. S.J.C. Spencer, 'Homosexuality Among Oxford Undergraduates', op. cit.

36. Denis Parr, 'Homosexuality in Clinical Practice', op. cit.

37. Criminal Law Amendment Act 1885

38. Roger Davidson, Gayle Davis, '"A Field for Private Members"', op. cit.

39. Wolfenden Report

40. Ibid.

41. Ibid.

42. *The Homosexual Condition*, BBC Home Service, 25 July 1957, BBC Written Archives
43. Roger Davidson, Gayle Davis, '"A Field for Private Members"', op. cit.
44 Roger Davidson, Gayle Davis, *The Sexual State: Sexuality and Scottish Governance, 1950-1980*, Edinburgh University Press, 2012
45. Wolfenden Report
46. Ibid.
47. Angus Wilson, *Hemlock and After*, op. cit.
48. Philip Norman, *Shout!: The True Story of the Beatles*, Pan Books, 2004
49. Wolfenden Report
50. Ibid.
51. Ibid.
52. Compton Mackenzie, *Thin Ice*, Chatto and Windus, 1956
53. Wolfenden Report
54. Recorded Crime Statistics 1898-2001/2, Home Office Statistics
55. *Homosexuality and Prostitution, A Memorandum of Evidence*, op. cit.
56. Wolfenden Report
57. Recorded Crime Statistics, op. cit.
58. Wolfenden Report
59. Ibid.
60. J. Tudor Rees, Harley V. Usill (ed.s), *They Stand Apart*, Heinemann, 1955
61. Gordon Westwood, *Society and the Homosexual*, op. cit.
62. Peter Wildeblood, *Against the Law*, Weidenfeld & Nicolson, 1955
63. Rupert Croft-Cooke, *The Verdict of You All*, Secker & Warburg, 1955
64. Wolfenden Report
65. Ibid.
66. Denis Parr, 'Homosexuality in Clinical Practice', op. cit.
67. Denis Parr, 'Psychiatric Aspects of the Wolfenden Report', *British Journal of Delinquency*, July 1958
68. J. Tudor Rees, Harley V. Usill (ed.s), *They Stand Apart*, op. cit.
69. Gordon Westwood, *Society and the Homosexual*, op. cit.
70. Donald West, *Homosexuality*, Duckworth, 1955.
71. *Homosexuality and Prostitution, A Memorandum of Evidence*, op. cit.

72. Ibid.

73. Memo from D.F. Boyd to Isa Benzie, 23 October 1953, *The BBC and the Closet*, BBC Radio 4, 29 January 2008

74. Memo from D.F. Boyd to J.C. Thornton, 27 April 1954, op. cit.

75. *Woman's Hour*, BBC Light Programme, 28 November 1955, BBC Written Archives

76. Theatres Act 1843

77. 'South', Lord Chamberlain Plays Correspondence Files, British Library

78. 'The Trial of Oscar Wilde', op. cit.

79. 'The Immoralist', op. cit.

80. 'Tea and Sympathy', op. cit.

81. 'The Lonesome Road', op. cit.

82. 'The Catalyst', op. cit.

83. 'No Retreat', op. cit.

84. 'Serious Charge', op. cit.

85. Philip King, *Serious Charge*, Samuel French, 1955

86. Reader's Report, 26 April 1954, BBFC file: *Tea and Sympathy*

87. Reader's Report, 12 May 1954, op. cit.

88. *Tea and Sympathy*, Metro-Goldwyn-Mayer, 1956

89. *The Strange One*, Columbia Pictures, 1957

90. Note from Examiners, 31 May 1957, BBC File: *The Strange One*

91. Anthony Carthew, 'New X Film is a Sensation', *Daily Herald*, 12 July 1957

92. 'A Vile Villain', *Daily Mail*, 11 July 1957

93. 'Gazzara Hatches Out – And Becomes a Star in his First Film', *Evening Standard*, 25 July 1957

94. Paul Dehn, *News Chronicle*, 26 July 1957

95. Derek Hill, 'Superb – But Will They Let You See This Film?', *Tribune*, 2 August 1957

96. *Spectator*, 2 August 1957

97. Wolfenden Report

98. Gordon Westwood, *Society and the Homosexual*, op. cit.

99. Martyn Goff, *The Plaster Fabric*, Putnam, 1957

100. Donald West, personal interview with author, 14 September 2012

101. Donald West, *Gay Life, Straight Work*, Paradise Press, 2012

102. Peter Wildeblood, *A Way of Life*, op. cit.

103. Fritz Peters, *Finistère*, Gollanz, 1951

104. Angus Wilson, *Anglo-Saxon Attitudes*, Secker & Warburg, 1956

105. Ibid.

106. Gillian Freeman, *The Liberty Man*, op. cit.

107. Audrey Erskine Lindop, *Details of Jeremy Stretton*, Heinemann, 1955

108. Donald West, *Homosexuality*, op. cit.

109. John Fraser, *Close Up: An Actor Telling Tales*, Oberon Books, 2004

110. John Fraser, personal interview with author, 11 January 2013

111. Martyn Goff, *The Plaster Fabric*, op. cit.

112. David Kynaston, *Family Britain, 1951-57*, Bloomsbury, 2010

113. Alkarim Jivani, *It's Not Unusual: A History of Lesbian and Gay Britain in the Twentieth Century*, Michael O'Mara Books, 1997

114. Donald West, *Homosexuality*, op. cit.

115. Gore Vidal, *The City and the Pillar*, John Lehmann, 1949

116. Bob Cant, *Footsteps and Witnesses: Lesbian and Gay Lifestories from Scotland*, Word Power Books, 2008

117. Alkarim Jivani, *It's Not Unusual*, op. cit.

118. Audrey Erskine Lindop, *Details of Jeremy Stretton*, op. cit.

119. *The Rattigan Versions*, BBC Radio 4, 8 June 2011

120. Adrian Brown, personal interview with author, 8 June 2012

121. Donald West, *Homosexuality*, op. cit.

122. Denis Parr, 'Homosexuality in Clinical Practice', op. cit.

123. Wolfenden Report

124. Ibid.

125. Robert Fabian, 'No Mercy – That Was The Rule Of This Rogue', *Empire News*, 10 July 1955

126. Robert Fabian, 'Downfall of a Mastermind', *Empire News*, 17 July 1955

127. Wolfenden Report

128. Ibid.

129. *Behind the News*, BBC Home Service, 11 November 1953, BBC Written Archives

130. Michael McManus, *Tory Pride and Prejudice: The Conservative Party and Homosexual Law Reform*, Biteback Publishing, 2011

131. Justin Bengry, 'Queer Profits: Homosexual Scandal and the Origins of Legal Reform in Britain', in Heike Bauer, Matt Cook (ed.s), *Queer 1950s: Rethinking Sexuality in the Postwar Years*, Palgrave Macmillan, 2012

132. Robert Boothby, *Recollections of a Rebel*, Hutchinson, 1978

133. Michael McManus, *Tory Pride and Prejudice*, op. cit.

134. Robert Boothby, *Recollections of a Rebel*, op. cit.

135. Michael McManus, *Tory Pride and Prejudice*, op. cit.

136. Peter Catterall (ed.), *The Macmillan Diaries, Volume I: The Cabinet Years, 1950-1957*, Macmillan, 2003

137. 'Law and Hypocrisy', *The Sunday Times*, 28 March 1954

138. Michael McManus, *Tory Pride and Prejudice*, op. cit.

139. Ibid.

140. John Wolfenden, *Turning Points*, op. cit.

141. Hugh David, *On Queer Street: A Social History of British Homosexuality, 1895-1995*, Harper Collins, 1997

142. Anthony Page, personal interview with author, 22 August 2012

143. Sebastian Faulks, *The Fatal Englishman*, Vintage, 1997

144. Brian Lewis, *Wolfenden's Witnesses: Homosexuality in Postwar Britain*, Palgrave Macmillan, 2016

145. Patrick Trevor-Roper, recorded interview, August 1990, Hall-Carpenter Oral History archive, British Library

146. Ibid.

Chapter 2

THE DOCTRINE OF SAINT WOLFENDEN

There's toffs wiv toffee noses and
Poofs in coffee 'ouses and
Fings ain't wot they used t' be.
…
I've got news for Wolfenden.
Fings ain't wot they used t' be.

Frank Norman, Fings Ain't Wot They Used T' Be [1]

When 15-year-old Louis McPhail from the Isle of Lewis could not get his hands on his favourite newspaper cartoons in early September 1957 he did not at first understand why. 'All of a sudden the blooming *Daily Record*s were going on top of the larder, right at the top,' he recalled. 'When my mother was out I stood on an enamel bread bin and I reached the very top and I took down the *Daily Record*. It was all about homosexuality. It was the Wolfenden Report, and it was my first contact with the word "homosexual".' [2]

News about the report was more accessible for Allan Horsfall in Lancashire: 'I remember going up town and buying all the papers I could get my hands on and taking them into the Sunbeck café in Nelson and reading through them all to see what the reaction of the papers was, and indeed what the committee had recommended.' [3]

For men like Horsfall the Wolfenden Report initially aroused a great deal of hope. It began by rejecting some common assumptions about homosexuality. There was no evidence, the report said, that homosexuality led to 'the demoralisation and decay of civilisations'. This notion was merely 'the expression of revulsion against what is regarded as unnatural, sinful or disgusting'. Homosexual men were also no more likely to be blackmailed (and therefore 'bad security risks') than 'drunkards, gamblers and those who become involved in compromising situations of a heterosexual kind'. Besides, the possible risk of blackmail was not a good enough reason for continuing to make private homosexual behaviour a criminal offence. Nor should homosexuality's supposedly 'damaging effect on family life' be a reason for legislating against it. While the committee deplored any 'damage to what we regard as the basic unit of society' (i.e. a marriage 'successfully and happily consummated'), male homosexuality was no more likely to do such damage than 'adultery, fornication or lesbian behaviour'. [4]

The report countered the suggestion that a change in the law would 'open the floodgates' of homosexuality and lead to 'unbridled licence'. Although law reform might 'amount to a limited degree of toleration', it would not lead to 'any considerable number of conversions' to homosexuality. Besides, it was not the function of the law to 'intervene in the private lives of citizens or to seek to enforce any particular pattern of behaviour'. Society and the law should allow 'individual freedom of choice and action in matters of private morality'. Unless the law was used to equate crime with sin, 'there must remain a realm of private morality and immorality which is, in brief and crude terms, not the law's business'. This premise formed the background to the Wolfenden Report's key recommendation: that 'homosexual behaviour between consenting adults in private should no longer be a criminal offence'. [5]

The committee thought that 'consent' should mean the same as it did for heterosexual sex, and that there were 'no grounds for differentiating between homosexual and heterosexual relationships'. The term 'in private' should mean a place where sexual activity did not 'outrage public decency'. The definition of 'adult' was more problematic. Some

Wolfenden witnesses and submissions of evidence proposed 16 as an appropriate age of consent – equal to that for heterosexual sex. Others thought that it should be as high as 30. The most common suggestions were 18 and 21. Taking into account the 'need to protect young and immature persons', the age at which a man's sexual preference was 'fixed', the meaning of 'adult' responsibility and the legal consequences of settling on a younger age, the committee finally recommended 21. In doing so, they also held out the hope that younger men might be prevented from dabbling in homosexuality. Youths, the committee thought, were 'incapable at the age of 16 of forming a mature judgement about actions of a kind which might have the effect of setting [them] apart from the rest of society'. Older youths aged 18 to 20 might be 'more mature in this respect', but they could still be 'induced by means of gifts of money or hospitality to indulge in homosexual behaviour with older men'. A key factor in influencing the committee's choice of 21 was also the likelihood of their main recommendation passing into law. Speaking 15 years later, John Wolfenden recalled: 'We plumped for this simply on grounds of expediency. We thought we could get 21, and we didn't think we could get anything lower.' [6, 7]

In order to protect under-age but sexually active youths from the full force of the law, the committee recommended that no proceedings should be taken against them unless their behaviour was accompanied by 'criminal or vicious' conduct, such as bullying, abuse of position, prostitution or blackmail. To ensure 'uniformity of practice', the committee also recommended that 'no prosecution for a homosexual offence committed in private should be commenced in England and Wales against a person under the age of 21 without the sanction of the attorney-general'. [8]

Concerns about the spread and visibility of homosexuality led the committee to call for an extension of legal controls on homosexual pick-ups. In the interests of 'public order', 'decency' and the protection of 'weaker members of society', they recommended that 'procuring or attempting to procure the commission of homosexual acts by third parties' should continue to be a criminal offence. The committee also thought that the crime of living on the earnings of female prostitution 'should be made to apply to the earnings of male prostitution', and that the law against brothels should be extended to include 'premises used for homosexual practices'. [9]

In an oddly contradictory move, the committee recommended retaining the distinction between buggery and other homosexual acts, even though they also stated that there was 'no clear case for attaching to buggery a penalty heavier than that applicable to other homosexual offences' and that it was 'ludicrous that two consenting parties should be liable to imprisonment for life simply because the act of indecency takes a particular form'. The committee's reasons for deciding to keep buggery as a separate offence centred on the kind of moral objections they had already rejected as being outside the law's concern: 'there is a long and weighty tradition in our law that this, the "abominable crime", is in its nature distinct from other forms of indecent assault or gross indecency'. The committee also thought that people felt 'a stronger instinctive revulsion' towards buggery because 'it involves coition and thus simulates the normal act of heterosexual intercourse', and because it 'may sometimes approximate in the homosexual field to rape in the heterosexual'. In order to smooth over the contradiction of recommending that men over 21 be allowed to engage in anal intercourse in private while retaining it as a criminal offence for everyone else, the report proposed a realignment of sentences. This involved lowering the maximum penalties for buggery but increasing them for gross indecency. [10]

Offences and Maximum Sentences Proposed by the Wolfenden Report

Existing offence	Existing maximum penalty	Proposed new offence	Proposed maximum penalty
Buggery	Life imprisonment	Buggery by a man aged over 21 with a youth aged 16-20	Five years' imprisonment
		Buggery by a youth aged under 21 with a consenting partner aged over 16	Two years' imprisonment
		Buggery in public	Two years' imprisonment
Indecent assault on a male by a male	Ten years' imprisonment	No change	No change
Gross indecency	Two years' imprisonment	Gross indecency by a man aged over 21 with a youth aged 16-20	Five years' imprisonment
		Gross indecency by a youth aged under 21 with a consenting partner aged over 16	Two years' imprisonment
		Gross indecency in public	Two years' imprisonment

Source: Wolfenden Report

The report further recommended that gross indecency cases should be tried at magistrates' courts rather than at assizes or quarter sessions, thus reducing maximum sentences from two years' imprisonment to six months. And if gross indecency between consenting adults in private were no longer a criminal offence, it followed that men over 21 who searched for sexual partners should not be prosecuted for procuring sex acts for themselves. But because the committee did not want to encourage 'exploitation of the weaknesses of others', they recommended that it should remain a crime for 'third parties' to procure sex for other men. They also thought that 'indecencies committed in lavatories and other public places' should be prosecuted under the Sexual Offences Act 1956 rather than under local bye-laws, leading to punishments harsher than a £5 fine. [11]

The report recommended that men charged with importuning should be allowed to request a jury trial. But in the event of a guilty verdict, the existing penalties of up to two years' imprisonment should be maintained. Penalties for this offence, the committee added, should also be harsher than those recommended in Part Three of the report for soliciting by female prostitutes.[*] The report explained: 'We do not think that it would be expedient to reduce in any way the penalties attaching to homosexual importuning. It is important that the limited modification of the law which we propose should not be interpreted as an indication that the law can be indifferent to other forms of homosexual behaviour, or as a general licence to adult homosexuals to behave as they please.' [12]

Because the committee was conscious of a 'haphazard element' in the operation of the law and did not want to raise 'suspicions of "witch-hunting"', they advised against 'out-of-the-way prying' by the police. They also recommended that, except in cases of indecent assault and offences committed against boys under 16, 'the prosecution of any homosexual offence more than 12 months after its commission should be barred by statute'. [13]

---

[*]   A £10 fine for a first offence; £25 for a second offence; three months imprisonment for a third offence

In the interests of 'good management', 'the preservation of discipline' and 'the protection of those of subordinate rank', the committee proposed that the armed forces should be exempt from its recommendations. Even if a solider aged over 21 engaged in a homosexual act in private with a consenting adult who was not in the services, he should still be subject to a court martial for 'disgraceful conduct of an indecent or unnatural kind' under the Army Act 1955. [14]

By way of contrast, the committee advocated a wider degree of latitude at approved schools. The report noted that school heads in England and Wales were required to report incidences of buggery and attempted buggery to the Home Office, while in Scotland they could decide whether or not to report them to the police. The committee favoured this lighter touch, suggesting that 'heads and managers of approved schools should enjoy the same measure of discretion as those responsible for the management of any other educational establishment'. The committee also called on the judiciary to deal 'dispassionately' with homosexual offences and to give 'proper weight to the reformative as well as to the deterrent or preventative aspects' of sentencing. The dilemma of doctors who were legally obliged to report cases of buggery to the police was addressed by the recommendation that buggery be re-classified as a misdemeanour rather than a felony. [15]

Other recommendations covered 'preventive measures' to reduce homosexual crime. These included a proposal to set up an 'appropriate body or bodies' to discover the origins of homosexuality and to investigate 'the effects of various forms of treatment'. The committee thought that research could be organised through the Medical Research Council, which might bring together 'psychiatrists, geneticists, endocrinologists, psychologists, criminologists and statisticians'. The committee also thought that the number of homosexual offences could be reduced through 'a healthy home background' for young people, the provision of medical advice for parents and children, 'sensible' sex education for children, teachers, youth leaders and student advisers and more information and support for medical students, probation officers and the clergy. The press, too, had a role to play by ensuring that stories about court cases kept details discreet and identities hidden. The committee noted: 'We have encountered several cases in which men have got into touch with homosexual offenders whose convictions were reported in the press, with the result that further homosexual offences were committed.' They approved of steps taken by the Ministry of Education and the Scottish Education Department to bar convicted homosexual offenders from teaching in schools. In addition, the committee thought that police officers should 'keep a vigilant eye on public lavatories', and they suggested that an extension of the practice in Scotland of using bye-laws to make it an offence to stay for more than a certain amount of time in a public toilet 'might further discourage the improper use of such places'. [16]

Not everyone on the Wolfenden Committee was happy with the final report. Mary Cohen, Desmond Curran, Lily Stopford and Joseph Whitby added a reservation which disputed the legal distinction between buggery and other forms of homosexual behaviour. They noted that other European countries which similarly criminalised homosexuality did not treat buggery as a separate offence. Nor did they think that the reasons for doing so were strong enough. Joseph Whitby also objected to the report's suggested penalties for indecent assault, buggery and gross indecency. He thought that there should be just two categories of offence: indecent assault and gross indecency, with maximum penalties of ten and two years' imprisonment respectively. 'It is hard to believe,' he wrote, 'that a young man needs to be protected from would-be seducers more carefully than a girl.' He also thought that 'psychological damage and moral corruption' were just as likely to occur in cases of indecent assault against females, where the maximum penalty was just two years' imprisonment. [17, 18]

The strongest opposition to the report from within the committee came from James Adair. He objected to the key recommendation that homosexual acts between consenting adults in private should be legal. This, he thought, was 'contrary to the best interests of the community' and would have 'very serious effects on the whole moral fabric of social life'. He predicted that 'adult male lovers' would live 'openly and notoriously under the approval of the law', and that this would have 'a regrettable and pernicious effect on the young people of the community'. Adair wanted homosexuality to be 'reduced in extent, or at least kept effectively in check', and he feared that a change in the law would be seen as 'condoning or licensing licentiousness' at a time when a 'relaxed attitude toward moral conduct and relationships' was 'prevalent everywhere'. [19]

Despite these reservations, the committee signed off the report at its last meeting in July 1957. John Wolfenden briefed journalists on 3 September and the report was released on 4 September. Five thousand copies of the first printed edition (priced at five shillings) were sold within hours. Counter staff at Her Majesty's Stationery Office also reported 'very brisk' sales of the second print run. Fifteen thousand copies were eventually sold in the first nine months of publication.

For the first time in British history a government report openly examined a subject which had only ever previously been discussed covertly or sensationally. 'It seemed to me an enormous breakthrough that the subject was at last talked about and that a change in the laws was at last officially recommended,' remembered English lecturer Tony Dyson. MP Robert Boothby, who had first pressed for an official enquiry, thought that the Wolfenden Report was 'wholly admirable'. John Wolfenden himself was surprised at the level of interest it generated. He later recalled: 'It is difficult for me, and it must be nearly impossible for anyone else to realise the to-do that followed.' [20, 21, 22, 23]

Press reaction was mixed. Seven out of 21 (33%) national and regional newspapers supported the report's recommendations. Fourteen (67%) were against them. But the seven supporters were all big nationals and, as the *New Statesman*'s Francis Williams pointed out, they had a combined readership of 22.5 million, representing 61% of the mature population of the country. [24]

Press Reaction to the Wolfenden Report

Newspaper	Reaction	Comment
Birmingham Post	Negative	'A weakening of restraints upon practices agreed even by those who take no moral view to be socially undesirable.'
Daily Express	Negative	'Why did the government sponsor this cumbersome nonsense? It is up to the home secretary to see that family life remains protected from these evils.'
Daily Herald	Negative	'Homosexual vice is so abhorrent to normal minds that public opinion will be slow to accept such a change.'
Daily Mail	Negative	'The main recommendations – that homosexual acts between consenting adults should cease to be a criminal offence – would certainly encourage an increase in perversion.'
Daily Mirror	Positive	'Sensible and responsible'
Daily Sketch	Negative	'Retrograde'
Evening Standard	Negative	'On no account must the Wolfenden recommendations on homosexuality ever be implemented. They are bad, retrograde and utterly to be condemned.'
Liverpool Post	Negative	'A deterioration of respect for normal human values'
News Chronicle	Positive	'Concealment may do more harm than good'
News of the World	Negative	'The moment the state officially condones such behaviour, an entirely new outlook would result. No longer would homosexuality be something to fear or be frowned upon, it would become rather respectable and a "thing to do". There is no knowing where it would end from a national standpoint.'

Source	Stance	Quote
Reynolds News	Positive	'Other forms of moral conduct are much more widespread, and socially more harmful, than homosexuality; yet they are not subject to the criminal law.'
Sunday Dispatch	Negative	'[We] shall not rest until [MP and Wolfenden Committee member Hugh Linstead] has been expelled from the Conservative Party.'
Sunday Express	Negative	'The Pansies Charter'
Sunday Graphic	Negative	'A smiling benediction to the sins of Sodom'
The Daily Telegraph	Positive	'The committee's findings, though necessarily controversial, are clear, conscientious and courageous.'
The Manchester Guardian	Positive	'A fine piece of work'
The Observer	Positive	'It was not to be expected that the report would win unanimous approval, for the subjects discussed arouse strong emotions in the public mind; and men and women are apt to be influenced in their opinions by immediate and emotional impressions.'
The Scotsman	Negative	'It can be no solution to any public problem to legitimise a bestial offence.'
The Sunday Times	Negative	'Basic national moral standard undermined by libertarian cults'
The Times	Positive	'Adult sexual behaviour not involving minors, force, fraud or public indecency belongs to the realm of private conduct and not criminal law.'
Yorkshire Post	Negative	'If this proposal is adopted by parliament, can anyone deny that society will have acquiesced in a weakening of its moral fibre?'

Sources: Francis Williams, Fleet Street Notebook, *New Statesman*, 14 September 1957; 'Wolfenden Committee and the Press', *The Lancet*, 14 September 1957

Early opinion polls showed what some newspapers, politicians and John Wolfenden himself suspected – that the British public was not yet ready for homosexual law reform. On 6 September the *Daily Mirror* printed a questionnaire coupon for its readers to cut out and send in. Out of the first 10,273 responses, 4,880 (48%) were in favour of law reform; 5,393 (52%) were against. Regional differences were marked. About one in two *Mirror* readers in the south of England supported the decriminalisation of homosexual acts, compared to three out of seven in the north, and just one in six in Scotland. On 10 September the *News Chronicle* published the results of a Gallup poll. It revealed that 42% of people saw homosexuality as a 'serious problem'. Twenty-seven per cent thought that it was 'not very' serious. Thirty-one per cent did not have an opinion. Thirty-eight per cent supported decriminalisation; 47% did not. In Scotland opposition to reform was even stronger. A poll for the *Daily Record* published on 11 September found that just 16% of readers supported decriminalisation. Eighty-four per cent were against. These early tests of public opinion showed that an average of 34% of people in Britain favoured law reform, while 61% were opposed. [25, 26, 27]

Following the publication of the report, John Wolfenden and other committee members did the rounds of television, radio and press interviews. William Wells told fellow MPs on 31 October, 'Members of the Wolfenden Committee received invitations to appear on television and were pursued with inquiries from the press. Sir John Wolfenden has been asked to address a meeting at Cambridge. I addressed a meeting at Oxford last weekend, and I have been invited to attend a debate in Liverpool University at the end of November and to address an Institute of Insurers in December on the subject matter of the report. Sir John Wolfenden himself, as he well deserves to be, is almost as well known to the British public as Mr Elvis Presley.' [28]

During a BBC television interview on 4 September Wolfenden explained the committee's key recommendation: 'We are concerned primarily with public order and not with private morality. We believe, rightly or wrongly, on the medical evidence we have had, that to permit adult males to behave in this way in private might itself be a protection of younger people.' The next day ITV broadcast a programme called *Homosexuality and the Law* in its north-west (Granada) and London (Rediffusion) regions which featured a discussion about the report with Liberal Party leader Jo Grimond and Derrick Sherwin Bailey, a Wolfenden witness and study secretary of the Church of England's Moral Welfare Council. The day after that, Wolfenden told BBC Television's *Press Conference*, 'We were not concerned with the private, personal, moral responsibility of an individual man or woman, or his or her private sexual behaviour. We don't approve of it morally, just as we don't approve of all sorts of other things morally – for instance, adultery and fornication. But we don't see why this particular form of sexual misbehaviour, as distinct from adultery, fornication, lesbianism, all the others – which most of us regard as morally repugnant – why that and that only should be a criminal offence.' [29, 30, 31]

Although aired late in the evening (and sometimes preceded by a contents warning*), these television and radio programmes introduced millions of people to the issue of homosexuality for the first time. Peter Robins, who worked as a teacher, thought that the coverage generated by the Wolfenden Report helped to bring about a small but discernible shift in public attitudes: 'This was the beginning of the change of tide. A loosening of the censoriousness about anybody who was gay.' Writing in the *New Statesman* three weeks after the report was published, writer and former police inspector C.H. Rolph (who, as Cecil Hewitt, gave evidence to the Wolfenden Committee on behalf of the Society of Labour Lawyers) thought that 'what the Wolfenden Committee has done – more than any royal commission for years – is to move forward the horizon of social thinking to a new point of no return'. Former Lord Justice of Appeal Norman Birkett agreed. He told a Howard League for Penal Reform conference in London in October 1957: 'I think we can console ourselves with the view there has been an advance. The subject can never be quite the same again.' [32, 33, 34]

The medical profession in general backed the Wolfenden Report. *The Lancet* described it as a 'balanced and comprehensive' document

---

* ITV viewers on 5 September were told, 'If you don't like frankness on this subject, you had better switch off.' [35]

which revealed 'so undesirable a state of affairs that it is difficult to feel sympathy for Mr James Adair's reservation in which he argues for the retention of this offence'. Later that month the archbishop of York (and future archbishop of Canterbury) Michael Ramsey also signalled his support. Writing in his monthly diocesan letter, he expressed his hope that 'the Home Office, under the enlightened leadership of Mr Butler, will introduce legislation to give effect to the main recommendations. Those who are critical of the relaxation of the criminal law in one respect need, I think, to distinguish clear moral thinking from moral sentiment. Christianity abhors the indulgence of lust, whether by fornication, adultery or homosexuality. But morality is not best promoted by giving criminal status to every kind of grievous sin; and the status of crime rightly goes with acts which, besides being sinful, inflict direct injury on the rights and persons of other people or imperil the community.' [36, 37]

Pressure from elements within the Church of England resulted in a vote to approve the Wolfenden recommendations at the Church Assembly in November 1957. The archbishop of Canterbury, Geoffrey Fisher, spoke for many when he told the assembly, 'If you say that a homosexual who violates manhood with another man is criminal, the heterosexual who violates his own manhood with a woman is doubly criminal in what he does to the community and the general good. I am concerned with the man who breaks up a home with adultery or habitually indulging in fornication who is still regarded as a respectable member of society guilty of no offence.' The bishop of Exeter, Robert Mortimer, called negative attitudes towards homosexuality 'a relic', although he was quick to add that all church men and women were united in their 'disgust and condemnation' of homosexual acts. After seven hours of debate the result was close but decisive: 155 votes to 138. The following day John Wolfenden told BBC Radio's *Any Questions*, 'If you had said five years ago that in 1957 the Church Assembly would have voted by a majority in favour of excluding from the criminal law homosexual acts between consenting adult males in private you would have been sent to a lunatic asylum. No one would ever have dreamt that that could have happened.' [38, 39]

In early December the Catholic Church also shifted its stance – albeit slightly. In a statement published in the *Westminster Cathedral Chronicle* the archbishop of Westminster, William Godfrey, set out the Church's views on 'the proposals regarding homosexual acts between consenting adults'. He explained that, in the interests of 'the common good', it might be necessary to 'tolerate without approving' such acts. Catholic belief still held that homosexual behaviour was 'grievously sinful' and that civil law would 'not exceed its legitimate scope' if it attempted to stop such conduct from becoming 'widespread or an accepted mode of conduct', but if the law tried to prevent 'private acts of homosexuality' it might 'do worse evils for the common good'. Godfrey ended by telling Catholics that they were 'free to make up their own minds'. [40]

Other influential voices supported the Wolfenden recommendations. Speaking at the Howard League conference in October 1957, judge Richard Elwes (who gave evidence to the Wolfenden Committee on behalf of the Roman Catholic Advisory Committee on Prostitution and Homosexual Offences) called for the law to be changed. He described the Criminal Law Amendment Act 1885 as 'experimental'. It had, he said, been on the statute book for 70 years and had 'completely failed'. At the same conference psychiatrist W. Lindesay Neustatter said he was 'in complete agreement with the [Wolfenden] committee's views that the law should not interfere with the private lives of individuals, even if they behaved in a way of which the majority of citizens disapproved'. In November 1957 the writer J.B. Priestley wrote in his *Reynolds News* column: 'I myself am strongly in favour of changing the law which does a great deal more harm than good.' He criticised 'all these gobbling red-faced types who make such a fuss of their hatred of homosexuality', and he warned that the opponents of law reform would frighten 'this spineless government into a hasty retreat from the Wolfenden Report'. [41, 42]

Priestley was right to doubt the government's willingness to move forward on homosexual law reform. When John Wolfenden first presented his report, the home secretary Rab Butler told him it was 'extremely interesting', but 'you are way out in front of public opinion'. In the middle of November Butler sent a memorandum to the cabinet home affairs committee stating that 'the balance of public and parliamentary opinion would be against' the decriminalisation of homosexual acts. He was therefore 'not disposed, at the present time, to accept this recommendation'. On 28 November the cabinet learned that the House of Lords intended to hold a debate on the issue, and they 'authorised the Lord Chancellor to indicate that there was no early prospect of government legislation to amend the law relating to homosexual offences'. [43, 44]

The Lords debate opened on 4 December with the Labour peer Lord Pakenham (Frank Pakenham, later Lord Longford) calling attention to the Wolfenden Report. He approved of the Wolfenden Committee's distinction between crime and sin and urged peers to be as tolerant-minded as the taxi driver who had driven Peter Wildeblood to Leamington magistrates' court in 1954. 'Personally, and speaking man to man,' the driver had told Wildeblood, 'I think it is a lot of bleeding nonsense. If two chaps carry on like that and don't do any harm to no one, what business is it of anybody else's?' Of the 17 other peers who spoke during the debate, eight broadly supported Pakenham's call for reform. They included the Conservative Lord Brabazon of Tara, who said, 'These people are self-eliminating. They do not breed. They do very little harm if left to themselves. When we speak about the repugnance and disgust of the [homosexual] act, we have to face the fact that all sexual intercourse, be it heterosexual or homosexual, if looked at anatomically and physiologically, is not very attractive.' Lord Lothian, the Conservative peer who had sat on the Wolfenden Committee, called for a more 'constructive attitude' towards the issue. Labour's Lord Huntingdon thought that the government should 'be brave and alter the law'. Lord Jessel, a Unionist, said that as long as they did not corrupt or exploit others, and that they behaved decently in public, homosexual men should be left 'in peace and obscurity'. He even knew of two men who had lived together for years 'on terms of great devotion and affection', and he did not think that 'any useful social purpose' would be served by 'prying into their exact physical relationship'. Archbishop Fisher favoured retaining buggery as an offence, but he repeated his view that 'the threat to general public moral standards from homosexual offences done in private is far less, and far less widespread, than the damage openly done to public morality and domestic health by fornication and adultery.' [45, 46, 47, 48]

Other peers were hostile to the report. The bishop of Rochester, Christopher Chevasse, thought that homosexuality was a 'contagious influence', similar to leprosy. He complained of 'sodomy clubs' frequented by homosexual men, and he did not think that 'the best way of getting rid of them was to allow them to indulge in this practise and exist'. Like 'half the people in the Church', he thought that 'no change in the general lines of the law should be made'. Lord Denning believed that 'natural sin was deplorable, but unnatural vice was worse. It struck at the integrity of the human race.' Just because 'an act of bestiality' took place in private, it did not necessarily follow that it should no longer be a criminal offence. 'The law,' he added, 'must either condemn or condone. In cases like this, the law must condemn. For so many people now, it is the law that sets an example. I am afraid that hell fire and eternal damnation hold no terror these days.' The bishop of Carlisle, Thomas Bloomer, thought that 'the abolition of this law would take away props from many people who need help'. Lord Lawson said that most people viewed homosexuality with 'horror', and if the government gave 'any kind of special preference to homosexuals, the country would probably never recover from it'. Strong condemnation came from the lord chancellor, Lord Kilmuir, who as home secretary David Maxwell Fyfe had appointed the Wolfenden Committee in the first place. He bemoaned the presence of 'sodomitic societies and buggery clubs' which encouraged 'lying, cruelty and indecency', and he thought that the proposal to decriminalise homosexual behaviour was 'tantamount to suggesting there was nothing socially harmful in such behaviour'. Young people would 'inevitably' be encouraged to 'indulge' in such behaviour, and society would be 'corrupted'. He believed that 'for every genuine invert there were many perverted by money or the desire for fresh sensation'. He also thought that legal change would be extremely difficult: 'Even if it were thought right to accept the committee's recommendation in principle, and Her Majesty's Government do not think that, very difficult consequential problems would arise. There would be the problem of definition. What is "in private" for this purpose? What is "consent"?' Kilmuir also made it clear that the government would have to 'take careful account of public opinion', and he did not think that 'the general sense of the community was with the committee in this recommendation'. There was, he concluded, 'no prospect of early legislation'. [49]

During the Lords debate the bishop of Carlisle also drew attention to the 'great gap between the thinking of many people on the subject of the relationship of law and morality and the thinking of ordinary folk, in the highways and byways of life, who do not think very much about it at all'. Carlisle was right in claiming that the majority of people knew little about homosexuality. When 15-year-old model Christine Keeler met the photographer Mark Henry for the first time at his London studio in 1957 she felt 'quite frightened of him because he was queer and I had never met one before'. At around the same time, Gillian Freeman and Edward Thorpe saw Robert Anderson's banned play *Tea and Sympathy* at the Comedy Theatre club in London. 'When we came out in the interval there were two old ladies in front of me,' Thorpe recalled, 'and one of them leaned across to the other and said, "You know, dear, I think he's got TB."' [50, 51, 52]

Despite chairing the committee which took his name, John Wolfenden stopped championing the report and refused to further promote the cause of homosexual law reform. He gave no more media interviews after 15 November 1957 and, apart from a short piece in the *New Statesman* in 1960, remained largely silent on the issue. Many felt let down. According to gay rights campaigner Peter Tatchell, the Lancashire councillor and founding secretary of the North-Western Homosexual Law Reform Committee Allan Horsfall was 'scathing' about Wolfenden's refusal to endorse a public campaign to implement the report's recommendations: 'Once the report was finalised, Wolfenden washed his hands of it. He didn't want anything more to do with homosexual law reform. Allan found that very disappointing. He'd seen the report, he'd seen its potential, and yet the architect, the author, was not willing to defend it.' [53]

It was left to others to take the lead. This began with a series of letters to the *The Spectator* in early 1958. The first was written by Robert Reid, an academic from Wells and a former headmaster of King's College, Taunton, who had resigned from his post in 1937 after being convicted of importuning. On 3 January *The Spectator* published a letter from Reid in which he complained of 'pogroms' of homosexual men in his area, the latest involving a 17-year-old boy. [54, 55]

> The pattern is much the same in all these cases. The police go round from house to house, bringing ruin in their train, always attacking the youngest men first, extracting information with lengthy questioning and specious promises of light sentences as they proceed from clue to clue, i.e. from home to home, often up to twenty. This time the age range is seventeen to forty, which is about the average. Last time, a man of thirty-seven dropped dead in the dock at assize. Just because this happens in country places and at country assizes, it all goes largely unreported. We had hoped that it might be finished, but if it is to continue we desperately need some society to afford support and comfort to the victims and their families. The real tragedy is that we still have moralists in high positions who imagine that they do good by this cruelty and in whose hands rest the destiny and happiness of so many of us, heterosexual and homosexual alike. [56]

By referring to 'so many of us, heterosexual and homosexual alike', Reid was taking a considerable risk. But his letter struck a chord. A.E. (Tony) Dyson, an English lecturer at the University of Wales in Bangor, wrote to *The Spectator* a week later supporting Reid's idea of a society 'to help the victims and their families of our homosexuality laws'. He also suggested that such a society should 'work for a change in the laws themselves'. It was time, he argued, 'that those who feel strongly on this issue should work together and attempt to make more widely known the compulsive moral and rational reasons in favour of a change in the law'. The following week novelist E.M. Forster joined the debate with his own letter to the *The Spectator*. He thought that 'Dr

Reid's disquieting account of the police prosecutions at Wells should receive all possible publicity. Evidently the scientific conclusions and humane recommendations of the Wolfenden Report cut no ice in that city. I have it on good authority that in another provincial city the police have under their control a homosexual whom they employ as a bait. He encourages homosexual advances and then reports them.' The 'provincial city' was probably Cambridge, where Forster lived, and the 'good authority' was possibly policeman Bob Buckingham, with whom Forster had had an intimate friendship since the 1930s. Forster maintained that the Wolfenden Report was 'not dead because the present government has chosen to ignore it', but rather 'a living document which will be constantly discussed and will gradually influence public opinion'. [57, 58]

MP Robert Boothby weighed in the debate with a letter on 24 January. Claiming to be 'the politician who was mainly responsible for getting the Wolfenden Committee set up', he welcomed Forster's opinion of the report as a 'living document', and he detected a 'sea change' in public attitudes towards homosexuality: 'Not for the first time public opinion is ahead of the House of Commons.' He also predicted with some accuracy what he thought would happen next. [59]

> There will be much animated discussion of the Wolfenden Report; and in the meantime the more disgraceful methods which have hitherto been used by the police against homosexuals will be greatly modified. After a time the argument will die down, but the climate of opinion will have been altered. Then some private member of parliament or, better still, some private lord will introduce a measure which will be carefully designated a Bill for the Further Protection of Young Girls. Into this bill a clause will be inserted to delete the Labouchère amendment to the similar bill of 1885. It will be passed, in an empty house on a hot August night, without discussion and without a division. [60]

Tony Dyson took the next step by drafting a letter to *The Times* in which he called on the government to legislate on the Wolfenden recommendations. Thirty years later, Dyson explained why he attempted to revive the report's flagging fortunes.

> I decided it must not be buried and forgotten. Somehow or other it must be kept alive. It must be talked about and talked about until everyone is so sick and tired of hearing it talked about that they just feel they have to do something, if only to stop the discussion. But the discussion still hadn't started, and I was waiting for somebody to start it, but nobody seemed to do it. In the end I just felt that if nobody else was going to do something I might have a go. [61]

After writing the letter, Dyson set about gathering influential signatures. Some of the people he approached refused to sign. The actor and theatre manager Donald Wolfit was appalled. 'He wrote a wonderful blockbuster,' remembered Dyson, 'all underlined, saying he would not sign such a preposterous letter, and how could one overlook the sinfulness of it.' John Wolfenden was dismissive: 'He said don't do it. It'll do more harm than good.' The former prime minister Anthony Eden apologised for not signing because, 'under strict medical advice', he was 'not making any statements for publication at the present time'. But thirty-two eminent people did sign the letter. They included two bishops (Birmingham and Exeter), Methodist minister and peace campaigner Donald Soper, Anglican cleric Trevor Huddleston, former prime minister Clement Atlee, writers Cecil Day Lewis, Stephen Spender, Angus Wilson, J.B. Priestley and his wife Jacquetta Hawkes, academic Noel Annan, historian A.J.P. Taylor, philosophers A.J. Ayer, Isiah Berlin and Bertrand Russell, doctors Alex Comfort and Kenneth Walker, sociologist Barbara Wootton and MP Robert Boothby. The letter was published on 7 March 1958. [62]

> Sir,– We, the undersigned, would like to express our general agreement with the recommendation of the Wolfenden Report that homosexual acts committed in private between consenting adults should no longer be a criminal offence. The present law is clearly no longer

representative of either Christian or liberal opinion in this country, and now that there are widespread doubts about both its justice and its efficacy, we believe that its continued enforcement will do more harm than good to the health of the community as a whole. The case for reform has already been accepted by most of the responsible papers and journals, by the two Archbishops, the Church Assembly, a Roman Catholic committee, a number of non-conformist spokesmen, and many other organs of informed public opinion. In view of this, and of the conclusions which the Wolfenden Committee itself agreed upon after a prolonged study of the evidence, we should like to see the government introduce legislation to give effect to the proposed reform at an early date; and are confident that if it does so it will deserve the widest support from humane men of all parties. [63]

Reaction was swift. On 21 March Lord Brabazon, who had supported the Wolfenden proposals in the House of Lords debate, wrote to Dyson.

I went the other day with Lord Pakenham to see the chancellor, relative to the possibility of him implementing at least some of the report of the [Wolfenden] committee. He was very sympathetic and said that the home secretary is sympathetic too, but the home secretary thought that they should have a debate in the House of Commons first of all to see what the feeling was there. Don't think for a moment that we're going to get recommendation one[*] through. That is going to be a long uphill fight. But if you get on with your society and try and raise hell when there is a witch hunt by foolish chief constables and that sort of thing, we shall be making a start. I think the law will finally be changed, and we shall look back on the present situation as odd as capital punishment for the theft of five shillings. [64]

On 19 April a group of 15 well-known married women (including the writers Iris Murdoch, Myfanwy Piper and Elizabeth Pakenham) wrote

---

[*] 'Homosexual behaviour between consenting adults in private should no longer be a criminal offence.' [65]

to *The Times* agreeing with the 7 March letter and challenging the government's assertion that public opinion was against implementation of the Wolfenden Report.

> We believe the government statement that public opinion is not ready for a change in the laws is too pessimistic; and that most humane and thoughtful people in this country would welcome early implementation of the report's findings on this subject. [66]

Some of those who signed Dyson's 7 March letter wanted to do more. Kenneth Walker and Jacquetta Hawkes persuaded C.H. Rolph, W. Lindesay Neustatter and the publisher Victor Gollancz to attend a meeting at the Priestleys' flat in the Albany building on London's Piccadilly. This led to the founding of the Albany Trust, a fundraising and charitable organisation to 'promote psychological health in men by collecting data and conducting research, publish the results thereof by writing, film, lectures and other media [and] take suitable steps based thereon for the public benefit to improve the social and general conditions necessary for such healthy psychological development'. Shortly afterwards what eventually became the Homosexual Law Reform Society held its first meeting on 12 May 1958 at Kenneth Walker's Harley Street surgery. Only three people were present: Walker, Tony Dyson and his friend the Anglican clergyman Andrew Hallidie Smith. Walker became chairman and Dyson vice chairman. Smith was later appointed secretary of both the HLRS and the Albany Trust. An executive committee was formed which included Gollancz, Hawkes, Neustatter, Rolph, Stephen Spender and Labour MP Kenneth Younger. An honorary committee was also appointed in order to, as Dyson explained, 'convince people that we were not just a set of cranks, or indeed a set of homosexuals, but that we were representing an actual liberal and intellectual strand in British opinion'. Honorary members included some of the signatories to the 7 March and 19 April *Times* letters, and also fashion designer Hardy Amies, novelist Graham Greene, actress Vivien Leigh, art historian Herbert Read, actress Sybil Thorndike, theatre critic Kenneth Tynan and writers L.P. Hartley, Compton Mackenzie and V.S. Pritchett. [67, 68]

The HLRS was an eclectic mix of the great, the good and the sympathetic. Antony Grey, who succeeded Andrew Hallidie Smith as secretary of the HLRS and Albany Trust in 1962, remembered it as 'a very broadly based society; people with all shades of religious and political opinions, and all shades of medical and psychiatric opinion. A lot of these people would have disagreed violently about the medical, moral and practical aspects of homosexuality. But one thing upon which they all agreed was that the existing law was unjust and should be done away with.' There was no question of adopting a radical agenda. Instead, law reformers rallied around the Wolfenden Report as the most acceptable model for legal change. As the Earl of Arran, who later became a prominent supporter of homosexual law reform, recalled: 'All I did was to preach the doctrine of Saint Wolfenden and to follow his major precepts.' [69]

Initial campaigning was done by a working party of volunteers. They included Antony Grey, who under his real name Anthony Garside Wright worked as a press officer for the British Iron and Steel Federation. The working party met at the home of Len Smith and Reiss Howard at 219 Liverpool Road in Islington, north London. Smith was a member of the Labour Party and had been a conscientious objector during the Second World War. Reiss, a Canadian, was an artist. Together they ran an antiques business. Their decision to allow the HLRS to use their address was a brave one, given the risk of police surveillance and arrest. Antony Grey later remembered the work of letter writing, envelope stuffing and record keeping there with great affection: 'It was the first time, I think, that I had known gay people in their own home background who had an atmosphere and an aura of calm and serenity, and maturity and enjoyment.' [70]

In the second half of 1958 much-needed funds started to come in. 'Letters appeared, many of them containing small amounts of money, encouragement, offers of help,' recalled Tony Dyson. Radio and television personality Gilbert Harding gave £50 after a 'rather harrowing' talk with Dyson in which he 'appeared completely broken in spirit by having to be a repressed homosexual in public life'. The poet Edith Sitwell donated £50 with 'a nice little letter'. Even John Wolfenden sent a letter (but no money) offering qualified support. He told Dyson it would take 'at least 17 years' to get the law changed. 'You might do it,' he added, 'although I doubt it. But I wish you luck now you've started.' E.M. Forster was 'very helpful', sending occasional cheques – sometimes for 'three or four thousand pounds at a time'. Artists Henry Moore and John Piper donated valuable pictures. By the beginning of October the HLRS had enough money to move into offices on the second floor of an 'outwardly imposing but inwardly squalid Victorian block' at 32 Shaftesbury Avenue in central London. [71, 72, 73]

The move came as the House of Commons was finally scheduled to debate the Wolfenden Report. In readiness, the HLRS circulated copies of *Homosexuals and the Law* – a pamphlet partly written by Peter Wildeblood – to all MPs. Further mailings of Wildeblood's *Against the Law* and Eustace Chesser's *Live and Let Live** caused anger among some MPs, who claimed that it was evidence of undue interference in the parliamentary process by a subversive homosexual lobby.

Ahead of the debate, a deputation of HLRS members met the home secretary, Rab Butler. As Brabazon had earlier told Dyson, Butler seemed to favour implementation of the Wolfenden Report. On 17 November he and Scottish Office minister Niall Macpherson met with the Tory backbench home affairs committee to discuss the report. The meeting did not go well. Fifteen years later Butler recalled how he 'did make very careful soundings of the party', but many of his Conservative colleagues 'would not have supported the reform. I wouldn't have got it through. If you're going to get your bill through you've got to get a majority, and there wasn't a majority at that time, because I tried.' On 18 November the cabinet agreed that during the forthcoming debate 'it would be necessary to oppose any proposal that the recommendations dealing with homosexuality should be accepted'. [74, 75]

The case for homosexual law reform was not helped by a sex scandal. On 21 November the prime minister Harold Macmillan confided in his

---

* The book strongly supported the Wolfenden recommendations and urged readers to remember that homosexuality was not 'the most alarming feature of life in the Atomic Age'. [76]

diary: 'A most unfortunate new trouble. Ian Harvey (under secy, F.O.) and a very nice chap, was arrested on Wednesday night in St James' Park and has been charged with indecent behaviour with a young guardsman. If (as I fear) he is guilty, it means that he must resign his post in the govt and his seat in parlt. I saw him this morning, and did my best to comfort him. But it [is] a terrible thing and has distressed me greatly.' According to Harvey – the MP for Harrow East and joint under-secretary of state at the Foreign Office – on the night of 19 November, after a dinner at the Polish embassy and a late vote in the House of Commons, he was 'in need of some fresh air' so went for a walk in St James's Park. [77, 78]

> It was just after eleven o'clock and the guardsmen were returning to Wellington barracks as the pubs were emptying. I had decided to make a circle of the park and I was walking down the Mall which admittedly is a known place for homosexual pick-ups. A young guardsman in uniform passed me at a slow pace and I knew what that meant. I turned and caught up with him and we went together into the park. [79]

A policeman and a park keeper heard rustling noises in the bushes and saw 'two men standing under a tree misbehaving'. Whilst being taken to Cannon Row police station Harvey tried to make a run for it, and on arrival there he gave a false name. At Bow Street magistrates' court the following morning 44-year-old Harvey and 19-year-old Coldstream guardsman Anthony Plant were charged with gross indecency and breaching park regulations by 'behaving in a way likely to offend against public decency'. Harvey immediately gave up his parliamentary seat and tendered his resignation to foreign secretary Selwyn Lloyd, who passed on Harvey's ministerial portfolio to John Profumo. Only former prime minister Winston Churchill seemed amused. After hearing about Harvey's arrest, he supposedly remarked, 'On the coldest night of the year? It makes you proud to be British.' Harvey was tried at Bow Street magistrates' court on 10 December. Thanks to the efforts of his barrister John Lawrence, charges of gross indecency were dropped. Harvey and Plant were instead fined £5 for breaking park regulations. Harvey paid Plant's fine. 'I felt it was the least I could do,' he later explained. Harvey went on to endure two years of social ostracism, alcoholism and depression. He and his wife (with whom he had two daughters) were divorced. He resigned from his clubs or was asked to stay away, and he was only spared the indignity of a dishonourable discharge from the Territorial Army by the intervention of the under-secretary of state at the War Office Hugh Fraser. Harvey also consulted doctors, including psychiatrist and Wolfenden witness Clifford Allen, about his 'condition'. Allen, he recalled, was 'clearly disappointed that I was neither on the verge of insanity nor desperately anxious to be cured of this terrible disease'. Harvey eventually went back to work in the advertising industry and became chairman of the Conservative Group for Homosexual Equality in 1980. [80, 81]

The House of Commons debate opened on 26 November. Like the Lords debate, it centred on a motion to 'take note' of the Wolfenden Report and did not lead to a final vote. 'It is a foregone conclusion,' said *The Times* that morning, 'that the homosexual laws will not be reformed yet.' But, it added, 'It is equally a foregone conclusion that reform must come eventually. The majority of well-informed people are now clearly convinced that these laws are unjust and obsolete in a society which refuses to punish lesbian practices, prostitution, adultery, fornication or private drunkenness.' During the debate MPs raised the usual objections against the decriminalisation of homosexual behaviour. Fred Bellinger, the Labour member for Bassetlaw, described homosexual men as 'a malignant canker in the community' who would 'eventually kill off what is known as normal life'. Cyril Black (Conservative, Wimbledon) warned that 'these unnatural practices, if persisted in, spell death to the souls of those who indulge in them. Great nations have fallen and empires been destroyed because corruption became widespread and socially acceptable.' Jean Mann (Labour, Coatbridge and Airdrie) feared an 'evil thread' running through the theatre, music halls, the press and the BBC which had international ramifications'. William Shepherd (Conservative, Cheadle) thought that there was 'far too much sympathy with the homosexual and far too little regard for society. I believe that it is our duty as far as we can to stop this society within a society. I want to discourage the homosexual by the discouragement of the law.' [82, 83, 84]

There were, however, some sympathetic voices. Peter Rawlinson (Conservative, Epsom), who had been junior defence counsel for Peter Wildeblood in 1954, opposed decriminalisation but recognised the defects in the law: 'To see a man, perhaps of talent and distinction, in the box, and to see the worthless wretched creatures being paraded there as witnesses for the crown, pampered by the police, is to feel that it is a mockery by society of the administration of the law.' Harford Montgomery Hyde (Ulster Unionist, Belfast North, and an honorary member of the HLRS) quoted from a letter he had received a few days earlier from a 'consenting adult' who had been sent to prison for 'an act committed in private'. The man had lost his job as a solicitor's clerk after someone sent his firm a press cutting about his trial and conviction.* Anthony Greenwood (Labour, Rossendale, and vice chairman of the Parliamentary Labour Party) told MPs: 'I believe that, ultimately, this reform will come. I am only saddened by the fact that it should come only after a still greater toll of human misery has been exacted by society.' [85, 86]

Home secretary Rab Butler signalled the government's unwillingness to implement the Wolfenden Report. He told the Commons: 'What is clear is that there is at present a very large section of the population who strongly repudiate homosexual conduct and whose moral sense would be offended by an alteration of the law which would seem to imply approval or tolerance of what they regard as a great social evil.' The debate closed with final remarks from under-secretary of state at the Home Office David Renton: 'We believe it is the instinct of most members of the public and most members of both Houses of Parliament to decline the Wolfenden proposals.' [87, 88]

But the fact that homosexuality had been discussed in parliament twice in one year was an achievement of sorts. On the morning of the Commons debate Kenneth Allsop of the *Daily Mail* wrote about 'the amazing changes' taking place in British society. [89]

---

* Hyde was deselected as Belfast North's Ulster Unionist parliamentary candidate before the 1959 general election. His constituency association remarked, 'We cannot have as our member one who condones unnatural vice.' [90]

Quietly, but inexorably, a startling revolution in morals is taking place in our society. Today's House of Commons debate on the Wolfenden Committee's recommendations is an expression at constitutional level of public acceptance of the necessity to discuss such problems publicly and candidly. It is a climate in which sex is being shorn of the leer and snigger. In the theatre, on the screen, on television, and in books a new honesty has emerged in this past year or two; the forthright examination of subjects that until very recently were taboo. [91]

The 'new honesty' in publishing had been underway for some time. A small but steady stream of novels featuring homosexual characters and themes had been published since the early 1950s. They included G.F. Green's *In the Making* (1952), Angus Wilson's *Hemlock and After* (1952) and *Anglo-Saxon Attitudes* (1956), Audrey Erskine Lindop's *Details of Jeremy Stretton* (1955), Gillian Freeman's *The Liberty Man* (1955), Compton Mackenzie's *Thin Ice* (1956) and Mary Renault's *The Last of the Wine* (1956). American titles were also available in Britain, such as Gore Vidal's *The City and the Pillar* (1949), Fritz Peters' *Finistère* (1951) and James Barr's *Quatrefoil* (1953). The most popular pre-Wolfenden 'homosexual' novel was Rodney Garland's *The Heart in Exile*, an exposé of London's homosexual scene, published by W.H. Allen in 1953.

The release of the Wolfenden Report and the media and parliamentary debates that followed prompted a further opening up of the market for homosexual novels. The first was Martyn Goff's *The Plaster Fabric*, published by Putnam in 1957. Goff's publisher supposedly warned him that the novel could land both of them in court, but a positive review by the poet John Betjeman discouraged the authorities from taking any legal action. *The Plaster Fabric*'s modest success encouraged other publishers to take on homosexual-themed fiction. Post-Wolfenden titles included Robin Maugham's *The Man With Two Shadows* (Four Square, 1958), Michael Nelson's *A Room in Chelsea Square* (Jonathan Cape, 1958), James Courage's *A Way of Love* (Jonathan Cape, 1959), Paul Buckland's *Chorus of Witches* (W.H. Allen, 1959), Simon Raven's *The Feathers of Death* (Anthony Blond, 1959), Mary Renault's *The Charioteer* (Pantheon Books, 1959) and

Alfred Duggan's *Family Favourites: A Roman Scandal* (Peter Davies, 1960). Foreign titles included James Baldwin's *Giovanni's Room* (Michael Joseph, 1957) and Maxence Van der Meersch's *Mask of Flesh* (William Kimber, 1960). In addition, homosexual characters appeared in mainstream fiction – in John Braine's *Room at the Top* (Eyre & Spottiswood, 1957; filmed in 1959), John Boland's, *The League of Gentlemen* (T.V. Boardman & Company, 1958; filmed in 1960), John Wiles' *The Asphalt Playground* (Gollancz, 1958), Angus Wilson's *The Middle Age of Mrs Eliot* (Secker & Warburg, 1958), Colin MacInnes' *Absolute Beginners* (MacGibbon & Kee, 1959), J.R. Ackerley's *We Think the World of You* (The Bodley Head, 1960), Lynne Reid Banks' *The L-Shaped Room* (Chatto & Windus, 1960; filmed in 1962), Andrew Salkey's *Escape to an Autumn Pavement* (Hutchinson, 1960), Colin MacInnes' *Mr Love and Justice* (MacGibbon & Kee, 1960) and David Storey's *This Sporting Life* (Longmans, Green & Co., 1960; filmed in 1963).

But the biggest change in the cultural landscape was the lifting of the blanket ban on homosexuality in the theatre. On 31 October 1958 the Lord Chamberlain issued a memorandum to his staff at St James's Palace alerting them to a 'change in policy' on the 'forbidden subject'. 'For some time,' he wrote, 'the subject of homosexuality has been so widely debated, written about and talked about, that it is no longer justifiable to continue the strict exclusion of this subject from the stage. Now that it has become a topic of almost everyday conversation, its exclusion from the stage can no longer be defended as a reasonable course.' He recommended that 'serious and sincere' plays which provided worthy 'contributions to the problem' should be allowed. To this end, he issued a set of guidelines: [92]

(a) Every play will continue to be judged on its merits. The difference will be that plays will be passed which deal seriously with the subject.
(b) We would not pass a play that was violently pro-homosexuality.
(c) We would not allow a homosexual character to be included if there were no need for such inclusion.
(d) We would not allow any 'funny' innuendos or jokes on the subject.

(e) We will allow the word 'pansy', but not the word 'bugger'.

(f) We will not allow embraces between males or practical demonstrations of love.

(g) We will allow criticism of the present homosexual laws, though plays obviously written for propaganda purposes will fall to be judged on their merits.

(h) We will not allow embarrassing display by male prostitutes. [93]

Kenneth Allsop called the Lord Chamberlain's move 'a sudden and unexpected concession to the spreading mood of enlightenment'. But Lord Scarborough's examiners had been uncomfortable with the homosexual ban for some time. In September 1953, while scrutinising Julien Green's *South*, assistant examiner St Vincent Troubridge noted, 'This play raises once again the question of the degree and extent to which the perversion of homosexuality may be dealt with on the public stage'. Because of the ban, Troubridge was 'not in doubt that I must pronounce against it', but he did so 'with the proviso that, if the Lord Chamberlain should have in mind any possible relaxation of the present attitude, this would provide the occasion'. Troubridge expressed similar uneasiness four years later while examining Ronald Duncan's *The Catalyst*. The play concerns three characters, one male and two female, who come to realise that they are all homosexual. Troubridge thought that it was a 'superb probing of human hearts and of the springs of love, affection and sexuality in men and women by a true poet with no intention to shock'. He recommended it for a licence, but his decision was overruled. In a highly unusual move, Troubridge challenged that decision: 'I have only once before offered advice in favour of a play of this nature; that was *Sud* [*South*] by Julien Green, when I said that *if* there were to be any relaxation, that was a suitable object; now I say (exceptionally) that I think there *should* be relaxation.' Once again he was overruled. [94, 95, 96]

In early 1958 the censors examined *Valmouth*, Sandy Wilson's adaptation of Ronald Firbank's 1919 novel – 'a risqué, ribald musical' which 'would not have easily found public acceptance just a few years ago'. The script was peppered with homosexual innuendos, including 'a dubious passage' about 'a Catholic priest with apparently a penchant for footmen' and a joke about male partridges doing 'curious things amongst themselves'. Even after being accepted with cuts for runs at Liverpool's New Shakespeare Theatre and the Lyric Theatre in Hammersmith, London, it remained for Troubridge 'about the most horrid musical I have ever read'. [97]

More problematic was the all-male revue *We're No Ladies*, written by and starring drag artists Phil Starr (Arthur Fuller) and Terry Dennis. Since the show included 'nothing immediately discernible as homosexual', it was passed for performance. But as soon as it opened on 4 February 1958 at the Twentieth Century Theatre in west London letters of complaint began to arrive. Examiner R.J. Hill went to see the show and reported that it was all fairly innocuous. Indeed, 'it would have called for little comment had not all the female parts been played by men. Some of the actors approximated to the dame type, others were pathologically effeminate. Nevertheless, apart from one or two questionable gestures, the actors' conduct on the stage was simply that of women. There were no "cissy" gestures or attempts to impose a male personality on that of the womanly one. There is no law which prevents female impersonation on the stage; it is in fact as old as the stage. Some of these actors were so good they might have been thought to be women.' Hill found that among the audience 'there was one almost certain homosexual, but apart from him the company present all looked most respectable and there were many accompanied by wives or girlfriends who obviously had no perverted interest in the proceedings. I listened, and certainly in my vicinity there was no questionable conversation. I saw no undesirables making themselves conspicuous during the interval.' The audience was 'large and enthusiastic' and familiar with 'camp' ('specialised actors' slang for a homosexual gathering'). Hill also noticed 'a rapport between audience and stage – in some cases Christian names were known, e.g. shouts of "Bravo Wally" at some piece of acting'. He concluded: 'I can offer no concrete evidence of the Twentieth Century Theatre becoming a focal point for pederasts.' In the end Phil Starr was ticked off by the Lord Chamberlain for departing from the licenced script and ordered to stop his drag queens singing the national anthem during the show. [98]

It was *We're No Ladies* rather the Wolfenden Report which prompted the Lord Chamberlain to rethink his policy on homosexuality. Writing to the clerk of the London County Council on 10 February to reassure him that action had been taken on the revue, assistant comptroller Norman Gwatkin admitted, 'The Lord Chamberlain finds himself in some difficulty over pieces of this kind. He has no apparent grounds for refusing to license a play merely because it is to be performed by female impersonators. Nevertheless the increase in homosexuality could give such performances a new implication.' [99]

With a change of policy already on the cards, Shelagh Delaney's *A Taste of Honey* had an easier time getting a licence – despite the inclusion of a homosexual character, Geoff Ingram. The play was staged by Joan Littlewood's experimental Theatre Workshop at the Theatre Royal in Stratford, east London on 20 May 1958 and transferred to the West End early the following year. Examining the script on 5 May, reader Charles Heriot found it 'a surprisingly good play – though God knows it is not to my personal taste. But the people are strangely real and the problem of Geoff is delicately conveyed.' He also thought that it was 'the perfect border-line case, since it is concerned with the forbidden subject in a way that no one, I believe, could take exception to.' References to Geoff as a 'pervert' and a 'castrated little clown' were, however, ordered to be cut. [100]

Even before he issued his memorandum, the Lord Chamberlain was looking for a play to trumpet his anticipated new policy. Joan Henry's *Look on Tempests*, which deals with the effect on a family of a man's conviction for an unspecified homosexual crime, was initially considered. On 6 October Charles Heriot wrote, 'This is what is known as a "sound" play on a forbidden subject. It is serious and sincere, but it is not well constructed. It could never, I believe, be a suitable *point d'appui* for any change of policy.' On the same day, assistant comptroller Norman Gwatkin informed comptroller Terence Nugent: 'Heriot does not consider this a worthwhile enough play with which to initiate a new policy. He is rather in favour of waiting for one by a well-known author.' Nugent wrote back to Gwatkin, 'I am afraid that I agree with Heriot that this play is not a worthy vehicle for so momentous a change of policy. It may be sincere and serious, but to my mind it is a very amateurish affair. I think that the change of policy, when it comes, should be heralded by a really worthwhile play, which I fear I do not think *Look on Tempests* to be.' Henry's play was refused a licence. [101]

In the event, there was no new play to herald the policy. But after it was announced in a letter to the chairman of the Theatres National Committee, Charles Killick, on 6 November, the effect was immediate. On 17 November Robert Anderson's *Tea and Sympathy* was passed for performance, followed by Ruth and Augustus Goetz's *The Immoralist* on 25 November. Julien Green's *South* and Joan Henry's *Look on Tempests* received licences on 19 February and 25 September 1959 respectively.* The first new play with homosexual characters and references to be licenced under the new regime was Frank Norman's *Fings Ain't Wot They Used T' Be*, which opened at the Theatre Royal, Stratford on 17 February 1959. Joan Littlewood's improvisatory direction got her into trouble with the Lord Chamberlain, but the 'queer interior decorator' Horace Seaton (who 'behaves mincingly' in tight-fitting white trousers) and references to 'iron hoofs', 'poofs', 'drag' 'bums' and 'gay' did get through. [102]

The British Board of Film Classification also felt obliged to open up to depictions of homosexuality. Film audiences seemed ready for change. When Metro-Goldwyn-Mayer's cinematic version of *Tea and Sympathy* opened in Britain in October 1957 there were derisive comments from critics, who described its treatment of the original play as 'toned down', 'hardly a whisper', 'boredom and embarrassment', 'drivel' and 'sickly and innocuous as nougat'. Most agreed with the *Daily Mail*'s Edward Goring that 'after so much fuss over banned plays and the theatrical vogue thrust into the shade by the Wolfenden Report, *Tea and Sympathy* will make about as much impact as a cup of cold cocoa.' [103, 104, 105, 106, 107]

A German import, *The Third Sex*, might have excited more interest, but most cinema goers never got to see it. Premiered in Vienna in August 1957 and released in Germany the following October under the title *Different From You and Me*, the film deals with the experiences of 17-year-old Klaus Teichmann, who falls in with a group of louche young

* *South* was also broadcast by ITV as a Play of the Week on 24 November 1959.

men at the home of art and antiques dealer Boris Winkler. In an attempt to save her son from what she fears will be a homosexual lifestyle, Klaus's mother fixes him up with their live-in home help Gerda. Mr Teichmann also reports Winkler to the police for seducing minors. But their plan backfires when Winkler reports Mrs Teichmann for procuring Gerda for her son, and she is convicted and sentenced to six months in prison.

The film fell foul of the BBFC almost as soon as it was submitted by Anglo Amalgamated Film Distributors in December 1957. 'We all felt that *The Third Sex* was not a serious work on the problem of homosexuality,' reported the examiner. 'It had neither the artistry, gravity or integrity to enable us to give it a certificate and thus establish a new precedent with possibly far reaching consequences. The film touches the fringes of homosexuality (soon after the publication of the Wolfenden Report and the government's recent refusal to act on its proposals about homosexuality). Its only moral is: "If a young man seems to be in danger of becoming homosexual, find him a pretty girl."' [108]

The following year distribution rights for the film passed to Gala Film Distributors, who, 'in view of the recent statement by the Lord Chamberlain with regard to plays dealing with homosexuality', tried to get it a certificate. Again, they were turned down. The new secretary of the board John Trevelyan (appointed in May 1958) explained: 'This film deals with homosexuality more extensively and overtly than any film which we have previously passed, and even if certain scenes are removed, there will still be a clear picture of a homosexual group led by a most unsavoury character. While the mother goes to considerable lengths to save her son from entanglement with this group by awakening his heterosexual feelings, it is she who is punished by six months' imprisonment. Winkler is not seen to be punished. This may be German law but to British eyes is seems somewhat unjust. The danger of it is that it leaves the implication that in the eyes of the law in Germany homosexual relations are favourably treated.' Gala instead had to apply to individual local authorities to have the film screened in their areas. Without a BBFC certificate this was difficult, and when local authorities asked the censor why the film had not been passed in the first place, very few gave their permission. Out of 22 councils approached by Gala, just ten allowed screenings of *The Third Sex* between 1959 and 1962. [109]

It was not that the subject of homosexuality itself was prohibited. Rather, as Trevelyan explained, *The Third Sex* was 'crude and trival and shows no understanding of the problems that [homosexuality] produces both for the individual and for society'. Like the Lord Chamberlain, Trevelyan was looking for a suitable film to signal a change of direction. In late 1958 the BBFC plumped for a version of Philip King's play *Serious Charge*. Producer Daniel Angel had bought the film rights in 1955 but held off from making a movie because of objections by the BBFC. By January 1958 the rights had passed to Mickey Delamar, who adapted the play with screen writer Guy Elmes and invited composer Lionel Bart to write some rock 'n' roll songs (including *Living Doll*) to give it more youth appeal. Cliff Richard was cast in his first film role as Curly, the younger brother of juvenile delinquent Larry Thompson (Andrew Ray). [110]

The BBFC's reader made few objections to the script, reporting in September 1958: 'I do not think that the treatment of the "homosexual" aspects of the story goes too far in view of the long way we have gone since 1955 in regard to this particular subject.' Controversy only arose when Delamar and director Terence Young insisted that the film should be released with an 'A' rather than an 'X' certificate to allow their target audience of under-16-year-olds to see it. But Trevelyan insisted, 'We have not yet accepted the theme of homosexuality for anything other than the "X" category, and I see no likelihood of our changing our policy. That being so, we can only accept this film for the "A" category if the nature of the charge is not clearly that of homosexuality.' Delamar was forced to abide by the ruling and to accept some minor cuts. These included the post-production synching of the word 'cissy' in place of 'fairy'. [111, 112, 113]

Critics were unimpressed with the film. 'Its worst fault is that it fails to face up to its big theme,' complained the London *Evening News*. David Robertson of the *Financial Times* wrote: 'It has a passing interest as the first British film to refer directly to the subject of homosexual offences; but the theme is never seriously discussed.' In the *Birmingham Evening Despatch* Ivor Jay even felt obliged to spell out to readers that the 'athletic vicar' Howard Philips (Antony Quayle) was 'framed by the local chief swaggerer of wayward youth. And the local flock, maybe because they are sheep, believe the vicar is a third sex type.' [114, 115, 116]

Several other films with homosexual references were passed by the BBFC between 1959 and 1960. They included *Suddenly Last Summer* ('I think the statement of homosexuality is handled as tactfully as possible'), *The Savage Eye* ('remove all shots of the stout man dressed as a woman showing false breasts through a diaphanous costume'), *League of Gentlemen*, *Spartacus*, *The Long and the Short and the Tall* and *Carry On Constable*. The latter was released in February 1960 with a U certificate, despite the appearance of Constable Benson (Kenneth Williams) and Special Constable Gorse (Charles Hawtrey) in full drag and some highly suggestive dialogue, including talk of 'a camp concert', 'something bright and gay for the poor indisposed constables' and 'when Mars is in conjunction with Uranus it's going to be a bumpy night'. Film writer Derek Hill derided the censor's allowance of this type of camp comedy at the expense of serious portrayals of homosexuality. In July 1960 he wrote in *Encounter*, 'Homosexual characters are permitted to mince through many English U-certificate comedies, providing they do it for laughs. There has, of course, been progress, and never more than during the past year or two. Scarcely a month now passes without an example of something which a few years ago would have been cut. One reason is television. When it was found that homosexuals, nudists, prostitutes, strip-tease dancers, and the victims of frigidity and sexual assault were able to appear and talk freely on television – without a single complaint being received from the watching millions – the board's failure to keep abreast of what the public will accept was brutally exposed. The film industry, upon whose support it so relies, has not been slow to point out the advantages enjoyed by its rival'. [117, 118, 119]

In response to this kind of criticism, Trevelyan and his examiners looked more kindly on two films about Oscar Wilde which simultaneously crossed their desks in 1960. The first, directed by Gregory Ratoff, had a screenplay by producer Jo Eisinger based on Leslie and Sewell Stokes' play *Oscar Wilde*, which had been refused a licence by the Lord Chamberlain in 1936. Producer David O. Selznick had originally submitted the play to the BBFC in 1952 in advance of a possible production, but the then secretary of the board Arthur Watkins advised him, 'We would be unable to see our way to grant a certificate to a film based on it'. In April 1959 the BBFC's reader looked again at the play after it was re-submitted by Twentieth Century Fox, and reported: 'I no longer think, in the changed climate of public opinion, that the board could refuse to certificate a film based on it. If we have to have films about homosexuals at all – and I am afraid we have – there is something to be said for choosing as the subject of such a film a man who is chiefly remembered for other things than his sexual aberrations.' The film went into production the following year with Robert Morely in the lead.* The second Wilde film was *The Trials of Oscar Wilde*, a big-budget technicolour production starring Peter Finch in the title role. It was written and directed by Ken Hughes, who based it on Harford Montgomery Hyde's 1948 book of the same name and John Furnell's 1955 fictional drama *The Stringed Lute*. [120, 121]

Both films were passed with 'X' certificates in May 1960 and released later that month. Neither dealt directly with Wilde's homosexuality. In *The Trials* Constance Wilde only hints at it when she tells their friend, the writer Ada Leverson, 'To have a woman come between yourself and your husband, that's something a wife can understand. But another man… I never understood it Ada. I just never understood it.' In *Oscar Wilde* the disgraced writer roars with laughter in the final scene after he asks an accordion player at a Paris café to 'play something gay'. [122, 123]

The Trials was particularly well received by critics and audiences. Peter Finch won a BAFTA award for his portrayal of Wilde, and John Fraser (Lord Alfred Douglas) was nominated for one. Leonard Mosely of the *Daily Express* commented, 'Whatever else the Wolfenden Report on vice in Britain failed to achieve, it has certainly opened the floodgates so

---

* Morely had also starred in the original play, premiered at London's Gate Theatre club in September 1936.

far as films, theatre and literature are concerned. The walls of prejudice and prudery may not have tumbled down yet, but they are certainly crumbling at the foundations. Two years ago, for instance, no film company in the English-speaking world would have dared to make a film about Oscar Wilde and tell the whole truth about him. Yesterday I saw the first of two films which try to do exactly that.' [124]

A drama about Wilde was also screened on television. On 5 August 1960 ITV broadcast *On Trial: Oscar Wilde*, a sixty-minute reconstruction of Wilde's court case. A month earlier it had broadcast an episode about Roger Casement, another infamous homosexual criminal, executed for treason in 1916. Both programmes were produced by Peter Wildeblood, who had gone on to work for Granada Television. The programme about Wilde (played by Michael MacLiammoir) included a commentary by J.B. Priestley and featured verbatim trial evidence from Wilde's young lovers – Charles Parker, Frederick Atkins and Edward Shelley. This angered *The Trials* director Ken Hughes, who had been forced by the BBFC to tone down the original dialogue in his film. He wrote to producer Irving Allen, 'This TV production, going out as it does to several million people in their own homes, family audiences and children, was outspoken to say the least. You may remember that you and I agreed most vehemently to avoid introducing any of Wilde's "little boys", and although they were referred to, their evidence was never heard. The TV production put three of them in the box. Wilde's performance in the TV production left no doubt, in my mind at any rate, that he was a "screaming fag", another point which we were at pains to avoid. Frankly, alongside the TV production, which is (I am led to believe) a "family entertainment", *The Trials of Oscar Wilde* is a children's film. Incidentally, this is not the first time that I have seen subjects treated on television in a most outspoken and forthright manner. Plays on prostitution, abortion and features on homosexuality and so on are quite common these days, and whilst our censor can keep the families out of the cinema, no one can stop them turning on a TV set.' [125]

The two films and the television programme were reminders that the law which had condemned Oscar Wilde to two years' imprisonment with hard labour for gross indecency in 1895 was still in force. In 1957 the total number of reported homosexual offences in England and Wales reached 6,327 – their highest since 1955. In 1958 there were 5,471 offences; in 1959 5,732; in 1960 5,240. Three weeks after the House of Commons debate in November 1958, newspapers reported on the suicide of 66-year-old Travis Baker and 41-year-old Joseph Knight, who gassed themselves in the kitchen of their home in Bilston, Staffordshire. They had, the coroner explained, made 'what is commonly known as a suicide pact' after being questioned by detectives about 'certain unnatural sexual offences'. The case prompted HLRS secretary Andrew Hallidie Smith to write to *The Spectator*, 'It is hard to see how the government can feel justified in continuing to allow this type of intrusion into the private lives of responsible adults. Only by the most twisted reasoning could it be argued that the result in this case was in the public interest.' In February 1959 Peter Wildeblood called attention in *Encounter* to 'many others who have had their careers dismembered and their lives exposed to view in the cooked-up stories of the Sunday press'. [126, 127, 128, 129]

> The prosecution of homosexuals has become a kind of grotesque lottery, in which a hundred men out of a possible 500,000 are annually selected to face the further hazard of coming up before either Mr Justice A, who signed the Wolfenden Report, or Mr Justice B, who would rather sign his own death warrant. No one has attempted to explain how this is consistent with even the most elementary standards of justice. In the meantime, in dull provincial towns where the niceties of political expediency are not understood, men go on putting their heads in gas ovens and leaving notes asking their relatives to bury them together. [130]

The HLRS reported 11 prosecutions involving 65 consenting adult men between December 1958 and May 1959. Typically they were rounded up in chain prosecutions. One case heard at Appleby assizes in January 1959 involved 13 men. In another at Penzance quarter sessions the following month, six men were charged with 'offences centred around a public lavatory'. In May two men aged 22 and 28 were sentenced to nine months in prison at the Old Bailey after pleading guilty to buggery. [131]

Blackmail remained a problem, although to what extent was unclear. Between 1957 and 1960 there were 686 reported incidences of blackmail in England and Wales. The number of homosexual-related cases was probably small (the HLRS cited just two between January and February 1959), although they usually went unreported. In November 1957 the *News of the World* reported on two cases. In the first, 'a young company director' was forced to hand over promissory notes and cash and cheques worth more than £140 to 28-year-old former boxer and 'professional artist' Samuel Davies. The two men had met outside a club in London's Soho and, after 'a small sip of sherry' at the businessman's flat, indulged in 'improper behaviour'. The prosecuting counsel at Davies' trial said that the case 'was by no means a pretty picture. One of the IOUs written by the director read: "In consequences of injuries by love-making I give you £100 damages."' [132, 133, 134]

Later that month Charles Melling, a 37-year-old churchwarden, Sunday school superintendent and income tax officer from Barnsley in south Yorkshire, was sent to prison for 18 months for blackmailing local men. In letters sent to two of his victims, Melling accused them of committing homosexual offences. The judge at Sheffield assizes told him: 'Great anxiety, strain and unhappiness is so often caused by this beastly method of trying to induce people to part with their money.' [135]

The case of Kelvin Randon held the attention of both *The Times* and the *Evening Standard* in January 1959. Twenty-six-year-old Randon was sentenced to seven years in prison for extorting £8,800 from a retired army captain. The two had met on Charing Cross Road in London in 1955 and had engaged in 'a minor act of impropriety' at the older man's home. Randon spent his hush money on 'riotous living and gambling', while his victim 'was terrified and prepared to do anything to avoid exposure'. He lived in fear 'every time the postman knocked, every time there was a telephone ring and every time he turned a street corner'. 'Mr X' changed his address several times, but his blackmailer always found him. His only respite came in 1958 when Randon spent six months in prison. [136, 137]

The Times followed two more cases of blackmail. In the first, Joseph Coleman – a cook from London – was bound over for 20 years after being found guilty at the Old Bailey of blackmailing 'a peer' over a period of 36 years. Following the guilty verdict the judge, Gerald Dodson, told the jury, 'Things happen in most men's lives which are mercifully covered up by the years, and the law does not allow the past to be dug up, or the skeletons and bones of past misdeeds rattled in front of a man in order to frighten him into paying up.' [138, 139]

In the second *Times* story 51-year-old manservant John Webb was found guilty at Clerkenwell magistrates' court of blackmailing his former employer, 'a clergyman of late middle age'. The victim admitted that 'something of an indecent nature' had taken place several times between them. Webb left the clergyman's employment in 1956, but over the next three years sent him 56 letters demanding payments of between £5 and £500. He eventually collected £1,500. Webb was sentenced to four years' imprisonment and ordered to pay back £584 of what remained of his ill-gotten gains to his victim. [140, 141]

Even the police were not averse to a little blackmail. In August 1958 the *News of the World* reported on the case of 22-year-old policeman Dennis Riddell from Sunderland, who was sentenced to four years' imprisonment for demanding with menaces £5 from two men in a public toilet. He had apprehended each of them, saying, 'I am a police officer. I think you are one of the ones we are after.' He then offered to let them go in return for cash. [142]

Meanwhile, pressure continued to mount on the government to implement the Wolfenden recommendations. In December 1957 a sub-committee of the Church of Scotland's Church and Nation Committee published a report favouring the decriminalisation of homosexual acts between consenting adults. The Church and Nation Committee later overruled its sub-committee, but the debate stimulated a wider discussion about the legal and moral aspects of reform. In 1959 barrister Quentin Edwards, a member of the Church of England's Moral Welfare Council, argued that a parliamentary bill would give reform advocates and parliamentarians the opportunity to 'declare that justice does not require that every homosexual act between men should be a crime'. [143]

The Quakers went further. In 1957 they set up a study group to look at the issue of homosexuality in response to enquiries from university students who had experienced 'the unfolding of homosexual conflicts'. The 11-member Group on Homosexuality and Other Problems of Sex published an account of their progress in *The Friend* in May 1960. [144]

> The social attitude current in this country hounds and penalises the male homosexual, causing the greatest hidden suffering to those who, for no fault of their own, have only known and are only capable of this form of expression, or who are torn by conflicting desires in both directions. In its consideration of the Wolfenden recommendations [the group] has found itself less and less able to distinguish between the evils of homosexual conduct and similar evils that occur in heterosexuality. The dedication of the self to the other person, and the acceptance of unlimited responsibility for each other. This unselfish and valuable type of relationship was found to be present in many homosexual liaisons, although the homosexual love affair seems to be typically riven through with doubts, passion and impermanence – not surprisingly, since social forces, by condemnation, tend to tear it apart. These social pressures create other evils: the closed society of homosexuals for example, and the reluctance of sympathetic people to speak up for homosexuals for fear of being so branded. [145]

The medical profession also re-joined the debate. In September 1959 *The Lancet* urged doctors to help 'ordinary people to understand the need for change and accept the necessary reforms'. It explained that 'where prosecution is undertaken – even unsuccessfully – the penalty can be appalling; and our present system has serious side-effects in blackmail and (often unexplained) suicide. In considering either the fairness or the efficacy of the punishment, we should note that though people may be able to choose what they do, they cannot choose what they are.' The following month HLRS chairman Kenneth Walker sent a letter to *The*

Lancet urging doctors to follow the Church of England's lead and to 'come down courageously and strongly on the side of implementation of the Wolfenden Report'. He cited the example of a 17-year-old boy from Consett in County Durham who had hanged himself in his cell while on remand awaiting trial for a sexual offence with another youth. Walker quoted the Durham assize judge as saying, 'In a decent world an adolescent would not be prosecuted on a criminal charge arising out of a sexual offence. He would be handed over to some intelligent sympathetic person who would help him out of his difficulties. If this boy had been at a public school he would have been handled intelligently. One can only hope that reform will be made easier by this dreadful thing.' [146,147]

But the government continued to resist calls for homosexual law reform. On 9 May 1960, in a written answer to the Conservative MP Henry Kirby, the home secretary Rab Butler told the House of Commons that it would be 'premature' to introduce legislation to amend the law. In order to revive reformers' flagging hopes and to push the issue up the political agenda, the HLRS organised an open meeting on 12 May at Caxton Hall near the Houses of Parliament. The meeting was attended by more than 1,000 people. Speakers included *New Statesman* editor Kingsley Martin, the bishop of Exeter Robert Mortimer, psychiatrist and HLRS executive committee member W. Lindesay Neustatter, surgeon and HLRS chairman Kenneth Walker and magistrate and newspaper columnist Anne Allen. Walker talked about the dangers of police raids and imprisonment. Allen spoke of her horror at the thought of her own sons being branded criminals if they were homosexual. Martin claimed that police arrests were deliberately targeted. 'They are more choosey,' he said, 'in the sense that they choose people who are less likely to make a fuss. I think it means that the working class man, the person whose reputation is not very high or distinguished or something, is picked on, and that the son of Lord So-and-So is given a hint that he'd better go and live abroad and is not noticed at all. I find this singularly repulsive myself. And I find it repulsive that our political parties should all be frightened; not sure, that is, that they could benefit by taking this off the statute book.' Neustatter expressed his disappointment that 'ordinary members of the public only know what they call the "nancy boy" – the very obvious homosexual. I am perfectly certain that many homosexuals are never recognised as such, and it is as absurd to judge all homosexuals by the unstable "nancy boy", as to judge all women by prostitutes.' [148, 149, 150]

Bernard Dobson remembered attending the meeting that day: 'It was packed out. By going to a place like that, you were proclaiming in a blaze of lights that you were one of these hundreds of homosexual men. On the platform was a man called Antony Grey. I was very excited by the meeting, so I went up to him and told him that he had given a marvellous speech and that I was very interested. He gave me his address and I joined the society.' A final vote called on the government to implement the Wolfenden recommendations. Only three people voted against. [151]

Pressure for change mounted again in the letters pages of the *The Spectator*. On 20 May Robert Reid complained about the prosecution of three men in his area and about police surveillance at a public toilet in Bristol, where 'a mirror is fixed to the ceiling so that a police spy may stand outside and see what is going on within'. The following week Ian Sainsbury from Sheffield wrote about two youths from south Wales who were convicted of 'homosexual offences committed in a prison cell'. He noted that the story had come from a report on overcrowding in prisons by the Labour MP Alan Brown. A week after, *The Spectator* published the first 'coming out' letter in British press history. Speaking 30 years later, estate agent Roger Butler explained why he and two other young HLRS volunteers – Raymond Gregson and Robert Moorcroft – decided to take the unprecedented and legally risky step of declaring themselves homosexual. [152, 153]

It was prompted by the heat of the moment. It was when the whole movement was really taking off. Because the HLRS had just got going, and there was a lot of publicity at that time. Letters were constantly being written to papers about the desirability of changing the law and generally opening things up. More books were being written, and people were being generally a bit more open. But not open enough. People were writing letters in favour of it in a very detached way, as though it wasn't anything to do with them. Practically nobody said directly in plain words, "I am." And I thought it was about time that somebody did. The other two were other volunteers who were doing the envelope addressing and all that, and talking about this one evening, I said, "Why not?" So I drafted the letter and we all signed it. [154]

They sent their letter to several newspapers and magazines, but only *The Spectator* and the *New Statesman* published it, on 3 and 4 June respectively.

> We are homosexuals and we are writing because we feel strongly that insufficient is being done to enlighten public opinion on a topic which has for too long been shunned. Furthermore, because we deplore a situation which requires that most homosexuals who write letters for publication are obliged to do so under a pseudonym, we have determined deliberately to sign our real names, even though, by doing so, we realise that we are making only a token gesture which may well be foolhardy. Over the past few years an enormous amount has been spoken and written about the homosexual situation. Most of it has been realistic and sensible, some has been vicious and singularly ill-informed. But whatever its form we welcome it, because we must welcome anything which brings this topic, for so long taboo, into open discussion. Only in this way can prejudice, which is born of ignorance, be overcome. We who sign this letter are anxious to do everything in our power to bring about better general understanding of our situation; it is often called a problem, but is only a problem because of the prevailing attitude towards it and because of the ludicrous law which encourages such an attitude and hinders every attempt to overcome it. The reform of this law, which has often brought more discredit to the police than to homosexuals, is, of course, inevitable, and we can only hope that the government will soon have the courage to realise and accept this. [155, 156]

Later that month the Labour MP for St Pancras North (and HLRS honorary committee member) Kenneth Robinson secured time for a

House of Commons debate calling on the government to 'take early action' to implement the Wolfenden recommendations. Unlike the two previous parliamentary debates, this motion would end in a final vote. Robinson set out his reasons for wanting to change the law in an article in the *New Statesman* on 25 June.

> The threat of imprisonment hanging over every homosexual must intensify the sense of guilt and shame which psychiatrists, clergymen and others find so common among those who seek their help. Such feelings can and do lead to suicide, even in cases where no criminal proceedings are pending and no exposure threatened. Press reporting of homosexual prosecutions, especially of persons known to the public, serves not only to keep the topic in the public mind but also to invest it with an air of unhealthy sensationalism. One partner in a private homosexual act is an easy victim, should the other decide upon blackmail. Equally unsatisfactory is the incidence of the law as between different police areas and between different courts. A few years ago a constituent of mine, aged 21 and on the threshold of a promising professional career, was sentenced as a first offender to four years' imprisonment for homosexual acts with a man much older than himself, who incidentally received a lighter sentence. [157]

When the debate took place on 29 June the arguments aired in the Lords and the Commons in 1957 and 1958 were again repeated. Robinson told MPs that homosexuality 'leads so often to unhappiness, to loneliness and to frustration because it entails in many cases heavy burdens of guilt and shame on those affected by it'. Roy Jenkins (Labour, Birmingham Stechford) urged MPs not to be 'too eager to stand out as an island against the general current of civilised world opinion'. Terence Clark (Conservative, Portsmouth West), on the other hand, had visions of 'a couple of hairy old males sitting on each other's knees and liking it'. Godfrey Lagden (Conservative, Hornchurch) thought that homosexual men were 'a dirty-minded danger to the virile manhood of this country'. Eirene White (Labour, Flint East) described homosexuality as 'difficult', 'embarrassing', 'distasteful' and 'extremely repugnant' – although she went on to support the motion. William Shepherd (Conservative, Cheadle) complained about the increasing publicity surrounding the issue. With unintended irony, he explained how 'two or three years ago the man who in middle age had not married would be able to say of himself, and other people would say of him, that he was probably a gay bachelor. Today, individuals know more about this subject. They have heard a great deal more talk about it and they say other things about the man whom they had previously called a gay bachelor.' The home secretary Rab Butler again made it clear that he had no intention of implementing the Wolfenden Report: 'I do not believe that the full case for a change has yet been made. Nor am I convinced that we are yet in a position to take the final decision on what the precise nature of the change should be. In a period when religious and ethical restraints are weak, as undoubtedly they are now, the restraints of the criminal law acquire a special significance.' Kenneth Robinson later recalled how Butler's speech came as 'a cold douche', and that 'after this strong indication of the official view it was clear, despite the fact that members enjoyed the rare privilege of a free vote, that the motion would be lost.' It was defeated by 213 votes to 99. [158, 159, 160, 161, 162, 163]

The day after the debate Harold Macmillan wrote in his diary: 'The House of Commons (whips off) voted heavily against homosexuality last night. This should end the parliamentary controversy for a time.' Macmillan and Labour leader Hugh Gaitskell did not vote on the motion. Nor did Butler. But Liberal Party leader Jo Grimond did, and he was in favour. So was the minister of power, Richard Wood. A voting record kept by the HLRS shows that Robinson's motion was also backed by other MPs who would have bigger roles to play in the future of both homosexual law reform and British politics. [164]

MPs Voting in Favour of Homosexual Law Reform, 29 June 1960

MP	Party	Constituency
Leo Abse	Labour	Pontypool
Anthony Benn	Labour	Bristol South East
Humphrey Berkeley	Conservative	Lancaster
Barbara Castle	Labour	Blackburn
Anthony Crosland	Labour	Great Grimsby
Richard Crossman	Labour	Coventry East
Desmond Donnelly	Labour	Pembrokeshire
Tom Driberg	Labour	Barking
Charles Fletcher-Cooke	Conservative	Darwen
Jo Grimond	Liberal	Orkney and Shetland
Roy Jenkins	Labour	Birmingham Stechford
Margaret Thatcher	Conservative	Finchley
George Thomas	Labour	Cardiff West
Jeremy Thorpe	Liberal	North Devon

Source: MPs' Voting Record in June 1960, Hall-Carpenter Albany Trust files, London School of Economics

Faced with its first parliamentary defeat, the HLRS took on the task of trying to influence politicians and the public in readiness for another vote. 'The main work that we did was the work of public education,' recalled Antony Grey. 'We did a great deal of writing, of speaking, lecturing and debating. The aim was not so much to put over simply a case for changing the law, [but] it was explained to people the nature of homosexuality and the sort of people homosexuals were, because this was something that we found people were generally abysmally ignorant of.' They faced a long struggle ahead. [166]

Chapter 2 references

1. Secker & Warburg, 1960
2. Bob Cant, *Footsteps and Witnesses: Lesbian and Gay Lifestories from Scotland*, Word Power Books, 2008
3. Alkarim Jivani, *It's Not Unusual: A History of Lesbian and Gay Britain in the Twentieth Century*, Michael O'Mara Books, 1997
4. *Report of the Committee on Homosexual Offences and Prostitution*, Her Majesty's Stationery Office, 1957 [Wolfenden Report]
5. Ibid.
6. Ibid.
7. *Measure of Conscience: Consenting Party*, BBC 2, 26 April 1972
8. Wolfenden Report
9. Ibid.
10. Ibid.
11. Ibid.
12. Ibid.
13. Ibid.
14. Ibid.
15. Ibid.
16. Ibid.
17. 'Reservation by Mrs Cohen, Dr Curran, Lady Stopford and Dr Whitby', Wolfenden Report
18. 'Further Reservation by Dr Whitby', op. cit.
19. 'Reservation by Mr Adair', op. cit.
20. Frank Mort, *Capital Affairs: London and the Making of the Permissive Society*, Yale University Press, 2010
21. A.E. Dyson, recorded interview, February 1990, Hall-Carpenter Oral History archive, British Library

22. Robert Boothby, *Recollections of a Rebel*, Hutchinson, 1978

23. John Wolfenden, *Turning Points: The Memoirs of Lord Wolfenden*, The Bodley Head, 1976

24. Francis Williams, Fleet Street Notebook, *New Statesman*, 14 September 1957

25. David Kynaston, *Modernity Britain: Opening the Box, 1957-59*, Bloomsbury, 2013

26. George H. Gallup, *The Gallup International Public Opinion Polls: Great Britain, 1937-1975, Volume One*, 1976

27. Stephen Jeffery-Poulter, *Peers, Queers and Commons: The Struggle for Gay Law Reform from 1950 to the Present*, Routledge, 1991

28. Michael McManus, *Tory Pride and Prejudice: The Conservative Party and Homosexual Law Reform*, Biteback Publishing, 2011

29. 'Keeping Vice Off the Street', *The Daily Telegraph*, 5 September 1957

30. '"I Am a Homosexual" Says a Doctor on TV', *Daily Mirror*, 6 September 1957

31. *Press Conference: Sir John Wolfenden*, BBC Television, 6 September 1957

32. Alkarim Jivani, *It's Not Unusual*, op. cit.

33. C.H. Rolph, 'Wolfenden Revisited', *New Statesman*, 28 September 1957

34. 'Homosexuality Law "Grave Injustice"', *The Times*, 14 October 1957

35. "I Am a Homosexual" Says a Doctor on TV', op. cit.

36. 'Homosexual Offences and Prostitution', *The Lancet*, 14 September 1957

37. 'Dr Ramsey Supports Report on Vice', *The Times*, 27 September 1957

38. 'Church Assembly Approve Report on Homosexuality', *The Times*, 15 November 1957

39. *Any Questions?*, BBC Home Service, 15 November 1957

40. 'The Wolfenden Report', *The Tablet*, 7 December 1957

41. 'Homosexuality Law "Grave Injustice"', *The Times*, op. cit.

42. J.B. Priestley, 'Outlaws We Should Bring Within the Law', *Reynolds News*, 10 November 1957

43. John Wolfenden, *Turning Points*, op. cit.

44. Michael McManus, *Tory Pride and Prejudice*, op. cit.

45. 'Government Caution on Wolfenden Reforms', 5 December 1957

46. Harford Montgomery Hyde, *The Other Love: An Historical and Contemporary Survey of Homosexuality in Britain*, Heinemann, 1970

47. Antony Grey, *Quest for Justice: Towards Homosexual Emancipation*, Sinclair-Stevenson, 1992

48. Matt Cook, 'Queer Conflicts: Love, Sex and War, 1914-1967', in Matt Cook (ed.), *A Gay History of Britain: Love and Sex Between Men Since the Middle Ages*, Greenwood Publishing, 2007

49. 'Government Caution on Wolfenden Reforms', op. cit.

50. Matthew Grimley, 'Law, Morality and Secularisation: The Church of England and the Wolfenden Report', *The Journal of Ecclesiastical History*, October 2009

51. Christine Keeler, *Scandal!*, Xanadu Publications, 1989

52. Gillian Freeman, Edward Thorpe, personal interview with author, 31 November 2012

53. *Last Word*, BBC Radio 4, 14 September 2012

54. www.lgbtarchive.uk

55. Letters to the Editor, *The Spectator*, 3 January 1958

56. Ibid.

57. Letters to the Editor, *The Spectator*, 10 January 1958

58. Letters to the Editor, *The Spectator*, 17 January 1958

59. Letters to the Editor, *The Spectator*, 24 January 1958

60. Ibid.

61. Tony Dyson, recorded interview, February 1990, Hall-Carpenter Oral History archive, op. cit.

62. Ibid.

63. Letters to the Editor, *The Times*, 7 March 1958

64. Tony Dyson, recorded interview, op. cit.

65. Wolfenden Report

66. Letters to the Editor, *The Times*, 19 April 1958

67. Antony Grey, Quest for Justice, op. cit.

68. Tony Dyson, recorded interview, op. cit.

69. *Measure of Conscience: Consenting Party*, op. cit.

70. Antony Grey, recorded interview, February 1990, Hall-Carpenter Oral History archive, op. cit.

71. Tony Dyson, recorded interview, op. cit.

72. C.H. Rolph, recorded interview, August 1990, Hall-Carpenter Oral

History archive, op. cit.

73. Antony Grey, *Quest for Justice*, op. cit.

74. *Measure of Conscience: Consenting Party*, op. cit.

75. Michael McManus, *Tory Pride and Prejudice*, op. cit.

76. Eustace Chesser, *Live and Let Live: The Moral of the Wolfenden Report*, Heinemann, 1958

77. Peter Catterall (ed.), *The Macmillan Diaries, Volume II: Prime Minister and After, 1957-1966*, Macmillan, 2011

78. Ian Harvey, *To Fall Like Lucifer*, Sidgwick & Jackson, 1971

79. Ibid.

80. '£5 Fine on Ian Harvey. He Will Pay to End of Life' *The Times*, 11 December 1958

81. Ian Harvey, *To Fall Like Lucifer*, op. cit.

82. Tim Newburn, *Permission and Regulation, Law and Morals in Postwar Britain*, Routledge, 1992

83. Antony Grey, *Quest for Justice*, op. cit.

84. David Kynaston, *Modernity Britain: Opening the Box, 1957-59*, Bloomsbury, 2013

85. Michael McManus, *Tory Pride and Prejudice*, op. cit.

86. Harford Montgomery Hyde, *The Other Love*, op. cit.

87. Stephen Jeffery-Poulter, *Peers, Queers and Commons*, op. cit.

88. Harford Montgomery Hyde, *The Other Love*, op. cit.

89. Kenneth Allsop, 'Suddenly… SEX Without a Snigger', *Daily Mail* 26 November 1958

90. Harford Montgomery Hyde, *The Other Love*, op. cit.

91. Kenneth Allsop, 'Suddenly… SEX Without a Snigger,' op. cit.

92. Minute by the Lord Chamberlain, 31 October 1958, Lord Chamberlain Plays Correspondence Files, British Library

93. Ibid.

94. Kenneth Allsop, 'Suddenly… SEX Without a Snigger', op. cit.

95. 'South', Lord Chamberlain Plays Correspondence Files, op. cit.

96. 'The Catalyst', op. cit.

97. 'Valmouth', op. cit.

98. 'We're No Ladies', op. cit.

99. Letter from Assistant Comptroller to The Clerk of the London County Council, 10 February 1958 op. cit.

100. 'A Taste of Honey', op. cit.

101. 'Look on Tempests', op. cit.

102. Frank Norman, *Fings Ain't Wot They Used T' Be*, Secker & Warburg, 1960

103. Edward Goring, 'Toned Down', *Daily Mail*, 5 October 1957

104. Milton Shulman, *Sunday Express*, 6 October 1957

105. Why Call This 'Hot'?, Leonard Mosely, Daily Express, 3 October 1957

106. C.A. Lejeune, *The Observer*, 6 October 1957

107. Peter Forster, *Financial Times*, 7 October 1957

108. Examiner's report, 10 December 1957, BBFC file: *The Third Sex*

109. Letter from John Trevelyan to Kenneth Rive, Gala Film Distributors, 21 November 1958, op. cit.

110. Letter from John Trevelyan, BBFC file: *The Third Sex*

111. Reader's report, 8 September 1958, BBFC file: *Serious Charge*

112. Letter from John Trevelyan to Mickey Delamar, 23 September 1958, op. cit.

113. Letter from Mickey Delamar to John Trevelyan, 9 March 1959, op. cit.

114. *Evening News*, 14 May 1959

115. David Robinson, *Financial Times*, 20 May 1959

116. Ivor Jay, *Birmingham Evening Despatch*, 28 August 1959

117. Examiner's report, 9 June 1959, BBFC file: *Suddenly Last Summer*

118. Minutes of Exceptions: *The Savage Eye*, BBFC

119. Derek Hill, 'The Habit of Censorship', *Encounter*, July 1960

120. Letter from Arthur Watkins to David O Selznik, 25 January 1952, BBFC file: *Oscar Wilde*

121. Reader's report, 14 April 1959, op. cit.

122. *The Trials of Oscar Wilde*, Warwick Film Productions, 1960

123. *Oscar Wilde*, Vantage Films, 1960

124. Leonard Mosely, *Daily Express*, 20 May 1960

125. Letter from Ken Hughes to Irving Allen, 9 August 1960, BBFC file: *The Trials of Oscar Wilde*

126. Recorded Crime Statistics 1898-2001/2, Home Office Statistics

127. 'Men Die After "Suicide Pact"', *Daily Telegraph*, 16 December 1958

128. Letters to the Editor, *The Spectator*, 26 December 1958

129. Peter Wildeblood, 'The Boys Who Cried Wolfenden', *Encounter*, February 1959

130. Ibid.

131. *Homosexuality – The Administration of the Law*, June 1959, HLRS, Hall-Carpenter Albany Trust files, op. cit.

132. Recorded Crime Statistics 1898-2001/2, op. cit.

133. *Homosexuality – The Administration of the Law*, op. cit.

134. 'Company Director Went to Soho', *News of the World*, 10 November 1957

135. 'Brought Shame on His Family', *News of the World*, 23 November 1958

136. 'Blackmailer "Bled" Mr X in Terror of the Phone', *Evening Standard*, 9 January 1959.

137. '£8,800 by "Slow Torture"', *The Times*, 10 January 1959

138. 'Alleged Demands to "Mr. X"', *The Times*, 3 June 1959

139. 'Threatening Letters After 30 Years', *The Times*, 3 July 1959

140. 'Clergyman Says He Paid £1,500', *The Times*, 22 August 1959

141. 'Clergyman's Ex-Valet Gaoled', *News of the World*, 20 September 1959

142. 'The PC Turned to Blackmail', *News of the World*, 3 August 1958

143. Quentin Edwards, *What is Unlawful? Does Innocence Begin where Crime Ends? Afterthoughts on the Wolfenden Report*, Church Information Office, 1959

144. 'Towards a Quaker View of Sex', *The Friend*, 20 May 1960

145. Ibid.

146. 'Homosexuality and the Law', *The Lancet*, 12 September 1959

147. Letters to the Editor, *The Lancet*, 31 October 1959

148. 'Minister's Reply on Homosexuality', *The Guardian*, 10 May 1960

149. Harford Montgomery Hyde, *The Other Love*, op. cit.

150. Douglas Plummer, *Queer People: The Truth About Homosexuals*, W.H. Allen, 1963

151. *Walking After Midnight: Gay Men's Life Stories*, Hall-Carpenter Archives Gay Men's Oral History Group, Routledge, 1989

152. Letters to the Editor, *The Spectator*, 20 May 1960

153. Letters to the Editor, *The Spectator*, 27 May 1960

154. Roger Butler, recorded interview, August 1990, Hall-Carpenter Oral History archive, op. cit.

155. Letters to the Editor, *The Spectator*, 3 June 1960

156. Correspondence, *New Statesman*, 4 June 1960

157. Kenneth Robinson, 'The Time for Decision', *New Statesman*, 25 June 1960

158. Michael McManus, *Tory Pride and Prejudice*, op. cit.

159. David Kynaston, *Modernity Britain: A Shake of the Dice, 1959-62*, Bloomsbury, 2014

160. Geoffrey Gorer, 'Man to Man', *Encounter*, May 1961

161. Peter Scott-Presland, *Amiable Warriors: The Official History of the Campaign for Homosexual Equality and Its Times, Volume One: Space to Breathe*, Paradise Press, 2015

162. Harford Montgomery Hyde, *The Other Love*, op. cit.

163. Matthew Grimley, 'Law, Morality and Secularisation: The Church of England and the Wolfenden Report', op. cit.

164. Peter Catterall (ed.), *The Macmillan Diaries, Volume II*, op. cit.

165. *Measure of Conscience: Consenting Party*, op. cit.

Chapter 3

THE GERM INSIDE

'The question of homosexuality has always intrigued me. It's a fascinating problem for a psychologist, you see. It's so complicated. And the human tragedies that lie behind it!'

Maxence Van der Meersch, *Mask of Flesh* [1]

On the evening of 5 September 1957 viewers in ITV's Granada (North of England) and Rediffusion (London) regions were faced with an unusual spectacle. An anonymous doctor, seated with his back to the camera, admitted on live television to being a homosexual. When the interviewer Elaine Grand asked him, 'Would you prefer to be normal?' the 35-year-old doctor responded enthusiastically: 'Oh yes, I would. If there was a guaranteed cure – a hope – that I could become an ordinary normal person I would certainly welcome it. I think all homosexuals would like to be cured and marry and have children.' [2, 3, 4]

The doctor's remarks reflected the confused and contradictory attitudes of the medical profession towards homosexuality in the 1950s and 1960s. During their deliberations the Wolfenden Committee had pondered the vexed question of whether or not homosexuality was a sickness or disease. To this end they examined the views of a wide range of medical witnesses, including representatives of the British Medical Association, the Institute of Psychiatry and the British Psychological Society. Two of the committee's members were also doctors – psychiatrist Desmond Curran and general practitioner Joseph Whitby.

The idea that homosexuality was a medical condition had a long history. As early as the 1860s the German writer Karl-Heinrich Ulrichs had begun to define homosexual men (or 'Urnings', as he called them) according to their psychological characteristics. In 1869 the Austro-Hungarian writer Karl-Maria Kertbeny invented the term 'homosexual' for his classification of sexual types. By the time German psychiatrist Richard von Krafft-Ebing published *Psychopathia Sexualis* in 1886 homosexuality was widely regarded as a pathological condition. In 1896 the British physician Havelock Ellis published *Sexual Inversion*, co-authored with the writer and poet John Addington Symonds, in which he argued that homosexual behaviour had biological as well as psychological origins. This theory culminated in the work of German sexologist Magnus Hirschfeld at the Institute for Sexual Research in Berlin, which opened in 1919. Hirschfeld believed that homosexuality was a congenital condition – possibly caused by glandular secretions – which gave rise to physical as well as behavioural characteristics. The Austrian psychoanalyst Sigmund Freud, on the other hand, argued that all humans had a fundamental bisexuality and that various psychological factors during childhood and adolescence led them towards 'homosexual and heterosexual object choices'. In a 1935 letter to the American mother of a homosexual man Freud stated that homosexuality was not an illness: 'We consider it to be a variation of the sexual function, produced by certain arrest of sexual development'. [5]

From the outset, the Wolfenden Committee was sceptical of theories which saw criminal behaviour in medical or psychological terms. They were influenced by the sociologist Barbara Wootton, who in 1956 remarked on how offenders and the generally disturbed or unhappy were 'today liable to be referred, or to refer themselves, to the psychiatric doctor. The modern psychiatrist is expected to deal with practically every variety of personal problem'. Quoting Wootton in their report, the committee argued that if homosexuality was regarded as an illness, then homosexual men could not be held fully responsible for their actions. They decided that 'the evidence put before us has not established to our satisfaction the proposition that homosexuality is a disease'. Citing

Alfred Kinsey's research in the US, the committee also acknowledged that homosexual tendencies might be present in most individuals. This, they added, 'leads to the conclusion that homosexuals cannot reasonably be regarded as quite separate from the rest of mankind'. They further pointed out that what some people considered 'abnormal' was often more 'a matter of degree or of what is accepted as the permissible range of normal variation'. Where mental health problems did affect homosexual men, these were more likely to be 'products of the strain and conflict brought about by the homosexual condition'. The committee noted that 'associated psychological abnormalities are less prominent, or even absent, in countries where the homosexual is regarded with more tolerance'. [6, 7]

The Wolfenden Committee cast doubt on the claims of doctors to cure homosexuality. They examined S.J.C. Spencer's study of Oxford undergraduates (which formed part of the British Psychological Society's submission of evidence) and found that out of five students receiving psychotherapy to deal with their homosexuality, 'our witness, while certainly not prepared to say that none would outgrow their condition, felt that such a change was unlikely'. Desmond Curran and Denis Parr similarly found that 25 of their patients who were treated with psychotherapy at St George's Hospital in London 'derived no apparent benefit in terms of changed sexual preference or behaviour'. In a particularly damning paragraph, the Wolfenden Report reiterated the committee's belief in the mutability of human sexuality and the unlikelihood of switching between 'absolute' homosexuality and heterosexuality: 'We were struck by the fact that none of our medical witnesses were able to provide any reference in medical literature to a complete change of this kind. Some of them have since sent us one or two examples in which such a change is claimed, but it is extremely difficult to assess the results in such cases. Our evidence leads us to the conclusion that a total reorientation from complete homosexuality to complete heterosexuality is very unlikely indeed.' The best thing that the medical profession could do, the committee concluded, was to help men live with their homosexuality. [8, 9]

A homosexual, like any other person who suffers from maladjustment to society, may be regarded as successfully treated if he is brought to a more nearly complete adjustment with the society in which he lives. This can happen without any radical change in his propensity itself. It can happen by his being made more fully aware of his condition. The object of the treatment is to relieve mental stress by producing a better adjustment. For this reason there may be good grounds, from the medical point of view, for not attempting any fundamental reorientation of the sexual propensity of a homosexual who is already well adjusted and is a useful member of society.' [10]

Although they rejected claims of cures, the Wolfenden Committee were still concerned to make homosexual men 'more discreet or continent' in their behaviour, and to 'reduce the number of homosexual offences and offenders'. It opposed castration as a preventative measure, but only because there was 'no guarantee that this operation removes either the desires or the ability to fulfil them; it would certainly have no effect in the case of the man who is addicted to the passive role of acts of buggery or to other forms of homosexual behaviour not involving the use of his own genitalia'. The committee did, however, think that the use of female hormones to dampen homosexual desire had 'its place'. They were reassured by doctors' claims that oestrogens could be successfully administered to 'diminish the strength of these desires', so that 'the disposition to commit offences will be correspondingly lessened'. Although oestrogen treatment was forbidden in English and Welsh prisons, it could be given to offenders as part of a probation order under the Criminal Justice Act 1948. It was this treatment which was prescribed for mathematician and computer pioneer Alan Turing as a condition of probation following his conviction for gross indecency in 1952. The Wolfenden Committee thought that there was 'much to be said for a wider use of probation with a requirement that the offender submits to medical treatment', either as an out-patient or as a 'voluntary' in-patient at a mental hospital. They duly recommended lifting the ban on hormone therapy for prisoners in England and Wales, provided that prisoners gave their consent and that prison medical officers thought that it would be useful.

Such treatment was already available in Scottish prisons. The Scottish Home Department recommended that all male prisoners convicted of sexual offences be interviewed by a psychiatrist and, if suitable and willing, given out-patient treatment at psychiatric clinics. Certain inmates were additionally selected for oestrogen therapy, on condition that they signed a consent agreement and remained under strict medical supervision. T.D. Inch, a medical adviser to the Scottish Prisons and Borstal Services, told the Wolfenden Committee that female hormones made prisoners less anxious and more 'adaptable'. The treatment was not, he said, 'pushed to its limits' or used 'to the extent of producing atrophy [shrinking] of the testicles or gynaecomastia [enlargement of men's breasts]'. Rather, it was administered 'only to the point of eliminating or at least greatly reducing libido'. Nor was the treatment widely publicised. The Scottish prison service 'never said anything' about it. 'We have,' said Inch, 'just kept very quiet.' But apart from Barlinnie prison in Glasgow – where a new psychiatric unit was being built – Scottish prisons had no specialist treatment centres. In England there were just two – one at Wormwood Scrubs in London; the other at Wakefield. In 1955 six inmates were selected for psychiatric treatment at both prisons. [12, 13]

Despite the Wolfenden Report's conclusions, the medical profession remained divided on the nature of homosexuality and how to deal with it – although doctors did generally support the decriminalisation of homosexual acts. In an editorial on the report in September 1957 *The Lancet* lamented that 'the claim of doctors to be heard on homosexuality is weakened by deep divisions of opinion within the profession. To the psychiatric wing homosexuality is a medical disorder, but at the opposite extreme there are doctors to whom homosexual behaviour is the abominable offence – in the realm of morals, not medicine.' The journal itself weighed in on the side of the 'psychiatric wing', and it criticised the Wolfenden Report for its assertion that 'homosexuality cannot legitimately be regarded as a disease or illness'. [14]

The Lancet's view was shared by many. In *Society and the Homosexual* Michael Schofield (who later changed his opinion) described homosexuality as 'in some ways analogous to the incidence of tuberculosis. Doctors say that many people have the germ inside them. Whether it will develop into the disease or not depends upon chance in the form of the environment in which they find themselves. Homosexuality is a severe mental sickness.' In the foreword to Audrey Erskine Lindop's *Details of Jeremy Stretton* an unnamed 'consultant in psychiatry' claimed that 'some of the unfortunates' who came to him could be made 'whole and clean again' if they stood up to 'the rigours involved in mental treatment'. The novel itself is constructed around the archetypal Freudian notion of homosexuality acquired through childhood experiences. The eponymous hero – who is brought up by his aloof vicar father and his spinster aunt after his mother dies in childbirth – develops homosexual tendencies and attempts to combat them by undergoing treatment from a psychotherapist, Dr Presnor. During one treatment session Presnor makes a plea to 'the man in the street' to accept homosexuality as a medical rather than a criminal problem. [15, 16]

'At the moment he either condemns it, ignores it or makes fun of it. But public opinion could make free clinics possible.'

'You mean put de-pansying under the National Health?'[Jeremy] laughed.

'Why not? There should be free treatment for those who can't afford it and who want it.' [17]

In the *British Medical Journal* James Hadfield, a lecturer in psychopathology and mental hygiene at London University, challenged the Wolfenden Report's assertion that homosexuality could not be reversed. 'There must be many psychologists,' he wrote, 'who could point to cures of this radical kind.' Psychiatrist Clifford Allen also insisted that homosexuality was 'a psychological disorder' and that it was 'definitely not true that homosexuality is incurable'. Psychologist

Richard Hauser went further. In his 1962 book *The Homosexual Society* (funded by grants from a Home Office research unit – the only Wolfenden recommendation to be acted on) he described homosexual men as a 'handicapped' minority and 'biological freaks'. This was said, he explained, 'with full sympathy for them; few of them are happy and nature has played them a dirty trick'. Hauser also described homosexuality as a 'social infection' which could be 'inborn in a small number of cases' – similar to a 'congenital deformity such as a hare-lip'. There was an urgent need, he added, to 'contain the evil' and to provide 'safeguards to prevent homosexuality spreading and becoming a threat to society'. Another doctor – E. Ganz, a medical examiner for Kent police – even claimed that he could detect physical evidence of homosexuality. In 1962 he wrote to the *British Medical Journal* to explain his methods. [18, 19, 20]

> In the past thirteen years I have been asked by the police to assist them with certain examinations of homosexuals. I found that the request to provide medical evidence for homosexual practices of the passive partner was a major problem. Most of my cases were teenagers or in their early twenties. I could not find any references in my books and had to rely on findings as I went along. My observations may help other practitioners who do police-surgeons' work. When one performs a per rectum examination one usually finds that the anal folds are tightly closed by the anal sphincter, and that on separating the cheeks with one's left hand one finds that there is a certain amount of resistance of the cheeks and also the folds are tightly interlocking. In the majority of homosexuals, particularly those who have been indulging in these practices almost up to the date of the examination, there is a certain readiness felt to receive the examining finger when the cheeks are separated, and the sphincter, almost as a reflex, dilates and a central hole appears when the folds separate. A normal sphincter would resist the insertion of the finger while the anal in the homosexual dilates almost in a reflex-like manner. [21]

Television and radio programmes also helped to promote the idea that homosexuality was a medical condition that could, and should, be cured. In 1958 Clifford Allen appeared on BBC Radio's *Woman's Hour* to answer questions from a listener in Essex who had written to the programme, asking, 'Am I right in thinking that homosexuality is inborn in a small percentage of individuals? Is it inevitable? Or can something be done to divert the sexual impulse into the usual channels? Is there a modern "miracle drug" that works? Can it be discovered early enough for something to be done – if there is anything to be done?' After the presenter Marjorie Anderson warned listeners who were 'not interested' that the item would last for eight minutes, Allen gave his advice. [22]

> It can sometimes be cured, not by magic drugs, but by painstaking psychological treatment. First we should try to prevent it, since prevention is easier than cure. Where homosexuality has developed, it can sometimes be cured, but this needs careful psychological treatment and may take some time. Naturally, like other diseases, the earlier it is treated, the more likely it is to respond. [23]

There were, of course, opposing opinions. After publishing *Society and the Homosexual*, Michael Schofield received more than 50 letters of complaint about his use of the term 'mental sickness' to describe homosexuality. Psychiatrist W. Lindesay Neustatter firmly believed that homosexuality was not a disease because homosexual men were 'in other ways perfectly normal and valuable citizens'. He questioned whether homosexuality was even 'abnormal' and suggested that it was instead 'an extreme variant of sexuality'. Two Wolfenden witnesses, doctors Eustace Chesser and Edward Glover, also thought that homosexuality was 'not a disease in the traditional sense', and that there was little difference between homosexuals and heterosexuals. In 1959 an anonymous homosexual doctor wrote to *The Lancet*: 'A true picture of male homosexuality in the community cannot be given if it is based on material drawn only from psychiatric practice, prisons, mental hospitals and venereal disease clinics. So long as the only doctors who write on this subject are heterosexual, so long as public opinion is based on emotional prejudice, so long as the law makes it dangerous for the homosexual himself to express an opinion, the present profound ignorance of the subject will continue.' He added that the causes of homosexuality were not known, and that most homosexual men were 'well-adjusted' and 'no different from their fellows'. Talk of a cure, he believed, was unrealistic and harmful. [24, 25, 26, 27, 28, 29]

Some churchmen and religious groups also rejected the suggestion that homosexuality was an illness. Outlining Catholic opinion in 1959, Michael J. Buckley wrote that homosexuality was 'most certainly not a disease', although he did regard it as 'a disorder and deviation' that was 'contrary to God's plan for mankind'. In a letter to the *New Statesman* in 1960 D.A. Rhymes, vicar of All Saints Church in New Eltham, south London, thought it 'very dubious whether homosexuality can ever be "cured"'. He suggested that people should 'stop thinking of homosexuality as either unnatural or a disease' and instead 'understand how best to help the homosexual'. The most effective way of doing this, he thought, was to 'help him find someone whom he can love and not to place any legal or social barriers in the way of his finding that love. As a Christian priest I would say that the fulfilment of love is never wrong.' The Quakers were even more forthright. They affirmed that homosexuality was 'not a psychiatric curiosity', and that 'homosexuals are not necessarily to be seen as "patients". True, many have psychiatric complaints; but in view of the ostracism that surrounds them this is scarcely surprising.' [30, 31, 32]

Caught in the middle of these debates were homosexual men themselves. Many accepted medical explanations for their sexuality – partly because they allowed them to argue that theirs was a condition beyond their control rather than a conscious criminal choice. Psychiatrist L.H. Rubinstein pointed this out, albeit critically, at a symposium on male homosexuality in 1956: 'It is all too easy for the homosexual to claim that his condition is constitutionally [i.e. genetically] determined, that it is a biological variant without any psychological cause. Homosexuals themselves favour this aetiology in self-defence, in order to counter-balance social disapproval as well as to maintain a façade of psychological normality.' Denis Parr agreed that medical explanations gave homosexual men a justification for their behaviour: 'Many homosexuals reach a stage of wanting medical confirmation of their own belief that they are irretrievably homosexual, so that they can feel free to go on practising for the rest of their lives.' [33, 34]

For men who accepted medical models of homosexuality, the possibility of a cure was an appealing proposition. The attractions of treatment were also strong when, under a punitive legal system, men were prevented from forming relationships and were threatened with prosecution, imprisonment, social rejection, loss of career and family break-up if their sexuality was discovered. Added to this was an almost unquestioning faith in doctors and a belief that modern science and medicine could cure all ills.

Taking the first step towards a cure could, however, be an embarrassing and disappointing experience. Peter Price from Merseyside went to see his family doctor about his homosexual feelings aged 12 in 1958.

> I sat down in Dr Lansley's surgery. 'Well what seems to be the problem?' he asked.
>
> 'I… I think I'm a homosexual.'
>
> 'Don't be stupid,' he said. 'You're 12 years old. How could you possibly know?' He smiled. 'You'll grow out of it.' [35]

Noel Currer-Briggs consulted his doctor shortly before he got married because he felt 'rather worried that I had fantasies about men not women'. The doctor reassured Noel, telling him, 'If you're not an artist and you're not effeminate you can't be homosexual.' Tony Kildwick similarly turned to his GP when his own marriage began to falter: 'I went to him and I said, "Now look, I get no sexual satisfaction at all in my married life. I still have these male fantasies. Do you think I'm homosexual?" And he said, "Well, I don't know. We weren't taught about this in my days at medical school."' He referred Tony to a psychiatrist. [36, 37]

By the late 1950s the theory that homosexuality was the result of a glandular disorder was largely discredited. In 1954 endocrinologist

G.I.M. Swyer told *The Practitioner* that there was 'no convincing evidence that human homosexuality is dependent upon hormonal aberrations. The use of sex hormones in the treatment of homosexuality is mainly disappointing.' In the same journal W. Lindesay Neustatter warned about the side-effects of injecting men with female hormones. As well as experiencing nausea, 'the subject may put on weight, and there may be development of mammary fat. It has, of course, no curative effect.' The BMA told the Wolfenden Committee that synthetic oestrogens such as stilboestrol and ethinyl oestradiol only temporarily stopped or reduced sexual desire. It added: 'In some who have been repeatedly punished and despair of avoiding further imprisonment, the drug may break a vicious circle and allow them to give up homosexual associations, [but] the method is useful in only a minority of cases, and is really valuable in a very small proportion.' In their 1958 study of 64 homosexual prisoners at Leyhill and Horfield Prisons, R.E. Hemphill, A. Leitch and J.R. Stuart noted that five inmates had been given oestrogen therapy because of 'difficulty in controlling sex drive'. Although they all showed a 'reduction or abolition of libido', none of them changed from being homosexual to heterosexual. The three doctors also found 'only minor differences between homosexuals and normals' and 'no evidence of endocrine disorder or any evidence that a particular kind of constitution or body build is associated with homosexuality'. They suggested a possible 'genetic factor' in the origin of homosexuality, and concluded: 'We have yet to find any evidence that the direction of intensely homosexual drives can be successfully altered.'[38, 39, 40, 41]

Even in Scotland, where hormone treatment was given to homosexual prisoners, some doctors questioned the practice. W.M. Miller, professor of mental health at Aberdeen University, told *The Scotsman* in 1959 that 'fiddling around' with hormones was 'utterly useless'. He believed that homosexual men should instead make a 'moral decision' to change, and that 'spiritual power' could give them the motivation to do so. The use of male hormones such as testosterone to make 'effeminate' men more 'masculine' also proved disappointing. A consultant endocrinologist at a London teaching hospital told BBC Television's *Lifeline* programme in

1957, 'You can't make a male homosexual more masculine by treating him with male sex hormones. In fact, if you give male sex hormones you merely intensify their homosexual desires.' [42, 43]

In their continued attempts to cure homosexuality, doctors instead turned to behaviour therapy. The idea was simple. Homosexuality, explained Clifford Allen in 1958, was the result of hostility to either the mother or the father, or of excessive affection for one or the other parent during infancy and childhood. The homosexual, he argued, 'must be made to realise that he is not irrevocably homosexual but has drifted into such behaviour. Homosexuals are such because they are afraid to be anything else'. James Hadfield explained the theory further in the *British Medical Journal.* [44]

> The case of homosexuality differs little from other perversions such as fetishism, which can be cured by discovery of their infantile origins. The orientation of homosexuality, and the deviation from the normal, appears to go back to a much earlier age than is usually supposed; and only when these factors are revealed and dealt with is the patient radically cured. Homosexuality can be cured in the full sense, provided we can trace the condition to its basic causes. Instances like that of suffocation at the mother's breast and consequent fear of females is not such an impossible experience for a child to have; nor is it inconceivable that this should produce a fear of women; nor that this should make him turn into himself and then to others of his own sex for gratification. [45]

Curing a homosexual's fear of the female or fixation with the male was a matter of psychological re-education: learning to be normal and unlearning to be homosexual. This could be achieved through psychoanalysis, through which a patient was equipped with the self-knowledge necessary to understand his condition and revert to heterosexual behaviour. It is this type of treatment which Dr Presnor recommends to Jeremy in *Details of Jeremy Stretton.* So does Dr Burgraeve in Maxence Van der Meersch's 1960 novel *Mask of Flesh.* At first, businessman Emmanuel Ghelens tries to rid himself of his homosexuality through the love of a good woman and the help of the church. When both fail he turns to Burgraeve, who offers him a simple diagnosis.

'In my opinion the trouble does not lie in your organism, but in your mind. At the age of puberty, at the age when the soul is still malleable, you forged for yourself a false conception. It is late, very late to back-pedal. We are only given a certain time, a single chance to forge our soul, you see. Now we shall have to start all over again to break and remould it; in fact, give you a new life. And that is no easy matter. But don't despair, we'll have a try all the same.' [46]

Psychotherapeutic cures for homosexuality were introduced to the wider public in an article in the *Sunday Pictorial* in February 1961. Reporter Ronald Maxwell went to the Marlborough Day Hospital in St John's Wood, north London to see the treatment for himself.

After the reason or reasons for the homosexuality have been discovered, the psychiatrist tries to put things into their true perspective. He will illustrate that the thing that caused the homosexuality is really something trivial. Then the psychiatrist attempts to reawaken the latent sex instincts. Sometimes he uses drugs to help the treatment. He gives the patient lysergic acid, known as LSD, which will enable him to remember details of his life, right back to birth. This speeds up the analysis, during which the psychiatrist learns of the events which may have caused the homosexuality. It also helps to bring those events to the front of the patient's mind. He can relive the moments of drama and re-experience the conflicts which preceded his diversion from normality. The patient is conscious under the drug so the psychiatrist can talk to him and guide him through those conflicts, changing his viewpoint on the issues which altered his life. [47]

Maxwell spoke to a 40-year-old television actor who explained why he was undergoing therapy: 'I want more than anything to be able to love a woman and marry her, and settle down and have children. I want to have a normal life like other people. I don't want to become just another of those awful old queers who hang around obscene places in the West End.' The man was enthusiastic about the treatment: 'It is amazing. I have reached the stage now where I can get some excitement from thinking about women.' [48]

Not everyone was convinced. Psychologist Donald West went to see an analyst to deal with his homosexuality in the 1950s. 'It certainly didn't work,' he recalled. 'The particular analyst was rather uninvolved because he tended to fall asleep.' In 1955 Mary Woodward, a psychiatrist at the Fountain Hospital in London, found that only seven out of forty-eight men (15%) who completed psychotherapy and hormone treatment at the Portman Clinic ended up with 'no homosexual impulse and increased heterosexual interests'. A major drawback of psychotherapy was the length of time it took to complete. James Hadfield cited the case of a 25-year-old naval officer who needed 164 sessions. Eustace Chesser thought that 'deep analysis' over five years or more was necessary – 'and not many people have the time or the money to make this possible'. Clifford Allen bemoaned the 'tragedy' that 'under the National Health Service there [was] too little provision for treating these cases'. [49, 50, 51, 52, 53]

In the early 1960s an alternative form of behaviour therapy was developed which seemed to provide a solution. Chemical aversion had first been tried in the US to cure alcoholism, and by the early 1950s it was being used by Czech psychiatrist Kurt Freund to treat homosexuality. The first use of the technique in Britain was described in March 1962 by Isaac Oswald and Basil James in two separate papers in *The Journal of Mental Science* and the *British Medical Journal*. Oswald reported the case of a 25-year-old married father of two who had volunteered for treatment to 'try and salve his marriage, for he had been living away with a man for eight months'. The man was 'usually a passive partner' and was 'principally interested in fellatio'. He was also 'greatly excited by male urine and sometimes drank it'. His treatment began with a thirty-minute taped interview in which he described his 'homosexual practices'. He was then given an injection every two hours of the vomit-inducing drug apomorphine. Simultaneously, the interview tape was played back to him through a loud speaker, and glasses of urine sometimes placed next to him. While the patient was being sick, another recording was played on a loop, with a voice saying, 'It makes me sick, it makes him sick. Sex with men? Oh, it makes him sick now. He gets sex with men. It must make him sick now. He'd meet men in lavatories. Ugh. Sex with men makes him sick. He looks at men's bodies. It must make him sick now.' The treatment continued for four days and three nights. But the results were inconclusive. The patient subsequently reported that during a sexual encounter with a man he had felt 'physically sick', but less than two months later 'he had left his wife and gone off to live with a man'. [54]

Meanwhile, in the *British Medical Journal* Basil James described the aversion therapy he had administered to a 40-year-old businessman at Glenside Hospital, Bristol in August 1961.

Treatment was carried out in a darkened single room, and during this time no food or drink was allowed. At regular two-hour intervals he was given an emetic dose of apomorphine by injection followed by 2 oz. of brandy. On each occasion when nausea was felt, a strong light was shone on a large piece of card on which were pasted several photographs of nude or near-nude men. He was asked to select one which he found attractive, and it was suggested to him that he re-create the experiences which he had had with his current homosexual partner. Thereafter a tape was played twice over every two hours during the period of nausea. This began with an explanation of his homosexual attraction along the lines of father-deprivation.* The adverse effect of this on him and its consequent social repercussions was then described in slow and graphic terms, ending with words such as 'sickening', 'nauseating', etc., followed by the noise of one vomiting. After a period of 24 hours the treatment was restarted with another tape, which concentrated more wholly upon the effect his practices had had on him, again ending histrionically. The following night the patient was awakened every two hours and a record played which was frankly congratulatory

---

* The man's father had died of cancer when he was 16.

and which explained in optimistic terms what would have been accomplished if his homosexual drive had been reversed. On the third, fourth and fifth days after the apomorphine treatment had finished a card was placed in his room, pasted on to it being carefully selected photographs of sexually attractive young women. Each morning he was given an injection of testosterone propionate and told to retire to his room when he felt any sexual excitement. He was provided with a record-player and records of a female vocalist whose performance is generally regarded as 'sexy'. [55]

Unlike Oswald, James claimed complete success. He reported that his patient 'felt no attraction at all to the same sex since the treatment'. The man's sexual fantasies were 'entirely heterosexual', and he had even found 'a regular girl friend'. The patient himself described the therapy as 'fantastically successful'. In a follow-up letter to the *BMJ* in February 1963 James confirmed that 18 months after treatment the patient had experienced no 'recurrence of his homosexual drives'. He was now 'courting' a woman, and the relationship showed signs of 'becoming a very serious one'. James did concede, however, that the man's 'considerable physical satisfaction' with his girlfriend did not have 'the same emotional component as his homosexual experiences', and that he 'occasionally found himself admiring pretty boys'. [56, 57]

James' treatment was given widespread publicity in an article in *The Observer*. The newspaper's medical correspondent Abraham Marcus repeated James' assertion that the patient's personal life was now 'better', and that 'for the first time his talent for writing has become productive and profitable'. The writer Antony Burgess may have heard about James' work. His 1962 novel *A Clockwork Orange* includes a remarkably accurate account of contemporary and future aversion therapy techniques. Halfway through the novel the anti-hero Alex undergoes Dr Brodsky's 'Ludovico Technique' while in prison in order to cure him of his criminal violence and so qualify him for early release. [58]

A woman nurse came in and she had a tray and a hyperdermic. All she did was to slam the needle into my left arm. Then the white-coated guy who was like a male nurse came in with a wheelchair. Where I was wheeled to was like no cinema I had ever seen before. One wall was all covered with a silver screen, and direct opposite was a wall with square holes in it for the projector to project through, and there were stereo speakers stuck all over the place. One white-coated guy strapped my head to a like head-rest. 'What's this for?' I said. And this guy replied that it was to keep my head still and make me look at the screen. And then I found they were strapping my hands to the chair arms and my feet were stuck to a foot-rest. One thing I did not like, was when they put like clips on the skin of my forehead, so that my top eyelids were pulled up and up and up and I could not shut my eyes no matter how I tried. 'Everything ready?' said Dr Brodsky in a very breathy voice. And then the lights went out. And then on the screen the picture came on. Then I began to feel sick. I had like pains all over and felt I could sick up and at the same time not sick up, and I began to feel like in distress. I could not shut my eyes, and even if I tried to move my eyeballs about I still could not get out of the line of fire of this picture. I knew I had to sick up, so I screamed: 'I want to be sick. Please let me be sick. Please bring something for me to be sick into.'[*][59]

In 1964, six years after first visiting his doctor, 18-year-old Peter Price was referred to a Chester psychiatric hospital for chemical aversion treatment. He later recalled the experience: 'I sat down in the doctor's room. An old-fashioned reel-to-reel tape recorder was sitting on his desk. He started to speak to me about sex acts between men. He asked me if I realised how revolting homosexuality was; how vile and revolting anal and oral sex were. His questions became more and more graphic, and it went on for an hour. Then he stopped the tape and told me we would be starting the therapy the next day.' The following day Peter was taken to 'a small windowless room' in a hut on the edge of the

[*] Burgess' original Russian-Romany-rhyming 'nadsat' (teenage) slang has been changed.

hospital grounds. Inside was a 'stack of "dirty" books' and a tape player with the recording of his interview with the psychiatrist. A male nurse asked him what he liked to drink, so Peter told him Guinness: 'There I am in this bed, listening to a tape which lasted an hour, and drinking beer and looking at the books. [The nurse] then gets up and gives me an injection. And the injection made me violently ill. I just wanted to throw up. I said, "I'm going to be sick." And he said, "Go on then, just be sick in the bed." And I was just vomiting everywhere. That lasted an hour, and every hour they gave me an injection. I felt dirty, grotty, filthy. I was petrified. It was like being in a horror movie.' Three days later Peter discharged himself from the hospital. [60, 61, 62, 63]

As well as patient intolerance to the procedure, chemical aversion therapy had other disadvantages. In an article in the *BMJ* in January 1964 Robert McGuire and Michael Vallance pointed out that the time taken between the patient viewing the 'stimulus' of the photographs and the sickening effect of the combined apomorphine and alcohol was unpredictable. In some cases the patient might not even feel nauseous. McGuire and Vallance also warned of 'dangerous side-effects'. This was highlighted by the case of 29-year-old Gerald William ('Billy') Clegg-Hill. A captain in the Royal Tank Regiment, Billy was convicted of homosexual offences at Somerset assizes in 1962 and put on probation for three years on condition that he undergo in-patient treatment for six months at the Royal Victoria military hospital in Netley, near Southampton. Three days after being admitted, Billy was dead. During treatment he was injected with apomorphine, which caused stomach haemorrhages, convulsions and a coma. To spare his family's embarrassment, Billy's death was quietly attributed to 'natural causes'. [64, 65, 66]

A similar case was reported at an inquest in Westminster, London in February 1964. 'W.T.', a 34-year-old hotel manager, underwent chemical aversion therapy after psychotherapy, electroconvulsive treatment and tranquilisers had failed to cure him of his homosexuality. He was initially given apomorphine and LSD, but by the third day of treatment the apomorphine had not resulted in vomiting so he was given injections of emetine and a tincture of ipecacuanha (a plant-derived drug also containing emetine). This toxic mix led to heart failure and the man's death a week later. [67]

These cases went unreported in the press, but medical practitioners knew about them. Donald West referred to the Westminster case in the 1968 Penguin reissue of *Homosexuality*, and in December 1964 psychiatrist Stanley Rachman submitted a paper to *Behaviour Research and Therapy* in which he noted: 'Some of the drugs which have been used in chemical aversion treatment have unpleasant side-effects and can be dangerous.' In a probable reference to both the Clegg-Hill and Westminster cases, he added: 'Chemical aversion cannot be used for the treatment of patients with gastric ailments or cardiac complaints.' He also repeated McGuire's and Vallance's point about the time taken between the presentation of 'various stimuli' and the onset of sickness resulting from the combined ingestion of the emetic and alcohol, which made the precise planning and measurement of treatment difficult. The drugs used might also depress patients or induce aggression and hostility. Chemical aversion, said Rachman, was lengthy, 'unpleasant' and 'arduous' for both patients and medics. [68]

In the white heat of the mid-1960s scientific revolution doctors instead developed another means of curing homosexuality: electrical aversion therapy. Electric shocks had first been used to treat homosexuality by the American psychologist Louis Max in 1935. In Britain the technique was first attempted by John Thorpe and Elsa Schmidt at Banstead Hospital in Sutton, Surrey in 1963. In an article published in *Behaviour Research and Therapy* the following year they described how a 28-year-old secretary and shorthand typist had come to them for help. [69]

Throughout his life, he had always experienced sexual arousal to male figures, particularly the buttocks, while he had never experienced such arousal to females. In spite of this, he had never indulged in homosexual practices as he felt that "there was no future in it". He masturbated three times weekly to pictures of male nudes and semi nudes which had been purchased specially for this purpose. It was decided to administer electrical aversion therapy in an attempt to produce an aversive response to the male pictures he had been using in his masturbation sessions. The patient was required to stand in a small room 3x3x10 feet, which was in darkness. He wore his ordinary garments with the exception of a specially prepared pair of shoes which contained an electrically conductive sole, which was connected to an electricity generator in the room adjoining. Before him was a microphone and a picture-viewing apparatus. By the use of the latter, the appropriate pictures could be illuminated by the experimenter when required. The patient was instructed to keep his eyes open during the treatment sessions and to look straight ahead. The experimenter, who was in the adjoining room, had before him an amplifier for the microphone, a switch to control the presentation of the picture and a GPO hand-operated a.c. generator. The picture in the treatment room was illuminated for one second 84 times in 15 minutes at random intervals. In 30 of these, randomly interspersed, the illumination was accompanied by a shock to the feet which began approximately 0.5 seconds after the picture had appeared. After a few shocks had been given a conditioned 'gasp' could be heard through the amplifier each time the picture became visible to the patient. It was therefore clear that he was observing the picture. [70]

The man was given three therapy sessions over two days, but during each session he became 'extremely disturbed', 'wept bitterly' and 'doubted whether he could continue'. During the fourth session he took off the shoes 'and continued to weep bitterly'. He talked for an hour about his various problems and his fear that the electric shocks would give him cancer. Treatment was stopped and the patient was referred elsewhere for psychotherapy. [71]

Thorpe and Schmidt were undeterred, however. They continued to develop their therapeutic technique and, together with fellow psychologist David Castell, tested it out on another patient – a 35-year-old man who had asked for help after reading the *Observer* article about Basil James' treatment at Glenside Hospital. The man specifically demanded aversion therapy, and he resigned from his job and rented out his flat in order to receive full-time treatment. He was duly admitted to Banstead's psychology department, bringing with him a collection of sixty nude male photographs 'which he had been using in his masturbation sessions'. This time treatment began with 'positive conditioning' in an effort to stimulate heterosexual desire. [72]

> In front of the patient, at head height, was a picture of an attractive, scantily dressed female which was visible only when illuminated by the operation of a switch by the psychologist. The patient was supplied with tissues and instructed to masturbate in the darkness, using whatever fantasy he desired. He should, however, keep his eyes open, look ahead of him and report 'now' when he felt that orgasm was being reached. This report served as the experimenter's cue to illuminate the female picture, which remained illuminated until the patient reported 'finished' immediately following ejaculation. [73]

By the sixteenth session the patient had still not learned heterosexual desire and was complaining about the lack of an aversive element in his treatment, so 'negative conditioning' was applied. He was shown his photographs of naked men, and given electric shocks on his bare feet through the floor grid every time they were lit up. In a development reminiscent of Ivan Pavlov's experiments on dogs in the 1900s, 'the patient was very soon reporting sensations of electric shock when the picture was illuminated, irrespective of whether shock actually followed'. The man was then subjected to more positive conditioning. After three sessions of this he was reportedly masturbating '100%' of the time to heterosexual fantasies. But this apparent success did not last. A week after leaving hospital the man admitted slipping back into his old ways, telling the doctors that he had 'masturbated three times over the weekend, always to homosexual fantasy'. After another positive conditioning session he became 'extremely emotional, accusing the psychologists of a complete lack of understanding of him as a person'.

He claimed that they were 'critical of him right from the start' and were 'more interested in [their] experimental results than in him'. [74]

Treatment was later resumed, and after three months in hospital and 138 positive and negative trials the patient was discharged. But the longer-term results of his treatment were inconclusive. Eight months after leaving hospital he wrote to the doctors to say that he had been 'prevented from putting into practice his new found heterosexuality after leaving hospital because he could not get rid of the person to whom he had sub-let his flat'. He had tried and failed to have sex with a woman, and had decided instead to wait 'until he would meet the right girl and fall in love'. According to Thorpe, Schmidt and Castell, the man continued to indulge in 'occasional homosexual patterns of behaviour'. But whereas before treatment he had only been aroused by men and boys, 'he now considered persons of both sexes. This occurred only in hot weather, of which there was not much in an English summer.' [75]

Despite mixed results, doctors continued to develop electric shock therapy. In 1964 Robert McGuire and Michael Vallance introduced their portable Do-It-Yourself aversion kit: a 6x6x2-inch box fitted with a nine-volt battery and electrodes connected to arm cuffs. McGuire and Vallance claimed that their device saved both time and money. It cost less than £1 to make, and after initial training patients could 'take the apparatus home to continue the treatment there', especially 'when the symptom is one usually indulged in alone – for example masturbation to perverse fantasies'. The device drew praise from Clifford Allen, who wrote to the *BMJ* in February 1964 to express his gratitude for this 'harmless and useful method of aversion therapy'. In a possible reference to the Clegg-Hill and Westminster cases, he added: 'The difficulty in the past has been that this form of treatment was uncertain, time-consuming and even dangerous, since patients died owing to idiosyncrasy to apomorphine. Electrical aversion eliminates these disadvantages and should be of great use for out-patients.' J.C. Barker of Shelton Hospital in Shrewsbury agreed: 'The technique is indeed simple and the apparatus cheap and easy to operate. Since the technique can be self-administered at home, the patient can give himself a boosting treatment should he notice a return of symptoms, or whenever he feels the need.' [76, 77, 78]

In May 1964 Thorpe, Schmidt, Castell and Paul Brown told *Behaviour Research and Therapy* about their own apparatus for 'aversion-relief therapy'. This was a wooden box with a turntable inside and a rectangular opening cut into the top. A cardboard disk with 'appropriate' words and phrases type-written onto it was glued to the turntable. As the turntable moved round, each word or phrase was illuminated by a small lamp fixed above the opening. In an adjoining room a psychologist controlled the turntable and operated an electricity generator or 'an apparatus described by McGuire and Vallance'. As the patient read the highlighted words or phrases aloud, he was given an electric shock through 'specially prepared shoes'. The words and phrases included 'homosexual', 'sodomy', 'in bed with a male', 'gay pub' and 'flapping wrists'. Once this aversive conditioning phase was complete, a final word or phrase appeared on the turntable which did not result in a shock, and which the patient would instead associate with relief. These included 'heterosexual', 'women', 'girl friend', 'sex with a woman' and 'female breasts'. Although they admitted that the treatment was 'extremely unpleasant', the four psychologists claimed that their patients were 'eager to continue with it' until they felt that they had been 'cured'. [79]

Further techniques were developed by Maurice Feldman and Malcolm MacCulloch, two of electrical aversion therapy's most enthusiastic advocates. In January 1965 they described their Pavlovian 'attempt to reproduce the method used with dogs' at Crumpsall Hospital in Manchester. This involved patients selecting photographic slides of both men and women and putting them in 'a hierarchy of attractiveness'. The female slides were placed in reverse order, with the most attractive first – although 'for some patients this [was] more accurately described as the least unattractive'. Feldman and MacCulloch accumulated an extensive collection of slides, including pictures 'which suggest various types of homosexual activity'. These images were mostly taken from magazines 'for the general public and from those which appear to have been specifically designed for homosexuals'. Patients were also encouraged to bring pictures 'of which they were particularly fond', including photographs of wives, girlfriends and, in one case, 'a recent homosexual "affair"'. The slides were projected onto a screen at the back of a small viewing box which patients put their head into. Electrodes were fitted around their lower legs and connected to a battery-powered electrical circuit 'similar in type to those on the market for entertainment purposes'. The treatment took place in a dark room 'in a quiet corner of the department', and so that there were no distractions, patients wore ear muffs specially made by MacCulloch himself. During the procedure patients were allowed to remove or recall slides by means of a hand switch. But if they viewed pictures of men for more than eight seconds, they were given electric shocks which would increase in intensity until they said 'no' and switched off the slides. Once the slides were removed and the shocks suspended, pictures of women were shown in an attempt to 'associate relief of anxiety with the introduction of the female'. Patients could ask to see the female slides again by pressing the switch and saying 'yes'. In this way, explained Feldman and MacCulloch, 'the absence of a female slide means that a male slide, by now associated with shock and hence anxiety-provoking, may reappear. Hence the patient gradually becomes motivated to request the return of the female slide. The whole situation is designed to lead to the acquisition of two responses: firstly, attempts to avoid males; and secondly, attempts to approach females.' Doctors had ultimate control over the process, however. To ensure that patients did not view female slides simply to avoid or terminate shocks, their requests to see them again were not always granted, and a master switch controlled by the therapist delayed patients' attempts to remove the male slides. [80]

Colin Fox underwent this treatment at Crumpsall Hospital when he was 19. 'I was convinced that deep down my homosexuality could be cured,' he recalled. 'I was shown slides of men and women and asked to say on a scale of one to ten how sexually exciting I found the slide of the male; and then I was given electric shocks, and it increased or decreased according to my request, reaction and attraction.' Colin remembered the electric shocks as 'sometimes excruciating. The pain terrified me.

It was much worse than touching a live electric cable. I knew it was coming, and would tense up in anticipation.' Yet he persisted because 'I was doing something wrong by having homosexual feelings. The punishment was part of the cure.' [81, 82]

There was a great deal of interest in Feldman and MacCulloch's work. In November 1964 an anonymous donor gave the North Manchester Hospital Management Committee more than £6,000 to pay for a research unit 'to extend the work which has been carried out by the department of psychiatry at Crumpsall Hospital into homosexuality'. [83]

By 1965 Feldman and MacCulloch were investigating pulse rate changes among homosexual patients undergoing 'avoidance learning'. In 1966 they and their colleagues J. Pinschof and Valerie Mellor – a probationer psychologist who had administered the shocks to Colin Fox – told *Behaviour Research and Therapy* about their high-tech method of checking if patients were genuinely cured of their homosexuality. The 'sexual orientation method' required patients to answer a questionnaire about male and female attractiveness in which they could describe men and women as 'interesting', 'attractive', 'handsome', 'beautiful', 'hot', 'pleasurable' and 'exciting'. Their responses were fed into Manchester University's Atlas computer and the results compared with patients' own self-assessments of their sexual reorientation. [84, 85, 86]

For Stanley Rachman the possibilities of electrical aversion therapy were endless: 'With the possible exception of patients with cardiac complaints there is virtually no danger involved, providing the equipment is well-designed and constructed.' He looked forward to the use of 'stimulant drugs' and the development of 'unpleasant auditory' techniques during treatment. He did, though, draw the line at an 'ill-advised' method developed in the US which involved injecting patients with a curare plant drug that temporarily stopped them from breathing and induced paralysis for between thirty seconds and two-and-a-half minutes. [87]

Other doctors hailed the success of their own aversive therapies. In January 1965 Stanley Gold and I.L. Neufeld from the department of child psychiatry at Guy's Hospital in London told *Behaviour Research and Therapy* how they had tested an imaginary form of persuasion on a 16-year-old youth who had been arrested for soliciting men in the toilets of a railway station.

> He was encouraged to visualise himself in a toilet alongside a most unprepossessing old man. It was suggested that he would not under any circumstances solicit such a person. When the patient agreed to this suggestion (by signal), he was rewarded with the words 'well done'. The image of the man was slowly changed to a more attractive form, but at the same time surrounded by prohibitions, such as the image of a policeman standing nearby. With this technique the patient quickly learned to reject an otherwise acceptable and attractive young man, even in the absence of prohibitions. [88]

Gold and Neufeld claimed that the youth eventually learned to choose women rather than men, and that 'after frequent reinforcements of the correct (heterosexual) choice [he] was able to choose the heterosexual object consistently'. After ten sessions he managed to 'avoid the temptation of homosexual contacts', despite retaining 'some feeling of attraction for young men'. At the end of seven follow-up interviews conducted over the course of a year the youth reported 'progressive improvement with no relapse'. He claimed that he no longer felt the urge to make physical contact with men, and that he had 'formed a relationship with a girl, which involved "petting", but not intercourse'. [89]

At St George's Hospital, meanwhile, John Bancroft, H. Gwynne Jones and B.R. Pullan were working on a 'transducer for measuring penile erection'. Their 'strain gauge' or 'penis plethysmograph' tested the degree of sexual arousal in patients and gave doctors more control over the timing and intensity of electric shocks. Made of mercury and rubber, the device was first tested on a 25-year-old paedophile. By the end of 1966 it had been used in more than 2,000 aversion therapy trials to treat transvestites, transsexuals, sadomasochists, fetishists and paedophiles, as well as homosexuals. [90, 91, 92]

Treatment methods were refined in other ways. By 1966 patients at Crumpsall Hospital could lie down in comfort on a bed in a darkened room and view images projected onto a ceiling screen via an angled mirror. Film clips as well as photographic slides were also used to 'increase the verisimilitude of the treatment situation'. The control system was redesigned so that patients themselves could switch off the male slides and their accompanying shocks. Valerie Mellor also devised a mercury switch which sensed when a patient looked away from a male slide and then made it leave the screen. This, it was hoped, would teach homosexuals to stop looking at other men in the street. [93, 94]

At Shelton Hospital J.C. Barker and fellow psychiatrist Mabel Miller began treating up to three patients at a time. Patients viewed the same slides but were screened off from each other and given shocks by three different operators. 'Light music' was played when the female slides were shown in order to stimulate heterosexual attraction and relaxation. At Highcroft Hospital in Birmingham consultant psychiatrist B.H. Fookes conducted positive conditioning sessions in an 'informal atmosphere', and he allowed patients to choose music to be played when pictures of women were shown. Charles Seager, a psychiatry lecturer at Sheffield University, thought that using pictures 'representing sweetness and kindness in a woman rather than the aggressively active sexual pictures which may be obtained from some of the more pornographic magazines' encouraged older homosexual men to build relationships with women as part of their 'social rehabilitation' after treatment. [95, 96, 97]

Treatments like these were carried out at private clinics and National Health Service hospitals across Britain without any oversight or standards of care. There were no regulations, for example, governing the strength of electric shocks given to patients. McGuire's and Vallance's portable DIY box contained a nine-volt battery. Feldman and MacCulloch used 18 volts or more at Crumpsall Hospital. At Banstead Hospital Thorpe, Schmidt, Brown and Castell went up to 120 volts. When Stanley Rachman and J. Teasdale analysed various aversion techniques in 1968 they counselled against the use of shocks that were 'too mild' in case patients became used to them. 'Shock intensities,' they advised, 'need to be fairly high.' [98]

Despite such painful, frightening and humiliating treatment, there was no shortage of patients. Positive press reports encouraged many homosexual men to seek a cure. In 1959 a former patient at the Portman Clinic in London wrote to the *New Statesman* praising the 'amazingly helpful' treatment he had received there. Thorpe's, Schmidt's and Castell's patient in 1962 actively sought aversion therapy after reading about it in the press. So did four out of ten men treated by John Bancroft in 1968. Family pressures also induced men to seek treatment. In Martyn Goff's 1961 novel *The Youngest Director* Leonard's mother persuades her husband that their son is ill and needs psychological help. Mr Bissel goes along with the idea in the hope that it might normalise Leonard. 'I'm not much of a believer in that sort of thing,' he tells him, 'but your mother feels we owe you the right of helping you.' Billy Clegg-Hill's half-sister Alison Garthwaite remembered how her mother was 'just glad that Billy was getting treatment because being gay was seen as such a shameful thing'. It was Peter Price's mother who persuaded him to see his doctor after she found out about his sexuality. Colin Fox submitted to treatment because 'my life was hell for years. I just hoped and prayed my homosexuality could be cured.' [99, 100, 101]

Even after the passing of the 1967 Sexual Offences Act – which decriminalised homosexual acts between consenting adult males in private – feelings of shame and guilt persisted for many. As John Bancroft noted, 'This increase in tolerance was not associated with any lessening of stigma.' Many of the homosexual offences which remained in place were still subject to medical treatment orders. Feldman and MacCulloch claimed that some of the offenders referred to them by the courts were 'grateful for the opportunity to have treatment – an opportunity which they never previously had, either because of shyness or because treatment was not available'. They even argued that their work helped to extend the boundaries of human liberty. [102, 103]

We have confined our treatment efforts to those individuals who sought help themselves, or at least welcomed legal intervention as an opportunity to seek help which they had previously avoided, through embarrassment or ignorance. Whilst it is wrong to impose alterations of behaviour on those who have not sought help, it would be equally wrong to withhold the chance of changing their behaviour from those who have done so because of a belief that it is not the individual who is out of joint but society itself. It is no consolation to an individual who feels that he is suffering through his homosexual interests and practices to suggest that if he only waits for a sufficient length of time society may eventually alter. By offering treatment to those who desire it, we are enlarging the area of human freedom, and the extent to which individuals have control over their own lives. [104]

Law reform organisations were ambivalent about medical cures. In April 1967 Allan Horsfall wrote to psychiatrist and North-Western Homosexual Law Reform Committee member Maurice Silverman about a 21-year-old man who had asked his GP to refer him to Crumpsall Hospital for aversion therapy. Silverman replied that he was 'by no means against utilising aversion therapy in appropriate problems'. At an NWHLRC meeting the following August the committee expressed concern at 'the continued use of aversion therapy as a "treatment" for homosexuals', but they agreed that 'so long as the treatment was undertaken voluntarily, it was a matter for the individual'. [105, 106]

The Albany Trust had strong links with psychologists and psychiatrists, many of whom accepted the validity of homosexual cures. In 1968 Trust supporter and social worker Tom Frost asked Paul Brown, a clinical psychologist at Central Hospital in Hatton, Warwickshire, to help set up an advice and support network in the West Midlands. 'Like us,' Frost told Antony Grey, '[Brown] feels that "cure" would be a possibility in only a small proportion of cases, chiefly in the 16-19 bracket. Paul would be willing to treat specially selected clients, using behaviour therapy procedures.' Grey himself was in close contact with psychiatrist Doris Odlum (a Wolfenden Committee witness), who passed him information about the Paddington Clinic and Day Hospital in London. According to Odlum, doctors there had 'for a number of years dealt with cases of homosexuality'. Grey wrote to her in May 1968: 'We will certainly want to get in touch with them, and I hope will find it possible to send them some prospective clients.', [107, 108, 109]

Others, however, had grave doubts about the efficacy and morality of homosexual cures. On BBC Television's *The Brains Trust* in June 1960 the writer and reviewer Marghanita Laski questioned the purpose of treatment: 'It does appear that there are people who are homosexuals by disposition, and "cure" isn't the right word because it implies putting them back to a normal state they've departed from, and their normal state is homosexuality.' In the *New Statesman,* writer Edward Hyams asked whether homosexuality was really a 'problem' at all. He also poured scorn on the notion of a cure. 'Forced psychological treatment', he wrote, was 'simply brainwashing', and the argument that curing homosexual men would help to reduce homosexual crime was 'tantamount to suggesting that in white communities the colour-bar problem could be solved by bleaching negroes; and in negro communities, by dying the whites black'. [110, 111]

Some medical professionals also opposed treatment. In 1958 W. Lindesay Neustatter warned of the dangers of 'brain-washing and of moulding people's minds'. Two years later A. Soames, an Oxford University academic, wrote to the *New Statesman* challenging Clifford Allen's assertion that homosexuality was a 'neurosis' because it was 'curable'. Soames countered that if 'one of the main fears of legislators is that of homosexuals making "converts" out of heterosexuals, it would appear that heterosexuality must also be a neurosis – i.e. that any sexual direction that can be changed must be a neurosis'. A homosexual doctor interviewed by Michael Schofield in 1960 described medical treatments as 'a waste of time'. He added: 'No one has ever changed a real queer into a normal. I think adapting oneself to one's condition is a better solution than attempting something that would almost amount to being reborn.' A psychiatrist at Edinburgh's Royal Infirmary agreed. He told 24-year-old Alan Alexander in 1961, 'I can see you think you've got problems, but you seem well enough adjusted. You're fine.' Writing in the *BMJ* in February 1964, psychiatrist F.A. Whitlock from Newcastle General Hospital warned that 'in our enthusiasm to apply the techniques employed in the psychological laboratory, we appear to be in danger of bringing ourselves into disrepute by the use of "scientific" treatments which are essentially painful and inhumane'. He argued that giving patients electric shocks was like 'the flogging, ducking and canonfiring of the past', and that 'good intentions do not justify the means employed'. Whitlock also wondered how far psychiatrists were 'justified in imposing on our patients "normal" values which conflict with the patient's own tendencies'. Seven years later, psychotherapist Reginald Beech told the *Sunday Times*: 'I can't imagine any Iron Curtain country has ever inflicted on captured spies the kind of treatment which may be handed out during electrical aversion.' [112, 113, 114, 115, 116, 117, 118]

Nurses, too, were uncomfortable with aversion therapy. In his criticism of chemical aversion methods in 1963 Stanley Rachman noted that the treatment sometimes aroused 'antagonism in some members of the hospital staff', who found it 'unaesthetic and even harrowing'. He added that it was 'not uncommon for attendants to object to participating in this form of treatment'. Feldman and MacCulloch also acknowledged the 'heavy demands' on nurses, who frequently complained about 'the distastefulness of the treatment'. In 1965 Charles Seager told *Nursing Times* that aversion therapy was 'in many cases alien to all that has been taught to the nurse and the doctor about the handling of psychiatric patients. The days of chains, of padded cells, of flogging and ducking as a means of exorcising the devil from the lunatic are past. Yet one must ask whether the difference between the former methods of treatment, applied no doubt with good intention, are different only in degree from the vomiting and electric shocks of aversion treatment.' He advised nurses who were asked to assist in aversive procedures to 'carefully consider' their own opinion 'rather than merely accepting orders. In its present stages the treatment is experimental, and it must remain a necessity for all concerned with its administration to look at it carefully and make their own decisions about their participation.' One nurse, Elizabeth Granger, took Seager's advice on board: 'I remember reading an article in the *Nursing Times* about aversion therapy. I recall it saying that if a nurse [was] asked to administer aversion therapy, and they didn't really want to for ethical reasons, then she should say "no". I distinctly remember thinking that's what I would do if I had to do it. I thought it was barbaric, and I really had no faith in the treatment. The science it was based on was very weak.' [119, 120, 121, 122]

Public attitudes were also changing. In 1964 the journalist Monica Furlong took issue with aversion therapy in an article in the *Daily Mail*. 'What baffles me,' she wrote, 'is that people do not consider [aversion therapy] infinitely more immoral, more damaging to everyone who takes part in it, than the condition it sets out to cure. That brainwashing as a treatment can be seriously entertained suggests how unhealthy and unbalanced our thinking on this whole subject has become.' Fellow *Daily Mail* writer Claire Rayner agreed: 'The alcoholic, the drug addict, the homosexual already carry a lot of suffering. Are doctors justified in stripping these people of their little remaining dignity by inflicting pain and shame in the name of therapy?' In 1965 Michael Schofield described behaviour therapy as a kind of 'thought reform' or 'brain washing', aimed at 'imposing one person's will upon another'. He added: 'The idea that doctors can rid the world of homosexuality, as they hope to rid the world of smallpox, is a medical fantasy. We should give up our attempts to eradicate the homosexual condition.' Richard Hauser, who in 1962 had described homosexual men as 'biological freaks', spoke out against medical cures in a radio discussion three years later. He described aversion therapy as a 'vomit or sulphurs' theory, and he argued: 'One can't fiddle with the problem, as psychotherapy does now. Are we going to have all these people vomit, or do all of these people have wrong cultures?' [123, 124, 125, 126]

In September 1965 the *Newcastle Evening Chronicle*'s Roy Smith visited 'a northern hospital' to see electrical aversion therapy for himself. [127]

The man in the chair in the blacked-out room is a homosexual. There is a projection screen before him. On it flashes a picture of a male model with a fine physique. Seconds later, as the photograph lingers on the screen, an electric shock races through the body of the watcher. As the sensation passes, the picture of the male is replaced by the image of an attractive woman. The sequence is repeated again and again. The image of the man is thus linked with displeasure and that of the female with pleasure. [128]

Smith was not convinced of the usefulness of the treatment. He described it as 'frontier medicine' and reminded readers that homosexuality was 'a form of behaviour that will always be with us. It cannot be legislated against or eradicated like a disease. Homosexuality is not something "catching" like measles or whooping cough.' In 1966 the writer and broadcaster Bryan Magee ridiculed the very notion of sexual reorientation: 'One can give anybody an aversion to anything. Presumably if one made the treatment violent or prolonged enough one could give a happily married man a violent aversion to heterosexual intercourse by associating it with nausea, vomiting and electric shocks. Would this mean he had been "cured" of being heterosexual? I suspect rather that it would mean he had been frightened off. Aversion therapy seems to me to be not so much a cure as a violently conditioned repression of symptoms.' Three years later, Geoffrey Gorer interviewed almost 2,000 people for his book *Sex and Marriage in England Today* (1971). Only 2% thought that 'people who fall in love with their own sex' needed 'psychiatric or medical help'. This compared with a National Opinion Poll published in the *Daily Mail* in 1965 which had found that 93% of people were in favour of 'medical or psychological treatment' for homosexual men. [129, 130, 131, 132]

Although many homosexual men continued to submit to treatment, many more were sceptical and even antagonistic towards the idea of a 'cure'. When Peter Wildeblood's book *Against the Law* was published in 1955 he was visited by a young man who told him, 'I haven't got a disease; I was just born that way. The doctors talk about "curing" you. I don't want to be cured.' Many of the men whom Michael Schofield interviewed in 1960 'berated the books which suggested that homosexuals needed treatment'. One young man imprisoned for a homosexual offence in 1961 told his MP, Godfrey Lagden, 'I don't want to have treatment. I just want to get out and start again.' In John Osborne's 1964 play *Inadmissible Evidence* John Maples faces a charge of importuning, but he rejects the idea of medical treatment to make 'a better impression' in court. He tells his solicitor, 'I don't want to change. I want to be who I am.' In Osborne's next play, *A Patriot for Me* (1965), guests at Baron von Epp's drag ball openly mock medical treatments and their practitioners. [133, 134, 135, 136]

Ferdy: Have you heard about the extraordinary Dr Schoepfer?

Kupfer: No. Who is he? What's he talk about?

Ferdy: Why, us. He sounds an absolute scream. Can't stop talking about it.

Baron: What's he say then, Ferdy?

Ferdy: Oh, that we're all demented. That we're all potential criminals, and some of us should even be castrated.

Kupfer: But who is he?

Kunz: A neurologist, I believe.

Albrecht: I went to a doctor once, and he just said 'pull your socks up'. Do you know what he told me to do? Go into the army! And find yourself a nice girl. Get married.

Baron: I went to a doctor like a silly thing when I was a student. He just looked very agitated and told me there was nothing he could do and go away. A few years later I heard he'd cut his throat.

Ferdy: I only went to a doctor once and he just said take more exercise. [137]

On BBC Two's *Man Alive* programme in 1967 a homosexual hairdresser told viewers that he had no interest in being cured: 'I'm perfectly happy the way I am. I have no desire to be heterosexual. I don't see any advantages in being heterosexual, except from the fact that one might have police protection.' Medical models of homosexuality were even given comic treatment in the popular radio show *Round the Horne*. In an episode broadcast in April 1967 Kenneth Horne visits Julian (Hugh Paddick) and Sandy (Kenneth Williams) for some medical advice. [138]

Horne: Outside the recognised branches of medicine there are a number of fringe practitioners. Now I myself recently suffered from insomnia, so when I came across an advertisement in my copy of the *Naturist Pictorial*... The advertisement read: 'Nervous disorders – consult Bona Nature Clinic, Harley Street'. And I decided to pay them a visit.

Sandy: Yes, we are actual homeopathic practitioners. We are, oh yes. We're not recognised by doctors.

Julian: Yes, you see Sand and me, we're on the fringe, aren't we? [139]

Even men who underwent treatment did not always take it seriously – particularly if they accepted it only at the behest of the courts as an alternative to prison or as part of a lighter sentence. In 1965 Feldman and MacCulloch reported that one offender sent to them for electrical aversion therapy 'found after two sessions that he was actually enjoying the treatment, and decided that in any event he did not really want to change'. Another man underwent a single session and then asked for further treatment to be carried out under an anaesthetic. Percival Thatcher was convicted of importuning in 1966 and was given the option of imprisonment or psychological treatment. He chose the latter: 'I knew it was not going to make me straight. I lied, and told them that it had worked.' One psychiatrist remembered how men referred to him were often 'motivated to say things that weren't actually true'. Former mental health nurse Benedict Henry recalled how offenders often lied about the effectiveness of treatment: 'I remember the consultant saying, "How do you feel?" One of the best responses to the doctor at the time was to say, "I feel repulsed by who I am." Or, "I have been thinking of some of the pictures you have shown me, and I realise now how distasteful that is." There was never actually any way of checking whether the patients believed in what they were saying.' [140, 141, 142]

Voluntary patients discovered for themselves that medical treatments were ineffective. 'I desperately wanted the treatments to work,' remembered one man, 'but they didn't.' Another former patient recalled a conversation with his psychiatrist: 'I said, "When am I going to find a breakthrough? You keep saying things will change, and everything's going to be ok." She said, "Well, I'm going to have to tell you now I don't think we are going to get anywhere. To be quite honest, I never expected we would in the first place."' Some patients were relieved when their treatment failed. Tony Kildwick went for aversion therapy at a hospital in Bristol (possibly Glenside): 'This chap explained to me that he would present pictures of attractive young men, and if I suddenly got sexually aroused I should be given an electric shock, which would hopefully turn me off. Gradually, he would substitute the handsome young men [with] nubile young ladies. Well, he started off by showing me a lot of brunette moustachioed Latins, and I was really rather more attracted to blond Nords, so it didn't work very well. I didn't have a shock, and I thought, "I really can't do this. This is ridiculous."' When Peter Price walked out of his chemical aversion treatment at Crumpsall Hospital he went to a gay bar and then spent the rest of the evening with a friend: 'It was almost as if I thought, this is it, I'm going to start living my life.' [143, 144, 145 146, 147]

The extremes of aversion therapy were sensationally exposed in an article by Peter Pringle in *The Sunday Times* in May 1971. Pringle reported on the case of Robert John, a patient who had suffered a heart attack while undergoing electrical aversion therapy at a London hospital. Pringle also described a recent experiment in which 'a group of psychologists found that, after only one hour, they could get a sexual response from looking at a screened picture of an old boot when it was continually followed by a series of sexy pin-ups'. This point was further demonstrated by Maurice Feldman and Malcolm MacCulloch, who, as part of a BBC Television programme on behaviour therapy, conditioned two 'normal' volunteers – a male and a female student from 'a Midlands university' – to become repelled or attracted by pictures of a squirrel and a toad. After several sessions the male student learned to avoid the squirrel, while the female student became attracted to the toad. [148, 149]

The *Sunday Times* article also pointed to 'an increasing amount of clinical data which shows that the treatment is more often a failure than a success'. Indeed, doctors were unable to prove convincingly that their 'cures' really worked. Many of the reports they produced were based on single case studies, and patients' longer-term sexual reorientation was rarely followed up. Where larger follow-up studies were made, 'success' rates were low. In 1958 Kurt Freund published a report in an Argentinian journal about his work in Czechoslavakia. It showed that only 12 out of 47 patients (25%) treated with chemical aversion therapy showed significant changes in their sexual responses. None of these 12 'heterosexually adapted homosexuals' (seven of whom were married) were completely rid of their homosexual desires at the end of the treatment. Freund concluded: 'There does not appear to be any method of treatment the efficacy of which could be said to be very apparent.' Freund's research was published in English in 1960 and widely circulated, but most doctors ignored his findings. [151, 152]

The only large-scale British study was conducted by MacCulloch and Feldman, and published in 1967. They found that just 13 out of 43 patients (including two women) treated with electrical aversion therapy between 1963 and 1965 had 'active heterosexual intercourse' one to two years later. Even this 30% success rate masked a number of factors which cast doubt on the doctors' claim to effect a cure. 33 out of the 43 patients had already had past heterosexual experiences, 'accompanied by satisfaction in all cases but one'. At the time of treatment, 18 of them were still engaged in 'some form of heterosexual behaviour', including seven who were having sexual intercourse with women – five of them with their wives. It is likely that these seven were counted among the 13 patients supposedly cured at the end of treatment. That left just six others (14% of the original 43); and even these may have been among the 33 patients who had already had previous heterosexual experience. [153, 154]

The results of Feldman's and MacCulloch's next largest study, published in 1971, were even more dubious. Thirty patients (again including two women) were given either psychotherapy or electrical aversion treatment. Twelve of the 30 had not even had previous homosexual experiences, as they had only engaged in 'phantasy'. Fourteen (47%) were described as 'improved' at the end of treatment, although the doctors did not explain what this meant. Thirteen out of the 14 were described as 'secondary homosexuals' – i.e. they had already had 'prior pleasurable heterosexual experience'. Only one 'primary' (i.e. exclusively) homosexual patient was deemed to have been cured. Feldman and MacCulloch concluded their study by recommending that in future patients should be selected for treatment through a 'triple sieve'. This meant excluding 'primary' homosexuals, people with a 'poor personality' and those with a low 'pre-treatment heterosexual score'. In other words, treatment should only be given to the most heterosexually-inclined patients. The doctors, it seemed, were rigging the results of their own treatment in advance. [155]

Results of Medical Treatment, 1957-1971

Practitioner	Hospital/Clinic	Type of Treatment	Results Published	No. of Patients Treated[*]	No. of Patients 'Cured'	% 'Cured'
D. Curran & D. Parr	Private practice	Psychotherapy	1957	100	0	0%
J.A. Hadfield	Unknown	Psychotherapy	1958	9	9	100%
R.E. Hempill, A. Leitch & J.R. Stuart	Leyhill & Horfield Prisons, Bristol	Oestrogen	1958	5	0	0%
M. Woodward	Portman Clinic, London	Psychotherapy & hormones	1958	81	7	9%
S.J.C. Spencer	Warneford & Park Hospitals, Oxford	Psychotherapy	1959	86	4	5%
S. Coates	Portman Clinic, London	Psychotherapy	1962	45	7	16%
I. Oswald	Unknown	Chemical aversion	1962	1	0	0%

* Including patients who did not complete full courses of treatment

B. James	Glenside Hospital	chemical aversion	1962 & 1963	1	1	100%
R.J. McGuire & M.J. Vallance	Unknown	Electrical aversion	1964	6	3	50%
S. Gold & I.L. Neufeld	Guy's Hospital, London	Psychotherapy	1965	1	1	100%
E. Schmidt, D. Castell, P. Brown	Banstead Hospital, Surrey	Electrical aversion	1965	16	8	50%
M.P. Feldman & M.J. MacCulloch	Crumpsall Hospital, Manchester	Electrical aversion	1967	43**	13	30%
J. Bancroft & I. Marks	Maudsley Hospital, London	Electrical aversion	1968	10	1	10%
B.H. Fookes	Highcroft Hospital, Birmingham	Electrical aversion	1969	15	9	60%
M.P. Feldman & M.J. MacCulloch	Crumpsall Hospital, Manchester	Electrical aversion	1971	30**	14	47%
			Total:	449	77	17%

** Including two women

With its attitude of celebration and defiance, the Gay Liberation Front of the early 1970s strenuously opposed aversion therapy and other forms of medical treatment. In 1972 members of the West London GLF Anti-Psychiatry Group sent a letter to a local GP protesting about his referral of patients for aversion therapy: 'Many members of the GLF can testify to the ineffectiveness of aversion therapy in reorientation of their sexual desires. Our plan is for homosexuals seeking advice from you to be given reassurances from you that they are fully capable of living a full, worthwhile and happy life. This positive attitude substituted for attempts to provide treatment and cure will spare many from intense and undue suffering.' [156]

In January that year the film version of Anthony Burgess' *A Clockwork Orange* was released in Britain. Speakers at a London symposium on 'Aversion Therapy and the Patient's Freedom' the following November clearly had the film in mind when they were challenged from the floor by GLF activist and *Gay News* writer Peter Tatchell. He interrupted proceedings to tell delegates about people he knew who had become 'chronic depressives' after undergoing aversion therapy. Others, he claimed, 'remained totally uncured and had become asexual "vegetables"'. He added that men were 'virtually blackmailed' into treatment when it was offered by the courts as an alternative to prison, and that there was an 'exaggeration of the success rate and playing down of the pain and discomfort'. Psychiatry professor Hans Eysenck responded by telling the audience that aversion therapy was 'just like a visit to the dentist'. Psychiatrist Isaac Marks (who had treated patients with electrical aversion therapy at Maudsley Hospital in London) argued that *A Clockwork Orange* was 'a totally inaccurate portrayal of aversion therapy', and that doctors were justified in using aversive techniques when 'the patient asks for help' or when 'society asks to be relieved of the burden of an individual'. No one, he added, objected 'when people with smallpox are quarantined' or when 'sadists or murderers are removed from society'. Tatchell was subsequently surrounded by 'ten heavies' and 'dragged out and carried from the symposium'. [157]

No one knows exactly how many men in Britain were treated for homosexuality in the 1950s and 1960s, but the evidence suggests that several hundred underwent hormonal, psychological and aversive 'cures'. The last treatments took place in the mid-1970s. In 1974 the American Psychiatric Association removed homosexuality from its influential *Diagnostic and Statistical Manual of Mental Disorders*. The World Health Organisation dropped homosexuality from its *International Statistical Classification of Diseases and Related Health Problems* in 1992. Some men who received treatment adjusted to their sexuality and reconfigured their lives. For others the experience was more troubling. 'I still have terrible flashbacks of my time in hospital,' recalled one former patient forty years after he received treatment. Some medical practitioners continued to defend their methods. 'Here were people coming along who seemed to be asking for help,' explained one psychologist. 'It was against the law. They wanted to change their behaviour. That's how it was presented to us. You never thought about the morality of what you were doing. You were effectively a technician.' Another psychologist argued that homosexual men were 'people who were disordered and needed treatment and psychiatric help'. But most doctors accepted John Bancroft's assertion in 1970 that 'it should be made clear that a person can still have homosexual tendencies and be a likeable, decent person. It should be stressed that homosexuality is a normal variant of sexual behaviour.' [158, 159, 160]

Chapter 3 references

1. William Kimber, 1960
2. 'Discussion by TV Panel' *Daily Telegraph*, 5 September 1957
3. 'A Doctor Tells on TV', *Daily Mail*, 6 September 1957
4. "'I Am a Homosexual" Says a Doctor on TV', *Daily Mirror*, 6 September 1957
5. Tommy Dickinson, *Curing Queers: Mental Nurses and Their Patients, 1935-74*, Manchester University Press, 2015
6. Barbara Wootton, 'Sickness or Sin?', *The Twentieth Century*, May 1956
7. *Report of the Committee on Homosexual Offences and Prostitution*, Her Majesty's Stationery Office, 1957 [Wolfenden Report]
8. Ibid.
9. Desmond Curran, Denis Parr, 'Homosexuality: An Analysis of 100 Male Cases Seen in Private Practice', *British Medical Journal*, 6 April 1957
10. Wolfenden Report
11. Ibid.
12. Roger Davidson, Gayle Davis, "'A Field for Private Members": The Wolfenden Committee and Scottish Homosexual Law Reform, 1950-67', *Twentieth Century British History*, Vol. 15, No. 2, 2004
13. Roger Davidson, Gayle Davis, *The Sexual State: Sexuality and Scottish Governance, 1950-1980*, Edinburgh University Press, 2012
14. 'Homosexual Offences and Prostitution', *The Lancet*, 14 September 1957
15 Gordon Westwood, *Society and the Homosexual*, Gollancz, 1952
16. Audrey Erskine Lindop, *Details of Jeremy Stretton*, Heinemann, 1955
17. Ibid.
18. J.A. Hadfield, 'The Cure of Homosexuality', *British Medical Journal*, 7 June 1958
19. Clifford Allen, *Homosexuality: Its Nature, Causation and Treatment*, Staples Press, 1958

20. Richard Hauser, *The Homosexual Society*, The Bodley Head, 1962

21. Correspondence, *British Medical Journal*, 27 January 1962

22. *Woman's Hour*, BBC Radio Light Programme, 10 July 1958, BBC Written Archives

23. Ibid.

24. Gordon Westwood, *A Minority: A Report on the Life of the Male Homosexual in Great Britain*, Longmans, 1960

25. W. Lindsay Neustatter, 'The Wolfenden Report. I. – Homosexuality', *The Howard Journal*, Vol. 10, No. 1, 1958

26. Eustace Chesser, *Odd Man Out: Homosexuality in Men and Women*, Gollancz, 1959

27. Edward Glover (ed.), *The Problem of Homosexuality: A Memorandum Presented to the Departmental Committee on Homosexual Offences and Prostitution by a Joint Committee Representing The Institute for the Study and Treatment of Delinquency and the Portman Clinic*, ISTD, 1957

28. 'Two Valuable Pamphlets', The Lancet, 20 April 1957

29. 'Male Homosexuality', *The Lancet*, 12 December 1959

30. Michael J. Buckley, *Morality and the Homosexual: A Catholic Approach to a Moral Problem*, Sands & Co., 1959

31. Correspondence, *New Statesman*, 30 July 1960

32. 'Towards a Quaker View of Sex', *The Friend*, 20 May 1960

33. L.H. Rubinstein, 'Psychotherapeutic Aspects of Male Homosexuality', *British Journal of Medical Psychology*, 1958

34. Denis Parr, 'Homosexuality in Clinical Practice', *Proceedings of the Royal Society of Medicine*, September 1957

35. Pete Price, *Namedropper*, Trinity Mirror North West & North Wales, 2007

36. Miriam Akhtar, Steve Humphries, *The Fifties and Sixties: A Lifestyle Revolution*, Pan Macmillan, 2001

37. Steve Humphries, Pamela Gordon, *A Man's World: From Boyhood to Manhood, 1900-1960*, BBC Books, 1996

38. G.I.M. Swyer, 'Homosexuality: The Endocrinological Aspects', *The Practitioner*, April 1954

39. W. Lindsay Neustatter, 'Homosexuality: The Medical Aspect', op. cit.

40. *Homosexuality and Prostitution, A Memorandum of Evidence Prepared by a Special Committee of the Council of the British Medical Association for Submission to the Departmental Committee on Homosexuality and Prostitution*, British Medical Association, 1955

41. R.E. Hemphill, A Leitch, J.R. Stuart, 'A Factual Study of Male Homosexuality', *British Medical Journal*, 7 June 1958

42. Graham Turner, 'Control Must Come Before Cure', *The Scotsman*, 6 June 1959

43. 'The Problem of the Homosexual', *Lifeline*, BBC Television, 26 November 1957, BBC Written Archives

44. Clifford Allen, *Homosexuality*, op. cit.

45. J.A. Hadfield, '*The Cure of Homosexuality*', op. cit.

46. Maxence Van der Meersch, *Mask of Flesh*, William Kimber, 1960

47. Ronald Maxwell, 'Twilight Men – Now They Can Be Cured', *Sunday Pictorial*, 5 February 1961

48. Ibid.

49. Donald West, personal interview with author, 14 September 2012

50. Mary Woodward, 'The Diagnosis and Treatment of Homosexual Offenders', *British Journal of Delinquency*, July 1958

51. J.A. Hadfield, '*The Cure of Homosexuality*', op. cit.

52. Eustace Chesser, *Odd Man Out: Homosexuality in Men and Women*, op. cit.

53. Correspondence, *New Statesman*, 25 June 1960

54. Isaac Oswald, 'Induction of Illusory and Hallucinatory Voices with Considerations of Behaviour Therapy', *The Journal of Mental Science*, March 1962

55. Basil James, 'Case of Homosexuality Treated by Aversion Therapy', *British Medical Journal*, 17 March 1962

56. Ibid.

57. Correspondence, *British Medical Journal*, 23 February 1963

58. Abraham Marcus, 'How Doctor Cured a Homosexual', *The Observer*, 18 March 1962

59. Anthony Burgess, *A Clockwork Orange*, Heinemann, 1962

60. Beverley D'Silva, 'When Gay Meant Mad', *The Independent*, 4 August 1996

61. *Dark Secret: Sexual Aversion*, BBC 2, 8 August 1996

62. Alkarim Jivani, *It's Not Unusual: A History of Lesbian and Gay Britain in the Twentieth Century*, Michael O'Mara Books, 1997

63. Pete Price, *Namedropper*, op. cit.

64. R.J. McGuire, M. Vallance, 'Aversion Therapy by Electric Shock: A Simple Technique', *British Medical Journal*, 18 January 1964

65. Beverley D'Silva, 'When Gay Meant Mad', op. cit.

66. *Dark Secret: Sexual Aversion*, op. cit.

67. 'Recent Cases: Fatal Emetine Poisoning from Aversion Treatment', *The Medico-Legal Journal*, Part Two, 1964

68. Stanley Rachman, 'Aversion Therapy: Chemical or Electrical?', *Behaviour Research and Therapy*, April 1965

69. Louis William Max, 'Breaking Up a Homosexual Fixation by the Conditioned Reaction Technique: A Case Study', *The Psychological Bulletin*, November 1935

70. J.G. Thorpe, E. Schmidt, 'Therapeutic Failure in a Case of Aversion Therapy', *Behaviour Research and Therapy*, March 1964

71. Ibid.

72. J.G. Thorpe, E. Schmidt, D. Castell, 'A Comparison of Positive and Negative (Aversive) Conditioning in the Treatment of Homosexuality', *Behaviour Research and Therapy*, March 1964

73. Ibid.

74. Ibid.

75. Ibid.

76. R.J. McGuire, M. Vallance, 'Aversion Therapy by Electric Shock: A Simple Technique', op. cit.

77. Correspondence, *British Medical Journal*, 15 February 1964

78. Correspondence, *British Medical Journal*, op. cit.

79. J.G. Thorpe, E. Schmidt, P.T. Brown, D. Castell, 'Aversion-Relief Therapy: A New Method for General Application', *Behaviour Research and Therapy*, May 1964

80. M.P. Feldman, M.J. MacCulloch, 'The Application of Anticipatory Avoidance Learning to the Treatment of Homosexuality – I. Theory, Technique and Preliminary Results', *Behaviour Research and Therapy*, January 1965

81. Beverley D'Silva, 'When Gay Meant Mad', op. cit.

82. *Dark Secret: Sexual Aversion*, op. cit.

83. 'Hospital Projects to Help Mentally Ill', *The Guardian*, 25 November 1964

84. M.J. MacCulloch, M.P. Feldman, J.M. Pinshoff, 'The Application of Anticipatory Avoidance Learning to the Treatment of Homosexuality – II. Avoidance Response Latencies and Pulse Rate Changes', *Behaviour Research and Therapy*, August 1965

85. Beverley D'Silva, 'When Gay Meant Mad', op. cit.

86. M.P Feldman, M.J MacCulloch, Valerie Mellor, J.M. Pinschof, 'The Application of Anticipatory Avoidance Learning to the Treatment of Homosexuality – III. The Sexual Orientation Method', *Behaviour Research and Therapy*, November 1966

87. Stanley Rachman, 'Aversion Therapy: Chemical or Electrical?', op. cit.

88. S. Gold, I.L. Neufeld, 'A Learning Approach to the Treatment of Homosexuality', *Behaviour and Research Therapy*, January 1965

89. Ibid.

90. J.H.J. Bancroft, H. Gwynne Jones, B.R. Pullan, 'A Simple Transducer for Measuring Penile Erection, with Comments on its Use in the Treatment of Sexual Disorders', *Behaviour Research and Therapy*, August 1966

91. John Bancroft, Isaac Marks, 'Electric Aversion Therapy of Sexual Deviations', *Proceedings of the Royal Society of Medicine*, August 1968

92. John Bancroft, 'A Comparative Study of Aversion and Desensitisation in the Treatment of Homosexuality', in Laurence E. Burns, James L. Worsley (ed.s), *Behaviour Therapy in the 1970s: A Collection of Original Papers*, John Wright & Sons, 1970

93. Northage J. de Ville Mather, 'The Treatment of Homosexuality by Aversion Therapy', *Medicine, Science and the Law*, October 1966

94. M.P. Feldman, M.J. MacCulloch, *Homosexual Behaviour: Therapy and Assessment*, Pergamon Press, 1971

95. J.C. Barker, Mabel E. Miller, 'Some Clinical Applications of Aversion Therapy', in Hugh Freeman (ed.), *Progress in Behaviour Therapy: Proceedings of a Symposium Held at the Postgraduate Medical Institute, University of Salford*, John Wright & Sons, 1968

96. B.H. Fookes, 'Some Experiences in the Use of Aversion Therapy in Male Homosexuality, Exhibitionism and Fetishism-Transvestism', *British Journal of Psychiatry*, March 1969

97. C.P. Seager, in Hugh Freeman (ed.), *Progress in Behaviour Therapy, op. cit.*

98. S. Rachman, J. Teasdale, *Aversion Therapy and Behaviour Disorders: An Analysis*, Routledge & Kegan Paul, 1968

99. London Diary, *New Statesman*, 31 January 1959

100. Martyn Goff, *The Youngest Director*, Putnam, 1961

101. Beverley D'Silva, 'When Gay Meant Mad', op. cit.

102. John Bancroft, 'Abnormal Sexual Behaviour: Homosexuality in the Male', *British Journal of Hospital Medicine*, February 1970

103. M.P. Feldman, M.J. MacCulloch, *Homosexual Behaviour*, op. cit.

104. M.P. Feldman, 'The Treatment of Homosexuality by Aversion Therapy', in Hugh Freeman (ed.), *Progress in Behaviour Therapy*, op. cit.

105. Letter from Maurice Silverman to Allan Horsfall, 5 June 1967, Peter Scott-Presland, *Amiable Warriors: The Official History of the Campaign for Homosexual Equality and Its Times, Volume One: Space to Breathe*, Paradise Press, 2015

106. Minutes of NWHLRC meeting, 3 August 1967, op. cit.

107. Letter from Tom Frost to Antony Grey, 28 January 1968, Hall-Carpenter Albany Trust files, London School of Economics

108. Letter from Doris Oldum to Antony Grey, 30 April 1968, op. cit.

109. Letter from Antony Grey to Doris Oldum, 12 May 1968, op. cit.

110. *The Brains Trust*, BBC Television, 23 June 1960

111. Edward Hyams, 'The Spurious Problem', *New Statesman*, 25 June 1960

112. W. Lindsay Neustatter, 'The Wolfenden Report. I. – Homosexuality', *The Howard Journal*, Vol. 10, No. 1, 1958

113. Correspondence, *New Statesman*, 25 June 1960

114. Correspondence, *New Statesman*, 23 July 1960

115. Gordon Westwood, *A Minority*, op. cit.

116. Bob Cant, *Footsteps and Witnesses: Lesbian and Gay Lifestories from Scotland*, Word Power Books, 2008

117. Correspondence, *British Medical Journal*, 15 February 1964

118. Peter Pringle, 'Fears Over Aversion Therapy Grow: Using Shock Tactics to Bend the Mind', *The Sunday Times*, 9 May 1971

119. Stanley Rachman, 'Aversion Therapy: Chemical or Electrical?', op. cit.

120. M.P. Feldman, M.J. MacCulloch, *Homosexual Behaviour*, op. cit.

121. C.P. Seager, 'Aversion Therapy in Psychiatry', *Nursing Times*, 26 March 1965

122. Tommy Dickinson, *Curing Queers*, op. cit.

123. Monica Furlong, 'The Law and the Homosexual', *Daily Mail*, 21 October 1964

124. Claire Rayner, 'Should Shame Be the Cure?', *Daily Mail*, 10 September 1970

125. Michael Schofield, *Sociological Aspects of Homosexuality: A Comparative Study of Three Types of Homosexuals*, Longmans, 1965

126. *Male Homosexual*, BBC Home Service, 12 January 1965, BBC Written Archives

127. Roy Smith, 'The Men Apart', *Newcastle Evening Chronicle*, 7 September 1965

128. Ibid.

129. Ibid.

130. Bryan Magee, *One in Twenty*, Secker & Warburg, 1966

131. Geoffrey Gorer, *Sex and Marriage in England Today: A Study of the Views and Experience of the Under-45s*, Nelson, 1971

132. Gordon Greig, 'Homosexuality: Alter the Law', *Daily Mail*, 28 October 1965

133. Peter Wildeblood, *A Way of Life*, Weidenfeld & Nicolson, 1956

134. Gordon Westwood, *A Minority*, op. cit.

135. *In the News*, ITV, 10 March 1961, Hall-Carpenter Albany Trust files, London School of Economics

136. John Osborne, *Inadmissible Evidence*, *John Osborne Plays 3*, Faber & Faber, 1998

137. John Osborne, *A Patriot for Me*, op.cit.

138. *The Men Man Alive: Consenting Adults 1. The Men*, BBC 2, 7 June 1967

139. 'The Admirable Loombucket – Lost Island Of Gonga', *Round the Horne*, BBC Light Programme, 2 April 1967

140. M.J. MacCulloch, M.P. Feldman, 'The Application of Anticipatory Avoidance Learning to the Treatment of Homosexuality I., op. cit.

141. Tommy Dickinson, *Curing Queers*, op. cit.

142. Michael King, Glenn Smith, Annie Bartlett, 'Treatments of Homosexuality in Britain since the 1950s – An Oral History: The

Experience of Professionals', *British Medical Journal*, 21 February 2004

143. Tommy Dickinson, Matt Cook, John Playle, Christine Hallett, '"Queer" Treatments: Giving a Voice to Former Patients Who Received Treatments for their "Sexual Deviations"', *Journal of Clinical Nursing*, May 2012

144. Glenn Smith, Annie Bartlett, Michael King, 'Treatments of Homosexuality in Britain since the 1950s – An Oral History: The Experience of Patients', *British Medical Journal*, 21 February 2004

145. Miriam Akhtar, Steve Humphries, *The Fifties and Sixties: A Lifestyle Revolution*, Pan Macmillan, 2001

146. Beverley D'Silva, 'When Gay Meant Mad', op. cit.

147. Alkarim Jivani, *It's Not Unusual*, op. cit.

148. Peter Pringle, 'Fears Over Aversion Therapy Grow', op. cit.

149. M.P. Feldman, M.J. MacCulloch, *Homosexual Behaviour*, op. cit.

150. Peter Pringle, 'Fears Over Aversion Therapy Grow', op. cit.

151. Kurt Freund, 'Sobre el Problema del Tratamento de la Homosexualidad', *Acta Neuropsiquiátrica Argentina* 1958

152. Kurt Freund, 'Some Problems in the Treatment of Homosexuality', in H.J. Eysenck (ed.), *Behaviour Therapy and the Neuroses: Readings in Modern Methods of Treatment Derived from Learning Theory*, Pergamon Press, 1960

153. M.J. MacCulloch, M.P. Feldman, 'Aversion Therapy in Management of 43 Homosexuals', *British Medical Journal*, 3 June 1967

154. M.P Feldman, M.J. MacCulloch, *Homosexual Behaviour*, op. cit.

155. Ibid.

156. Tommy Dickinson, *Curing Queers*, op. cit.

157. Peter Tatchell, 'Aversion Therapy "Is Like a Visit to the Dentist"', *Gay News*, No. 11, November 1972

158. Tommy Dickinson, Matt Cook, John Playle, Christine Hallett, '"Queer" Treatments', op. cit.

159. Michael King, Glenn Smith, Annie Bartlett, 'Treatments of Homosexuality in Britain since the 1950s – An Oral History: The Experience of Professionals', op. cit.

160. John Bancroft, 'Abnormal Sexual Behaviour', op. cit.

Chapter 4

A HUGE HOMOSEXUAL KINGDOM

'I know that around the world this country has now earned the dreadful title of "The Capital of Queerdom".'

Noyes Thomas, *News of the World*, 26 July 1964 [1]

On 22 October 1964, in front of millions of television viewers, a softly spoken office manager politely but firmly rejected the suggestion that what he and other homosexual men did was 'disgusting'. He told Bryan Magee on ITV's *This Week*, 'Personally I find that what a heterosexual couple do is just the same to me. I find it unnatural and repulsive. And whilst they consider they lead a normal life, I lead as completely a normal life as they do.' He added that he had lived with another man for seventeen years as 'a married couple' and that there was 'a very great love, a very great feeling' between them. [2]

The man's comments gave an insight into the everyday lives of gay men and showed how far the discussion about homosexuality had moved on since the publication of the Wolfenden Report seven years earlier. Just four years before, Michael Schofield had published the first major sociological study of homosexual men in Britain – *A Minority: A Report on the Life of the Male Homosexual in Great Britain.* Under his pseudonym Gordon Westwood, Schofield interviewed 127 men aged between 18 and 84. He found that 41 (32%) shared accommodation with other gay men, including men who were not their partners. One interviewee explained: 'I've lived with Simon for the last three years. It's completely asexual. If we had sex together we'd just laugh. But I couldn't possibly share with someone who wasn't queer. It works quite well. There's a certain amount of sisterly affection between Simon and me and it provides the means to live well and a certain amount of security.' Schofield noted that this kind of arrangement also resulted in 'more sexual freedom' and provided 'understanding and companionship with a like-minded man'. Playwright Joe Orton came across two such friends in Highbury, north London in 1967. After picking up Irishman Alan Tills in the public toilets on Holloway Road, Orton went with him to his home. There he met flatmate Dave from Burnley, and all three had sex together. [3]

'Come again sometime,' Dave said, switching on the television set. 'We'd love to have you.'

'The best night for us is Monday or Wednesday,' Tills said, as he let me out of the front door. I thought they were both very nice fellows.' [4]

One man told Schofield that he thought some homosexual men behaved 'badly in public' because they were 'living with their families or in some situation where they cannot find relief after a day at the office. I don't mean I scream as soon as I get home or talk sex all the time, but it's such a relief not to be on my guard all the time.' Schofield found that six out of 11 of his contacts who 'regularly engaged in homosexual activities in public places' lived in homes where it was impossible to bring back sexual partners. Others were forced to keep their sexuality secret from the friends and family they lived with and to 'build up a complex fabrication of lies and deceit in order to explain their absences'. One man complained: 'The whole thing is so often bedevilled with nervousness and also by the dreadful business of lies, wangles, subterfuges and time-table manipulation. The double-life aspect of the thing is a constant irritant.' [5]

Thirteen (10%) of Schofield's contacts lived in houses owned by other gay men. Three landlords had a policy of only renting their properties to gay tenants. One let rooms in his house to twelve men. Such *ménages* were not uncommon. In 1967 the actor Kenneth Williams told Joe Orton about an arrangement he had heard about in north London.

'There's this doctor – a queen, but good-natured – and she's bought this house and stocked it with boys. They're all working lads. All from borstal. And she's allotted them their various tasks. One is responsible for the plumbing, another for the electricity. And so it goes on. I said to one of the boys, called Chris, 'You do all the plumbing – all copper – for cost price?'

'Well,' Chris said, 'he's been good to us. Very good. See I was in borstal and nobody cared about me. And he took me in. Give me a roof over my head.'

There's even a boy responsible for the goldfish. And if any of them neglect their tasks she calls him into her surgery, wags her finger and says, 'Now then, Dennis, you've neglected to feed the goldfish. What is your excuse?

And the lad might say, 'Well, you see, I had the trade in and I forgot.'

'Forgot!' this queen will say. 'Had the trade in and forgot? You've no right to have the trade until you've fed the fish!' [6]

Landlords who were not gay – and especially women – often preferred gay tenants because they thought that they were more responsible and tidier than heterosexuals. In Jay Gilbert's 1963 novel *The Goose Girl* French landlady Madame P. tells Roger and Lewis, 'You are good boys. I never had better tenants.' Relationships between tenants and landladies sometimes became close. One of Schofield's interviewees told him how his landlady had seen off a potential trouble-maker. [7]

Our landlady is Irish and a sweety. The boy in the next room was having an affair with another boy, and this boy's ex-boyfriend came to the door and showed a photograph of Martin to the landlady and asked if he visited this house. The landlady said: 'Sure enough he does. They're two very nice boys. They make no secret of what they are and they're no trouble at all. They like their bit of fun the same as everyone else but they keep the place nice and clean so don't you be interfering with them. They're very respectable and have women up there and all. So be off with you.' [8]

But living too closely with a friend or partner could be stressful – even destructive. Joe Orton confided in his diary in 1967 his concerns about living with Kenneth Halliwell in their one-bedroom flat at 25 Noel Road in Islington, north London: 'I think it's bad that we live in each other's pockets twenty-four hours a day, 365 days of the year. When I'm away Kenneth does nothing, meets nobody.' Three months later Halliwell murdered Orton and then killed himself. [9]

To defuse tensions some men chose not to live with their partners, or else agreed on more open arrangements. Elizabeth Montagu, the half-sister of Lord Montagu, was hired by the HLRS in 1964 to make a publicity film for them.* Her script depicted a gay couple living in semi-independent households. Hospital doctor John Brown and his banker boyfriend Peter occupy the same house, but Peter has a self-contained flat on the top floor because 'he likes to be independent'. Previously he has had a relationship with 22-year-old Luke, who still has a key to the house and later robs and blackmails the pair. [10]

Some couples preferred exclusively monogamous relationships and even entered into marriage-like arrangements. Desmond Plummer (the pseudonym of John Montgomery) described one such union in his 1963 book *Queer People*.

I know two young men who were determined to start their partnership with a stronger bond than mere affection. They were proud of one another, and they wanted their love to last, as all lovers do. So they arranged a wedding ceremony in a private house, invited their friends,

---

* The film project was eventually abandoned due to lack of funds and because it was 'not considered suitable by the trustees'. [11]

160

and standing before a table adorned as a simple altar, they swore fidelity to each other. Then their friends gathered round and drank to their happiness. Their feelings were genuine. It was a gay occasion. [12]

Day to day, gay men's domestic lives were as routine and ordinary as their heterosexual counterparts'. Joe Orton's diary makes frequent references to cooking, cleaning and watching television with Halliwell. When *Nova* journalist Irma Kurtz interviewed Benno Premsela, the president of Holland's national gay association,* and his 'friend' Hans at their Amsterdam home in 1967, she noted that they 'share the housework, care for their two male beagles, and seem to maintain a harmonious household'. Michael Schofield found that many of his contacts first mentioned household chores when they were asked about their spare-time activities: 'When two men are sharing an apartment, it is not surprising that a large amount of time is spent in cooking, laundering, keeping the place clean, etc.' This further endeared them to their landladies, three of whom 'preferred to have two men sharing an apartment'. [13, 14]

In his 1966 book *One in Twenty* Bryan Magee listed two advantages of being gay: first, 'a homosexual is usually independent and without ties'; second (but 'first and foremost'), 'almost every unmarried homosexual has a higher standard of living than he would have if he were heterosexual'. If they could afford to, gay men liked to spend a significant proportion of their incomes on their homes. In an exposé of London's commercial sex scene for *Encounter* in 1960, Simon Raven wrote that soldiers and sailors who were picked up by 'well-to-do homosexuals' were always impressed by 'a smashing flat'. In 1965 Quentin Crewe of the *Daily Mirror* interviewed a 15-year-old boy who told him about the 'beautiful flats' men took him to. Some homes were indeed luxurious. In Colin Spencer's 1963 novel *Anarchists in Love* Reg Pearson attends a house party at the home of theatre critic Sir Percy Dickins** in Adelaide Square, Brighton. [15, 16, 17]

---

*   Cultur en Ontspanningscentrum (C.O.C), founded in 1946
**   A character partly based on the writer and literary critic John Lehmann

The room was long and gold, the muted lights shone on gilt and silver, large mirrors and candelabra; books, pieces of blue and white china and nude bronze figures; taste and money, the cultivation of beauty and of being smart, it was lush. [18]

In Martyn Goff's 1967 novel *Indecent Assault* art student David Coulsdon is similarly impressed by the London flat his stockbroker uncle Julian shares with his 'friend' Cantor (a 'better-looking, less talented Kenneth-Williams-of-an-actor'). Situated in a 'huge' Victorian house, the flat occupies the whole of the ground floor – 'four large and two small rooms six steps up from the road'. [19]

For many gay men, having a smart address and a well-appointed home was something to aspire to. Leonard Bissel in Goff's 1961 novel *The Youngest Director* novel lovingly attends to the décor of his house in Chelsea, south-west London.

Leonard wondered what impression the [drawing] room had made. Unlike the rest of the house it was sparsely furnished in modern style. There was a long, low coffee table with plants set in sunk trays at each end; a lime coloured couch with an arm at one side only; and a large Bratby on one wall. A piece of stone sculpture on the thin mantelpiece looked Barbara Hepworth but was by a friend of Leonard's. [20]

Following the arrest of the spy John Vassall in 1962, it emerged that in addition to blackmail over his homosexuality, the Admiralty clerk's espionage had been motivated by large cash payments from his Russian handlers. He used these extra earnings to rent an eighth floor flat in the exclusive Dolphin Square complex in London's Pimlico district. Number 807 Hood House cost him £400 a year to rent, even though his annual salary at the Admiralty was only £700. As well as providing a discreet location for undercover activities, the flat was a place where Vassall could bring back gay friends and lovers without attracting attention. After his arrest in February 1962 a neighbour told the *Daily Telegraph*, 'This block of flats is ideal for anyone who wants to keep himself to himself.' [21]

Later the following year, the *Sunday Pictorial*'s crime reporter Norman Lucas visited the flat. He found the bedroom and bathroom 'full of perfume bottles', and there was a teddy bear and a cuddly cheetah on the bed. He thought that a casual visitor would 'get the impression of someone with a reasonable income because of the quantity of glass and furniture'. If it had not been for the fragrances on display in the bathroom ('roughly nine or ten bottles of various perfumes, colognes and talcs. I think Elizabeth Arden was one of the manufacturers'), Lucas would not have known that it was 'a flat of a homosexual'. According to the Radcliffe Tribunal, which investigated the spy case, Vassall furnished his flat with a 'Jacobean chest, antique bureau, desk chair, gate leg table, Sheraton chair, wall cabinet and another table' – all bought at a discount from the estate of a female friend, Mrs McNaughton. The *Daily Telegraph* also claimed that Vassall also owned a 'Queen Anne wardrobe' costing £400 and a £300 cupboard. The rest of Vassall's furniture and household items – including a fitted carpet from Peter Jones, a Persian rug, curtains from a shop in Wigmore Street, a second-hand carriage clock from Harrods, two antique tables from Maples, a Rediffusion radio, a Deccalion record player and a drinks cupboard containing glassware – were purchased by him or given by friends and relatives. For the *Daily Sketch* it was all part of Vassall's 'dream-world bid to be somebody'. [22, 23, 24, 25]

Vassall was also very house proud. He hired a daily cleaner and home help, Doris Murray, who became a personal friend. She even visited him in his cell after his trial at the Old Bailey in October 1962, 'sobbing and wiping away tears on the arm of her fur coat' as she left. In a 'life story' published by the *Sunday Pictorial* the following November, Vassall said of his flat: 'I spent many long hours putting the finishing touches to it and making it cosy for all my visitors. On my dressing table stood a miniature toy white poodle and other furry animals. And on my bed lay my favourite friend – a cuddly toy cheetah. I had a photograph specially taken in colour of me and my cheetah. I wish I had it with me now.' The infamous cheetah was apparently bought during a skiing trip to Germany: 'It just reminded me of my cat, which I could not have in my flat. I just kept it as a memento.' [26, 27, 28]

Unlike Vassall, most gay men did not receive bundles of £50 to £200 from Russian spy masters to spend on their homes. But having creature comforts and the latest mod cons was important for many. In *Indecent Assault* American art student Grant Dellon invites David back to his flat. Although the building and the street are 'dilapidated Victorian', the flat itself is 'luxurious'. In contrast, Joe Orton's and Kenneth Halliwell's home was spartan. But (unlike Vassall) they did own a television set, and also a hi-fi system – the most expensive item in their flat. A solicitor's letter sent to Orton's brother Douglas after the couple's deaths gave an insight into their domestic lives. [29]

> Of the articles remaining in the flat it would appear that the most valuable are your brother's typewriter, two student-type table lamps which appear to be new, and a considerable number of gramophone records and books. There is also what appears to be a valuable hi-fi set. Copies of your brother's plays of course will eventually form part of his estate, and all the paintings in the flat appear to have been collages done by Halliwell. [30]

The solicitor also noted the presence of two single beds – indicative of the legal restrictions governing gay men's private lives as well as of Orton's and Halliwell's particular relationship. Other couples chose to sleep together, despite the law. Dave Ongar and Eddie Ranscombe in *The Youngest Director* are in 'little more than a marriage of convenience', and 'each had his own sex partners', but they still share the same bed and do not bother to hide the fact. This and their shabby flat disturbs Leonard when he visits them in north London.

> A huge, disordered living room: unmade double divan, wardrobe with open doors, oval table piled with unwashed dishes, armchairs littered with clothes. The cheap 'camp' set-up was typical of many in the seedier districts of London; the disordered sexual lives spilled into even more disordered daily ones. [31]

Single gay men on low incomes tended to live in rooms and bedsits in poorer parts of town. In the 1961 film *Victim* Jack Barrett and Eddy Stone live in adjoining basement bedsits in a rundown terrace house in Fulham, west London. In Meg Elizabeth Atkins' 1964 novel *The Gemini* David Quest visits the cheap bedsit occupied by his lover Rex Fielding.

> His room was bright and cheap and chaotically untidy; it was like all the rooms I had lived in as a young man, alone in London: some dingy, some gay, some spacious, some cramped, all flavoured with impertinence. [33]

The cheapness and availability of multiple occupation houses appealed to many young men moving to the big cities. Such houses sometimes developed into microcosmic gay communities. Jack and Eddy have keys to each other's rooms. When David comes to see Rex he encounters 'a plump creature with a careful hair-do' on the landing. 'Are you looking for Rex?' he asks. 'I have the room down there.' [34]

For those at the bottom of the income scale, accommodation was basic. Denis, a hotel lift boy in *The Youngest Director*, occupies dingy basement rooms in a 'squat Victorian house with a broken red balcony along the first floor'. Tellingly for any self-respecting householder, 'the front steps were dirty'. When Leonard visits, he is repelled both by Denis and by his living quarters. [35]

> Light on, comic in hand, Denis lay on a divan that faced the door. Fair, frail and almost coquettish at any time, in bed he looked like a permanent invalid. The room smelled strongly of cheap perfume and unwashed socks and there were worn clothes piled on the floor. 'Hello ducky.' Denis put down the comic paper. 'Fancy you coming to see little me.' [36]

In Jenni Hall's 1964 novel *Ask Agamemnon* (adapted as the film *Goodbye Gemini* in 1970) 18-year-old Julian Dewar flees to a squalid bedsit near London's Paddington station after murdering his blackmailer Clive Landseer. His twin sister Jacki finds him hiding there.

The room was cold and dark. The only light was reflected from the street lamps. The window was shut. The little room was airless. She looked around the room. Julian was sitting on the small double bed. There was a wash-basin, a cupboard, a small table by the bed with a lamp on it, two wooden chairs and on the floor by the fire was an electric hot-plate with a battered kettle on top. She felt the floor vibrate as a train passed under the house. There were two bursting carrier-bags under the basin, spilling out rubbish onto the rubbish already spilled. [37]

Because of its size, relative anonymity and established homosexual population, London was a magnet for gay men. Sixty-three per cent of Michael Schofield's contacts lived there, even though only a quarter were born in the city. Within London there was a distinct geography of homosexual settlement. 'Chelsea, Earl's Court and Notting Hill Gate were all mentioned as districts with large concentrations of homosexuals,' observed Schofield. With its artistic heritage, fine houses and Thames-side location, Chelsea attracted wealthier men like Leonard in *The Youngest Director*. By contrast, Leonard's boyfriend John Cramer, who works as a hotel porter, lives in nearby Earl's Court, where the high volume of bedsits and Victorian houses sub-divided into flats tended to accommodate younger, less well-off gay men. So too did Notting Hill. One of Schofield's interviewees described the gay population there as 'a kingdom within a kingdom'. Other areas frequently mentioned as centres of homosexual habitation were leafy Hampstead (where *Indecent Assault*'s Uncle Julian and Cantor reside), Belsize Park (where *The Youngest Director*'s Dave and Eddie have their 'shabby flat') and Pimlico (home to *Indecent Assault*'s Grant Dillon and to John Vassall). [38]

Men also congregated in these districts to socialise and immerse themselves in an emerging gay scene. Schofield's Notting Hill contact told him, 'I expect you know there is a huge homosexual kingdom just below the surface of ordinary life, with its own morals and code of behaviour. When I walk through Notting Hill Gate I feel I'm at a giant homosexual party.' Indeed, house parties were still the main *entrées* into gay society. Ian Christie remembered 'the usual routine' of going to parties in Edinburgh and Glasgow on Friday and Saturday nights: 'We danced, drank, gossiped, joked and entertained each other until five or six in the morning. We didn't have commercial discos, but we had far more parties in each other's houses and flats. It was nothing for one hundred people to crowd into one small apartment, word having gone round the cafés and pubs like wildfire.' Mike, who lived in London, remembered: 'Every Saturday night there was a choice of at least half a dozen parties to go to, which you'd travel to the other end of London to get to – lots of people getting together, bring a bottle, maybe 50 people in a flat. It was a place where you went to enjoy, and also to meet people.' Brian Sewell had similar memories of the London party scene. [39, 40]

> Three young men living in the rambling basement of Christabel Aberconway's house in North Audley Street held parties almost every Saturday. Jack Harriman, one of Eric's* friends, was another regular party-giver in a mews cottage near Portman Square. To these gatherings we were expected to take a bottle of wine for immediate consumption and a friend to exchange for the night. [41]

Some commentators were alarmed by the increasing visibility of gay men. In June 1959 *The Scotsman*'s Graham Turner complained that in Glasgow 'the problem of homosexuality becomes real indeed when one is accosted oneself on the entrance to one of the city's large railway stations'. According to Turner, Dundee also had a 'small problem of homosexuality' involving 'the grosser physical kind' of behaviour, 'centred around certain of the public lavatories in the city'. In July 1964 the *News of the World*'s Noyes Thomas warned readers about the 'creeping menace of homosexuality in Britain today'. There was, he added, 'a vast "queer" brotherhood with tentacles reaching around the globe'. In a *vox pop* street interview in the 1965 film *Darling,* a man tells TV reporter Robert Gold (Dirk Bogarde) that what he is most 'ashamed of in Britain today' is 'how rife homosexuality has become. Two or three

---

*   Eric Bewsey, a civil servant

years ago you were very blatantly approached by different people in different places. I think in actual fact it has become worse over a period of time. But it's one of those things that you have to live with.' [42, 43, 44]

Despite the law against it, making sexual contacts was fairly easy. Playwright Nicholas Wright (who made a fleeting appearance as a TV runner in *Darling*) remembered 'masses of sex around'. Myles Antony, art director for the John Stephen chain of clothes shops, also thought that finding sex was never a problem 'if you were even vaguely attractive'. John, a waiter from London, told *This Week* how he picked up men in the street: 'If someone looks at me knowingly, and I may be interested, then I will endeavour to get into conversation in the usual, conventional way. But it can happen stepping out of one's door, or getting onto a bus or tube train, or even at work.' [45, 46, 47, 48]

Public toilets were still popular places for casual pick-ups or on-the-spot sex. 'I don't think people were stuck in those days for loos to go to,' remembered Alan Alexander from Edinburgh. 'It was very easy if you went into one and got a nod from somebody and they wandered a few blocks down. Along Queen Street for example there was one of those French iron *pissoirs,* and the same along Abercromby Place.' Other favoured locations in Edinburgh included the toilets at Regent Terrace, Royal Terrace, Albert Street, London Road, Carlton Hill and, most infamously, Princes Street – known as the 'Carousel' or 'Wheel of Fortune'. There were also well-known cottages in Manchester, including one on Bridgewater Street and another on Knott Mill. The lavatories at Leeds railway station had a reputation for sexual encounters, as did the men's toilets at Birmingham New Street station. Jonathan Blake remembered frequent visits to that particular location: 'It was wonderful, with all that ceramic and brass. It was a way of making contact with people.' [49, 50]

London had an especially large number of cottages. *The New London Spy*, Hunter Davies' 1966 'discreet guide to the city's pleasures', recommended them as an 'immediate way of discovering the way into more general homosexual activity in the city'. [51]

The main railway stations are [a] source of prospective encounters for lavatory-lovers, although, for some obscure reason, the main termini on the Southern Region are by far the most popular. The men's cloakrooms of West End hotels where there is a constant traffic of men in and out are another easy means of contact, especially where they are situated not far from a public lavatory and it is therefore possible to promenade between the two without occasioning too much notice. In one or two hotels very close to the heart of the West End it is a commonplace for the ground-floor cloakroom to be used for making an initial contact while the quieter lavatories on the upper floors provide cover for – to use a legal phrase – indecent acts. Every suburban area has its pissoir serving the local queers. Some become so notorious that they are the frequent object of a special pilgrammage by queers living on the other side of London. Nearly all parks and recreation grounds (and there are literally scores in the greater London area) have 'cottages' where the odd queer may be found cruising. In addition many pubs have outside lavatories which, during drinking hours – and often all hours – are well known for their homosexual possibilities. Department stores all over London have men's lavatories where occasional activity takes place; in fact the possibilities are limitless in this field if the itinerant queer is ready to run the not inconsiderable risks attached to this form of hunting. [52]

Some public toilets in the West End had national and even international reputations. Douglas Plummer wrote about one in Soho which was 'almost permanently manned by plain-clothes policemen'. Magistrate Clyde Wilson described it as 'perhaps the most notorious place of its kind in London'. The conveniences in Leicester Square were also well known – both to gay men and to the police. Bryan Magee received a letter about them from a member of the public, concerned about police operations there. [53]

Yesterday, for purely normal functional purposes, I went into the toilet at Leicester Square. As I was about to leave, two plain clothes detectives arrested a young man standing nearby. I had watched the bigger man of the two and seen him deliberately provoke the interest of the man they later arrested. The other detective – who incidentally was young and quite effeminate looking, far more so than the man they arrested – was watching from a toilet stand a few feet away. [54]

Other public toilets outside central London were also well frequented. When a local newspaper published a report about arrests made at one convenience in Kennington, south London, a reader rang the editor to complain, 'Me and my mates don't like your story. And anyway, where else is there to go?' Joe Orton was a regular visitor to the public toilets on Holloway Road. Music producer Joe Meek, who lived and worked at nearby 304 Holloway Road, preferred the toilets at Madras Place. He was arrested there in November 1963 for 'persistently importuning for an immoral purpose', and fined £15. *The Evening News* carried the story and helpfully published details of the toilets' location. [55, 56]

London encompassed a constellation of other meeting points. Piccadilly Circus still had a reputation for gay pick-ups – in the underground station toilets and at the railings by the County Fire Offices. Jonathan Blake recalled going there as a teenager: 'We used to come as a family to London and stay in a hotel. I remember when I was 13 coming up and for the first time I got to have my own room. I remember getting up at about two o'clock in the morning and going down to Piccadilly Circus, which I'd heard about.' According to *The New London Spy*, the capital's parks, commons and fields were also a 'sure-fire means of contact'. The guide listed several 'open-air rendezvous'. [56, 57]

Wimbledon Common
Homosexual activities take place around the perimeter of a small lake, known, appropriately enough, as Queen's Mere. From dusk onwards individuals begin to arrive and stroll around the lake and the immediate paths. Contacts are of all types, old and young, butch and bitch, with quite a large proportion of leather and motor-cycle fans.

Hampstead Heath
After dark, from April to October, the paths are quite busy with promenading queers; even on a January night with snow falling a few hardy habituees can be seen searching for al fresco partners.

Richmond
These fields are used by queers for nude sunbathing so that the venue is essentially a summer-time one. A little way back from the towpath the grasses grow long and clumps of bushes afford cover for amorous associations.

Highgate Ponds
An official enclosure where nude sunbathing is possible. Naturally this affords easy opportunities for queers to solicit one another. A natural segregation takes place between the queers at one end and the muscle-men from the adjoining gym and swimming club at the other. Outside the enclosure, on the grass, more circumspect sunbathing takes place and while no actual sexual activity takes place, many queers find it, on a summer's day, a pleasant place to contact each other.

Hyde Park Lido
Another summer-time rendezvous for queers which has the advantage of being right in the heart of London. Once again the homos and the heteros divide themselves up fairly obviously, and the picking-up process is confined to the casual exchange of a glance or a word. [59]

For indoor experiences men could visit any one of a number of Turkish baths. Douglas Plummer thought that these were 'frequented by the more promiscuous type of homosexual'. *The New London Spy* explained their attraction. [60]

Because it is possible to stay all night in these places they obviously provide quite a lot of cover for homosexual activities. The staff mostly turn a blind eye to much of the midnight prowling or conveniently ignore the more or less obvious fact that a cubicle designed for one is occupied by two; at least they do if the activity is not too blatant. Periodically the management carries out a purge or, following a complaint, maintains a stricter watch which seems to lapse a little after a week or two. [61]

The Savoy baths in Jermyn Street remained open throughout the 1960s. The Metro Turkish Baths in Harrow Road were popular until they were demolished in 1963 to make way for the West Way flyover. The baths under the old Imperial Hotel in Russell Square were also well-frequented until the hotel was redeveloped in 1966 (the mosaic pavement sign pointing to the baths can still be seen). *The New London Spy* also recommended local council-run baths in east and south London: 'These vary a lot in comfort and cleanliness but they are all comparatively cheap and the customers are generally a lot younger – many of them the local dockers and factory workers who genuinely go to the baths in order to avail themselves of the facilities – but are not averse to enjoying the other activities. These baths are never open all night – they mostly close at about 8 p.m. – but the opportunities they present for a liaison are probably more concentrated because of it.' The baths in Bermondsey enjoyed a particularly widespread reputation. Plummer referred to them in *Queer People,* and Brian Sewell remembered visiting them. So did Bernard from Aberdeen, who recalled that there were 'always one or two boys on the make'. [62, 63, 64]

The New London Spy also told readers about certain cinemas 'where local queers concentrate some of their activities'. It noted that the interest of the audience was not primarily aroused by the action on the screen. [65]

In fact, the less the customers will be attracted by the programme the more they can be expected to go for each other. News cinemas are an obvious lure because the programme of news and "shorts" need not be taken seriously and in any case starts to repeat itself in an hour so that anything missed through amorous dalliance can soon be seen again. It is a common practice for queer customers to get up frequently and go to the lavatory; they then return to a different seat where something more attractive – or more responsive – can be found. [66]

The most notorious cinema was the Biograph on Wilton Road near Victoria station. Artist and film maker Derek Jarman called it 'a fleapit'. Writer Quentin Crisp remembered that the 'sound-tracks help[ed] to conceal the noise of creaking seat springs'. Gerald from Norfolk thought it was 'a hell of a place. Used to be fab.' He witnessed men 'sitting next to each other and carrying on just as if they were in bed. Some with their trousers half down, laying on top of each other. And nobody saying a word.' Allen Eyles remembered that 'the seats in there were very tight against each other and there wasn't any proper arm rest between them, and I noticed a great deal of movement of the audience there. You'd find whole rows of patrons continually standing up to let someone in or out, and constant activity. Men would come and sit next to you for about five minutes, and when there was no favourable response they would get up and try somewhere else.' Tony Papard had his first gay encounter at the Biograph and met his long-term partner there. [67, 68, 69, 70]

I quickly discovered the left-hand side of the auditorium where the younger men sat, and where they were all jerking each other off. The police turned a blind eye towards the Biograph. They were known to tell men masturbating and messing about in the toilets in Victoria station to 'go down the road to the Biograph if you want to do that sort of thing'. Flo was in the box office. Tubby and a miserable bald-headed old man sold ice-creams in the break between pictures – two of the most unglamorous ice-cream girls ever. Tubby was very bold and used to shout out, 'Half time, change partners'. Or, 'Half-time, change hands,' to the masturbating gay male couples in the audience. A few women wandered in by mistake. [71]

Journalist Anne Sharpley went to the Biograph in 1964 to gather information on homosexuality for the *Evening Standard*. One patron told her, 'You can't see the film for men getting up and going off in twos.' The following year the *Daily Mirror*'s Quentin Crewe went there and was horrified by what he saw. [72]

> I had not been in my seat in the cinema for more than ten minutes when a man came and sat next to me. After a few moments his knee pressed against mine. Then his hand touched my leg. I asked him to go and sit elsewhere. He did. I was repelled but not surprised. For I had been told that this particular cinema was a meeting place for homosexuals. Soon in this cinema, where people seemed to be playing musical chairs, a young boy sat in the seat next to mine. Again I felt a knee pressed against mine, then a hand on my leg. This time I did not send my would-be seducer away. Instead I talked to him. He told me his name was David. He was fifteen. I asked him if he visited this cinema often. 'Oh yes, my friend and I are here about twice a week.' His friend was the same age, lost somewhere in the darkness of this cinema. But what did they come for? To earn money? 'No, of course not,' said David. 'I mean I don't mind if someone gives me a few bob but I do it because it's fun. I want it. I like the men.' [73]

Other more discreet pick-ups could be had in theatres. The Crush Room at the Royal Opera House was a well-known hunting ground, as were the standing rows at Sadler's Wells. In Leonard James Harper's 1963 novel *Teddy Boy Ahoy* the fictitious East Ham Palace is the setting for one man's ill-judged attempt to arouse the interest of 15-year-old delinquent Terry Winslow. [74, 75]

> The show was about halfway through before Terry became fully aware of the man who was sitting beside him. The man's hand slid to his knee. The man became more daring, his hand kneading and caressing. Suddenly, a wicked-looking stiletto flashed in the half-light of the theatre. Terry brought it down again and again, savagely slashing at the man's unprotected hand. 'The filthy rotten bastard! He's a queer.' [76]

The business of exchanging sex for money or gifts continued in much the same way as it always had. Simon Raven revealed the extent of male prostitution in his 1960 article for *Encounter*. He began with the 'dreary truth that in London as in other large cities there is a substantial demand for the services of the male prostitute'. He proceeded to divide male sex workers into five groups. The first consisted of 'young men of the armed services who are either stationed or on leave in London'. The most prominent of these were guards of the royal household division who were happy to supplement their pay by hiring themselves out, and who had 'a traditional knowledge of and notorious capacity for all sexual activities of a venal nature'. Usually an older, more experienced soldier (often a non-commissioned officer) told a younger colleague where he could be picked up, and for what price. The case of 'Tom' was typical. [77]

> Tom was [told] not to accept less than thirty shillings and he must ask for at least three pounds if his client requested, and he himself allowed, the 'taking of a real liberty', by which euphemism one connotes the practice of buggery as opposed to the very much more usual manual or oral caresses. Thereafter, having discovered so easy a way out of his financial afflictions, Tom found himself 'on the streets' with increasing frequency. I strongly suspect that Tom, along with most soldiers who behave like him, has a definite if narrow homosexual streak. He is, in fact, bisexual – a judgment which, in its general implications, is confirmed by some remarks once made to me by a young lance-sergeant (also of the Brigade). 'Some of us get quite fond of the blokes we see regularly,' he said. 'You go to their flats and have some drinks and talk a bit – they're nice fellows, some of them, and interesting to listen to. And as for the sex bit, well, some of the younger ones aren't bad looking and I've had some real thrills off them in my time.' [78]

Raven's second category of sex worker was made up of 'boys and young men [with] full-time and respectable jobs of a more or less "refined" nature (hairdressers, shop walkers, low-grade couturiers, or interior decorators)' who were 'not above improving their incomes by an occasional evening "on the game"'. Their occupations gave them a taste for 'elegance and sophistication' which their salaries could not afford. Dabbling in commercial sex helped them, for example, to pay 'the rent overdue on too sumptuously furnished an apartment'. Rodney, a 17-year-old "'beauty shop" apprentice', told Raven, 'I've got my room to pay for, and the instalments on the gramophone to keep up, and I like nice things. So if I can get three or four pounds extra for my trouble, it comes in very handy.' [79]

The third category was formed of 'far less prepossessing' boys of 'poor intelligence and low town background'. They had 'neither the ability to get a good job nor the application to stay with it' and drifted between low-skilled, low-paid casual jobs. Len, an unemployed warehouse hand, told Raven, 'My friend told me that I could get some money by flogging myself to some rich geezer that liked boys.' Raven later heard that Len had beaten up a client and had stolen clothes and money from him. [80]

The fourth group included the 'classical type of "layabout"', who engaged in 'shady enterprises', including 'petty theft, dope-passing, running for low bookmakers, hired violence and crude confidence tricks'. Micky, 'a typical boy of this kind', made quick money from dodgy dealings, but 'drinks, frolics or gambles the lot away'. He sometimes spent money on female prostitutes, although 'his sexual flexibility is such that he has been known to produce a very young "fancy boy" of his own'. Micky told Raven, 'I spend the lot and then look around. But wherever I look I see steamers and suckers, so I don't have to look for long.' [81]

The fifth type was the 'full-time professional male prostitute'. Some of them lived 'in very good circumstances' and were able to find a rich patron to 'set [them] up', or at least take them on 'luxurious foreign holidays'. Conrad was 'a finished article' in this respect – 'polished, witty, by no means unread, highly vocal and even knowledgeable about current plays, exhibitions and scandals; a good cook, a light but sophisticated drinker; above all, to judge from his conversation, a person of inexhaustible resource in matters of sexual technique'. Raven thought that Conrad could easily have been mistaken for 'an amusingly epicene member of an exacting cosmopolitan set', except for two unfortunate disadvantages: he did not speak a foreign language, and his accent was 'quite undeniably Welsh'. [82]

Sex, whether paid for or free, could, however, be dangerous. Extortion and intimidation were common. 'There may not be much direct blackmail,' explained one of Michael Schofield's contacts, 'but there is a great deal of subtle blackmail. I got to know a man; I didn't even like him from the start, but he came to stay with me. I didn't want him but I didn't dare refuse. I lent him a lot of money which of course I'll never get back. He still turns up occasionally and I don't know any way of getting rid of him without bringing down my own life in ruins.' Another interviewee told Schofield how he had picked up a guardsman, who told him, '"Are you going to give me your wallet, or are you going to be beaten up?" The guardsman took the wallet and handed me back five shillings and said, "Come and have a drink". When I protested he said, "It's no use being upset by these things. You'll just have to get used to it." We went for a drink and we talked about it. He said that even if I went to the police, he was 21 and I was over 40 so I wouldn't stand a chance.' Anne Sharpley met a gang of boys who specialised in 'robbing homos'. One of them told her, 'It's easier than breaking and entering. We pretend we're queer, let them take us back home, then rob them of everything. They're too scared of the police to do anything. They don't make the least resistance. I know one boy who got £350 straight off that way, just by threatening a queer.' A friend of Douglas Plummer told him how he had been forced to hand over his gold watch and £80 to a young man he had met on Hampstead Heath. The youth later demanded a further £5. Plummer's friend asked him for advice: 'He was frightened that his mother would receive a letter revealing that he was homosexual; he knew she would never understand. I told him to go to Scotland Yard, where I knew a "queer" detective. A meeting was arranged outside Green Park tube station. The police grabbed the blackmailer as he was handed an envelope containing dummy money. No action was taken against my friend. But all "queers" are not so fortunate.' [83, 84, 85]

Some sexual encounters led to violence. 'I picked up a man and brought him back to my rooms,' recounted another of Schofield's contacts. 'After we'd had sex, we were sitting drinking beer when suddenly he picked up a bottle and hit me over the head. Then he went berserk, breaking everything in sight and weeping at the same time.' In November 1962 a casual pick-up by former Labour Party chairman George Brinham led to his death. After meeting 16-year-old Laurence Somers near Charing Cross in London, 46-year-old Brinham took him for a coffee and 'a spin in his car'. Following a couple of brown ales and a trip to the cinema, Brinham brought Somers back to his flat in Pembroke Square, Kensington. Brinham then allegedly made a pass at Somers, who grabbed a glass decanter and repeatedly hit him with it. Somers fled to his mother's house in Matlock, Derbyshire but was arrested two weeks later. He was put on trial at the Old Bailey in January 1963. The jury found him not guilty of both murder and manslaughter on the grounds of Brinham's supposed 'provocation'. In an interview with the *News of the World* after his acquittal, Somers pledged in future to 'stick to mates I know'. He added, 'Don't pal up with older men. That's my advice to any other young country lads who go up to the city.' [86, 87]

The killers of police canteen manager Vincent Keighery got off less lightly. Keighery lived in Craven Terrace, Paddington, west London. In November 1964 he invited three men – Bill Dunning, John Simpson and Michael Odham – to his flat for drinks. As the men left, Keighery supposedly tried to hug and kiss Dunning. The three men then beat him to death and stole two lighters from his jacket. All three were found guilty of murder in March 1965 and sentenced to death. But following parliamentary debates on capital punishment and its suspension in November 1965, their sentences were commuted to life imprisonment. They eventually served between 11 and 12 years. [88]

Five other murders in the 1960s had their origins in 'the twilight world of the homosexual'. Norman Rickard and John Vigar were both killed in February 1962, probably by the same killer. Rickard's body was found inside the wardrobe of his basement flat in Elgin Avenue, Maida

Vale, west London. He had been beaten and strangled with the cord of his dressing gown, and his hands tied with a flex. Vigar's body was discovered by his landlady in his bedsit in St George's Drive, Pimlico. He had also been strangled with a twisted vest, and his hands tied with the cord of his dressing gown. The so-called 'wardrobe killer' was never found. But during their investigations Metropolitan Police detectives noticed similarities with the so-called 'carbon copy' killings of William Elliott and Gerry Stubbs in Chesterfield in June 1960 and March 1961. The Met shared their information with Derbyshire Constabulary, leading to the arrest of Michael Copeland in 1963. Copeland admitted to the two murders and also to that of 16-year-old Guenther Helmbrecht, whom he had killed in November 1960 while serving in the army in Verden, West Germany. Like Keighery's killers, Copeland was found guilty of murder in March 1965 and sentenced to hang, but his sentence was commuted to life imprisonment. [89, 90]

Two years later police investigated the murder of 17-year-old warehouse worker Bernard Oliver. Oliver, who lived with his parents in Steeds Road, Muswell Hill, north London, went missing in January 1967 after an evening out with friends. Ten days later his body was found strangled, cut into eight pieces and packed into two suitcases in a field near Tattingstone, Suffolk. Detectives 'swooped on the haunts of known vice criminals in the London area', but the 'suitcase killer' – 'thought to be a homosexual pervert' – was never found. [91]

As well as being vulnerable to blackmail, robbery, violence and murder, gay men faced the added risk of exposure to sexually transmitted infections without being able to get access to medical help and advice. As the Wolfenden Report had pointed out, doctors and medical staff had a legal duty to report homosexual offences to the police. This discouraged many gay men from visiting surgeries and clinics. In a 1964 report on venereal disease Michael Schofield wrote: 'It is clear that the existing law puts the homosexual, and in a sense, the venereologist, in an awkward position. In small communities a visit to the local clinic may cause more embarrassment because there is a chance that the patient may be known to the doctor or others working there.' Several men told

Schofield about their negative experiences at sexual health clinics. 'If I'd stamped on a baby I couldn't have been given darker looks,' said one. 'It's ghastly in that clinic,' commented another. 'One is treated like a criminal. The doctor is off-hand and unpleasant.' Schofield understood that the problem of sexually transmitted infection was also related to the lack of safe meeting places for gay men. 'It is worth noting,' he wrote, 'that the young inexperienced homosexual does not know where to find sexual partners and that he is more likely to have homosexual relations with a man he has picked up in a public lavatory. Quite often the ones who have the most sordid episodes are the least experienced. The man who knows his way around the homosexual merry-go-round is better able to look after himself.' [92]

Young men felt the absence of social spaces most keenly. Sociologist Jeffrey Weeks remembered that the 'queer' scene in the 1960s 'didn't feel very welcoming'. Tony Papard lived in Welwyn Garden City with his mother. He longed to meet other gay men but did not know where to go. 'My mother had a gay boss at the time,' he recalled, 'and I asked her to ask him where I could meet other gay men. She never did ask him of course, saying it must just be a "phase" I'd grow out of.' Derek Jarman also lived with his parents in suburban Northwood, Middlesex while he was studying humanities at King's College, London: 'I was unaware of queer bars and clubs. I was a nice middle-class boy. I didn't go drinking in Soho. The bars were an illegal world, far away from Metroland.' When he did finally venture into a gay pub – the William IV in Hampstead – Jarman felt uncomfortable and alienated: 'The William IV was thoroughly middle-aged; elderly models and artistic antique dealers. There were very few young people "out"; mostly old queens who'd sat at the bar for years on end hoping that some "chicken" would come in. And when we did, we were totally uninterested in them.' Record producer Peter Wadland visited the same pub in 1966 and found himself sitting near the playwright Noel Coward: 'On one of the opposite seats was a man in a green Tyrolean hat with a poodle. He looked at me, and asked me to look after his dog while he went to the toilet. When he came back he asked if his dog could have one of my crisps. I gave him one, but the dog wouldn't eat it, and Coward tried to give me the crisps back. He said, "Of course, you know who I am?" I hadn't the foggiest. He said, "I'm the man who wrote *Bitter Sweet*."' [93, 94, 95, 96, 97]

The New London Spy gave some tips about where to go, although for legal reasons it could not publish the names and addresses of gay clubs, pubs and bars. History student Philip Rescorla saw the book in Foyle's bookshop on Charing Cross Road in London in early 1967. 'I was actually looking for a guidebook of London,' he recalled. 'I picked it off the shelf and I looked at the index, and lo and behold it said 'Homosexual London'. I closed it and I thought, this I've got to buy. So I rushed back to the hall of residence [at Queen Mary and Westfield College] and read the chapter. It didn't give any names of places, but it gave areas. And it talked about cruising areas like Piccadilly and Putney towpath [and] Hampstead Heath. It also talked about Earl's Court, and there was something about Earl's Court which attracted my attention. I thought, if I go to Earl's Court one Saturday evening, I'm going to be able to find them and find out where they go. I eventually found an outrageous queen, so I followed him and he eventually disappeared into a pub called the Colehearne.' [98]

Most men discovered the gay scene in their local area by word of mouth, by overhearing conversations, or else by initiating discrete enquiries. Allan Horsfall remembered a standard ploy: 'The story goes of someone who went to work in a strange town and didn't know where the gay community was. So he went into a pub and said, "I've only been here two days. The first pub I went in was full of nancy boys. I can't quite remember the name of it." And two or three people turned round and said, "Oh, you mean the Rose and Crown." So he drank up and went down the Rose and Crown.' This tactic was described in more detail by Anthony Rowley in an article for *Axle Spokes* magazine in 1963. Rowley posed the question of how 'a young man, a student for example, who arrives at the conclusion that he is irrevocably queer', might 'discover the whereabouts of others like himself'. [99, 100]

A remembered fragment of late-night conversation springs suddenly to mind, the man-of-the-world tone, perhaps, of a pipe-smoking rowing enthusiast in the same lodgings, to whom you think it politic to offer coffee from time to time:- 'You know such-and-such a pub? Well, I was in there the other night and, Christ, the whole place was heaving with bloody poufs. Or that's what Tom who was with me said they were. He says someone told him it's their main meeting place around here.' [101]

After taking 'the plunge' of locating the fictitious Stitch-in-Time pub, the student goes there one evening. [102]

The place is packed. Ordinary looking types, most of them. Here perhaps a rather hysterical laugh; there a slightly flamboyant gesture; and over there a schoolgirl-like complexion surmounted by a thick head of curly blonde (peroxide?) hair; but such things would pass unremarked in any conventional context. On your way out you spot a face you know – someone from your own college – a chemist in the year ahead of you: God, the last person you would ever have suspected, a quiet, level-headed Yorkshireman. Two pints have made you forget the possibility of his normality; you catch his eye; he nods in your direction. A day or two later in the common room he makes a point of getting into conversation with you, opening casually: 'Why doesn't anyone ever bother to empty these bloody ash trays? Sorry, I don't know your name. Didn't I bump into you somewhere a day or two back? The Stitch, wasn't it? Wasn't exactly at its gayest the other night, was it?' This last said with no special emphasis, but 'gay' is the operative word you recognise and are meant to follow up. [103]

For Eustace Chesser, knowledge of the 'special slang which gives a double meaning to quite ordinary words' was the key to entering 'the homosexual underworld'. He noted how 'a newcomer might be addressed by some such remark as, "Rather a queer spot, isn't it?". If he misses the emphasis laid on the word "queer" he evidently is not interested. The word may be repeated in different contexts to test whether he is merely being cautious. But if he replies, "Yes, it's quite gay," with a significant inflexion, he has accepted the gambit. He knows the passwords.' [104]

Rowley also provided a glossary of 'slang and double-entendres' which gay men used to identify each other. [105]

> 'Gay', 'kinky', 'bent' and 'queer' are synonyms for 'homosexual'; but they are so widely known among the laity that they have to be carefully used. So also 'camp' is applied to anything one might conceivably associate with homosexuality: thus one might speak of a 'camp shirt', or a 'camp book', or a 'camp joke'. 'Screaming' is an adjective used to describe anyone whose behaviour is too outrageous; if a boy is 'rent' or 'on the game' he is a male prostitute; 'trade' is the argot word for 'sex'; a 'queen' is an old or unattractive homosexual, and so on. [106]

According to Rowley, London was 'the Mecca of the practising homosexual', with Piccadilly Circus and Leicester Square forming 'a decidedly queer mile'. He claimed that in Soho there were 'at least a dozen' gay clubs, and 'various pubs and coffee bars which have come to cater, whether by design or accident, for a special clientele.' Richard Hauser thought that there were 'about 50 clubs in the London area'. Other cities, too, had their gay locales. Douglas Plummer claimed that Birmingham had two gay pubs. Glasgow had one club 'with several hundred members', a 'big hotel' and a restaurant catering mainly to gay men. Aberdeen hosted 'more than one meeting place'. Nottingham had 'a world-famous rendezvous'. Portsmouth had 'several' places. Blackpool had two 'well-known' meeting places. Plymouth had three; Leeds two; Bath two; and Bristol two. Brighton had three clubs and two bars that were 'mainly "queer"'. Gay men, said Plummer, could also meet 'every weekend at two hotels near Edinburgh', and at a pub 'in an unlikely back street in a Staffordshire town' which had been, for many years, 'one of the most famous meeting places in the Midlands'. [107, 108, 109]

Venues were usually one of three types: private clubs, pubs and coffee bars. Private clubs were licensed to sell alcohol from 3 pm to 11 pm to members who paid a subscription. Members could also bring friends as guests. According to Rowley, such clubs were 'frequently invested with an aura of decadent elegance in the imagination of those who have never visited them. In reality they differ very little from any other efficiently conducted and moderately well-furnished West End club. There will be a juke-box, perhaps, thundering out the latest Cliff Richard or Sinatra disc; a fruit-machine; one or two armchairs, and a chaise longue – but most people prefer to stand so that they can survey the field of action.' Michael Schofield thought that these venues were 'no different from the 22,000 registered clubs in the country, except that their membership is almost exclusively made up of homosexuals. The proprietor is not always a homosexual and is sometimes a woman. In these clubs the homosexual can relax, throw off the mask, reveal his real interests and talk in his own vernacular. Many a contact has commented on the relief he feels in these clubs after spending most of the day in normal company where he has to keep up appearances, watch that he does not give himself away and pretend to feelings he does not have.' One of Richard Hauser's contacts also told him that when he went to a club 'the mask drops and I can be myself for the first time.' [110, 111, 112]

The most famous gay clubs in London were the A&B (Arts and Battledress) and the Rockingham. The A&B was opened by Stan Cowley in 1941 and fictionalised as the Aldebaran in *The Heart in Exile*. The Rockingham was opened in 1950 by George ('Toby') Roe, who had the distinction of being the first ever proprietor of a gay club to be questioned by an official government inquiry. The Radcliffe Tribunal summoned him in February 1963 to find out if John Vassall had been a member (he had not).* Roe told the tribunal that his club had 4,500 members but that it did not advertise or have a sign outside the premises. Douglas Plummer was probably referring to the Rockingham when he invited readers of *Queer People* to 'visit one of these clubs'. [113, 114]

This is a tall, attractively decorated room whose windows are hung with expensive curtains. The taste is excellent if slightly theatrical. In this

---

* The tribunal also questioned the Alibi's club secretary John Murray. In January 1963 Vassall himself was asked if he had ever visited the Rockingham, Alibi, Spartan, 50, A&B, Music Box and Leo clubs. He replied that he had been to the Rockingham, A&B and Spartan but had never been a member. [115]

particular club the motif is Edwardian, and the huge cut-glass chandelier that hangs from the centre of the ceiling reflects the beauty of a past age. Under its light, the grey closely fitted carpet and the comfortable chairs and highly polished long bar look as if they might be part of a big European hotel. There is a washroom, a cloak-room, and an attendant to keep out intruders. If you are a member you may bring guests, but you must sign their names in the register, as in any other club in Britain. The barman is a young man in a white jacket. You will probably discover, if you ask, that his last job was as a waiter at the Hotel Angleterre in Copenhagen or the Metropole at Brighton. He is one of the thousands of international hotel servants, probably Swiss or French, who understand all the vagaries of human nature, and are never surprised. He may or he may not be 'queer'; it isn't our concern, and it doesn't affect his job. When we enter the club it is half-past eight, and it is unlikely that the room will fill up until nine or later. We buy two whiskies and sodas and we sit near the piano and look around. A middle-aged pianist is softly playing popular music, and we noticed that most of the other ten or twelve people in the room looked over when we came in, and eyed us up and down, as if summing us up. [116]

Other clubs were less salubrious. In *The Gemini* David visits one of them.

There was the dingy, unmistakable stink of lust. There were not-very-young men wearing make-up and younger men with hard eyes and harder mouths. A crowded Saturday night. There was a great deal of noise in the bar and amongst the regulars a soundless symphony of nudges and winks; somewhere a high, hysterical laugh rang. [117]

Many men found the atmosphere of clubs stultifying and preferred instead to go to traditional pubs. Some, like the Colehearne in London's Earl's Court or the Salisbury on St Martin's Lane, had long attracted a theatrical, bohemian crowd (the interior of the Salisbury was filmed as The Chequers in *Victim*). Others were well-known pick-up spots. In Stuart Lauder's 1962 novel *Winger's Landfall* seaman Harry Shears observes the action at his local in Lewisham, south London.

He watched in the mirror the comings and goings to and from the door marked 'Gentlemen', and presently strolled out there. Just idle curiosity, for this was a fairly notorious 'cottage'. The red-faced buck navvy and the rat-faced little man in a raincoat had overstayed their time. As Harry entered, the little man buttoned up hastily and scuttled out, and Harry and the navvy eyed each other sidelong in the gloom. But this wasn't worth the risk, for it was well known to the police as well. [118]

East London pubs were especially popular with gay men. *The New London Spy* explained their attractions.

Several of them have music, either professional groups or local talent. Some, near the docks, attract the shipboard homosexuals and their tolerant sailor boyfriends. Twenty years ago they would almost all have been full of rough, tough, friendly East-Enders, indifferently dressed except for the odd 'wide boy' of the period in his American draped suit. Now, worthy of a full sociological study to themselves, the local boys – still tough, still friendly – are elegantly dressed in silk and mohair suits, expensive shoes, shirts and ties; all very sharp, very sophisticated. These burly, worldly dockers are the natural bait for the itinerant homosexuals who make their forays from further west and amuse the locals with their jokes and mannerisms. Some of the pubs have gained real social distinction and it is not an uncommon sight to see Jaguars, Lancias and Mercedes jostling in the car parks with the less exotic machinery of the locals. [119]

Kenneth Williams and fellow actor and entertainer Stanley Baxter went slumming to one such pub – the Bridge Tavern in Canning Town – in July 1967.

Once in the bar we got besieged by young lads asking for the autograph etc., and met a very nice lad called Alan who was a boxer, and a friend called Paul who said, 'I'm the wife.' There was a dreadful youth boasting that he'd been in *Oliver* who kept shouting, 'I'll fuck you', &

I said, 'Charming!' rather weakly and kept laughing it off. Another boy started taking his trousers off but the landlady said 'That's enough', & I said to the landlord, 'It's too much' v. grandly. I must admit I enjoyed it v. much myself. A great pleasure to be surrounded by thoroughly unpretentious men. [120]

Younger gay men were more drawn to the energy and modernity of coffee bars, which sprang up across Britain from the late 1950s. Many of them attracted regular gay clienteles. This, *The New London Spy* explained, was less the result of an 'easing of sociological tension over the subject' and more to do with the commercial acumen of businessmen who realised that 'a cellar room, sparsely furnished but equipped with a juke box and fruit machine and serving coffee and coke will be a lucrative means of attracting quite a lot of queers who want to continue the hunt after the bars have closed'. [121]

Entrance to these often does not demand even a nominal membership; it is just a matter of paying half a crown entrance fee and then something over the odds for each cup of espresso coffee or bottle of coke. There is always a juke box blaring incessantly and dancing is not discouraged. In fact, on busy Saturday nights it becomes more like a rugger scrum and has even been known to approach the orgiastic. The crowd is very mixed: mods, rockers, beatniks, layabouts, hustlers, simpering young hairdressers, crew-cut truck-drivers, students and tourists, blue jeans and leather gear. At week-ends the scene survives into the small hours. This sort of club is very much a product of the sixties and has done a lot to enliven the homosexuals' milieu. [122]

Michael Schofield's partner Anthony Skyrme remembered going to coffee bars 'whether they were gay or not because coffee bars were the latest thing'. He was especially fond of The Coffee House in London's Haymarket, famed for its cascading water fountain sculpted from coloured Perspex sheets. He also frequented the Calabash in Drayton Gardens, Chelsea, run by the photographer Laon Maybanke. Journalist

Peter Burton also went there and remembered its 'flock wallpaper and red plush. The walls were decorated with framed photographs of stars – there was a stunning shot of Vivien Leigh – all taken by the owner. The entrance and the cloakrooms were guarded by a squat old woman – Spanish, I think, dressed in black bombazine.' Some coffee bars, like Le Gigolo on the Kings Road in Chelsea, had small dance floors. Derek Jarman went there and remembered 'a narrow staircase [that] led straight down onto a red-tiled dance floor, at the most 15 feet square, probably less; the place was painted white. There was a bar where you could only get Coke and Nescafé. At the back was a raised area – about 10 feet square – with two toilets off. Music as far as I can remember came from the jukebox. We weren't allowed to touch when dancing. If you touched anyone the doorman would say, "Hey lads, come on, you know the rules."' But illicit sexual activity did take place. Robert, a merchant seaman, remembered: 'It was very crowded and hot, and when I went on to the dance floor, I discovered that it was not so much a dance but more of an orgy, and the further one got sucked into the heaving mass of bodies, the more overt the sexual activity became.' [123, 124, 125, 126]

The most famous gay coffee bar in London was Le Duce on D'Arblay Street in Soho. Modelled on The Scene mod club in nearby Ham Yard, it was owned by ex-policeman Bill Bryant and his partner Geoffrey Worthington. There was a coffee bar on the ground floor and a dance area with a juke box and a large fish tank in the basement. Jarman described Le Duce as 'the most exciting club of the 60s, where the "hip" hung out'. Architect John Chesterman remembered the atmosphere there as 'electric': 'You got these 16 to 17-year-old kids dancing like machine guns all through the night. All the people who fancied young boys used to come around and hang outside.' Clubbers often used drugs, as Philip Rescorla recalled: 'A lot of them were drugged up to the eyeballs. It seemed in order to get them through the weekend.' Le Duce was mainly a place to socialise and dance rather than find sex. Peter Burton, who managed the club from 1966 to 1968, remembered encounters there as shy, bashful affairs: 'I remember the pattern – Saturday night. Le Duce. Standing against a wall. Looking around. Seeing someone. Thinking: he's cute. But that might be as far as it would go on that occasion. However, the following weekend you'd maybe nod to each other, dance together a few times. Maybe make a date to meet later in the week – for a drink, a movie. Sex was led up to, rather than an instant inevitability.' [127, 128, 129, 130]

If sex was not inevitable at Le Duce then police raids were. It was said that the fish died so often because clubbers threw their drugs into the tank when police officers arrived. Derek Jarman remembered similar raids at Le Gigolo, where people were arrested 'more by bad luck than design. You waited your turn to be frisked and given a numbered piece of paper which you showed at the door upstairs before you were allowed home. After the police left, the floor was a sea of recreational drugs jettisoned in the dark.' [131]

The police carried out raids on other gay venues throughout the 1960s. The Kandy Lounge in London's Chinatown was busted in 1962. Plainclothes officers reported seeing pairs of men 'dancing the twist to a juke box' in an 'overbearing' atmosphere. They also saw 'three young men in bright shirts and tight jeans' talking 'effeminately' and a middle-aged man showing two teenagers how to dance the twist. The club's owner David Browne and its secretary Paul Broadbent were both convicted of allowing disorderly conduct and were each fined £23. In 1966 The Other Place coffee bar in Chelsea was also raided. According to police officers, nearly 200 men were 'trying to dance together or swaying to the music. They were like the proverbial sardines. Some were kissing passionately and fondling each other in an indecent way. They were also indulging in unnatural sexual practices. Most of the men there were of an effeminate kind and obviously homosexual.' The owner, John Toole, was sentenced to nine months' imprisonment for keeping a disorderly house. The judge at the trial described the coffee bar as 'an absolute sink of filth and iniquity'. [132, 133]

The authorities were disturbed as much by the social, generational and racial mixing at these venues as by the homosexual behaviour they saw there. Anthony Rowley thought that a 'striking feature' of gay venues was the absence of social barriers: 'A 17-year-old railway worker will be seen chatting unselfconsciously and on Christian name terms with the sons of peers. During the Kandy Lounge court case police sergeant Albert Corrie, speaking for the prosecution, noted with disapproval that 'patrons were aged from 14 to 45'. In a study of black immigrants in Stepney, east London in 1955 sociologist Michael Banton observed that 'a number of white homosexuals come round the cafés and the public houses of the coloured quarter looking for coloured "friends"'. One of Richard Hauser's contacts told him that men at the gay club he went to were 'my own people, whether they are white or brown. They're fellow queers, despised by everybody'. For some, this was evidence that gay men were ahead of the curve of the change in social attitudes beginning to take place. John Chesterman sensed 'a gay scene evolving well in advance of the popular swinging 60s image'. Nicholas Sharpe, a young Oxford academic in Julian Mitchell's 1961 novel *Imaginary Toys*, thinks that 'one of the advantages of being homosexual is that one is prevented from being class-conscious.' Bryan Magee thought that this 'freedom from class barriers' enabled gay men to achieve a unique kind of solidarity: 'There is naturally a tendency for them to stick together, to support each other, and this bond can transcend other barriers which in different circumstances would be strong.' [134, 135, 136, 137, 138, 139, 140]

Despite their popularity, the seedy reputation and legally precarious nature of gay venues discouraged many men from visiting them. Christopher Spence thought that the gay scene in Britain was 'pretty limited and pretty tacky. I can remember going to Amsterdam, and to Paris and to Brussels, and being absolutely amazed at how way behind we were. Particularly in Holland – the openness, and the fact that gay men were so relaxed going out in public, which was so much in marked contrast to what it was like here.' One of Michael Schofield's contacts told him he longed to go to 'proper places to meet friends of similar outlook. At present I feel a bit unsafe in clubs. They may be raided at any time.' [141, 142]

Gay men knew that having their sexuality revealed in the course of a police raid could spell disaster. 'There was a lot to lose by being known as a queer,' remembered Schofield, who was himself subject to background checks while undertaking Home Office-funded research. The psychiatrist Peter Scott was asked to make an assessment of him. 'We didn't talk for very long,' recalled Schofield. 'He just said, "They've asked me to find out if you're a homosexual, and I think you probably are, but I'm not going to tell them.'" An anonymous interviewee on *This Week* was less fortunate. He told Bryan Magee how he had lost his job after his company received an anonymous telephone call from 'a friend': 'I was summoned into the office and told that they had received a phone call saying I was homosexual. Did I deny this? And of course I didn't deny it, because living a lie is one thing, and living a bigger lie is even more. So I said no, I was homosexual, and [they] said they no longer wished my services, and I was fired.' [143, 144]

The situation was worse for men with convictions for homosexual offences. 'People who have been in prison and come to us asking for help in finding jobs are a big problem,' explained Antony Grey in an Albany Trust talk in 1963. 'Unfortunately there is more prejudice against ex-prisoners who have been in prison for a homosexual offence than there is against somebody who has merely stolen a few thousand pounds from the petty cash, for instance. I know of some professionally qualified men who have been six or nine months without succeeding in getting even the most menial job after they have come out of prison.' On a radio programme in 1965 one man explained how 'at the present moment I've got employment because I lied to them about the reasons for being out of employment for the number of months I was in prison.' Another man wrote to the Brighton *Evening Argus* to complain that he faced long term unemployment because he was unwilling to lie about his conviction: 'The average homosexual wishes only to give loyal service to his employer, just the same as a normal person would do. Surely if one is honest, someone somewhere could at least give persons like myself a chance to prove their loyalty to them.' Even being suspected of homosexuality could prevent men from getting a job. One young man from Manchester told BBC Radio in April 1966, 'People look at you and think, oh, he's one of those. And they say no thank you.' [145, 146, 147, 148]

Gay men in work also faced difficulties. An interviewee on *This Week* recounted how he had to conceal his sexuality from colleagues by 'pretending the whole time; guarding your language the whole time. I guard what I say, even on perfectly ordinary topics.' A man on the 1965 radio programme explained how he lived 'two lives – private life and a public life. There is this pressure of make-believe all the time. It's pretty artificial, having to live with one's colleagues and simply act a part all day. You have to do it day in, day out, year after year.' Another man described the uncomfortable conversations he faced at work. [149, 150]

> Naturally they ask, 'Are you married?' And you say, 'No,' and they give you a funny look. You can almost hear a mental, 'Why?' And then I always feel they're thinking, there's something wrong with him. Thirty, not particularly ugly, why isn't he married? They're always asking me about girls. 'Do you have a girlfriend?' And of course if you say no you're more or less admitting to the fact you're a homosexual. And if you say yes then you start weaving a web of lies. [151]

Young professionals in the corporate world faced particular pressures in this regard. 'I think that when one begins to turn 30 companies will begin to wonder why someone isn't married,' one man told the radio programme. In *The Youngest Director* the chairman of Leonard's American-owned trading corporation tells him: 'We'll have to find you a wife pretty soon.' Company manager Fred Wise explains why. [152, 153]

> 'American companies have proved that the married executive is happier and therefore a better worker than the unmarried. But there's also a corollary. If a young, hardworking, imaginative director won't toe the line in this one detail, perhaps there'll soon be others where he'll want to stop outside corporation rules. Do you see? This marriage business will become a test. Don't you think it would be the same story at the next company, and the next, and the next? [154]

The chairman eventually finds out about Leonard's homosexuality and forces him to resign on the grounds of 'mental ill-health'. [155]

Working class men also felt the strain of hiding their sexuality. One man on the 1965 radio programme described himself as 'a bag of nerves' at work. 'I'm worried all the time – what are people thinking?' Another man talked about having to 'put on the big man act'. [156]

I have to be like the fella that works on the bench next to me, my mate at work. I have to be the same as he is. He's married with a couple of kids. I've got to chase the girls in the shop, to make it look as though I'm a man. I'm not in the least bit interested in them girls. But I've got to put that atmosphere on to make people think I'm a normal man. Because if they once find out that I am queer I've got to leave my job again, and I lost a three-year apprenticeship through it. I only had twelve months to go on my apprenticeship as an electrician in a big store and I lost it because of the men making a fool out of me in town. [157]

The creative and artistic professions were hardly havens of homosexual tolerance either. Theatre director Anthony Page remembered visiting Dundee in 1962 with the actors Edward Fox and David Andrews. During an evening's drinking on a boat with some local sailors, one of them suggested partnering up. 'David and Eddie got absolutely enraged,' recalled Page. 'I was longing to go off to their cabins, but I couldn't.' John Fraser was told by his agent to end a fling with ballet dancer Rudolf Nureyev: 'If you don't stop this madness instantly, your career will be over, and I will have nothing more to do with you! He'll leave you unemployable with your reputation in tatters!' Nicholas Wright remembered the forbidding atmosphere of movie-making in the 1960s: 'I think the only time I ever thought I might have to conceal my sexuality, and did, was when I was a runner on *Far From the Madding Crowd.* * Back then the culture of big movies was so macho you just wouldn't out yourself as gay.' Brian Sewell recalled how he was rejected for promotion at auction house Christie's because of his sexuality. One of the directors, David Carritt (a former lover of Liberal MP Jeremy Thorpe), told him about a meeting he had had with the other directors at which the possibility of Sewell joining the board had been discussed: 'All but one had been in favour, but the decision had to be unanimous. Patrick [Lindsay] had objected, and objected in such terms as had humiliated David – "We've got one homosexual on the board; we don't

---

*   Directed by John Schlesinger and released in 1967

need another.'" In *The Youngest Director* Leonard's friend Tony Newman works in the publishing industry, but he is careful to make sure that his 'inversion' is kept 'well out of sight'. In David Stewart Leslie's 1963 novel *Two Gentlemen Sharing* Roddy Pater tells his friend Jane that in order to 'forge ahead' in advertising it is best to 'unlearn fast' any homosexual habits. 'It's not, as they say, a very gay profession'. [158, 159, 160, 161, 162, 163]

Some men who were not prepared to hide their sexuality instead decided to run away to sea. The merchant navy had long had a reputation for taking on gay crew members and for turning a blind eye to homosexual behaviour on board ship. Even the National Union of Seamen admitted as much. At its annual general meeting in 1966 a speaker remarked, 'Whilst I would hesitate to say that the British merchant navy has become a haven for homosexuals, we have them on board in increasing numbers.' Chris joined Cunard in 1958 because 'it was generally known, underground, that it was quite gay in the merchant or, come to that, the Royal navy.' Pubs in port cities were also well known as meeting places for gay men. Former seaman Don Trueman remembered visiting one of them in Liverpool: 'The gay guys used the little back room, the snug. We were in the public bar. We'd blow them kisses from time to time. They'd walk through the pub bar to the gents and we'd say, "Nice arse" or something, and they'd say, "Ooh, thank you." They'd flash their tackle in the gents – you could tell what they were by the way they were standing at the stone.' In Gillian Freeman's 1961 novel *The Leather Boys* (written under the pseudonym Eliot George) Dick gets a foretaste of life at sea at the dockside pub he visits after signing up. [164]

'My name's Dick,' Dick said.

The men gave a chorus of giggles and shrieks and the one next to him said, "Ow camp!' Dick blushed.

'I love Dick,' one screamed. And they all shrieked with laughter again.

'You'll 'ave to put Dick on the list, won't you?' said the man with rings. 'Listen to Mother.'

'What list?' asked Dick.

'The queers list, dear. Mother keeps it in 'er cabin.' They all laughed. 'What ship you getting?'

'The Armada.'

'Oh my Gawd! Big Mary's on that ship, darling. You'll 'ave to do just what she says. She'll draw a knife if she's upset.' [165]

In *Winger's Landfall* Harry takes a job as a steward on the cruise ship Cyclamen, sailing from Sydney to Tilbury. On board he meets Marilyn ('a slim little queer, aged about 16'), Diamond Lil ('a tall blonde in a green brocade dressing-gown, very discreetly made up, like a well-bred *Tatler* woman), Patience (an 'old cow'), Rita ('a tall, middle-aged, languid queer with receding hair and a ravaged, beaky face'), Bubbles ('hitting the bottle hard') and Prince, a young steward who agrees to be Harry's 'boy'. The high point of the voyage is a party for passengers and crew to celebrate crossing the Equator. [166]

> Lil stepped out onto the deck. 'Dear subjects, they said you were calling for me!' she said, in a shrill, South Kensington tone. 'I've just come out on the balcony for a moment.' She wore a long, white clinging gown, white gloves, drop earrings, silver high heels, and what looked like a silver fox stole over an unobtrusively false bust. Lil was followed by Rita in red velvet, Patience in a gay print frock and a flowered straw hat, and others in less successful travesty. Rita and Patience were manifest imposters, sending themselves up by walking hand on hip and wagging their rumps; the rest of the rabble dropped inelegant curtseys, finger to chin, and jostled for precedence. But Lil exhibited an absolute mastery in her impersonation. Several passengers were gaping down from the promenade, and Harry wondered what they made of the scene. [167]

Such antics were not only fictitious. Martin sailed on the P&O liner Canberra as a steward on its maiden voyage from Southampton to Sydney in 1961: 'I could honestly say there was a thousand crew, and out of the thousand there were 500 gays on that ship. It was like heaven.'

A few years later Martin went with his friend Gerty G-string to a pub in a small port town in Wales. 'Gerty used to wear a crushed velvet blue jacket and King Charles shirts, plus a full face of make-up. She also had masses of bleached blonde hair. I was darker and smaller, and I'd got my eyes blue with eye shadow and back-combed my hair. It looked as if we'd just come off a space ship.' By then, however, the British public had seen enough of gay men not to be completely shocked by them, or by what they wore. [168]

Chapter 4 references

1. 'Into The Twilight World'
2. *This Week: Homosexuals*, ITV, 22 October 1964
3. Gordon Westwood, *A Minority: A Report on the Life of the Male Homosexual in Great Britain*, Longmans, 1960
4. John Lahr (ed.), *The Orton Diaries*, Friday 24 March 1967, Da Capo Press, 1996
5. Gordon Westwood, *A Minority*, op. cit.
6. John Lahr (ed.), *The Orton Diaries*, Sunday 30 April 1967, op. cit.
7. Jay Gilbert, *The Goose Girl*, Hutchinson, 1963
8. Gordon Westwood, *A Minority*, op. cit.
9. John Lahr, *The Orton Diaries*, Sunday 30 April 1967, op. cit.
10. *The Colour of His Hair*, A Film Treatment for The Homosexual Law Reform Society, Prepared by Elizabeth Montagu for Samaritan Films, 5 November 1964, Hall-Carpenter Albany Trust files, London School of Economics
11. Albany Trust Report, 1963-66, op. cit.
12. Douglas Plummer, *Queer People: The Truth About Homosexuals*, W.H. Allen, 1963
13. Irma Kurtz, 'Homosexuality: The Unlocking of a Law', *Nova*, February 1967
14. Gordon Westwood, *A Minority*, op. cit.
15. Bryan Magee, *One in Twenty*, Secker & Warburg, 1966
16. Simon Raven, 'Boys Will be Boys: The Male Prostitute in London', *Encounter*, November 1960
17. Quentin Crewe, 'The Boy Who Sat by Me in the Cinema', *Daily Mirror*, 15 April 1965
18. Colin Spencer, *Anarchists in Love*, Eyre & Spottiswoode, 1963
19. Martyn Goff, *Indecent Assault*, André Deutsch, 1967
20. Martyn Goff, *The Youngest Director*, Putnam, 1961

21. John Owen, 'Admiralty Man in Secrets Case', *The Daily Telegraph*, 14 February 1962

22. George Martin, 'Secrets of the Scented Flat'; 'The Cuddly-Toy Spy', *Daily Sketch*, 24 January 1963

23. *Minutes of Evidence Taken at Public Hearings Before the Tribunal Appointed to Inquire into the Vassall Case and Related Matters*, Her Majesty's Stationery Office, 1963

24. 'Weaknesses That Led to Vassall's Fall', *Daily Telegraph*, 23 October 1962

25. 'How They Caught Him After 6 Years', *Daily Sketch*, 23 October 1962

26. Ibid.

27. 'The Men Who Came to See Me – and the Women? They Gave Me Mother Love', *Sunday Pictorial*, 11 November 1962

28. *Minutes of Evidence*, op. cit.

29. Martyn Goff, *Indecent Assault*, op. cit.

30. Letter from Laurence Harbottle to Douglas Orton, 16 August 1967, Matt Cook, *Queer Domesticities: Homosexuality and Home Life in Twentieth-Century London*, Palgrave Macmillan, 2014

31. Martyn Goff, *The Youngest Director*, op. cit.

32. Ibid.

33. Meg Elizabeth Atkins, *The Gemini*, Peter Owen, 1964

34. Ibid.

35. Martyn Goff, *The Youngest Director*, op. cit.

36. Ibid.

37. Jenni Hall, *Ask Agamemnon*, Cassell, 1964

38. Gordon Westwood, *A Minority*, op. cit.

39. Bob Cant, Susan Hemmings (ed.s), *Radical Records: Thirty Years of Lesbian and Gay History*, Routledge, 1988

40. 'Mike', recorded interview, 1995, Tony Dean Gay Commercial Scene interviews, British Library

41. Brian Sewell, *Outsider: Always Almost; Never Quite*, Quartet Books, 2012

42. Graham Turner, 'Growing Problem of the Homosexual', *The Scotsman*, 5 June 1959

43. Noyes Thomas, 'Into the Twilight World', *News of the World*, 26 July 1964

44. *Darling*, Vic Films, 1965

45. Nicholas Wright, telephone interview with author, 25 May 2012

46. Jeremy Reed, *The King of Carnaby Street: The Life of John Stephen*, Haus Publishing, 2010

47. *This Week: Homosexuals*, op cit.

48. 'John', recorded interview, 1996, Tony Dean Gay Commercial Scene interviews, op. cit.

49. Bob Cant, *Footsteps and Witnesses: Lesbian and Gay Lifestories from Scotland*, Word Power Books, 2008

50. Jonathan Blake, recorded interview, March 1991, Hall-Carpenter Oral History archive, British Library

51. Hunter Davies (ed.), *The New London Spy: A Discreet Guide to the City's Pleasures*, Anthony Blond, 1966

52. Ibid.

53. Douglas Plummer, *Queer People*, op. cit.

54. Bryan Magee, *One in Twenty*, op. cit.

55. Douglas Plummer, *Queer People*, op. cit.

56. 'The Man Who Wrote "Telstar"', *The Evening News*, 12 November 1963

57. Jonathan Blake, recorded interview, op. cit.

58. Hunter Davies (ed.), *The New London Spy*, op. cit.

59. Ibid.

60. Douglas Plummer, *Queer People*, op. cit.

61. Hunter Davies (ed.), *The New London Spy*, op. cit.

62. Matt Houlbrook, *Queer London: Perils and Pleasures of the Sexual Metropolis, 1918-1957*, Chicago University Press, 2005

63. Hunter Davies (ed.), *The New London Spy*, op. cit.

64. Jeffrey Weeks, Kevin Porter, *Between the Acts: Lives of Homosexual Men, 1885-1967*, Rivers Oram Press, 1998

65. Hunter Davies (ed.), *The New London Spy*, op. cit.

66. Ibid.

67. Derek Jarman, *At Your Own Risk: A Saint's Testament*, Hutchinson, 1992

68. Quentin Crisp, *The Naked Civil Servant*, Jonathan Cape, 1968

69. Jeffrey Weeks, Kevin Porter, *Between the Acts*, op. cit.

70. Margaret O' Brien, Allen Eyles (ed.s), *Enter the Dream House: Memories of Cinemas in South London from the Twenties to the Sixties*, British Film

Institute, 1993

71. Tony Papard, e-mail to author, 6 June 2009

72. Anne Sharpley, 'London's Hidden Problem', *Evening Standard*, 20 July 1964

73. Quentin Crewe, 'The Boy Who Sat By Me In The Cinema', op. cit.

74. Nicholas Wright, *The Reporter*, Nick Hern Books, 2007

75. Hugh David, *On Queer Street: A Social History of British Homosexuality, 1895-1995*, Harper Collins, 1997

76. Leonard James Harper, *Teddy Boy Ahoy*, Thames-Side Publications, 1963

77. Simon Raven, 'Boys Will be Boys, op. cit.

78. Ibid.

79. Ibid.

80. Ibid.

81. Ibid

82. Ibid.

83. Gordon Westwood, *A Minority*, op. cit.

84. Anne Sharpley, 'London's Hidden Problem', op. cit.

85. Douglas Plummer, *Queer People*, op. cit.

86. Gordon Westwood, *A Minority*, op. cit.

87. 'The Night I Killed George Brinham', *News of the World*, 27 January 1963

88. Robert Traini, 'Murder Squad Ask: Did You See Him?', *Sun*, 7 December 1964

89. Jack Miller, 'Murders in a Half World', *News of the World*, 25 February 1962

90. 'Strangler: List of Names is Found', *Evening Standard*, 22 February 1962

91. 'Killer Hunt In Vice Haunts', *The Evening News*, 21 January 1967

92. Michael Schofield, 'Social Aspects of Homosexuality', *British Journal of Venereal Diseases*, June 1964

93. Jeffrey Weeks, Stonewall 40, South Bank Centre, 16 July 2009

94. Tony Papard, e-mail to author, op. cit.

95. Derek Jarman, *At Your Own Risk*, op. cit.

96. Derek Jarman, *Kicking the Pricks*, University of Minnesota Press, 2010

97. Philip Hoare, *Noel Coward: A Biography*, Sinclair Stevenson, 1995

98. Philip Rescorla, recorded interview, November 1985, Hall-Carpenter Oral History archive, op. cit.

99. '1967 And All That', Lesbian and Gay Newsmedia Archive, www.lagna.org.uk

100. Anthony Rowley, 'Another Kind of Loving: What is it Like to be a Homosexual?', *Axle Spokes,* 4, 1963
101. Ibid.
102. Ibid.
103. Ibid.
104. Eustace Chesser, *An Outline of Human Relationships*, Heinemann, 1959
105. Anthony Rowley, 'Another Kind of Loving', op. cit.
106. Ibid.
107. Ibid.
108. Richard Hauser, *The Homosexual Society*, The Bodley Head
109. Douglas Plummer, *Queer People*, op. cit.
110. Anthony Rowley, 'Another Kind of Loving', op. cit.
111. Gordon Westwood, *A Minority*, op. cit.
112. Richard Hauser, *The Homosexual Society*, op. cit.
113. *Minutes of Evidence*, op. cit.
114. Douglas Plummer, *Queer People*, op. cit.
115. *Minutes of Evidence*, op. cit.
116. Douglas Plummer, *Queer People*, op. cit.
117. Meg Elizabeth Atkins, *The Gemini*, op. cit.
118. Stuart Lauder, *Winger's Landfall*, Eyre & Spottiswoode, 1962
119. Hunter Davies (ed.), *The New London Spy*, op. cit.
120. Russell Davies (ed.), *The Kenneth Williams Diaries*, Friday 14 July 1967, Harper Collins, 1993
121. Hunter Davies (ed.), *The New London Spy*, op. cit.
122. Ibid.
123. Anthony Skyrme, Michael Schofield, personal interview, op. cit.
124. Peter Burton, *Parallel Lives*, GMP Publishers, 1985
125. Derek Jarman, *At Your Own Risk*, op. cit.
126. Paul Baker, Jo Stanley, *Hello Sailor! The Hidden History of Gay Life at Sea*, Longman, 2003
127. Derek Jarman, *At Your Own Risk*, op. cit.
128. John Chesterman, recorded interview, September 1993, Hall-Carpenter Oral History archive, op. cit.

129. Philip Rescorla, recorded interview, op. cit.

130. Peter Burton, *Parallel Lives*, op. cit.

131. Derek Jarman, *At Your Own Risk*, op. cit.

132. 'Goings On at The Kandy Lounge', *News of the World*, 16 September 1962

133. 'Sink of Filth: Coffee Bar Man Jailed', *Chelsea News*, 2 December 1966

134. Anthony Rowley, 'Another Kind of Loving', op. cit.

135. 'Goings On at The Kandy Lounge', *News of the World*, op. cit.

136. Michael Banton, *The Coloured Quarter: Negro Immigrants in an English City*, Jonathan Cape, 1955

137. Richard Hauser, *The Homosexual Society*, op. cit.

138. John Chesterman, recorded interview, Hall-Carpenter Oral History archive, op. cit.

139. Julian Mitchell, *Imaginary Toys*, Hutchinson, 1961

140. Bryan Magee, *One in Twenty*, op. cit.

141. Christopher Spence, recorded interview, September 1990, Hall-Carpenter Oral History archive, op. cit.

142. Gordon Westwood, *A Minority*, op. cit.

143. *The BBC and the Closet*, BBC Radio 4, 29 January 2008

144. *This Week: Homosexuals*, op. cit.

145. Antony Grey, *Speaking Out: Writings on Sex, Law, Politics and Society*, 1954-95, Cassell, 1997

146. *Male Homosexual*, BBC Home Service, 5 January 1965

147. 'Surely Someone Somewhere Could Give Me a Chance', *Evening Argus*, 13 March 1965

148. *The Night People*, BBC Home Service, 4 April 1966

149. *This Week: Homosexuals*, op. cit.

150. *Male Homosexual*, op. cit.

151. Ibid.

152. Ibid

153. Martyn Goff, *The Youngest Director*, op. cit.

154. Ibid.

155. Ibid.

156. *Male Homosexual*, op. cit.

157. Ibid.

158. Anthony Page, personal interview with author, 22 August 2012

159. John Fraser, *Close Up: An Actor Telling Tales*, Oberon Books, 2004

160. Nicholas Wright, telephone interview with author, op. cit.

161. Brian Sewell, *Outsider: Always Almost; Never Quite*, op. cit.

162. Martyn Goff, *The Youngest Director*, op. cit.

163. David Stuart Leslie, *Two Gentlemen Sharing*, Secker & Warburg, 1963

164. Paul Baker, Jo Stanley, *Hello Sailor!*, op. cit.

165. Eliot George, *The Leather Boys*, Anthony Blond, 1961

166. Stuart Lauder, *Winger's Landfall*, op. cit.

167. Ibid.

168. Paul Baker, Jo Stanley, *Hello Sailor!*, op. cit.

Chapter 5

DO I LOOK LIKE A BLOODY PANSY?

'A lot of people assume we're bitchy and effeminate and go round jangling bracelets, which isn't true.'

Male Homosexual, BBC Home Service, 5 January 1965 [1]

On 29 June 1960, the day the House of Commons voted on the Wolfenden Report, a script reader at the British Board of Film Censors was hard at work scrutinising a script for an as yet untitled film. 'It is a good script,' she noted, 'but may well be tricky. We have never had such an explicit survey of this subject on the screen, or such a great number of different types of "queer" assembled in one film. I really am rather nervous. A lot of the material here is in itself pretty sensational.' The film was eventually released as *Victim*, and it brought cinema audiences face to face with gay men for the first time. [2]

Victim took more than a year to complete and was the result of careful planning and co-operation between its makers – husband-and-wife screen writers Janet Green and John McCormick, producer Michael Relph and director Basil Dearden – and the BBFC's secretary John Trevelyan. As early as May 1960 Trevelyan had discussed the film project with Relph over lunch – the first of many convivial meetings and correspondences. Trevelyan, a liberal-minded former examiner for the board, was conscious of the need to reflect the post-Wolfenden debate about homosexuality on film. But, as his objections to *The Third Sex* in 1958 had shown, he was wary of explicit representations of gay men. He advised Relph to 'approach the subject with caution'. In particular, Trevelyan expressed concern that the film might 'give an impression of a world peopled with no one but "queers", since in the story there are few characters who are not of this kind. The more we can see of the characters going about their daily lives in association with other people who are not "queers", the less we have of groups of "queers" in bars and clubs and elsewhere, the better. Indeed, I hope that you will keep the homosexual relationships as far as possible in the background.' Trevelyan further spelled out his concerns in a letter to Janet Green on 1 July. [3]

We have never banned the subject of homosexuality from the screen but we have not until recently had very much censorship trouble with it, partially because American film producers were prevented from dealing with the subject by the inflexible ruling of the Code[*] and because British film producers knew that the subject was not one of general discussion in this country and was one that would probably not be acceptable to British audiences. Recently the situation has changed in this country due on the one hand to the Wolfenden Report, which was followed up by a good deal of free discussion in the press and on radio and television, and on the other hand to the Lord Chamberlain making a public announcement in the press that he was now willing to accept homosexuality as a theme for stage plays. As far as the film is concerned, we have so far only had the problem as presented in the two films about Oscar Wilde. As you know, on the subject of homosexuality there is a division of public opinion, and, if this week's debate in the House of Commons is anything to go by, it appears that there is still a majority opposed to any compassionate treatment of it. What presents difficulties is that, in order to develop the story, you have shown groups of homosexuals of different social classes and, since

* The Hays Code, which governed the motion picture industry in the US

there are few characters in the film who represent normality in sex, you have conveyed the impression, quite unwittingly, that the world is largely peopled with queers. The more normality you can bring into this very sombre world the better. Frankly we would not want this amount of emphasis on homosexual practices nor the somewhat frank dialogue about it that is in the present script. [4]

Despite the censor's doubts, Green persevered with her original vision. She charmed Trevelyan with offers to visit her and her husband in France ('If you ever come to Paris, either for business or pleasure, my husband and I would be delighted if you would let us know since you would be a very welcome visitor to our home') and she resisted Relph's suggestion that she add more humour 'of the kind that we know from experience emulates when inverts are around'. She told him that this was 'asking for trouble as far as the censor is concerned, since it will seem to him "camp"'. [5, 6]

Green and McCormick were no strangers to film controversy. Their 1959 screenplay for *Sapphire* (also produced and directed by Relph and Dearden) had explored the theme of race relations in a whodunit murder mystery format. Their initial treatment for *Victim* (provisionally titled *Boy Barrett*) centred on a married 50-year-old judge and Queen's Counsel called Melville Carr who is blackmailed by 'a boy who rides a Lambretta' called Butch Cut. But the film grew into something much more than a blackmail detective story. As Relph explained to Green and McCormick in August 1960, 'It is likely to be the first wholly adult and serious approach to homosexuality that the British cinema has made. This imposes great responsibilities and obligations upon us. To make our audience shed its long accumulated prejudice against these people we must show our characters in such depth that the audience will not only pity them (the easiest of all emotions), but understand them and identify themselves to some extent with their problems and emotions.' [7, 8]

This approach was not initially to the censor's liking. The film, Trevelyan told Relph, 'seems to us to come down rather heavily in favour of the homosexual. There are certain dialogue lines which seem to us to be examples of "special pleading". I think you should be careful also not to give ideas to potential blackmailers on how they could extend their practice. We are told it "offers unrivalled opportunities to any extortionist". This may be true, but is it wise to point it out?' [9]

By the time the third draft screenplay reached Pinewood Studios in October 1960 these issues had largely been ironed out. Green reported that the studio bosses thought it was 'great' and 'completely compelling'. She added, 'Since it was written with the shadow of the censor's axe right across the paper, we are pleased at any rate with that reaction. But, oh! what more could we have done had we been left alone.' Meanwhile, Allied Film Makers – Relph's and Dearden's production company – was beginning to cast roles. Dennis Price took the part of Calloway the actor. Norman Bird, Nigel Stock and Charles Lloyd-Pack became bookshop owner Harold Doe, car salesman Phip Mortimer and hairdresser Henry. Darren Nesbitt was the renamed blackmailer Sandy Youth. Twenty-year-old Peter McEnnery took the role of Jack 'Boy' Barrett. 'I was very green at the time,' he recalled. 'My agent persuaded me to do it, and it was the right decision. This was a leading part, and a good part.' Sylvia Syms, who was pregnant at the time, accepted the part of the judge's wife, Laura (previously named Loretta) after several actresses had turned it down. 'I came from a politically aware background, and tried to seek roles that were interesting,' she later recalled. 'I had a lot of gay friends. I knew it was important to do this film.' Casting the homosexually-inclined judge (renamed Melville Farr, in order to avoid objections from a real QC called Arthur Comyns Carr) was more problematic. Jack Hawkins was initially asked, but he faced a filming clash with *Lawrence of Arabia* and also expressed doubts about the script. [10, 11, 12, 13, 14]

The film's title, too, caused difficulties. Relph disliked *Boy Barrett* and suggested *The Blackmailers* or *Boy on the Scaffold* instead. But both were rejected by Green. Dearden was also unhappy with some aspects of the script, particularly with what he saw as the characterisation of gay men as 'types rather than human beings; human beings, let's face it, different in only one respect from heterosexuals. Which brings me to Eddy, a vital character, who must be written in depth. He seems to be justifying himself all the time. Have you ever known a "queer" to justify himself to anyone? Why should he? He doesn't feel that he is queer. He feels that he is normal to himself, and misunderstood by everybody else!' [15]

At the end of 1960 Green and McCormick decided to stop amending their screenplay. In a letter to Relph and Dearden they reminded them about their expertise on the subject of homosexuality, having 'studied the subject for years, read almost every book written about it during recent years, and talked with doctors, policemen and *inverts themselves.*' Green also balked at the suggestion that gay men should be involved in making the film: 'We were quite horrified in retrospect at your suggestion that the screenplay should be given to an invert to read. Any comments would only be biased and disastrous to our respective objective viewpoints.' [16]

Filming on *Boy Barrett* was due to begin on 30 January 1961, but it still had no lead actor. Jack Hawkins finally rejected the script. James Mason was approached, but for tax reasons could not make a film in England. Stewart Granger was considered, but he was not free, and John Davis, the managing director of Rank Organisation (Allied Film Makers' financial backer and distributor), did not want him anyway. Then in late December 1960 Earl St John, Rank's executive producer at Pinewood Studios, hit upon a solution. Relph explained to Green:

This is a story of a man whose marriage and career are threatened by the consequences of homosexual impulses. Provided he is old enough to have a brilliant career in the law, isn't it more moving and more urgent for predominantly youthful audiences if it is a younger man and a younger marriage? Young people might feel that for a man who was old enough to be a judge and had been married for nearly 30 years, the sexual side of life would not be of vital importance. The judge business was one obvious snag, but this situation could, we felt, very easily become that of a brilliant young barrister about to take silk. At this point Earl suggested Dirk Bogarde to us. We studied every scene in the script very carefully with him in mind and felt that astonishingly little adjustment was needed to make it fit him wonderfully well. We sent him the script, and in spite of obvious dangers for him, he jumped at it. Of course there is no doubt that this is the most commercial casting one could have hoped for, and that he will give a wonderfully sensitive performance. [17]

Dirk Bogarde later claimed to have accepted the role of Melville Farr with alacrity during Christmas 1960.

The telephone rang. It was Basil Dearden. 'Sent you a script over this afternoon, by messenger. Might interest you. Read it over the holiday and let me know, OK? You may not like it. No one else does. Everyone we offered it to has turned it down. You're our last chance.'

'Thanks. What's it about, paedophilia?'

'No. Homosexuality, actually. Middle-aged married man with a yen for a bloke on a building site.'

My father was struggling at the top of the tree trying to fix the fairy on top. 'Pa, would you mind if I made a rather difficult film. I mean difficult in the moral sense; serious stuff?'

'I don't think I quite follow you. Political do you mean?

'Homosexual.'

'Oh my dear boy, we get so much of that sort of thing on television. Mother and I find it dreadfully boring, all those doctors and psychiatrists bumbling on. Just remember that mother and I live in a small village, we have to get on with our neighbours. Not always easy. Try not to do anything which would embarrass her. People are so narrow, you know. [18]

Despite his professed nonchalance, Bogarde knew that he faced considerable risks taking the part. He was known privately in the film world to be gay, and had a long-standing relationship with his manager Anthony Forwood while publicly maintaining a liaison with French actress Capucine. Yet having starred in two recent Hollywood flops

(*Song Without End* and *The Angel Wore Red*) and at 39 no longer the youthful romantic lead in the popular *Doctor* films of the 1950s (*Doctor in the House*, *Doctor at Sea* and *Doctor at Large*), Bogarde was keen to move his career in a new direction. 'He wasn't getting any other great offers, and it was a wonderful part,' recalled friend and colleague John Fraser. Sylvia Syms thought that Bogarde also identified with Farr, even to the extent of amending the screenplay. His personal copy of the final shooting script, dated 23 January 1961, includes extra handwritten dialogue for the scene in which Laura confronts her husband about his relationship with Barrett. [19]

> Mel: Alright, alright, you want to know, I'll tell you. You won't be content until I tell you – until you've ripped it out of me. I stopped seeing him because I wanted him. Can you understand – because I wanted him. (Pause) Now what good has that done you? [20]

Bogarde's copy of the script also has '*Boy Barrett*' crossed out and replaced with '*Victim*'. Both Green and Dearden preferred the original title, but Relph still disliked it, and Rank bosses worried about the implications of '*Boy*'. By February 1961 the film was definitively titled *Victim*. [21]

According to Bogarde, the atmosphere at Pinewood Studios at the start of filming was tense.

> There was a sort of meeting before we started, and Basil Dearden and Michael Relphs quite rightly said, 'Look, we don't want any sending up of this. It's very serious; it's the first time it's been done, so you will not refer to homos, poofs, queens, queers, fags, faggots.'
>
> And I said, 'What the hell do we call them?'
>
> Basil said, 'We use the word on this set "inverts".'
>
> So we had a very closed set. We kept the press off it. We went through the whole first week in absolute agony, walking on eggshells. Nobody dared bend down. 'Til one super day on the second Monday, when I thought we really can't go through with this any more because it was so reverent, it was like making the life of Christ backwards.

One of the carpenters did actually bend down. And a voice from the gantry yelled out and cleared the air and said, "Watch yer arse Alfie!" And what was marvellous was from that moment onwards the film was plain sailing and we made, I think, a respectable job of it, and we thoroughly enjoyed it. Thank God for Alfie. [22]

The press soon heard about the film. On 17 February the London *Evening Standard* told readers that *Victim* would be about 'an eminent barrister, played by Mr Dirk Bogarde with greying temples, who has homosexual leanings but had never put them into practice'. It added that Bogarde had 'felt some misgivings about accepting the role, but in his 15 years as a Rank contract star he had not been offered so many good parts that he could afford to turn this one down.' The following month *Films and Filming* published an article which criticised the film's portrayal of its gay characters. Reporter Peter Warren complained that *Victim* made 'its central character, a middle-aged barrister, only a potential homosexual. The reason: the studios are afraid that their top contract star for fifteen years would lose his female following if he played an honest queer. If *Victim* at least points to the plight of millions who, because of parliament's refusal to amend the law, are open to blackmail because their promiscuity is homosexual rather than adulterous it may do some good. But if it implies, as is the case of some cheap literature, that homosexuals exist only among a low-life criminal group, then it will add little to public enlightenment.' [23, 24]

Relph and Bogarde responded with separate letters to the magazine. Relph explained that the script had been written long before Bogarde was offered the part of Farr, and he added: 'The crime side of the story arises purely from the fact that homosexuals under the present law are rendered liable to the most vicious forms of blackmail. The homosexuals in the picture are criminals in no sense other than that they break the law by the very fact of their homosexuality. The film puts forward the same point of view as the Wolfenden Committee, that the law should be changed. Contrary to suggesting homosexuals "exist only among a low-life criminal group", the film shows that homosexuality may be found in otherwise completely responsible citizens in every strata of society.' Bogarde, meanwhile, claimed it was 'distressing, in a paper of your kind, to read such inaccurate reporting, specially for once when one is trying to get out of the Simon Sparrow* category (however excellent and delightful he was to play) and join forces with a team who are honestly trying to develop with a new and exciting trend in the cinema today.' [25]

By April 1961 filming was complete. Bogarde later claimed it was 'one of the happiest films I've ever made'. Peter McEnnery also recalled moments of humour. Although they did not act alongside each other, he and Bogarde were photographed on the backlot of Pinewood Studios for the snapshot used to blackmail Farr, which he burns on the fire at the end of the film: 'George Courtney Ward, who was the famous Pinewood photographer, had got a car lined up at the back, and Dirk and I sat in the front. Dirk just sat there, sending me up, saying, "Ooh lovely, I want to get hold of you." He was very friendly.' [26, 27]

The BBFC made a number of objections to the finished film, which it viewed in May 1961. Trevelyan took exception to the Bogarde-scripted dialogue between Farr and Laura, and in particular to the repeat of 'I wanted him'. Trevelyan wrote to Relph: 'We realise that this is a dramatic ending, but we are worried about it.' He also disliked Laura's accusation that Farr was 'attracted to that boy as a man would be to a girl', the absence of a 'self-control' argument against homosexual behaviour and the final 'vindictive outburst' by blackmail ringleader Miss Benham. Relph held firm against most of these objections, arguing that the Mel-Laura scene should remain intact, as it was the 'dramatic kernel of the film' which embodied 'the honesty of our approach to the subject'. But he agreed to cut some dialogue in the scene between Laura and her brother Scott Hankin after they see the 'Farr is queer' graffiti on the garage door. Trevelyan thought that their subsequent conversation about Farr's influence on his young nephew Ronnie might prove 'a dangerous idea to put into the minds of young adolescents'. So the lines 'There's a moment of choice for almost every adolescent boy; I'm not going to risk Ronnie making the wrong choice' were cut. [28, 29]

---

*   The lead character in the *Doctor* films

Victim was given an 'X' certificate and sent for final editing and distribution. Relph was careful to thank Trevelyan for his 'understanding and enlightened attitude to this very difficult subject'. Janet Green also expressed her gratitude for his 'receptiveness and encouragement right from the beginning of this project'. For his part, Trevelyan was 'glad that it worked out all right'. He told Green, 'Michael and Basil made a very good job of the film and were greatly helped by having a really good script. Once again we were really able to get the real work of censorship done before the picture reached the floor, and I am sure that this is the best way of doing it.' [30, 31, 32]

Pinewood's publicity department went straight to work, deliberately promoting '*Victim*' as a controversial film. In a pre-recorded interview, Bogarde described his role as 'a marvellous part'. Without once mentioning the word 'homosexual', he described *Victim* as 'tremendously important because it doesn't pull any punches. It's quite honest. People will go and see this film and thoroughly enjoy it or be distressed by it; but they will be moved somehow by it.' In a Pinewood press release Green explained how she and McCormick had felt 'impelled to write an original screenplay which would reflect the plight and life of the homosexual in London. We feel strongly that this is a matter upon which the public are ill-informed and know only one point of view. We have talked to doctors, social workers and experts of all sorts, both for and against. And to inverts themselves.' Four days before *Victim*'s London opening, she told the *Daily Pictorial*'s show business editor Jack Bentley how she had dealt with a subject 'which many brilliant minds have failed to present conclusively'. She explained that as a married woman she was 'above suspicion of personal motives' and felt 'more strongly about the injustice of it all than most men'. She had also 'studied every book on the subject during the last eighteen months and mixed freely with male homosexuals. And when I read of them getting longer sentences than the beasts who assault little children, it makes my blood boil.' [33, 34, 35]

A paperback novel by William Drummond (the pseudonym of Arthur Calder-Marshall) based on the Green and McCormick screenplay was published by Corgi Books to coincide with *Vicitm*'s premiere at the Odeon in Leicester Square, London on 31 August 1961. The film was also chosen as the official British entry for the 22nd Venice Film Festival. Critical reactions were mostly positive. Many reviewers focused on Bogarde's courage in playing Farr. The *Evening Standard*'s Alexander Walker thought he risked 'curdling the adulation of his fans' but predicted that 'his brave, sensitive picture of an unhappy, terribly bewildered man will win him and this film a far wider audience'. Dilys Powell in the *Sunday Times* pointed out that *Victim* 'could not have been shown and would have excited horror or ribaldry up to a few years ago'. In *Woman's Mirror* Susan Mann declared *Victim* 'the most startlingly outspoken film Britain has ever produced. It may shock you. It may even disgust you. But it's a film that, sooner or later, had to be made, and deserves to be seen.' [36, 37, 38]

Other reviewers were less impressed. The regional press in northern England was particularly hostile. Sheffield's *The Star* called the scenes in The Chequers pub 'bizarre and frightening'. The *Yorkshire Post* thought that *Victim* was homosexual 'propaganda', and that it 'would have been just as good if it had contained no reference to perversion'. The *Financial Times* was disappointed that the 'cruel and unnecessary persecution' of gay men was 'hardly advanced by Janet Green and John McCormick's script, which is more concerned with hoodwinking audiences about the identity of the principal blackmailer than with any serious inquiry into the issues it professes to consider'. *The Guardian* likewise wished that, 'having taken the brave decision to deal with this perilous theme, the film makers had been just a little more charitable towards the homosexual "victims" of our laws; one senses that, in order to avoid outrage to the more backward sections of public opinion, they were a little less forthright in expressing their own real convictions.' James Breen in *The Observer* thought that the film was 'not primarily about homosexuality at all, but about blackmail, and it is shaped not as a social study but as a mild thriller. Mr Bogarde brings to it all an expression of gentle distress and a quantity of crows' feet and grey-streaked hair, but the film would have gained in dramatic guts if he had been more seriously implicated.' *Films and Filming* also criticised *Victim*'s timidity in dealing with homosexuality. But it did acknowledge the film's importance. [39, 40, 41, 42, 43]

> *Victim*, for all its faults, is a landmark in British cinema. The British have stopped being hypocrites and the censor has indicated that no subject, responsibly treated, is taboo. And when, as inevitably will happen, the law is changed and a man is no longer penalised for expressing his senses and sensibility as he will, *Victim* will have made its contribution to that understanding. [44]

Victim also made a positive contribution towards homosexual law reform. Antony Grey thought that it helped to raise public awareness of homosexuality at a time when 'the degree of unawareness of other people's sexuality was quite extraordinary'. Lord Arran, who later steered a reform bill through the House of Lords, thought it had 'a significant impact on the public', and that it 'probably made it easier to secure reform in the 1960s'. In 1968, after watching *Victim* 'on telly', Arran sent a letter to Dirk Bogarde expressing his admiration for his 'courage in undertaking this difficult and potentially damaging part'. He also told Bogarde that he thought the subsequent change in public opinion in favour of homosexual law reform was due in part to *Victim*. [45, 46, 47]

Audience reactions to the film were mixed. Kenneth Williams thought it 'all v. slick, same team as *Sapphire* (Relphs) and like that, superficial and never knocking the real issues. Never touching on what Kenneth Walker described as "playing out the tragedy of the heart alone, with no one knowing of their troubles."' John Fraser disliked *Victim* because 'I knew perfectly well it was all right to be gay, and I didn't need a film to tell me that.' Actor Dudley Sutton thought it was 'about blackmail, and it was about Dirk's hair style. And those awful little queens in the background. It brought in every cliché. I thought it was ghastly.' Others were even more scathing. According to the writer Christopher Isherwood, film producer James Woolf and director Tony Richardson 'hated' *Victim*. Woolf told Isherwood and fashion designer Raemonde Rahvis during a car journey to the house of actor and director Bryan Forbes (who co-owned Allied Film Makers), 'I can't imagine anything less interesting than a story about homosexuality.' Isherwood was disgusted by Woolf's hypocrisy:* 'How ugly! Disowning his nature like that, in the presence of outsiders. That's what causes persecutions.' [48, 49, 50, 51]

Other gay men were pleased and even grateful to see the film. John Chesterman remembered the sense of excitement when *Victim* was released: 'The minute anything came along in the way of a film that had any gay stuff in it, everybody went to it. The fact that it was often a very downbeat approach to the whole thing hardly mattered. All the gay people knew that Dirk Bogarde was gay. This was passed around as common knowledge. But the fact that he came out and acted in a movie about it was terrific.' Patrick Trevor-Roper saw the film at the Odeon, Leicester Square and remembered seeing groups of gay men waiting in a queue 'curling around the back' of the cinema. 'It seemed like a social party, with everyone's friends in it.' David George thought that *Victim* marked 'a really great improvement in our lives. It did make the general public aware of how difficult a homosexual life was, and how discreet and careful we had to be. It was an important film which helped enormously.' Screen writer and director Terence Davies recalled the effect of seeing *Victim* as a 15-year-old in Liverpool. [52, 53, 54]

> That moment when Dirk is in the police station and the policeman says, 'You of course knew that Barrett was a homosexual?' And the camera tracks in on Dirk and he says, 'Yes, I had gathered that.' 'Homosexual' was a word that no one ever said. The word in those days was 'queer', which was derogatory and very unpleasant. And I just thought, yes, and so am I. [55]

Both Dirk Bogarde and Peter McEnnery received many letters of thanks from gay men and their families. So did Relph and Dearden. Charles

---

* Woolf was gay and rumoured to be the lover of actor Laurence Harvey, whom he cast in numerous films

Holland from Amsterdam spoke for many when he wrote to them in February 1962: 'I am moved to thank you, and everyone concerned, especially Janet Green, John McCormick, Dirk Bogarde, Dennis Price, Sylvia Syms, Peter McEnnery, just about everyone for your fine, honest, beautiful film *Victim*. In a world, perhaps on the brink of a fall-out, it was most encouraging to have visual proof that there are strong, clean voices which are not afraid to be heard.' [56]

The film marked a watershed in the portrayal of homosexuality on film. For the first time, the public encountered gay men as ordinary, sympathetic individuals rather than as camp or sinister perverts. Tony Richardson may have hated *Victim,* but he benefitted from its pioneering passage through the censorship process while making his film version of Shelagh Delaney's play *A Taste of Honey*. Richardson's main difficulty in getting a BBFC certificate was the character of Geoff, who, a script reader warned in May 1960, should not be 'too "sexy" or too young in appearance'. John Trevelyan told producer Michael Holden in March 1961 that 'the cinema-going public here is not attracted by homosexuals on the screen. I am told that films dealing with homosexuality have not been a great success commercially. We have never had any ban on homosexuality on the screen, but, bearing in mind that the cinema-going public is in the main very different from theatre audiences, we usually suggest that where it is not a main theme but incidental, it should be suggested rather than directly shown.' Richardson, however, managed to reassure Trevelyan. [57, 58]

Certainly we don't intend to play Geoffrey in any excessively effeminate way and we will do everything we can to infer his abnormality and not force it on the audience. I do appreciate what you say about homosexuality in general and we will treat it in the most delicate way possible. However, I would remind you the same attitude does exist with theatre audiences, and it is only in the way that the character has been treated without sentimentality and with humour that has made the theme so attractive and appealing to people who have seen the play. In fact, watching it in America it was fascinating to see how completely the audience was won over by the character. In fact, they have always found it to be the most sympathetic character in the story. [59]

A Taste of Honey was given an 'X' certificate on 1 September 1961 and released two weeks later. It won the BAFTA award for best British film in 1962: and Murray Melvin received a best actor prize at the Cannes Film Festival for his portrayal of Geoff. Writing in the *Tribune*, Polish film maker Boleslaw Sulik thought that he played the role 'remarkably well', and that Geoff was 'a beautifully observed character, making Dirk Bogarde's recent film *Victim* look positively ridiculous'. Bogarde himself admitted as much to Melvin when the two of them worked together on the 1962 film *HMS Defiant*: 'You did more for the cause in one scene than the whole of bloody *Victim* put together.' [60, 61]

Geoff's gay identity is partly expressed by the way he dresses. In an early scene he walks into a shoe shop in Salford where Jo works.

Geoff: I want a pair of shoes.
Jo: What sort of shoes?
Geoff: Well, have you got any of them Italian…
Jo: Casuals?
Geoff: Yeh.
Jo: What size?
Geoff: Eight.
Jo: Any particular colour?
Geoff: No. Ay, nothing too startling. [62]

Geoff buys his Italian casuals for 18 shillings (reduced from 24s 11d) and later sports them at an Easter parade. The camera focuses in on them, and Jo instantly recognises both the shoes and their wearer.

Geoff's taste for foreign fashion was shared by a generation of young men. Michael Schofield noted in 1960 how 'in the last ten years there has been a marked change in men's clothing, especially in the lower social groups. The tendency has been for young men to wear informal clothes that accentuate the form of the male body. Ironically this has made it more, not less, difficult for one homosexual to recognise another. Ten years ago a man wearing, for example, very tight jeans would be suspected of dressing in a way that is said to be characteristic of the homosexual, but today a man whose mode of dress might have been considered ostentatious ten years ago would be horrified if it were suggested that he was "dressed up like a pansy".' [63]

Many of these young men styled themselves 'modernists', or 'mods' for short. Predominantly working class, they were inspired by French and Italian clothes and manners. The Fabulous Hoplite in Colin McInnes' 1959 novel *Absolute Beginners* is an early prototype. A former 'male whore's maid' who dabbles in a little 'freelancing' prostitution 'when conditions get too rough', he mainly supports himself and his clothes-buying habit by selling stories to newsapaper gossip columnists. He is 'handsome in an elfin, adolescent sort of style', witty, sharp-tongued, friendly and unashamedly gay. We first meet him 'nervously patting his hair, which was done in a new style of hair-do like as if a large animal had licked [his] locks down flat, then licked the tip of them over his forehead vertical up, like a cockatoo with its crest on back-to-front. He was wearing a pair of skin-tight, rubber-glove thin, almost transparent cotton slacks, white nylon-stretch and black wafer-sole casuals, and a sort of maternity jacket, I can only call it, coloured blue.' Later, the Hoplite arrives at a party in London's Knightsbridge wearing 'some Belafonte-style, straight-from-the-canefield (via the make-up room) kind of garments, with too many open necks, and tapering wrists, and shoes like tin-openers, all in light colours except for some splashes of mascara that gave his eyes melancholy and meaning'. [64]

By the time Gillian Freeman wrote *The Leather Boys* (1961) – a novel about 'two working class boys who fall in love' – the mod movement was in full swing. Dick is a fully fledged member. Less ostentatious than The Fabulous Hoplite, he is no less careful with his appearance. [65]

He liked to look really smart. He always took great care of his shoes, which he had hand-made and which cost him a lot of money. Tonight he was wearing a suit, but sometimes he wore a narrow-shouldered jacket with saddle stitching. He tied his tie carefully in front of the little looking-glass, and then bent his knees so that he could see to do his hair. It was thick and dark and wavy and grew to the tops of his ears. As he combed his hair he jutted his chin forward and narrowed his eyes. [66]

Philip Baker from Crawley in Sussex remembered the sense of daring and excitement of being a gay mod in the early 1960s.

I used to wear Italian suits with cloth buttons and a 'bum freezer' jacket. It was a smart outfit but I had to hide them from the couple I was fostered with, so I used to leave the house in one lot of clothes and go to a friend's to change. I also got my first pair of winkle-pickers. I went down to Devon and Cornwall with a friend on a scooter. I had a Lambretta. We used to enjoy ourselves. [67]

Most mods were not gay, but their obsession with appearance and their tendency to socialise in male-only groups meant that they were often assumed to be. 'In modernism you dressed for other blokes,' recalled Carlo Manzi. 'You were far more interested in a guy coming up and saying, "Great suit" than a girl coming up and saying, "Great suit", because the girls didn't look particularly good.' David May thought that 'there was a large gay element' in the mod movement. 'On Saturday afternoons we'd go to get our hair done in the women's hairdressers. We didn't fight rockers; we were far more interested in some guy's incredible shoes, or his leather coat.' Ken Browne also thought that there was 'a definite gay influence involved with the early mods. The London clubs would have a lot of gays in them wearing outrageous white suits with big high heels. Mods took that influence. It became a case of looking as pretty as possible, as nice as possible. They weren't that interested in girls. They were so wrapped up in themselves, interested in their scooters, clothes and pills. The clubs were just full of blokes.' Peter Burton agreed: 'The premier mod club – the Scene in Ham Yard – was basically a straight version of Le Duce. Those who frequented the Scene and Le Duce came from the same working class backgrounds. Both groups paid the same attention to clothes; both groups looked much alike. Not surprisingly, really, as their clothes came from the same shops.' [68, 69]

Carlo Manzi remembered shopping for clothes in London in the early 1960s: 'A mate of mine said, "You guys want to go down Carnaby Street, but watch it! It's full of poofs. It's where they go to get their clothes."' Another former mod remembered that in one shop he went to 'the only other person was a tall, well-dressed young negro who bought a pair of coloured denim hipster trousers. This negro was obviously homosexual and I realised that homosexuals had been buying that stuff for years. They were the only people with the nerve to wear it.' [70, 71]

Dressing in styles more commonly associated with gay men could cause mods trouble – as Carlo Manzi recalled: 'I bought a pink shirt. It had a giraffe collar and a tab front. I put it in the wash. The next day I went to get it and I couldn't find it. I said to my mum, "Where's that pink shirt?" She said, "I've torn it up. It's a duster now." I couldn't believe it. I said, "Why?" She said, "Because everyone will think you're a poof. I'll give you the money to buy a new shirt, but please don't buy pink."' Steve Marriott, lead singer of the pop group Small Faces, recalled having 'terrible rows with my dad for looking like a poof'. His mother Kay Marriott remembered: 'My Steve, the first time he wore white trousers, he was beaten up.' Mark Timlin knew about the risks of being a mod, but he thought that they were well worth taking. He recalled how, one payday, he and a friend went shopping for clothes: 'We both bought pink shirts. My mate took his back [and] got a white one because people were calling him a poof. But I thought, bollocks, I'm not taking mine back. So I wore mine on the Monday morning on the train to work. I was sweating. So many people were looking at me. I wore it with a blue knitted tie, a blue suit, Anello and Davide shoes. And I looked the business.' [72, 73]

Mods who were gay sometimes found themselves the focus of unwanted attention from the police. One man from Manchester told Michael Schofield, 'There's one policeman I know works on the traffic lights near my house. He sees me going home from work in all my dirty clothes. He sees me coming out of my house half an hour later dressed up to go to town. Then he knows I'm queer. He just gives me that filthy look.' George from Hove also remembered being targeted by the police: 'This guy, quite clearly a policeman in plain clothes, came up to me and said could he ask me questions about homosexuality? And I ran. I must have been pretty obvious for him to come up and do that. I was in tight black drainpipe trousers which were all the rage then, and brothel creepers and a cerise-coloured suede jacket.' [74, 75]

The lighter, brighter, tighter clothes beloved of gay and straight mods alike were often designed by gay men and stocked in shops owned and run by them. One of the first was Filk'n Casuals in Brighton, next to the Theatre Royal in Bond Street. It was run by Phil and Ken, who claimed to have trained in Paris – Phil at House of Worth. James from Brighton remembered the pair well: 'They were the first people to do beach shirts in gaudy, jazzy, Caribbean-type colours for gentlemen. Really, in those days you wouldn't be seen dead in that sort of thing. You'd be thought to be "that sort" of person. I can't think of anything in London quite as camp as that. They were so outrageous that it was always said that if you went to buy a tie, they'd measure your inside leg. Phil was always known as Rose Filk'n, and Ken was known as Esme Filk'n, and they really were very, very naughty.' [76]

The joke about buying a tie and being measured for an inside leg was supposedly first told by jazz singer George Melly in reference to Vince Man's Shop at 15 Newburgh Street in London's Soho. The shop (popularly known as Vince's) was opened in 1954 by Bill Green, who started out as a photographer taking physique pictures of young men who worked out at the nearby Marshall Street baths. In 1964 he told BBC Radio's *South East Special* how he had come to open Vince's.

> When I got demobbed I opened a studio, primarily to photograph children and actors and actresses. I used to carry on weight lifting at a gymnasium, and one day I was asked to photograph one of the boys at the club. Magazines started to use the pictures and asked me

to photograph other weightlifters. Now these boys used to turn up in rather unsuitable gear to be photographed in. So I got a girl friend to make some swimwear which I thought were right to photograph these boys in, and I kept them in the studio. They were actually made from women's roll-ons from a well-known chain store. They were cut down and made a very comfortable, very slick, very brief swim short so that boys could be photographed and would appear well. The result [was that] they all wanted to buy these swim trunks. I'd had to get these made wholesale, and we sold them. Within six months after that I had to close down the studio because the business on the swimwear, on the mail order side and people coming in to buy, had overwhelmed the whole thing. I was then in business, originally selling rather brief and – considered by many people – outrageous swimwear. Well, that was followed by a holiday in France, spending some of the ill-gotten gains from my swimwear business, in which I saw, in those days – this is the early fifties – that the younger people were wearing black jeans and black shirts. And I thought, this hasn't been seen in Britain. Everyone is so busy wearing blue jeans which they can smuggle in from America. So I got black jeans and black shirts and similar things made in this country, and they went like a bomb. I started designing stuff myself. People said the stuff was so outrageous that it would really only appeal and sell to the rather sort of eccentric Chelsea set, or theatrical way-out types. And my first shop, which I opened in October 1954, was given six weeks' life by the locals. [77]

The 'well-known chain store' was Marks and Spencer, and the 'eccentric Chelsea set' and 'theatrical way-out types' included actors and dancers from the nearby London Palladium. They were attracted by Green's innovative designs, colours and fabrics – narrow jeans, hipster trousers, light shirts, tight-fitting sweaters, polo-necks, matelot tops and snug briefs in bright red, yellow, purple, mustard, pale blue, pink and white, made from cotton, denim, suede, leather, velvet, silk and even bed ticking. Priced at about three guineas each, Green's trousers and shirts were not cheap. 'We catered to a very wide public, within an age range of 25 to 40,' he explained. 'They weren't teenagers, because teenagers couldn't meet our prices, but artists and theatricals, muscle boys and celebrities of every kind.' Clients included comedian Peter Sellers, actor Sean Connery (an early model for Vince's mail order catalogues), photographer Anthony Armstrong-Jones, boxer Billy Walker, artist Pablo Picasso and King Frederick IX of Denmark. Antiques dealer Christopher Gibbs remembered Vince's as 'faggy, theatrical, cock-a-snook at the folks who went there', but 'there was always enough of them to keep the show on the road'. Green advertised in gay-friendly magazines such as *Films and Filming*, and in 1960 he took out his first advertisement in a national newspaper, the *Daily Mirror*. 'It came out on Saturday,' he recalled, 'and on the Monday morning I took £200-worth of orders.' Green's clothes were stocked or copied by other shops, including Filk'n Casuals in Brighton, Bobby's in Bournemouth and Dale Cavana in London. He also secured wholesale contracts with department store Marshall and Snelgrove. [78, 79]

The association between men's fashion and gay identity was understood by clothing retailers, who deliberately targeted their merchandise at gay as well as straight men. Vince's catalogues were famous for their suggestive advertisements and photographs of attractive male models. A 1961 catalogue, for example, featured the 'torso shirt' – a tight white T-shirt 'with bicep-baring sleeves'. The shop's 'Corsair slacks' were described as 'beautifully cut Bermuda style (and that means made for a close fit everywhere)'. Retail rival Donis Man's Shop (with branches at 23 Carnaby Street and 156 Kensington Church Street) was similarly risqué. [80]

Top designers engaged by Donis have spent much time in gay and colourful Spain capturing the enchantment and romance, paying detailed attention to the trends which will be sure to dominate your wardrobe this year.

Gay beach colours in fine quality stretch nylon, this superb swim brief in colours Royal, black, sky blue and coral. [81]

The designer and retailer who made the most of the profitable crossover between gay fashion sensibility and popular consumerism was John Stephen. Born in Glasgow the sixth of nine children, Stephen briefly worked as a welder's apprentice before moving to London aged 18 in 1952. His first retail job was as a salesman in the military department of Moss Bros in King Street, Covent Garden. In 1955 he worked as a sales assistant at Vince's, and then for Nicholas Perry, helping him to set up and manage a boutique in Blandford Street, Marylebone. It was at this time that Stephen met his boyfriend and future business partner Bill Franks. In 1956 the pair pooled their £300 savings and rented a room on the second floor of a building at 19 Beak Street, Soho. They called the shop His Clothes and stocked items similar to the most popular designs at Vince's. When fire destroyed their stock the following year, Stephen and Franks moved to empty premises at nearby 5 Carnaby Street. The rent was cheap and the shop had a workroom at the back and a large window at the front to display merchandise. At the time, Carnaby Street was a shabby back street with small tailoring workshops, locksmiths and an electricity depot. But Vince's had already marked the area out as a shopping district for specialist menswear, and Soho was home to several gay clubs and coffee bars. Stephen's and Franks' masterstroke was to sell stylish clothes more cheaply and in larger quantities than their rivals, including Green, and to target them at the emerging youth market. His Clothes was bright, colourful and friendly. 'When we first started we didn't think about success,' recalled Franks. 'We were having fun. We had so little money that when we took over the first shop all we could do was paint the shop front canary yellow, so it stood out in the dreary back streets, and make the fixtures and fittings ourselves from old orange boxes, which we covered in felt.' [82]

In 1960 Stephen opened John Stephen The Man's Shop at numbers 49 to 51 Carnaby Street, and he employed Myles Antony as a window dresser. Antony later became art director for the John Stephen group, responsible for interior designs and displays. Mike McGrath was also hired as a publicist. He knew both John Stephen and Bill Green and understood the latter's eclipse by his one-time employee: 'There was a noticeable difference between Bill Green, who had started the whole thing, and John Stephen, who had worked for him in that shop. The problem was that Bill Green had this objectionable personality, which was tragic because his stuff was so good. In the 50s his summer and winter catalogues were the nearest to a gay publication because anybody who fancied men would pounce on these catalogues, and would be impressed by the clothes, and buy them. If he'd had a nicer personality and knew how to get on with people better, he could have been the one who took over. But John Stephen did because he was a totally different, very humble young man.' In 1961 Green moved Vince's to larger premises in Foubert's Place, around the corner from Carnaby Street. He eventually left the fashion business and opened a restaurant called Auntie's in Fitzrovia. John Stephen, meanwhile, took over most of Carnaby Street and opened further retail outlets in Regent Street, Old Compton Street, Old Bailey Street, Queensway, Earls Court Road, Kings Road, Loughton High Road and East Street in Brighton. [83]

Modernism went mainstream with a feature in *Town* magazine in September 1962. Journalist Peter Barnsley and photographer Donald McCullin profiled three young mods from Stoke Newington, north London – 15-year-old Mark Feld (later glam rocker Mark Bolan), Peter Sugar and Michael Simmonds, both aged 20. 'The most important thing in the world to them is their clothes,' wrote Barnsley. 'They have cupboards and shelves bulging with suits and shirts often designed by themselves in bright, strange and violent colours. In their vocabulary they, and the few other contemporaries of whom they approve, are described as "faces" – the necessary ingredients are youth, a sharp eye for dressing, and a general lack of mercy towards the rest of the world.' Feld claimed he owned 'ten suits, eight sports jackets, fifteen pairs of slacks, thirty to thirty-five good shirts, about twenty jumpers, three leather jackets, two suède jackets, five or six pairs of shoes and thirty exceptionally good ties'. Sugar explained that some of their clothes were specially made for them by Harry Bilgorri, a tailor on Bishopsgate in the City of London. 'We're all a bit exhibitionist,' he admitted. 'Some of our clothes are a bit effeminate but they have to be. I mean you have to be a bit camp.' Feld added, 'You get a lot of jeers and shouts round our way. If you wear something that's a bit different it's "Nancy" and "Look at that queer".' He also expressed his admiration for John Stephen: 'You've got to hand it to him. All those shops and he's still only 26 or something.' [84]

The 'king of Carnaby Street' himself always dressed in a classic dark suit, white shirt and tie. Occasionally – as during an appearance with pop group Manfred Mann on BBC 1's *A Whole Scene Going* in 1966 and during a fashion trip to Milan with Mary Quant the same year – he wore some of his own with-it wares. But sartorially and personally Stephen kept a low profile. Few knew that he shared his flat in Jermyn Street with Bill Franks. Like many of his gay contemporaries in the business and entertainment worlds, he colluded in a manufactured image of heterosexual possibility, as suggested in an interview he gave to teenage girls' magazine *Boyfriend* in 1966. [85]

> Quiet and unassuming, he appears more of a courtier than a king. He's got a funny, spluttery laugh that's infectious, and bites his fingernails. His best feature are grey/blue eyes that are very direct. He doesn't talk all the time, but if he misses a point in the conversation, he likes to recap just to make sure. [86]

Under Stephen's influence shopping became a fun, liberating experience – in contrast to the 1950s, when buying clothes was an awkward, furtive activity often carried out by mothers, wives or girlfriends. Stephen's shops were relaxed, trendy places where record players spun the latest hits and where film, pop and sports stars hosted new openings, special events and promotions. Shop assistants dressed in John Stephen designs and were young, good looking and often gay. In Montague Haltrecht's 1964 novel *Jonah and his Mother* 18-year-old Jonah is taken by his older lover Gray Linton to a men's fashion boutique, where he experiences the thrill of buying a new outfit.

> An assistant came forward. Gray spoke to him, and he went to a hanging case and drew back a curtain. Jonah's heart beat faster when he saw a row

of suede sleeves, gracefully inanimate. He unbuttoned his jacket, and Gray helped him off with it. The assistant took a suede jacket from the rail and slid it over his arms, fitted it on his shoulders, smoothed it over his chest. He paraded across the floor and looked in the mirror. [87]

Older men, too, adopted the new 'dandy' style of dress. Thirty-one-year-old Leonard in *The Youngest Director* spends much of his time and money on looking good.

Leonard checked the detail of his dress. Button-two dark blue suit, plain navy tie, spotless white shirt and dark brown suede shoes. He was not sure about the shoes. Glancing at his watch, he opened the cupboard in the wall opposite the window and took out a pair of black pointed shoes. He sat on the edge of the double bed, made the change, then surveyed the results in the mirror. He approved. [88]

Fifty-year-old antiques dealer Gray Linton also swings with the times. He is sharply critical of his younger shop assistant for his stuffy, old-fashioned dress sense: 'Why does he wear a pin-stripe suit in this weather? Doesn't he see what's going on in the world about him? Things are changing. You don't have to be so formal nowadays. At his age he should wear a suede jacket. He'd look quite nice in it.' HLRS committee member Norman St John-Stevas recalled how as a 35-year-old prospective parliamentary candidate he wore a brightly coloured shirt, tie and tasselled shoes to the selection committee meeting of the Chelmsford Conservative Association in 1964. A member of the committee later remarked, 'They sent us three people to choose from: a woman, a drunk and a queer. Of course, we had to take the queer.' In a further sign of how outward appearances had changed, a 'homo' told the *Evening Standard* in July 1964, 'Fifteen years ago almost anyone wearing light trousers and coloured ties and shirts was probably gay. But now the normals have taken over our kind of dressing and you simply can't tell from clothes any more.' [89, 90, 91]

As well as blurring homo- and heterosexual distinctions, gay-inspired fashion did much to break down class barriers. In 1965 US magazine *Business Week* noted that in Britain 'the population explosion and cultural upheavals have caused fashion to flow up from the masses and young people for the first time, instead of filtering down from the upper classes.' This is reflected in the way Leonard and his working class boyfriend John in *The Youngest Director* dress for a lunch with Leonard's parents and his company chairman. Whereas separate dress codes would once have set them apart, fashion now unites them against traditional values and authority. [92]

> They both took special care with their dress, Leonard wearing a new glen-check grey suit, red tie and brown suede shoes, John a suede jacket and narrow grey trousers. Leonard wondered for a moment whether John ought to wear a light suit, then decided that the opulent jacket would provide more of a challenge to the chairman. [93]

As appearance became a less reliable indicator of sexuality, writers, film makers and social commentators looked for other ways of identifying gay men. Physical and behavioural traits such as soft hands, cooking, sewing, artistic pursuits and an interest in sports were instead flagged up as tell-tale signs. In Lynne Reid Banks' 1960 novel *The L-Shaped Room* Caribbean immigrant John at first seems quite ordinary to Jane Graham, who lives next door to him in a shabby London bedsitter. But her boyfriend Toby points out some suspect traits.

> 'He's got those great brutal-looking hands that you'd think could snap your backbone like a twig, and then when he shakes hands with you and you feel them, damn me, they're like a baby's bottom. And you see him handling anything delicate – well, like an egg, for instance. He's a first-class cook, old John, you must get him to make you an omelette one day, and just watch him break those eggs. He does needlework too.' [94]

Dick Snape in Andrew Salkey's 1960 novel *Escape to an Autumn Pavement* has 'long fingers with manicured nails', and he handles a saucepan with 'brisk housewife movements'. Johnny Burney in J.R.

Ackerley's 1960 autobiographical novel *We Think the World of You* is a married working class lad with three children, but he too has 'very well-shaped hands, slender yet strong'. In Harold Pinter's 1961 television play *The Collection* Bill Lloyd is suspect because he is a dress designer, 'a man of taste' and an opera fan. TV make-up man Joe (Aubrey Lloyd) in Robert Muller's 1962 television play *Afternoon of a Nymph* flutters around actress Elaine in her dressing room. 'I'd love to be made a fuss of,' he lisps enviously. 'I suppose that's why I went into this business in the first place. You know, it must be really nice being a pretty girl like you.' Later he covetously holds up Elaine's dress in front of himself. [95, 96, 97, 98, 99]

Sandy Youth, the moped-riding, leather clad blackmailer in *Victim*, listens to classical music, practices boxing with a punch ball and has a picture of Michelangelo's David on his living room wall (itself hung with fashionable textured wallpaper). Ed and Sloane in Joe Orton's 1964 play *Entertaining Mr Sloane* similarly share a passion for boxing, wrestling and bodybuilding. In Philip King's 1963 play *How Are You Johnnie?* Derbyshire lorry driver Les Thornton proudly tells his workmate Johnnie Leigh's mother that he can 'cook as good a dinner as you can. *And* I do my own washing and mending.' He later proves his skill by sewing on a shirt button for Johnnie. In Terence Rattigan's play *Man and Boy* (1963) company director Mark Herries is supposed to be a 'silly, pink-faced old fairy' because he has 'literary leanings', and because there is 'something bohemian' about him. Likewise, newly-wed Lancashire lad Arthur Fitton in Bill Naughton's play *All In Good Time* (1963; adapted from his 1961 television play *Honeymoon Postponed*) rouses the disapproval of his father Ezra with his 'fancy music, fancy readin' and fancy bloody talk'. In David Storey's 1960 novel *This Sporting Life* and in Lindsay Anderson's 1963 film version of the book Mrs Hammond thinks that rugby league scout 'Dad' Johnson (William Hartnell) is 'unusual' because he has 'awful hands. They're all soft.' She tells her tenant and lover Arthur Machin (Frank in the film) that the old man ogles him 'like a girl'. Factory boss and rugby club owner Gerald Weaver is also 'supposed to be a fairy' because he watches the rugby players in the bath and does a lot of 'patting and arms-on-your-shoulder stuff'. He also has a 'short mincing stride'. In the film Weaver (Alan Badel) further demonstrates his suspect sexuality by putting his hand on Machin's knee while giving him a lift in his car. [100, 101, 102, 103, 104]

Gerald Weaver was the sort of predatory 'toucher' whom psychologist Richard Hauser warned people about in his 1962 book *The Homosexual Society*. The book defined 37 'homosexual types', including several subcategories. [105]

- The Bisexual
- The Married Man
- The Upper-Class Married Man
- The Middle-Class Married Man
- The Working-Class Married Man
- The Demoralized Married Man
- The Young Bisexual
- The Self-Isolated Homosexual
- The Fully Sublimated Homosexual or Bisexual
- The Homosexual Prostitute (including The Young Volunteer, The Call-boy, The 'Cottage' type, The Club and Pub Prostitute and The 'Roller')
- Sugar Daddies
- 'Married' Homosexual Partners ('who form a husband and wife relationship with one partner playing a feminine role and looking after the home')
- The Pub Type
- The Club Type
- The Homosexual 'Friend'
- The Prison Queer
- The Ship's Queer
- The War Queer
- The Homosexual Alcoholic
- The 'Guilty' Homosexual
- The Religious Homosexual
- The Paedophiliac

- The Psycopath
- The 'Cottage' Type
- The Self-Masturbator
- The Homosexual Voyeur
- The Sado-Masochist
- The 'Abnormal' Homosexual
- The 'Toucher'
- The Promiscuous Homosexual
- The Rebel
- The Woman Hater
- The Homosexual 'Virgin Chaser'
- The 'Body-builder'
- The True Transvestist
- The False Transvestist
- The Mentally Sick Homosexual [106]

Journalists, too, popularised the idea that gay men conformed to particular types. In February 1962 Jack Miller of the *News of the World* speculated that the 'wardrobe killer' of Norman Rickard and Alan Vigar was either 'a "Ronson lighter", which is what a puff calls the pimp who finds clients for him; a blackmailer; a homosexual whose lust suddenly turned to murderous frenzy; or, I suspect, a man who hates homos with the same soul-torturing bitterness that Jack the Ripper hated prostitutes.' Following the publication of the Radcliffe Report on the Vassall spy case in April 1963, Lionel Crane of the *Sunday Mirror* wrote a guide on 'How To Spot A Possible Homo'. He explained that gay men were either 'obvious' or 'concealed'. [107, 108]

OBVIOUS: Those who dye their hair, touch up their lips, and walk with a gay little wiggle could be spotted by a One-Eyed Jack on a foggy day in Blackwall Tunnel.
CONCEALED: They wear silk suits and sit up at chi-chi bars with full bosomed ladies. Or they wear hairy sports jackets and give their wives a black eye when they get back from the working men's club.

THEY wrestle, play golf, ski and work up great knots of muscles lifting weights. They are married, have children. THEY are everywhere, and they can be anybody. [109]

Crane went on to list eight specific types:

1. THE MIDDLE-AGED MAN, unmarried, who has an unnaturally strong affection for his mother.
2. The man who has a consuming interest in youth. He is ready to give ALL his spare time to working and talking with boys or youths.
3. THE CRAWLER. The 'umble man, the man who is always saying he's nothing and everybody else is marvellous, the man with the fixed and meaningless smile on his face. A prime suspect.
4. THE FUSSY DRESSER. When one, two or three button jackets are in, he is the first to wear them. His shirts are detergent bright, his tie has the latest knot and he is always just so, and he can never pass a mirror or a shop window without a sly glance at himself.
5. THE OVER-CLEAN MAN. His cheeks are smooth, his hair sparkles, his nails are manicured and he washes his hands a dozen times a day.
6. The man who is ADORED BY OLDER WOMEN.
7. The man in the bar WHO DRINKS ALONE and is forever looking at other customers over the top of his glass.
8. THE TOUCHER. The man who is always putting his hand on another man's shoulder or arm. [110]

The following year Noyes Thomas compiled his own list of 'popular suspects' for the *News of the World*. [111]

1. The man who has never married, shows little interest in women and lives alone, or with another man or perhaps his mother;

2. The fussy dresser, always slightly ahead of fashion, who pays what seems to be a little too much attention to his hair, face, manicure and so on;

3. The office or factory 'crawler', always ready to oblige, always ready with a smooth word, always with a fixed, smarmy grin on his face;

4. The man with an apparently excessive interest in youth activities;

5. The man who doesn't seem able to resist pawing you as he talks – the hand on the shoulder, the pat on the back, the clutch at your arm. [112]

With such wide ranging definitions, straight men sometimes found themselves wrongly accused of being gay. David Avery, a Conservative London councillor, remembered how, as an MI5 officer at the time of the Vassall inquiry, he received a knock on the door from a special branch police officer who wanted to interview him to find out if he was homosexual and therefore a security risk. The officer revealed that the source of the allegation was the secretary of state for the colonies, Duncan Sandys, who had noticed that Avery 'smoked his cigarettes like a woman'. [113]

The Vassal case prompted numerous descriptions in the press of gay men as weak, vain, blackmail-prone traitors. In October 1962 John Deane Potter of the *News of the World* described the 38-year-old spy as an 'evil elf', 'a creature from the twilight' and 'a member of the third sex to whom the ordinary human values mean nothing'. He added, 'What had all these words like patriotism and loyalty to do with him? Why should they mean anything, when other words like love and marriage meant even less?' In *The Meaning of Treason* (1965) Rebecca West wrote that Vassall evoked 'the image of homosexuality as it appears to all interested inhabitants of a great city, fascinating and repellent. Because of him the public imagination was haunted by visions of the slender figure in sweater and tight jeans who lurks in the shadow by the wall, just outside the circle of the lamplight, whisks down the steps of the tube-station lavatory, and with a backward glance under the long lashes offers pleasure and danger.' [114, 115]

Similar stereotypes found their way into John Osborne's 1965 play *A Patriot For Me*. The drama centres on the real historical figure of Alfred Redl, a homosexual counter-intelligence officer in the Austro-Hungarian army in the years before the First World War. Redl was blackmailed and paid large sums of money by Russian agents to betray military secrets before being unmasked in 1913. Rather than stand trial and dishonour the army and the empire, he was persuaded to shoot himself. Osborne's playscript was based on *The Panther's Feast* (1959), a fictionalised biography of Redl by the American military historian Robert Asprey. With its descriptions of Redl's lavishly furnished Prague apartment (which had 'the very strong odour of perfume') and his secret collection of women's clothes, the book prefigured journalists' revelations about Vassall's flat in Dolphin Square. [116]

A Patriot For Me created a *cause célèbre*, thanks to the Lord Chamberlain's outright refusal to give it a licence. Osborne's plays had caused problems for the censor before. In 1964 *Inadmissible Evidence* was inadvertently passed for performance despite a scene in which the character John Maples tells his solicitor about a sexual encounter he had with an employee in the back of a car. *A Patriot For Me* was more problematic, however. According to script reader Charles Heriot, it was 'a perfect example of a piece which might corrupt, since it reveals nearly all the details of the homosexual life usually left blank even in the newspaper reports.' He also thought that its blend of pity and special pleading for legal change made it 'the Pansies' Charter of Freedom'. The Lord Chamberlain refused to give The English Stage Company a licence to perform the play at the Royal Court theatre in London unless large sections of dialogue and whole scenes – including a drag ball in Act Two – were cut. Despite pleas from Arts Council chairman Lord Goodman, drama critic and author Harold Hobson, Edinburgh Festival director Lord Harewood and National Theatre director Laurence Olivier, the Lord Chamberlain (since 1963 the former Bank of England governor Lord Cobbold) held firm. The Royal Court responded by temporarily turning itself into a theatre club, enabling it to stage *A Patriot For Me* for audiences who signed up as members. [117]

This exploitation of a legal loophole outraged the Lord Chamberlain. On 11 August 1965 he sent comptroller Eric Penn to see the play. Although Penn noted the presence in the audience of the Lord Chancellor, Lord Gardiner, and his wife, he thought that the play was primarily 'devised to give homosexuals pleasure at seeing their own life depicted on the stage'. He concluded: 'I do not think that the tolerance of homosexuality in this country has yet reached a point where this play, in its present form, is suitable for public performance.' Charles Heriot agreed. He told Penn that 'the homosexual scenes, especially the "drag" ball would certainly attract all the perverts in London, and might even persuade the young and ignorant that such a life might not be so bad after all.' [118, 119]

But the Lord Chamberlain misread both the play and the public mood. *A Patriot For Me*'s director Anthony Page remembered that the Royal Court was 'absolutely packed out' for performances. 'The audience was largely old women. They absolutely adored it. It was very successful. You couldn't get tickets for it.' It also jointly won the *Evening Standard* award for best play, along with Frank Marcus's lesbian-themed *The Killing of Sister George*. Even the Lord Chamberlain's assistant comptroller John Johnston, who went to see a performance on 12 July, was surprised to find the theatre 'full, and the audience more sophisticated than I had expected'. Three days earlier, Ronald Brydon wrote in the *New Statesman*: 'Osborne has taken queerness as his subject precisely as Nabokov took the love of pubescent girls or Henry James the *donnée* of American innocence in Europe. He has rendered it for all it is worth, for its exoticism, spectacle, irony and sentiment: for its *interest*. And what, for God's sake, is wrong with that? It *is* interesting. Redl's country was as wrong 50 years ago as ours still is today.' A month later Arnold Goodman told the Lord Chamberlain that *A Patriot For Me* had 'an important topicality at this moment of time when the whole issue of the position of the homosexual in society is under discussion'. [120, 121, 122, 123]

Gay men, however, thought that the play was patronising and that it took an overly stereotypical view of their lives. Anthony Page considered it a 'very emotional, almost hysterical play'. Nicholas Wright, a future Royal Court director, called it 'a lousy play; and the gay stuff was absolute rubbish'. Derek Jarman remembered that for him the theatre generally in the mid-1960s was 'of no interest'. Plays, he recalled, 'reduced us to a load of laughable pantomime drag queens'. Traditional representations of gay men as comic, pathetic or repressed loners certainly persisted. In Peter Shaffer's *Black Comedy* (1965) antiques shop owner Harold Corringe is a camp clown. Stage directions require him to be 'possessive', 'emotional' and 'hysterical'. Ageing couple Charles Dyer and Harry Leeds in Charles Dyer's *Staircase* (1966) are even camper and more pitiable. Charles Heriot was not initially inclined to give the play a licence, but John Johnston thought that the 'comic setting' and the absence of 'offensive action' rendered it harmless and unlikely to corrupt anyone. In Noel Coward's *A Song of Twilight* (1966) Hugo Latymer is similarly anodyne because Coward (admiringly described by Heriot as 'the Old Master in tremendous form') took care to only gradually and discreetly reveal his homosexuality in the course of an old-fashioned drawing room plot set in a high class Swiss hotel. [124, 125, 126, 127, 128, 129]

The censor had more trouble with Joe Orton's *Loot* (another *Evening Standard* award winner in 1966). It was only given a licence after Orton and his producers met with John Johnston twice, in April and September 1965, to confirm dialogue cuts and substitutions. In any case, the principal characters Hal and Dennis only have a vaguely homosexual relationship. 'I don't want there to be anything queer or camp or odd about the relationship of Hal and Dennis,' Orton later explained. 'They must be perfectly ordinary boys who happen to be fucking each other. Nothing could be more natural.' The homosexual tension between Ian and Jimmy in *When Did You Last See My Mother?* (1966), written by 20-year-old student Christopher Hampton, is more explicit. This prompted the Lord Chamberlain to require whole passages to be cut. Charles Heriot also warned, 'This piece should be watched to prevent its unspeakable little author from getting away with anything'. The censor's feathers were further ruffled when the *Daily Telegraph*'s drama critic W.A. Darlington mistakenly referred to an end-of-scene fight and hug between Ian and Jimmy as 'a pair of young homosexuals locked in an embrace'. The confusion was only cleared up when the manager of the Comedy Theatre in London confirmed that 'before the final curtain there is no more than a spontaneous hug between the two young men'. The Lord Chamberlain duly notified his staff: 'No further action is called from us. The manager says he has had no complaints from patrons. What a relief!' [130, 131, 132, 133]

The problem of embraces between men again arose with a German language production of Frank Wedekind's 1891 play *Spring Awakening*. The Bremen Theatre Company was due to perform it at the Aldwych Theatre in London in 1967 as part of the Royal Shakespeare Company's World Theatre Season, but the censor forbade any 'embrace or other physical act of affection' between the characters Hans Rilow and Ernst Robel. Protests by the Bremen company that the play had been 'put on all over Europe for the last 60 years without alterations being made' and their threat to pull out of the planned visit prompted the intervention of the RSC and the cultural relations department of the Foreign Office. A hasty compromise was reached whereby 'one slight kiss' was allowed between the two boys. [134, 135, 136]

The British film industry was more daring in its treatment of homosexuality. In January 1964 the film version of Gillian Freeman's *The Leather Boys* was finally released after being kept on hold for almost a year. Freeman adapted her original gay romance to make more of the marriage difficulties of Reggie (Colin Campbell) and Dot, but she also scripted scenes which dealt frankly and sensitively with the unrequited love of Pete (Dick in the novel, played by Dudley Sutton) for his pal Reggie. The BBFC approved the final screenplay with few changes, even allowing a scene in which Reggie meets Pete's gay merchant navy friends at a dockside pub. But to avoid 'any over-emphasis on the homosexual angle', Pete's final line to Reggie – 'I love you' – was cut. Nevertheless, under Sidney J. Furie's direction the film stepped beyond the limits of what was permissible in the theatre by showing Pete and Reggie in bed together – albeit as mates lodging at Reggie's grandmother's house. The significance of the scene, however, was not lost on cinema audiences.

Edward Thorpe remembered seeing the film at the Empire in Leicester Square, London: 'There were a lot of motorcycle people, and there were quite a lot of noises – cheers and things – when they were in bed together.' *The Leather Boys* was well-received by critics. Dilys Powell of *The Sunday Times* praised Sutton's 'splendid performance which, with its complexity of feeling, would have been unthinkable in the British cinema of 20 years ago.' The *Spectator* thought that Pete was 'the antithesis of the general notion of a homosexual as frail and sissy', and that 'between them Mr Furie and Mr Sutton have made a film about loneliness so acute that it spills over from the particular to the universal rather than vice versa, as generally happens in pictures with a "problem" (like *Victim*, for instance).' [137, 138, 139, 140, 141]

While *The Leather Boys* broke boundaries by showing men in bed together, Gerry O'Hara's 1965 film *The Pleasure Girls* went a step further by featuring two gay men in an embrace. For director and screen writer O'Hara it was 'natural' to include gay couple Paddy (Tony Tanner) and Ivor (John Hanson) in his film about a weekend in the lives of young people sharing a house in west London. 'I knew so many gay people,' he recalled. 'What was the difference?' In the original script the scene in which Sally rushes into Paddy's and Ivor's room after a row with her boyfriend Keith made it clear that the two men had been 'engaging in a physical relationship'. O'Hara also remembered filming Paddy and Ivor kissing, but this was cut before the film's release in May 1965. [142, 143]

The first on-screen gay kiss in a British cinema did not take place until 7 November 1965, when the London Film Festival screened *Dream A40* at the Odeon, Leicester Square. Now regarded as a gay classic, *Dream A40* was an experimental 16-minute short by Jamaican-born actor and director Lloyd Reckord. It follows a young gay couple (Nicholas Wright and Michael Billington) on a road trip up the A40, which develops into a guilt fantasy after a girl travelling in another car sees them holding hands. At the end of the film Billington's character finds Wright hanging by a rope around his neck. He gently takes him down and kisses him on the mouth. Speaking decades later, Reckord remembered 'the fear and the guilt that gay people had. I wanted to show that. Why should a certain set of people have to live like that, with fear, and looking over one's shoulder?' Nicholas Wright also recalled working on the film: 'I was an out of work actor, and there was hardly any work. I went to see Lloyd and he sort of explained it to me and asked me if I'd do it, and of course I said yes. I didn't get paid for it. There was no money at all. I didn't meet Michael [Billington] until the first day we were shooting. He was very attractive, and we sort of got talking. And I was thinking, "Oh, is he gay? He's really rather sexy." And then he said to me, "Have you ever heard of a singer called Judy Garland?" I said yes, and thought well, he's obviously not gay! He said, "Because I'm going out with her daughter, Liza." So that was it. We shot it over about seven or eight days, something like that. We never discussed the gay issue at all.' [144, 145]

1965 also saw the release of director John Schlesinger's Oscar-winning film *Darling*. It too features an 'ordinary, fun guy who happens to be gay' – photographer Malcolm (played by Roland Curram). Although Malcolm's homosexuality is obvious – to the extent of him sharing a waiter boyfriend with friend and model Diana Scott while on holiday in Capri – it does not define him as a character. Actor Antony Sher saw the film in South Africa when he was 16 and was deeply affected by it. 'I watched *Darling* in a strange state of shock,' he recalled. 'There was a gay character, played by Roland Curram, and when he and Julie Christie take a Mediterranean holiday, he exchanges a funny look with the handsome waiter over breakfast one morning – a look I'd never seen before – and then the waiter comes to collect him on a scooter and they drive off into the night. They're going to have sex. You don't see it, but you know it.' [146, 147]

The possibility of having a gay son was gently broached in the 1966 comedy-drama *The Family Way*. Produced by John Boulting and directed by his brother Roy, the film was based on the 1963 play *All In Good Time* by Bill Naughton, who also wrote the screenplay. Marjorie Rhodes reprised her role as Lucy Fitton, defending her son Arthur (Hywel Bennett) from his father Ezra's insinuation that there is 'something very odd and very queer' about his love of Beethoven and reading. The film also hints at an ambiguous past relationship between Ezra (John Mills) and his former best friend Billy Stringfellow, who, it is intimated, might be Arthur's real father. When Arthur's parents-in-law, the Pipers, come to discuss Arthur's failure to consummate his marriage to their daughter, Lucy questions the nature of Ezra's friendship with Billy. [148]

> Lucy: Would you say there was anything odd or queer about a fella that went on honeymoon and took his pal with him?
> Mrs Piper: Another man?
> Mr Piper: On his honeymoon?
> Ezra: Do you mean Billy Stringfellow?
> Lucy: Who else? Just because our Arthur's marriage hasn't gone right yet, you've no call to talk about him being queer. The lad's no more odd and queer than you and Billy were. And goodness knows what that must have looked like. [149]

While films were beginning to include gay men in their portrayals of mainstream society, television was exploring the legal and personal challenges they faced. The BBC police series *Z Cars* was the first TV drama to include a gay storyline. In an episode called 'Somebody… Help' Frank Wood (John Paul), a middle-aged man living in the fictional Lancashire town of Newtown, is blackmailed about his homosexuality, but he is unwilling to seek help from the police. The episode was scripted by regular *Z Cars* writer John Hopkins and broadcast live on BBC 1 on 3 June 1964. The programme no longer exists and the script is lost, but an idea of its content can be gained from an article written by Hopkins for *Radio Times* that week.

> If your house was broken into, valuable property stolen, and you could not go to the police and ask them to help you get it back, to whom could you go? If you were stopped on the way home and beaten up and you could not tell the police, whom could you tell? This is the nature of the predicament which faces Frank Wood in tonight's *Z Cars* story. A man attempts to blackmail him. Wood has only to go to the police, tell them, and they will make every possible effort to catch the man. Given

normal circumstances Wood's course of action is plain but Wood is a homosexual, a man outside the law, unable to go to the police without incriminating himself. If he reveals the attempt to blackmail him he will also reveal why he is being blackmailed. Then he faces trial, possible conviction, prison, probation anyway, the certainty of local scandal, even the end of his business career. The man who preys on anyone like Wood can count on his reluctance to go to the police in nine cases out of ten, 'screw' money out of him until there is no money left and then pass on to the next victim. In nine cases out of ten he can practise safely, secretly, until the tenth man stands up and says, 'No.' [150]

A BBC file on the episode gives further details about the characters. Frank Wood is in his 40s, a 'respectable estate agent type, quiet and intense, slight'. His principal blackmailer, Peter Howe, lives in a bedsit. Another blackmailer called Price is in his 30s, 'rough' and married to an 'uncouth' woman. According to the file, Wood is 'upset, unsure of his action – tries to withdraw the complaint – and then gathers his courage to make a charge.' [151]

> He confesses that he is homosexual and is being blackmailed. The police visit Howe, who denies that he is blackmailing Wood. Howe is also homosexual, admits that he is a friend of Frank Wood and says that Wood is making the charge out of jealousy. He refuses to come to the police station or to have anything to do with it. It is one word against another. [152]

The file also notes that 'the story is careful and restrained and deals with the dilemma of Wood – faced on the one side with blackmail and on the other with confession to the police and the personal consequences of a trial'. The episode prompted some debate, and also several complaints. In an article in the Edinburgh *Evening News Despatch* on 20 June, journalist Alexander Reid referred to 'protests at a recent issue of *Z Cars* when the miseries that result from the present British laws relative to homosexuality were dramatised'. A week later a *Manchester Evening*

News reader complained that *Z Cars* had 'glorified the hideousness of homosexuality – the crime condemned in the Bible as an abomination before God. Two characters in *Z Cars* were "homos" – unashamed and vile – and I say that the BBC ought to have more taste and better regards for standards.' [153, 154, 155]

John Hopkins dealt with homosexuality again in his Wednesday Play *Horror of Darkness*, filmed in 1964 but not broadcast on BBC 1 until March 1965. The play was directed by Anthony Page and centres on the fraught relationship between commercial artist Peter Young (Alfred Lynch), his girlfriend Cathy and Peter's old art school friend Robin Fletcher (Nicol Williamson) after Robin turns up unexpectedly at the couple's home. Towards the end of the play Robin admits his love for Peter – the first such declaration on British television. Robin eventually leaves Cathy and Peter. Later his partner Philip Moss (Wallas Eaton) arrives to tell them that Robin has killed himself. Anthony Page remembered that the play was delayed for broadcast for a year 'because Nicol said "I love you" to Alfred Lynch. That was very shocking at the time, to the BBC at any rate.' [156, 157]

In 1965 the BBC also began broadcasting what became one of its most popular radio shows. *Round the Horne* was created by writers Barry Took and Marty Feldman and featured Kenneth Horne as the eponymous presenter. Episode four introduced the characters Julian and Sandy (Hugh Paddick and Kenneth Williams) – the first fictional gay couple to regularly appear in a radio or television series. Billed as a pair of out-of-work actors, the camp duo ('Oh hello, I'm Julian and this is my friend Sandy') introduced Horne in a variety of gay enterprises, invariably prefixed by the gay slang (polari) word 'bona'. They included Bona Books, Bona Guest House, Bona Caterers and Bona Nature Clinic. The pair's banter was risqué and peppered with *double entendres*. Paddick and Williams often ad libbed lines, making references to 'camping', 'cruising', 'queens', 'drag', 'mincing', 'rent' and 'fags'. In February 1967 they took a comedic swipe at the law in a sketch called 'Bona Law', in which they appeared as lawyers from 'a fashionable firm of solicitors in Lincoln's Inn'. [158]

Horne: Will you take my case?

Julian: Well depends on what it is. We've got a criminal practice that takes up most of our time.

Horne: Yes, but apart from that, I need legal advice.

Sandy: Oh, i'n' 'e bold! [159]

Julian and Sandy were effeminate and unthreatening, but they were treated sympathetically and even affectionately. *Round the Horne* cast member Betty Marsden recalled, 'It was the first time that a couple of camp gentlemen had really ever been heard on radio. And we were astounded, I think, that it got past the censor.' Kenneth Williams thought that Julian and Sandy helped to change public attitudes: 'We all thought that by familiarising people with funny aspects of what was then tending to be an esoteric clique with a private language and all the rest of it, if we made it popular, made it funny, people would see that sect of the population, so to speak, in another light; and perhaps an endearing, an enlightening light.' The audience at home and in the studio were certainly in on the jokes, and the programme pulled in eight million listeners a week. In March 1967 it won Took and Feldman the Writers' Guild of Great Britain Award for best comedy script. [160]

By 1965 the frequent appearance of gay men on both radio and television was enough to prompt Harry, the 68-year-old working class patriarch in Edward Bond's play *Saved*, to call the *Radio Times* a 'waste a good money' with a 'lot a lies an' pictures a nancies'. The following year the gay references in Hugo Charteris's Wednesday Play *The Connoisseur* passed with little controversy. The play looked at bullying and homosexuality at an English public school and was based on Charteris's own experiences at Eton. House captain Christopher Tenterden (Richard O'Sullivan) gets into trouble with the school authorities for writing an article for the fictitious *Daily Pictorial* headlined 'High Jinks in Famous Boys Public School – Prefect's Revelations'. In it, Tenterden describes the school's dormitories as 'Augean stables of privilege'. He later tells his father, the school chaplain, that 'this house is a brothel'. He is also bullied by 'Trooper'

Ballantyne (Ian Ogilvy) who, like Tenterden, is attracted to choirboy Harry Benson (Paul Guess). Tenterden tells his house master that 'Ballantyne is making Benson's life a misery with sexual advances which he doesn't want', but he is ignored. [161, 162]

The BBC returned to the problematic relationship between gay men and the police in an episode of *Softly, Softly*, a spin-off series of *Z Cars* set in Bristol. In 'Murder Reported', broadcast on 23 November 1966, Thomas Grant (Blair Stewart), a 27-year-old deputy department store manager and the married father of a six-month-old baby, is stabbed to death near railway sidings in an area of wasteland 'popular with "courting couples"'. The killer turns out to be a young man who works at a coal loading yard near the railway. He robs Grant of money and a watch, which he then sells. The video recording of the programme was wiped after broadcast, but the shooting script survives. One scene takes place in a gay pub. The script describes The Angel as 'a small pub with a scrubbed look, bare wooden tables and the like.' [163]

> It was once, clearly, a straight workingman's pub, and it has that bare look still. The contrast is thus heightened between it and the proprietor and customers. These are all queers, and there are fifteen or so. They should range widely in age and in type. Some of them can be startlingly obvious, some of them should be really beefy. Some of them should be nondescript. The only woman there is [the landlady] Auntie May. She is florid and old. She calls everybody "dear". She is capable of being very tough. We hear the lot first. A high-pitched buzz.' [164]

When detective sergeant Harry Hawkins and police constable Tanner visit the pub to investigate Grant's murder they talk to Auntie May about her customers.

> Auntie: Some of my customers are not as flush as they look.
> Hawkins: Spend it all on tarting themselves up?
> Auntie: Some of them. And some of them don't make much – they get found out and don't stay in the same job long enough.

Hawkins: You make them sound hunted.

Auntie: (not vehemently) They often are, aren't they dear? (as Hawkins makes a stir of dissent) They are, you know, dear. Not persecuted, I don't mean that. They're worried, frightened most of them.

Hawkins: (very quietly) And some of them are ashamed.

Auntie: (cheerfully) Yes dear. Some of them fight against it. It's worst for them. [165]

In a final scene which would have been unthinkable a few years earlier, Grant's 'special friend' Ron Gulliver (Anton Darby) visits his widow Connie to return a fountain pen that belonged to her husband. Quietly and simply he tells her the nature of their relationship. [166]

Connie: That's Tom's!

Gulliver: Yes. He gave it me.

Connie: Why?

Gulliver: He liked me.

Connie: Oh.

Gulliver: I loved him. [167]

ITV was more reluctant than the BBC to broadcast dramas with gay content. Bill Meilen's 1966 Play of the Week *The Division* was initially banned by the Independent Television Authority – although more for its portrayal of violence at a naval approved school than for its references to homosexuality. Granada Television was only permitted to broadcast it in May 1967 – almost a year after it was produced. The play concerns a young offender, Dando (Richard O'Callaghan), who is given extra tuition by a sympathetic officer and teacher, Commander Kerslake (Roddy McMillan). The school bully Mundy accuses Kerslake of being gay because of his interest in Dando's education. 'If the papers get to hear about it,' he tells Kerslake, 'it'd be awful for the ship, sir. Some of them would really go to town on a story like this.' To avoid scandal, the school's headmaster, Captain Bean, offers to transfer Kerslake and his wife to another school. [168]

Kerslake: Do you think I'm homosexual?

Bean: Of course I don't.

Kerslake: God damn and blast it man, do I look like a bloody pansy?

Bean: You don't have to make a case to me. I know it's a pack of lies. It could happen to any officer in this school. But the finger happens to be pointing at you. You must have seen this sort of thing happen to people before. We're wide open to it here. Place full of boys. A million people outside only too willing to believe it. [169]

By 1967 it was no longer easy to tell who was a 'pansy' and who was not. But an accusation of homosexuality could still stick, and it could still ruin a man's life and career – notwithstanding the changes in public attitudes then taking place.

Chapter 5 references

1. Anonymous interviewee
2. Reader's report, 29 June 1960, BBFC file: *Victim*
3. Letter from John Trevelyan to Michael Relph, 18 May 1960, Janet Green Collection, British Film Institute
4. Letter from John Trevelyan to Janet Green, 1 July 1960, op. cit.
5. Letter from Janet Green to John Trevelyan, 4 July 1960, BBFC file: *Victim*
6. Letter from Janet Green to Michael Relph, 13 July 1960, Janet Green Collection, op. cit.
7. *Boy Barrett*, first draft screenplay, June 1960, op. cit.
8. Letter from Michael Relph to Janet Green and John McCormick, 22 August 1960, op. cit.
9. Letter from John Trevelyan to Michael Relph, 31 August 1960, op. cit.
10. Letter from Janet Green, 25 October 1960, op. cit.
11. John Coldstream, *Victim*, Palgrave Macmillan/British Film Institute, 2011
12. Peter McEnnery, telephone interview with author, 15 June 2012
13. Stephen Bourne, *Brief Encounters: Lesbians and Gays in British Cinema, 1930-1971*, Cassell, 1996
14. *Victim* Q & A, British Film Institute, 3 August 2011
15. Letter from Michael Relph to Janet Green, 8 November 1960, Janet Green Collection, op. cit.
16. Letter from Janet Green to Michael Relph and Basil Dearden, 15 December 1960, op. cit.
17. Letter from Michael Relph to Janet Green and John McCormick, 2 January 1961, op. cit.
18. Dirk Bogarde, *Snakes and Ladders*, Chatto & Windus, 1978

19. John Fraser, personal interview with author, 11 January 2013

20. Dirk Bogarde, *Boy Barrett*, final shooting script, 23 January 1961, British Film Institute

21. Letter from Basil Dearden to Janet Green and John McCormick, 30 January 1961, Janet Green Collection, op. cit.

22. Dirk Bogarde, The John Player Lecture, National Film Theatre, November 1970

23. 'Dirk Bogarde Takes His Most Daring Role', *Evening Standard*, 17 February 1961

24. Peter Warren, 'Rank's "Victim" May End Up a Martyr', *Films and Filming*, April 1961

25. What YOU Think, *Films and Filming*, May 1961

26. Sheridan Morely, Dirk Bogarde, *Rank Outsider*, Bloomsbury, 1999

27. Peter McEnnery, telephone interview with author, op. cit.

28. Letter from John Trevelyan to Michael Relph, 15 May 1961, BBFC file: *Victim*

29. Letter from Michael Relph to John Trevelyan, 16 May 1961, op. cit.

30. Letter from Michael Relph to John Trevelyan, 30 May 1961, op. cit.

31. Letter from Janet Green to John Trevelyan, 12 September 1961, Janet Green Collection, op. cit.

32. Letter from John Trevelyan, 13 September 1961, BBFC file: *Victim*

33. *Dirk Bogarde in Conversation*, 1961, Carlton International Media

34. Letter from Janet Green to Malcolm Feuerstein, 7 April 1961, Janet Green Collection, op. cit.

35. Jack Bentley, 'Here's a Film to Start You Arguing', *Sunday Pictorial*, 27 August 1961

36. Alexander Walker, *Evening Standard*, 31 August 1961

37. Dilys Powell, *The Sunday Times*, 3 September 1961

38. Susan Mann, *Woman's Mirror*, 2 September 1961

39. Anthony Tweedale, *The Star*, 7 October 1961

40. *Yorkshire Post*, 7 October 1961

41. *Financial Times*, 1 September 1961

42. *The Guardian*, 2 September 1961

43. James Breen, 'Ten-Letter Word', *The Observer*, 3 September 1961

44. *Films and Filming*, October 1961

45. Antony Grey, recorded interview, February 1990, Hall-Carpenter Oral History archive, British Library.

46. Michael Mason, 'Arran's New Bill', *Gay News*, 23 September 1976

47. Letter from Lord Arran to Dirk Bogarde, 5 June 1968, www.dirkbogarde.co.uk

48. Russell Davies (ed.), *The Kenneth Williams Diaries*, Saturday 2 September 1961, Harper Collins, 1993

49. John Fraser, personal interview with author, op. cit.

50. Dudley Sutton, telephone interview with author, 22 May 2012

51. Katherine Bucknell (ed.), *Christopher Isherwood, The Sixties, Diaries, Volume Two: 1960-1969*, 8 October 1961, Chatto & Windus, 2010

52. John Chesterman, recorded interview, September 1993, Hall-Carpenter Oral History archive, op. cit.

53. Patrick Trevor-Roper, recorded interview, August 1990, op. cit.

54. Alkarim Jivani, *It's Not Unusual: A History of Lesbian and Gay Britain in the Twentieth Century*, Michael O'Mara Books, 1997

55. John Coldstream, *Victim*, op. cit.

56. Letter from Charles Holland to Michael Relph and Basil Dearden, 11 February 1962, Janet Green Collection, op. cit.

57. Reader's report, 8 May 1960, BBFC file: *A Taste of Honey*

58. Letter from John Trevelyan to Michael Holden, 2 March 1961, op. cit.

59. Letter from Tony Richardson to John Trevelyan, 9 March 1961, op. cit.

60. Boleslaw Sulik, *Tribune*, 22 September 1961

61. Murray Melvin, *A Taste of Honey* Q & A, British Film Institute , 7 November 2011

62. *A Taste of Honey*, Woodfall Film Productions, 1961

63. Gordon Westwood, *A Minority: A Report on the Life of the Male Homosexual in Great Britain*, Longmans, 1960

64. Colin MacInnes, *Absolute Beginners*, MacGibbon & Kee, 1959

65. Gillian Freeman, Edward Thorpe, personal interview with author, 31 November 2012

66. Eliot George, *The Leather Boys*, Anthony Blond, 1961

67. Hall-Carpenter Archives Gay Men's Oral History Group, *Walking After Midnight: Gay Men's Life Stories*, Routledge, 1989

68. Jeremy Reed, *The King of Carnaby Street: The Life of John Stephen*, Haus Publishing, 2010

69. Richard Weight, *Mod! A Very British Style*, The Bodley Head, 2013

70. Jeremy Reed, *The King of Carnaby Street*, op. cit.

71. Richard Barnes, *Mods!*, Plexus Publishing, 1991

72. Jeremy Reed, *The King of Carnaby Street*, op. cit.

73. Richard Weight, *Mod!* op. cit.

74. *Male Homosexual*, BBC Home Service, 5 January 1965

75. Peter Dennis (ed.), *Daring Hearts: Lesbian and Gay Lives in 50s and 60s Brighton*, QueenSpark Books, 1992

76. Ibid.

77. 'Gear Street', *South East Special*, BBC Radio, 22 August 1964

78. Richard Smith, 'What Are You Looking At?', *Gay Times*, July 1994

79. Jeremy Reed, *The King of Carnaby Street*, op. cit.

80. Sean Cole, *Don We Now Our Gay Apparel: Gay Men's Dress in the Twentieth Century*, Berg, 2000

81. Donis Man's Shop, 1959 Spring/Summer catalogue

82. Geoffrey Aquilina Ross, *The Day of the Peacock, Style for Men 1963-1973*, V&A Publishing, 2011

83. Paul Anderson, *Mods: The New Religion; The Style and Music of the 1960s Mods*, Omnibus Press, 2013

84. Peter Barnsley, 'Faces Without Shadows', *Town*, September 1962

85. John Stephen Collection, Victoria & Albert Museum

86. Personality Page, *Boyfriend*, 8 January 1966

87. Montague Haltrecht, *Jonah and his Mother*, André Deutsch, 1964

88. Martyn Goff, *The Youngest Director*, Putnam, 1961

89. Montague Haltrecht, *Jonah and his Mother*, op. cit.

90. Michael Bloch, *Closet Queens*, Little, Brown, 2015

91. Anne Sharpley, 'London's Hidden Problem', *Evening Standard*, 20 July 1964

92. 'Street Where "Mod" Look Was Born', *Business Week*, 28 August 1965

93. Martyn Goff, *The Youngest Director*, op. cit.

94. Lynne Reid Banks, *The L-Shaped Room*, Chatto & Windus, 1960

95. Andrew Salkey, *Escape to an Autumn Pavement*, Hutchinson, 1960

96. J.R. Ackerley, *We Think the World of You*, The Bodley Head, 1960

97. *The Collection*, Television Playhouse, ITV, 11 May 1961

98. Harold Pinter, *The Collection*, Eyre Methuen, 1963

99. *Afternoon of a Nymph*, Armchair Theatre, ITV, 30 September 1962

100. Philip King, *How Are You Johnnie?*, Samuel French, 1963

101. Terence Rattigan, *Man and Boy*, *The Collected Plays of Terence Rattigan, Volume Four*, Hamish Hamilton, 1978

102. Bill Naughton, *All in Good Time*, Samuel French, 1965

103. David Storey, *This Sporting Life*, Longmans, Green & Co., 1960

104. *This Sporting Life*, Independent Artists, 1963

105. Richard Hauser, *The Homosexual Society*, The Bodley Head, 1962

106. Ibid.

107. Jack Miller, 'Murders in a Half World', *News of the World*, 25 February 1962

108. Lionel Crane, 'How to Spot a Possible Homo', *Sunday Mirror*, 28 April 1963

109. Ibid.

110. Ibid.

111. Noyes Thomas, 'The Men Behind the Mask', *News of the World*, 2 August 1964

112. Ibid.

113. Ken Livingstone, *You Can't Say That: Memoirs*, Faber & Faber 2011

114. John Deane Potter, 'Twilight Traitors', *News of the World*, 28 October 1962

115. Rebecca West, *The Meaning of Treason*, Penguin Books, 1965

116. Robert B. Asprey, *The Panther's Feast*, Jonathan Cape, 1959

117. Readers' Report, 30 August 1964, Lord Chamberlain Plays Correspondence Files, British Library

118. Note from comptroller to Charles Heriot, 13 August 1965, op. cit.

119. Note from C.D. Heriot to comptroller, 14 August 1965, op. cit.

120. Anthony Page, personal interview with author, 22 August 2012.

121. Note from assistant comptroller, 12 July 1965, Lord Chamberlain Plays Correspondence Files, op. cit.

122. Ronald Brydon, 'Osborne at the Ball', *New Statesman*, 9 July 1965

123. Letter from Lord Goodman to Lord Cobbold, 5 August 1965, Lord

Chamberlain Plays Correspondence Files, op. cit.

124. Anthony Page, personal interview with author, op. cit.

125. Nicholas Wright, telephone interview with author, 25 May 2012

126. Derek Jarman, *At Your Own Risk: A Saint's Testament*, Hutchinson, 1992

127. Peter Shaffer, *Black Comedy*, Hamish Hamilton, 1968

128. Memorandum from assistant comptroller to Lord Chamberlain, 29 September 1965, Lord Chamberlain Plays Correspondence Files, op. cit.

129. Reader's report, 20 January 1966, op. cit.

130. John Lahr, *Prick Up Your Ears: The Biography of Joe Orton*, Allen Lane, 1978

131. Reader's report, 21 January 1966, Lord Chamberlain Plays Correspondence Files, op. cit.

132. W.A. Darlington, 'Playwright's Precocious Talent', *Daily Telegraph*, 5 July 1966

133. Note to the Lord Chamberlain, 12 July 1966, Lord Chamberlain Plays Correspondence Files, op. cit.

134. Reader's report, 17 April 1967, op. cit.

135. Letter from Jeremy Brooks to assistant comptroller, 21 April 1967, op. cit.

136. Letter from J.F.D. Johnston to Jeremy Brooks, 24 April 1967, op. cit.

137. Letter from John Trevelyan to Raymond Stross, 9 August 1962, BBFC file: *The Leather Boys*

138. Gillian Freeman, *The Leather Boys* script, 1963, British Film Institute

139. Gillian Freeman, Edward Thorpe, personal interview with author, 31 November 2012

140. Dilys Powell, *The Sunday Times*, 26 January 1964

141. *Spectator*, 31 January 1964

142. Gerry O'Hara, telephone interview with author, 12 May 2012

143. Letter from John Trevelyan to Gerry O'Hara, 9 October 1964, BBFC file: *The Pleasure Girls*

144. Lloyd Reckord, Lesbian and Gay Film Festival, BFI Southbank, 12 April 2011

145. Nicholas Wright, telephone interview with author, op. cit.

146. Roland Curram, personal interview with author, 18 May 2012

147. Antony Sher, *Beside Myself: An Autobiography*, Hutchinson, 2001

148. *The Family Way*, Boulting Brothers, 1966

149. Ibid.

150. John Hopkins, 'Z Cars: A Man Outside the Law', *Radio Times*, 28 May 1964

151. 'Somebody…Help', *Z Cars*, programme file, BBC Written Archives

152. Ibid.

153. Ibid.

154. Alexander Reid, 'Ban TV Sex? Not Me!', *Evening News Despatch*, 20 June 1964

155. Letters, *Manchester Evening News*, 27 June 1964

156. *Horror of Darkness*, The Wednesday Play, BBC 1, 10 March 1965

157. Anthony Page, personal interview with author, op. cit.

158. 'The Three Musketeers, Part 1', *Round the Horne*, BBC Light Programme, 19 February 1967

159. Ibid.

160. *Gay Times: The Sex Lives of Us*, BBC Radio 4, 13 September 2007

161. Edward Bond, *Saved*, Methuen Drama, 2000

162. *The Connoisseur*, The Wednesday Play, BBC 1, 4 May 1966

163. 'Murder Reported', *Softly, Softly*, BBC 1, 23 November 1966, BBC Written Archives

164. Ibid.

165. Ibid.

166. Ibid.

167. Ibid.

168. *The Division*, Play of the Week, ITV, 25 May 1967

169. Ibid.

Chapter 6

A WIND OF CHANGE

> Homosexuality is nowadays so fashionable a topic of conversation that many people must wonder just where it thrives in such remarkable profusion.
>
> Anthony Rowley, 'Another Kind of Loving:
> What is it Like to be a Homosexual?', *Axle Spokes,* 4, 1963 [1]

In the summer of 1960 the outlook for homosexual law reform looked bleak. On 30 June the House of Commons had voted heavily against the Wolfenden Report. Of the 312 MPs who voted, only 99 (32%) wanted the government to 'take action' on the report. The law and its administration by the police and the courts remained unchanged. Public opinion was unmoved by the debate. Most people did not want to know about homosexuality. A cartoon by Osbert Lancaster in the *Daily Express* on 1 July typified attitudes. In it, two smartly dressed ladies at a cocktail party discuss the Commons vote. 'What I particularly admired about the debate,' one of them remarks, 'was the way that every speaker managed to give the impression that he personally had never met a homosexual in his life.' [2]

Ignorance, embarrassment, ridicule and disgust were the most common attitudes towards homosexuality. 'There is a general tendency among the general public to think of all homosexuals as "pansies",' noted Michael Schofield in 1960. 'To many people homosexuality is a laughing matter, and this attitude is encouraged by the music hall jokes and the assumption that all homosexuals are effeminate.' Theatre shows and television comedies perpetuated such stereotypes. The original script by Alan Bennett, Peter Cook, Jonathan Miller and Dudley Moore for *Beyond the Fringe* – which opened at the Edinburgh Festival in August 1960 – included a sketch called 'Bollard…The Man's Cigarette', in which two 'dreadful queens' appeared in a mock cigarette advertisement. Another sketch about 'consenting males' and the Wolfenden Report was set in a public lavatory. ITV's popular sitcom *Bootsie and Snudge* (produced by Granada Television from 1960 to 1963) featured odd couple Claude Snudge (Bill Fraser), a club porter and ex-sergeant major, and his sidekick Montague 'Bootsie' Bisley (Alfie Bass). TV critic Maurice Richardson thought that the series, which drew 17 million viewers a week, was 'compulsive' viewing partly because of the 'strange by-play' of the actors: 'They carry the ambivalent, equivocal and sometimes almost flagrantly – though, I suppose, always sublimated – homosexual relationship between these two monsters as far as possible, exploiting all conceivable nuances and many that are inconceivable.' Richardson may have misread the homosexual element in Bootsie's and Snudge's relationship, but as Michael Schofield pointed out, this was a consequence of the greater alertness to homosexuality since the publication of the Wolfenden Report: 'Many people who were at one time scarcely aware of the existence of homosexuality now tend to see it in places where it does not exist. Some men and women now suspect any man over 30 who is not married, and sometimes even younger men come under suspicion because they decide to share a flat with other men for reasons of economy or companionship.' [3, 4, 5]

Views on homosexuality were shaped as much by social class, age and gender as by personal prejudice and morality. In the middle of the socio-economic scale attitudes were mostly characterised by ignorance, denial and disapproval. In *The Youngest Director* (1961) Leonard is 'close to his mother and friendly with his father', but he worries about them discovering his sexuality. When they do eventually find out, their reactions are typical.

'You, a nancy boy?' His father was, or pretended to be, incredulous.

'Yes, and you've always known it. Only you've never had the courage to admit it to yourself, that's all.'

'I just don't believe it.' The big man sat staring at his son.

'What do you mean, you don't believe it? I'm not a monster or a criminal. I didn't choose to be born as I am.'

'I don't want to see you again – ever! I don't want anything to do with you. I shan't change my mind, either. You've got into bad company and been perverted. The whole thing's disgusting and unnatural.' [6]

Leonard's mother is bewildered rather than disgusted.

'I had a feeling, Leonard, that something was not quite right. No, I don't mean that. I sort of felt you were different but I' – she laughed – 'it sounded so silly: I tried to avoid thinking about it.'

'It's not so silly,' said Leonard reassuringly as John came back with the coffee. The boy examined the tray then realised that he had forgotten the sugar.

'Leonard, is he also – you know, the same?'

'Yes,' agreed Leonard sadly, realising how little she still understood. Sharing his life, having a partner, living, in fact, a marriage of two people, all these concepts meant nothing to her. [7]

Harold Calvert in Angus Wilson's 1964 novel *Late Call* is a straightforward hypocrite. The headmaster of a secondary modern school in the fictional new town of Carshall, he is a pseudo-liberal snob who professes free thinking and open mindedness when it suits him. When his eldest son Ray leaves for London to live with another man he initially feigns acceptance.

'You mean he's homosexual.' He sounded deliberately casual, but his surprise would out. 'Ray! He's so popular, so good with everyone. Oh, well, it's not the end of the world. I'm not entirely Victorian, you know.' [8]

Later Harold writes his son 'a friendly letter', urging him to come back home. [9]

> I only blame myself that you never felt able to come and tell me of your difficulties. If you had, what was probably only a passing phase in every adolescent's life (I seem dimly to remember some 'crush' as we called them on a golden-haired, cherubic junior boy – now no doubt a hoary father of five – in my own school days) it need never have assumed the exaggerated proportions in your life that it has now. Anyway, come home, I do beg you. Sexual choice is a small, often exaggerated part of life. The pleasures, ideals and memories that unite you to your family and to your friends here at Carshall are so much more important than this one barrier that now seems to loom so large in your life.' [10]

When Ray decides to stay in London with his lover, Harold's real feelings come to the fore: 'It makes me sick. No one can say that I'm narrow-minded. I've long said the law's antiquated. But to trade on his abnormalities. Living with some rich old man.' Harold later describes his son as 'a little whore'. [11]

In *The Wanting Seed*, Antony Burgess' 1962 novel about a dystopian Britain, the threat of over-population and resource scarcity compels the state to reduce births and human fertility. Homosexuality is highly prized and promoted because of its supposed sterility and unproductiveness. But teacher's wife Beatrice Joanna Foxe remains disgusted by gay men. When she leaves the ministry of agriculture after compulsorily donating the body of her dead baby for fertiliser she encounters a group of gay men in the lift.

> That sort of thing was now encouraged – anything to divert sex from its natural end – and all over the country blared posters put out by the Ministry of Infertility, showing, in ironical nursery colours, an embracing pair of one sex or the other with the legend 'It's Sapiens to be Homo'. The Homosex Institute even ran night classes. At the

fifteenth floor the lift picked up a foppish steatopygous young man. He began, with swift expert strokes, to make up his face, simpering, as his lips kissed the lipstick, at his reflection in the lift mirror. 'What a world,' she thought. The world was mad; where would it all end? [12]

In *Victim* Miss Benham, the bookshop assistant and blackmail mastermind, is biblical in her loathing of gay men. When her accomplice Sandy Youth tells her that she is 'a sort of cross between an avenging angel and a peeping tom' she hisses back, 'They disgust me. They're everywhere. Everywhere you turn. The police do nothing, nothing. Someone's got to make them pay for their filthy blasphemy.' Such outrage against homosexuality often influenced professional decision-making. When Joe Orton and Kenneth Halliwell were each given the unusually harsh sentence of six months' imprisonment plus a £2 fine for defacing Islington public library books in May 1962, Orton claimed that their sentences were so severe 'because we were queers'. The presiding magistrate Harold Sturge was certainly hostile towards gay men. In 1956 he sent a memorandum to the Wolfenden Committee describing same-sex practices as 'morally wrong, physically dirty and progressively degrading'. [13, 14]

Younger middle class men and women often shared similar attitudes to homosexuality. In *The Youngest Director* Tony Newman, a gay friend of Leonard's, explains that he once knew a 'smart, well-to-do and interesting' married couple who were aware of his 'situation' and tolerated it 'as long as it was not waved in front of their noses.' Sally Bulmer, a social worker in *Late Call*, claims to have dealt with 'Ray's kind' before. 'I like them on the whole,' she says. 'I've always said the same to them. It's a stupid law but it's there. So if you can't be good, be careful.' In Julian Mitchell's 1961 novel *Imaginary Toys* student Elaine Cole pities Nicholas and his boyfriend Giles Mangles: 'Poor things. I wonder who's the boy and who's the girl. Perhaps they don't do it like that. I wonder why it happens. Don't have to worry about having babies, though, lucky things.' Fellow student Charles Hammond is deeply disturbed by homosexuality, but will only admit it to himself. [15, 16, 17]

Though I have no theoretical objection to men living together, in practice I find it terribly embarrassing. I don't know what it is – something to do with the prejudices one has been brought up with, perhaps, or perhaps it's just an incomprehension of why they don't want girls, and a feeling that they must be lacking somewhere. And I can't stand all that pansy prancing about and calling each other 'dear' and self-consciously being naughty. Like any minority, they have *en masse* certain qualities that I just can't take, and if I meet them *en masse*, which happens practically never, thank heavens, I squirm and feel depressed. [18]

Such attitudes were not exclusive to the middle classes, but working class men and women tended to be more open in expressing them. Jack Evans, Elaine Cole's boyfriend, is a coal miner's son who thinks that homosexuality is 'not natural'. He tells Nicholas and Giles, 'You can have sex your way, I suppose, but you can't ever have the feeling of partnership, of being a regular pair'. Fred the barman at the Chequers pub in *Victim* is more direct. 'They're good for a laugh all right,' he tells photographers' model Madge. 'Very witty at times. Generous too. I hate their bloody guts.' Madge at first demurs but then concedes, 'Well they're just not quite normal dear.' Jack, an 'assault and battery case' in *Teddy Boy Ahoy* (1963) thinks that 'a queer deserves to be sliced up'. Terry, his pal at the remand home, agrees – even though homosexuality is rife at the approved school he is sent to. [19, 20, 21]

One of the boys was getting into another boy's bed. He listened hard, discovering that the same thing was happening all around the dormitory, as if at a given signal. The place was alive with queers. They were practising homosexualism. It seemed as though none of them were afraid of voicing their feelings either. [22]

In *The Gemini* (1964) Rex's family does not understand his homosexuality. They think it might be some kind of sickness or handicap, like the disability which affects his younger brother Brian. Rex tells his lover

David that for his family 'being queer is something they pretend doesn't even exist, and they'll go on pretending until it's unavoidable – and then I'll be to them something disgusting, like Brian, only worse, because my mother can see the hand of God in him – but only of the devil in me'. When Rex's older sister eventually finds out about his sexuality she is disgusted: 'She was clearly at a loss; reference to normal sexual relationships was proscribed by her code. How then could she even approach the problem of the homosexual? She regarded Rex as a moral leper. He had opened her eyes to a condition she never wanted to believe really existed and she had no alternative but to condemn him.' [23]

Some working class communities were more accepting, and even protective, of gay relatives, friends and workmates. In *The Homosexual Society* Richard Hauser noted that 'the "homo" is, for many, an abomination. We do, however, know of a number of cases where people have regarded a homosexual with whom they have grown up with surprising tolerance. Once the animosity has been removed and people have got used to a workmate "with a kink", tolerance and even protection against the outside world comes to the fore.' Fred Dyson, a miner from Yorkshire, benefitted from this kind of solidarity after he was convicted of importuning in the early 1960s. His case was reported in the local newspaper under the headline 'Miner Admits to Being a Homosexual All His Life', and a copy was left in the canteen at Goldthorpe Colliery, Barnsley, where he worked as an overman. Fred went to see his union secretary, who told him, 'You've done nowt wrong. I've played with a bloke many a time.' The secretary then took him to the miners' club, where one of the men announced, 'Fred, if thou can admit to being a poof all thou life, thou are a better man than us. Have a pint.' [24, 25]

Millie Winders in *We Think the World of You* (1960) knows exactly the nature of her son Johnny's relationship with Frank. After Johnny is sent to prison for housebreaking, Frank goes to see Millie at her home in Stratford, east London. He senses her 'understanding' and detects 'a true perception of my feeling for her son'. Millie's acceptance is due in part to Frank's financial support for Johnny and his young family – part of a long-standing tradition of older middle or upper class men taking care of younger working class lovers. This kind of class patronage formed part of Robert Boothby's (Lord Boothby from 1958) relationships with east London lads. They included Leslie Holt, a club croupier and cat burglar whom Boothby met at Esmeralda's Barn, the nightclub in Knightsbridge owned by the gangsters Reggie and Ronnie Kray. Holt was previously Ronnie Kray's lover, and it was he who arranged an infamous meeting between Ronnie and Boothby at the latter's Belgravia flat in 1964. Homosexuality was tacitly accepted in east end gangland circles. Several of the Krays' associates were gay, including 'Mad' Teddy Smith, with whom the Labour MP Tom Driberg had an affair. Both Driberg and Boothby were regular guests at sex parties at Ronnie Kray's flat in Cedra Court, Cazenove Road, in Clapton, north London. The two politicians were also spotted by Conservative MPs Terence Clarke and Barnaby Drayson at the White City Stadium dog track in 1964, allegedly trying to pick up boys. [26, 27]

Most men, however, took care to hide their sexuality. The notion of 'coming out' was unthinkable. In *The Leather Boys* (1961) Dick longs to talk about his love for Reggie after he is killed in a gang fight, but he does not dare: 'There had been times when he had wanted to blurt out, cry out, "we loved each other". But he couldn't. There was no one to tell.' One of Schofield's interviewees in *A Minority* told him how he had tried to talk openly to friends about his sexuality, but with mixed results. [28]

I felt it is because people don't admit their homosexuality that heteros think all homos are pansy boys. Also I wanted to prove to myself that my close friends were so close that I would be accepted whatever I was. So I sat down and wrote to my five best friends and told them I was homosexual. One replied with a pompous letter saying he would talk to me if we met on the street, but he would prefer me not to visit his home again. One replied saying it wouldn't make any difference, and the other three never replied and they've never mentioned it, although we remain good friends. But once I began to collect homosexual friends I realised I would be endangering them by telling others of my homosexuality. It would bring them under suspicion, so I don't tell anyone now. [29]

As Antony Grey pointed out, a reluctance to talk about sex generally underpinned negative attitudes towards homosexuality.

> People don't want to know about sex. This is especially true of homosexuality because homosexuality is a subject about which one either knows a good deal or else one knows nothing at all; and those who don't want to know will not be told. I have heard of an 18-year-old boy who was troubled about his homosexual feelings, and who, having hesitated for months, came down to breakfast one day and said to his parents: 'I've got something very important to tell you: I'm homosexual.' His mother, who was pouring out the coffee, did not even bother to look up. She said, in reproving tones: 'Don't be silly, dear, that's not a funny joke at all.' [30]

Grey knew of several cases where parents had thrown their gay sons out of the house and had even assaulted them. In *The Youngest Director* John hides his sexuality from his parents because 'my old man's a copper and my mother's a leading light in the Mothers' Union. They'd have a fit if they had the slightest suspicion. They ask me when I'm going to get married sometimes, but they only laugh when I say "never". I wouldn't lie to them, so I hope they don't pry further.' In Philip King's play *How Are You Johnnie?* (1963) Johnnie's stepfather James Roberts is also a policeman, who uses his professional position to persecute gay men. When he finds out that Johnnie is friendly with his gay workmate Les, he threatens to tell the delivery firm where they both work. [31]

> Roberts: I know who the chap is; I know his name; I know where he lives, and I know the other queers he knocks around with. You ought to have nothing to do with him.
> Johnnie: He's with me on the job. We work together all the time. How can I have nothing to do with him?

Roberts: I could soon fix that. I've only to go down and have a word on the quiet with your boss. I know him. Either let me, or go to your boss yourself and tell him about him. And tell him you don't want to work with a bloody queer.

Johnnie: Yeh, yeh. And then what'll happen?

Roberts: If I know your boss, that chap'll be out on his backside in ten minutes. [32]

John Anselm, a 25-year-old poultry firm accountant in George Moor's novel *The Pole and Whistle* (published in 1966 but probably written in 1961-62) also lives in a small community where everyone knows everyone else's business. After he is beaten up by a gang of youths, news about his sexuality soon spreads around the fictional Lancashire town of Hawkward. 'The whole of Hawkward will know about you,' his mother warns him, as he waits for the inevitable knock on the door from the police (unnecessarily as it turns out). [33]

In *Sociological Aspects of Homosexuality* (1965) Michael Schofield pondered the difficulties faced by gay men living in small communities: 'The homosexual's predilections will soon become common knowledge and before long he will have to give up trying to appear normal to his friends and workmates, and there will be no point in trying to keep up any pretence.' Richard Hauser thought that this was why so many gay men moved to London: 'They avoid the risk of being "found out" and embarrassing their families as well.' In *Late Call* Ray refuses to return to Carshall. In *The Pole and Whistle* John emigrates to Japan. In *The Youngest Director* Leonard considers moving to another country where there are no 'vicious, outdated sexual laws'. But Ray, John and Leonard have the money and the professional contacts to escape their environments. Working class men were not so fortunate. 'It is harder for them to leave the family home and perhaps financially impossible for them to live alone in rooms,' noted Schofield. 'In fact it is more difficult for the working-class homosexual to resist the pressures from his family to get married. It is harder for him to take up a congenial career where his workmates will not demand proof of his heterosexuality. It is extremely difficult for financial and class reasons for him to set up home with another homosexual. All these things mean he is more likely to commit homosexual activities in public and so get involved with the law. And he will not be able to afford a good lawyer to defend him.' [34, 35, 36]

The vulnerability of gay working class men was highlighted by a chain of arrests in Bolton in 1963. Ten men – five of whom worked at the town's District General Hospital – were convicted of homosexual offences after the police obtained love letters from 24-year-old former hospital attendant John Redfern to his boyfriend Michael ('Vince') Lively, a 19-year-old soldier. Lively had deliberately arranged for another soldier to give the letters to his commanding officer in the hope that he would be dismissed from the army and then able to 'join John in Westhoughton'. The plan backfired when the officer reported Lively to the police, prompting a round-up of other men who had previously associated with Redfern. During their trial at Manchester Crown Court in July 1963 the names and addresses of all ten men were published in the local press. They included a hospital cook, a nurse, a nursing sister tutor, a nursing orderly, an assistant matron, a storekeeper and a plastics moulder. Despite his protests to the police that 'I am in love with Vince; I don't think we did anything wrong', Redfern was sentenced to 18 months in prison. Lively was put on probation for three years. The other men received fines of between £15 and £25, even though some of their offences had been committed three to six years previously. Several men lost their homes and jobs. One man tried to kill himself. [37, 38]

Police campaigns against gay men were particularly virulent in Lancashire in the early 1960s. In September 1963 *The Observer* reported on a sudden rise in prosecutions for importuning in the Manchester area. There had been just one prosecution for this offence in 1955; none in 1956; two in 1957; and two in 1958. In 1959 there were 30 prosecutions; in 1960 105; in 1961 135; and in 1962 216. *The Observer* noted that the increase coincided with the appointment of a new chief constable, John McKay, at the end of 1958. A man from Manchester also told Michael Schofield in 1963: 'Whenever I see a copper, I just avoid him because there's enough coppers in Manchester, and if you once get spotted by them as being queer that's it, your life's not worth living anymore.' [39, 40]

The arrests and prosecutions in the north-west prompted Colin Thomas, a 24-year-old BBC production trainee based in Manchester, to propose a radio programme about the lives of gay men. 'I suppose there was a sense of wanting to do something about this issue,' Thomas later recalled. 'It seemed to me [that] the most effective way of doing that was to simply hear the voices of gay men.' Through the Albany Trust he contacted Michael Schofield, who was interviewing gay men for *Sociological Aspects of Homosexuality*. The BBC's head of programmes in the north, Graham Miller, was broadly supportive of the programme idea. In September 1963 he wrote to BBC Radio's head of talks and current affairs George Camacho, 'Colin Thomas, whom you may know as a young and lively trainee, was attached to us earlier this year. He put to us a proposal for a 30 minute programme in which members of the homosexual minority talked about themselves and their place in society. We told him to go ahead and explore the possibilities without commitment. I have heard the recorded actuality and believe it could form the basis of an illuminating, moving and significant documentary.' Camacho, however, was unhappy about the proposal and was worried that the programme might 'whet the appetite' of latent homosexuals, who would 'have their interest awakened'. Miller responded with a memo which reflected a discernible shift in opinion beginning to take place: 'As a community we take an attitude towards homosexuality, an attitude given the sanction of law and enforced by the police. Responsible, sincere and practical people are now questioning whether our attitude is sound, and whether indeed it ought to be enforced by law. Surely the BBC has the right to broadcast radio versions of such studies as a serious contribution to the public debate.' The programme was eventually given the go-ahead but was delayed for broadcast for more than a year. [41, 42, 43, 44]

Young people like Colin Thomas were at the forefront of changing attitudes towards homosexuality. The generation of baby boomers born during and after the Second World War were now coming of age, free from the pre-war morality and social mores of their parents and grandparents. Young women in particular were sympathetic towards gay men. Writing in 1963, Antony Rowley noted the presence in gay clubs of numerous 'non-lesbian girls' who, 'rather than resembling the sort of girl who is unable to get herself a normal boyfriend and has to content herself with a mother-substitute role', found the company of gay men 'refreshing'. According to Antony Grey, the film *Victim* also did much to clear 'the sheer bewilderment of the wives and girlfriends of gay men'. Dirk Bogarde later claimed to have received letters from women thanking him for helping them to understand 'what was wrong with their son, their husband'. In *The L-Shaped Room* Jane knows about John's homosexuality and recognises its value in the help he gives her during her pregnancy: 'I knew what I owed to John, and that he couldn't have helped me in the way he had if he had been any different.' Another pregnant young woman, Jo in the 1961 film version of *A Taste of Honey*, similarly appreciates the support she gets from Geoff. At first she tells him that she is interested in 'people like you' and wants to know 'what you do, and why you do it.' But when her insistence offends him she relents: 'I don't care what you do. Honest I don't.' In Andrew Salkey's *Escape to an Autumn Pavement* (1960) Johnnie's landlady and occasional lover Fiona Trado likewise does not care about his sexuality: 'I do think you're homosexual, but I can't say to what extent or anything. And this doesn't mean that I don't want you as my lover. I couldn't care less. You're what I've been waiting for, homosexual or not.' [45, 46, 47, 48, 49, 50,]

But female sympathy carried little political weight. In March 1962 MPs rejected a private member's bill introduced by the Labour MP for Pontypool, Leo Abse. This would have addressed some of the harsher elements of the law by proposing that prosecutions for homosexual behaviour between consenting adults in private first be authorised by the director of public prosecutions, and that prosecutions for such offences should only be initiated within twelve months of their commission – thus preventing the prosecution of stale offences and eliminating prolonged blackmail. The bill also proposed that gross indecency cases should be tried at magistrates' courts (resulting in a fine rather than imprisonment in the event of a guilty verdict), and that the courts obtain medical reports before sentencing first-time offenders. But because the bill would not have implemented the key Wolfenden recommendation of decriminalising homosexual acts between consenting adult men in private, its failure to pass through parliament was welcomed by many campaigners. Desmond Donelly told *The Spectator* in February 1962 that if the bill succeeded, 'nothing more would ever be done to bring down the walls of prejudice and harshness that now lie behind the law'. Allan Horsfall also thought that 'it was such a meek proposal that, if passed, it would [have been] counterproductive' and may have 'put off the possibility of full reform for another decade or possibly more'. [51, 52]

Although the homosexual law reform process temporarily ground to a halt, a series of sex scandals kept the issue alive. The first came to light in spring 1962 when 62-year-old Ian Horobin, a former Conservative MP and minister for power, unexpectedly withdrew his name from a list of prospective life peers just two weeks after accepting a title. In a letter to the prime minister, Horobin blamed 'the amount of work which I now understand to be entailed by being an active member of the House of Lords'. In reality, criminal charges were about to be brought against him relating to his relationships with boys at the Mansfield House University Settlement in east London. The Settlement offered education and social activities for the working class residents of Canning Town and Plaistow, and Horobin had been warden there for nearly forty years. His success in raising funds had earned him a knighthood in 1955. He took a particular interest in the boys' club at Fairbairn House, where he also had a flat on the second floor. Actor Terence Stamp was a club member in the early 1950s, and he remembered 'all kinds of gossip about Sir Ian, the strongest being that he was a bit of a "ginger beer". I didn't really subscribe to this as there was nothing cissy about him at all. I just kept out of his way for the most part.' One Saturday afternoon, however, 14-year-old Stamp was invited to Horobin's flat to show him some paintings he had done. [53, 54]

> He pulled the heavy curtains across one of the four windows which overlooked the street, saying, 'We shouldn't look at them in direct

sunlight.' I opened my folder and he came and stood close to me, first looking over my shoulder, and then leaning over me, turning the paintings, resting his hand on my back. He slipped his hand lightly on to my neck. His other hand reached around me and rubbed the outside of my trousers. I spite of myself I was getting a hard on. He moved behind me. 'Yes,' he was saying, his head close to the back of mine. I could feel his breath. 'That's a nice rod, a very nice rod.' I felt him pressing himself against me, almost bending me over the table, his breathing becoming heavier. I was really petrified. I made a grab at his hand, pulled it away from me and edged along the table. I heard myself say, 'I've got to make a move now.' I heard him shuffling my paintings together, walking across the carpet towards me. I turned and took the folder without looking. He said, 'You won't lag on me, will you?' I just nodded. He pushed something into my top pocket; it was a ten-shilling note. [55]

Someone did eventually 'lag' on Horobin. In October 1961, while he was on holiday in Spain, word got out about his relationship with 17-year-old club member Roy Girard. On his return, Horobin admitted that he and Girard had been 'virtually married' for three years, and that he had also had other young 'sweethearts'. Although he resigned as warden, Horobin felt sufficiently in the clear to accept the offer of the peerage. But further accusations of sex with minors and revelations about Girard's role in encouraging boys to visit Horobin in his flat led to both of them being arrested and charged with indecency. At his trial at the Old Bailey in June 1962 Horobin pleaded guilty to ten charges and was jailed for four years. Girard admitted five charges and was bound over on probation for three years. [56, 57, 58, 59, 60]

Eight months later, junior home office minister Charles Fletcher-Cooke became embroiled in scandal. The Conservative MP for Darwen was a friend of the writer Robin Maugham, and through him he befriended 19-year-old borstal boy Anthony Turner. In February 1963 Turner was caught speeding down Commercial Road in east London in Fletcher-Cooke's Austin Princess car, despite being disqualified from driving and on remand for alleged trespass at Piccadilly Circus underground station. Following his arrest, Turner talked to newspaper stringer Laurence Bell about his relationship with 48-year-old Fletcher-Cooke. Bell, who knew Turner through his involvement with the New Bridge charity for ex-offenders, passed the story to the press, leading to Fletcher-Cooke's ministerial resignation.[*][61]

In March the sexual shenanigans of minister for war John Profumo and model Christine Keeler hit the headlines. Although the Profumo affair was essentially a heterosexual and security scandal, it too had a homosexual component. In May Laurence Bell was arrested and charged with nine counts of indecency with guardsmen from Chelsea barracks. At the same time, 18-year-old Jeffrey Leonard of the Coldstream Guards was sentenced to nine months' imprisonment at a court martial for 'impropriety' with Bell and for 'conduct to the prejudice of good order and military discipline'. It transpired that Leonard had given information about other guardsmen and their homosexual associates to Bell, who then passed on the information to the *Sunday Express*, the *Evening Standard* and other newspapers.[62]

When his case came to trial at the Old Bailey in October 1963, Bell claimed that the War Office was 'out to get' him in revenge for leaking stories to the press. He also claimed to have given information to the Labour MPs George Wigg and Emanuel Shinwell about the 'Profumo-Ward-Keeler affair', and to have given evidence to Lord Denning's judicial inquiry into the affair. In an outburst from the dock, Bell called Charles Fletcher-Cooke 'a homosexual' and 'one of those concerned in the conspiracy to get me convicted'.[63,64]

Bell also claimed that 'a present member of the government concerned with nuclear weapons' was homosexual, and that the minister had been 'present with me more than once in a London flat with guardsmen'. This was a reference to Denzil Freeth, a junior science minister and the Conservative MP for Basingstoke. In July 1963, at the height of the Profumo scandal, Liberal MP and HLRS executive committee member Jeremy Thorpe had told constituents in North Devon that, in

---

[*]   Fletcher-Cooke retained his parliamentary seat until 1983.

the wake of Profumo, 'two further ministers will soon have to resign for personal reasons'. He was alluding to Freeth and to transport minister Ernest Marples, who, wrongly as it turned out, was rumoured to have been the naked 'man in the mask' serving drinks to Christine Keeler, Mandy Rice-Davies and other guests at a sex party. In the course of his inquiry Denning discovered that in 1960 Freeth had indeed attended 'a party of a homosexual character and there participated in homosexual conduct'. Since Denning's brief included identifying ministers who might be security risks, Freeth was quietly persuaded to step down from his ministerial post. He was also asked not to stand at the 1964 general election. [65, 66]

Bell, meanwhile, was found not guilty after the trial judge, Justice MacKenna, told the jury that it would be 'unsafe' to convict him on such little evidence. MacKenna also suggested that the army's Special Investigation Branch, which was investigating information leaks by guardsmen to the press, might have used their knowledge of Bell's homosexuality to accuse him of 'immorality' with soldiers in order to punish him for embarrassing the army and the War Office – already bruised by the circumstances surrounding Profumo's resignation in June 1963. The subsequent discharge from the army of a key prosecution witness – 21-year-old grenadier guardsman Richard Hall – also added weight to Bell's claim of a politically-inspired frame-up. The only tangible outcome of the affair was an army ban on soldiers visiting two West End pubs – the Welsh Harp in Chandos Place and the Lemon Tree in Bedfordbury – where guardsmen and their gay admirers congregated. [67, 68]

1963 marked a turning point in public attitudes towards sex in general. The Profumo scandal exposed the hypocrisy of Britain's political and social elite and brought about a more open questioning of the laws governing sexual behaviour. Antony Rowley sensed a 'strong blast of a wind of change' that year. 'In recent months,' he wrote, 'the subject of queerness has begun to be one which can be discussed without blushes and euphemisms'. He speculated that 'with the law's alteration, the time might well come when, at worst, the sight of a pair of homosexuals dancing together at a party in, say, Edgeware, would arouse puzzled amusement; at best, it would pass unremarked as a comparatively common social phenomenon.' That actuality was some way off, but opinions on homosexuality were changing. In 1963 the Quaker group formed six years earlier to examine the issue of homosexuality, published its conclusions in a pamphlet called *A Quaker View of Sex*. It affirmed that 'the kind of morality that includes a vehement and categorical condemnation of the homosexual is not Christian, for it lacks compassion for the individual person and it lacks understanding of the human problem. Homosexual affection can be as selfless as heterosexual affection, and therefore we cannot see that it is in some way morally worse. Neither are we happy with the thought that all homosexual behaviour is sinful. An act which (for example) expresses true affection between two individuals and gives pleasure to them both does not seem to us to be sinful by reason alone of the fact that it is homosexual.' [69, 70]

Young people especially were becoming more relaxed about homosexuality. Paul McCartney and the other members of the Beatles (who released their first album in March 1963) knew that their manager Brian Epstein was 'queer' but 'didn't really have a problem with it'. In *How Are You Johnnie?* 25-year-old Johnnie cares little about Les's sexuality. 'Look, I'm not shocked,' he tells him. 'You've got your own life to live, mate, and it's up to you to live it the way you want.' Like Jo in *A Taste of Honey*, he is a 'bit nosey, p'raps. I've never come across one of you chaps before,' but ultimately his workmate's sexuality is 'no concern of mine'. He tells his stepfather that as long as Les 'pulls his weight on the job – and he does – I don't care whether he chases men, women or ruddy French poodles'. [71, 72]

Members of the older generation, too, were starting to loosen up. In *All In Good Time* Arthur's mother Lucy offers a robust defence of her son against his father Ezra's accusation that there is 'something odd or queer' about him: 'It's a father's duty to help an' protect a lad like that, not to turn on him like the mob would, an' tear his self-respect to ribbons, all over somethin' he had no say in.' Even Ezra softens his attitude: 'You know I'd never turn on the lad, Lucy, if he needed me.' [73]

The increased discussion of homosexuality on both radio and television even prompted the BBC to issue a directive to producers and announcers on how to say the word. 'Pronunciation of Homosexual' was circulated in February 1963 'to clear up any misunderstanding on the pronunciation of this word', because, according to a BBC spokesman, 'no one really knew how to pronounce it properly, and we have to be precise'. The guidelines – which were widely reported in the press – further helped to educate the public about homosexuality. In *Late Call* Ray's grandmother Sylvia Calvert confesses that she 'never knew how to pronounce it before. You see the word so often in the papers and books, and things nowadays, don't you?' [74, 75, 76]

The BBC also planned a *Panorama* programme on homosexuality and sent a camera crew to Amsterdam to film the city's The Link club. But the programme was never broadcast. The incoming editor, David Wheeler, decided that it did not 'make a self-contained story'. He was also concerned that the programme would 'raise an issue' if it were broadcast at the normal *Panorama* time of 8:25 pm on a Monday evening. According to the US entertainment industry magazine *Variety*, BBC executives who viewed the programme also decided that it was not 'of public interest'. [77, 78]

The BBC did at least think that the publication of the Radcliffe Report on the Vassall spy case in April 1963 was sufficiently in the public interest to give it coverage. The report cleared the civil service of failing to recognise Vassall's homosexuality, and it concluded that there was nothing 'improper' in the relationship between Vassall and his boss, the Civil Lord of the Admiralty Thomas Galbraith. The revelation that Galbraith had written letters to his clerk addressed 'My Dear Vassall' inspired a sketch on the BBC's satirical TV show *That Was The Week That Was,* which poked fun at the excessive security measures imposed since Vassall's exposure. In the sketch, civil service chief Lance Percival reprimands his subordinate David Kernan for using overfamiliar language in a draft letter.

Percival: You will simply end your letter without innuendo of any kind. Now, let's see what you've done. 'Yours faithfully'. I don't believe it!
Kernan: That's normal, sir.

Percival: Normal? In the context of a man writing to a man, it's nothing less than disgusting. 'Pursuant to your letter'? Pursuant?

Kernan: It's the usual phrase, sir.

Percival: The word has an erotic penumbra, you take it out. 'I'm hoping for the favour of an early reply'. 'Favour'? I believe you're one of those cranks who believe there are loyal homosexuals. I think you secretly believe that the way to stop homosexuals being blackmailed into subversive acts is to change the law so that they can't be.

Kernan: Well, it had crossed my mind, sir. [79]

Another *TW3* sketch, written by John Braine, featured Kenneth Cope in a monologue on the problems of being heterosexual – a comic inversion which satirised attitudes towards gay men and the increasingly commonplace discussion of homosexuality in the media.

Heterosexuality is an ugly word. Until recently it skulked in the obscurity of medical text books. Now, one hears it everywhere. There are few outward signs by which a heterosexual reveals himself. A heterosexual walks – or rather clumps in hobnailed boots and belted mac – alone. Not for him the joys of true comradeship; his energies are all spent in the pursuit of women. There is nothing he longs for more than a night out with the boys, but a night out with the boys – in the truest, deepest sense – is precisely what he can never enjoy. He is too busy making passes at the barmaid. What is being done about this problem? Very little. The prevalent official attitude is simply to make heterosexuality as difficult as possible, to scoop it under the carpet. It's a strange twilight world I live in. Mine is a sad story. I am not a criminal. Before you condemn me out of hand try and see me as I am – a lost and lonely soul with perhaps a more than passing resemblance to, dare I say it, yourselves. [80]

An unexpected defence of gay men and an implied criticism of the law came from Lord Radcliffe, the chairman of the tribunal which had investigated John Vassall. In a *Panorama* interview in August 1963, Radcliffe rejected the idea that gay men were automatic security risks and therefore more likely to be traitors. He told the reporter James Mossman, 'I have no sympathy at all for the view that because a man is a homosexual he is therefore peculiarly vulnerable in the way of character, in the sense that he is a weakling who will give way to pressure more easily than others, or that he is a person who is incapable of truth or anything like that. In any society which regards homosexuality as an unworthy vice, you are offering in homosexual practices a liability to being taken advantage of.' [81]

By 1963 another argument in favour of law reform had begun to emerge. According to some commentators, homosexuality was not a perversion of choice indulged in by a freemasonry of moral corruptors but a natural phenomenon affecting a disadvantaged social minority who needed the protection rather than the punishment of the law. Michael Schofield called his 1960 book *A Minority*, and Graham Miller used the same term in his memo to the BBC's George Camacho in September 1963. In *Imaginary Toys* Nicholas tells Charles that law reform is 'a question of being accepted as a human being. We're always being treated as separate, and not always as equal.' One of the men interviewed by Schofield for *A Minority* told him, 'It's my nature to be gay.' In *Victim* Henry the hairdresser blames nature for playing him 'a dirty trick', while Lord Fulbrook reminds Farr that 'the invert is part of nature'. Writing in *Family Doctor* in 1961, Eustace Chesser described 'homosexual impulses' as 'not abnormal in themselves. They are part of our ordinary human nature.' Similarly, in *All In Good Time* Lucy tells Ezra that even if Arthur were gay, 'nature would ha' done it, an' nature is not to be thwarted'. In an article in *Encounter* in August 1963 Colin MacInnes stated his belief that 'heterosexuals, bisexuals and homosexuals of both genders have existed in the world since Eden, and will continue to do so til the last trumpet sounds.' [82, 83, 84, 85, 86, 87]

This nascent minority rights argument was not yet employed in the campaign to change the law, however. Instead, the reform movement focused on widening its reach. In 1963 the HLRS approved the setting up of local committees in different parts of the country. As part of this process, Antony Grey put Lancashire councillor Allan Horsfall in touch with Manchester-based supporter Stanley Rowe, who then convened a meeting at his home on 4 June 1964. The meeting was also attended by Colin Harvey, a senior social worker for the Church of England's North West Board of Social Responsibility. Harvey reported back to the board, and its chairman, the bishop of Middleton Ted Wickham, offered the group the use of the board's meeting room on Blackfriars Road in Salford if it became a properly constitued committee. The North-Western Homosexual Law Reform Committee was duly launched at a public meeting at Church House in Manchester on 7 October. Allan Horsfall was appointed secretary, and local solicitor Niel Pearson became president. Clergyman Bernard Dodd was nominated chairman. He was succeeded by Colin Harvey in 1967.

Earlier in 1964 the government had effectively imposed the provisions of Leo Abse's failed 1962 bill. On 16 July the Home Office issued a statement explaining that the director of public prosecutions, Norman Skelhorn, had advised chief constables that, 'in order to achieve greater uniformity of enforcement of the law regarding homosexuality in private, they should seek his advice before bringing proceedings'. Added to an existing arrangement by which chief constables were required to consult the DPP on 'stale' homosexual crimes or those involving blackmail and extortion, this was at first seen as a liberal move. But as *The Sunday Times*' James Margach reported, the change was designed to tighten up rather than relax enforcement of the law. According to Margach, the home secretary, Henry Brooke, refuted 'the suggestion that the new procedure means the Home Office is encouraging the police to go "soft" on homosexuals. The official view is, in fact, that some authorities are too lax in administering the present law about consenting males committing an offence in private.' Brooke also denied that the new guidelines had anything to do with 'some infectious rumours which have been circulating during the week'. This was a reference to a story in the *Sunday Mirror* on 12 July which had alleged links between an unnamed 'prominent peer' (generally assumed to be Lord Boothby) and a 'leading thug in the London underworld' (Ronnie Kray). A week later the newspaper ran a story headlined 'The Picture We Must Not Print' about a photograph it had obtained showing Boothby, Kray and

Boothby's lover Leslie Holt sitting together on a sofa in Boothby's flat in Eaton Place. After intense political and legal pressure, the newspaper backed down and published a front page apology to Boothby and paid him £40,000 compensation. [88, 89, 90, 91]

On 15 October the general election brought a new Labour government to power. A week later ITV broadcast a thirty-minute documentary about homosexuality on its flagship current affairs programme *This Week*. For the first time on British television, gay men talked openly (albeit hidden from view) about their sexuality and the pressures they faced. Presenter Bryan Magee opened the programme by explaining that 'one person in twenty' was homosexual. [92]

> On any busy street you pass half a dozen every five minutes because, contrary to popular opinion, most of them don't look any different to anyone else. People can only tell the obvious ones, but they are a tiny minority. It means on average at least one in every large family; several in every street; several in every block of flats, in every office block, in every factory, in every club, in every society. In every large organisation, like every big firm, every civil service department, the armed forces and so on, there must be hundreds, even thousands. If all the homosexuals were to leave their jobs simultaneously, the economy of the country would be thrown into something like chaos. [93]

The BBC meanwhile felt safe enough to broadcast Colin Thomas' long delayed radio programme. The tapes for *Queer People* were sent to the Third Programme and the Home Service in late 1964, with a view to broadcasting them on either station. Third Programme controller Percy Newby thought that the subject was 'an important one which ought to be explored', but he did not think that the interviews were racy enough: 'The speakers sounded inhibited as though they were concealing far more than they were prepared to reveal. The queen who ran screaming round the town seemed alive, but the others…?' Instead, the programme, re-titled *Male Homosexual* and split into two parts, was broadcast by the Home Service in January 1965. The first part included interviews with six gay men. The second part, aired a week later, was a panel discussion with Michael Schofield and psychiatrists Richard Hauser, Anthony Storr and Hugh Freeman. Like Bryan Magee on *This Week*, Schofield emphasised the ubiquity of gay men. [94]

> They can be found in every walk of life, as the Wolfenden Report said, from the most intelligent to the dullest hobo. Not only are there homosexual criminals, but there are policemen who are homosexuals. Not only are there patients who are homosexual, but there are doctors who are homosexual. Spies are homosexual, and so are politicians. We all know that a few of them can be easily recognised, but most of them cannot. And this means, I think, that people don't realise quite how many there are. [95]

During the interviews gay men talked frankly about their lives. One spoke about his fear that his family might find out about his sexuality. Another talked about the support his parents had given him after he was arrested for a homosexual offence.

> My dread of the law before I did clash was that my parents would become aware that I was a homosexual, and I thought the world would kind of split apart. But they stood by me throughout it, as I think all parents will do.' [96]

Another interviewee voiced a growing assertiveness evident among some gay men.

> I think really we're just quite happy being the way we are, if people would only leave us alone, or just accept us a little bit. But they won't. They say, 'Oh, they're two queers.' And they sort of sneer when they say 'queer', as if you're a freak. I don't think I'm a freak. I don't think I'm any different from anybody else, except that I just happen to be in love with a man instead of a woman. What sort of love it is I don't know, but I think it's a great love. It's something far deeper than anybody could ever realise. [97]

Speaking forty years later, Colin Thomas hoped that the programmes 'made some small contribution to change the climate of public opinion'. Indirectly they did. Antony Grey recalled that 'within the space of a few weeks the prominent agony aunts of the day, people like Marjorie Proops, all came to me and said, "We feel it's time to open up this subject for our readers." Theirs were the first really positive articles, trying to explain it to mothers and sisters and so on.' [98]

BBC Radio's *Woman's Hour* also took up the issue of homosexuality. In March 1965 W. Lindsay Neustatter appeared on the programme to reassure 'many an anxious mother' who might be worried that their child was homosexual: 'Homosexuality based on love and respect is surely preferable both personally and socially to more conventional sexual expression which is devoid of affection. Much grief and loneliness suffered by relatives of homosexuals is based upon the false assumption that their loved ones are highly abnormal.' Neustatter added that gay men who resisted family and social pressures to get married were 'more worthy of our admiration than our contempt'. To prove the point, a letter was read out from a female listener who had married a gay man. [99]

> Life is one long pretence – pretence in front of our friends that we are a normal couple; pretence to him that I am content. For why should I add to his problems by making scenes when it is not his fault that he is what he is? He is not a vicious man. He is just a man who can't stand women. Occasionally he stays out all night. If friends ask, I make excuses, saying he's at a business dinner or something similar. I only pray they will never find out how near they are to the mark when they make their cheery little jokes about him 'having a night out with the boys'. [100]

The programme prompted a postbag of letters, mostly expressing gratitude to *Woman's Hour* for having aired the issue. 'Surely it's time we all realised that just as each of us has a different taste for the other good things in life, so each of us has a different taste for sex and affection,' wrote one listener. 'I don't believe that homosexuality is an illness any more than frigidity is.

Instead of acting like vindictive children in condemning people whose sexual desires are different from our own, let us modern mothers bring our children up to accept other people as they are.' Another listener thought that homosexuality was 'a subject the public needs help to understand, and more power to you for your part.' [101]

Journalist Monica Furlong weighed in the debate with a hard hitting article in the *Daily Mail* in November 1965. She told readers about Michael Brooke Baker, a 20-year-old whose lost wallet had been handed in to a Sussex police station. Officers at the station found a letter inside 'which suggested to them that Michael must be homosexual'. They arrested Baker and extracted from him the names of 'a number of friends with whom he had had homosexual relations'. Baker himself was prosecuted and sent to gaol for three years. An appeal court judge later ruled that his sentence was 'by no means excessive' and had been imposed for 'the protection of other young boys' – despite the fact that Baker himself was still a minor. 'What about the protection of Michael?' Furlong protested. 'What about the court's duty to try to re-integrate him into our society?' [102]

Baker's case showed that gay men still faced severe legal sanctions. In 1961 the total number of reported homosexual offences in England and Wales stood at 5,605. In 1962 4,866 offences were reported. In 1963 there were 5,435; in 1964 4,912; in 1965 4,389; in 1966 4,695. Despite the sense of change in the air, gay men still kept a low profile 'I [didn't] think the attitude towards homosexuality was particularly permissive,' remembered Jeffrey Weeks. Philip Rescorla lived a 'double life' at university and kept his homosexuality secret 'because I felt that people would disapprove'. One woman recalled how 'when my boyfriend found out that his flatmate at university was gay he went ballistic. Kicked him out. Refused to speak to him ever again. The works. It was terrible. But those attitudes were widespread. It was a brave man or woman who came out of the closet in the swinging 60s.' Those who did 'come out of the closet' often found it an awkward and painful experience. Christopher Spence decided to tell his family he was gay in 1965 when he was 21. [103, 104, 105, 106]

It was amazing how annoyed people were – not so much about the fact that I was having this sexual relationship and living with this man, but that I was wanting to tell anybody about it. I can remember my father kept saying, 'Well, why do you want to talk about it? Why do you want to tell anybody about it? It this really necessary? This is something you will grow out of. You don't think you will, but you will grow out of it, and why do you have to tell anyone?' [107]

This led Spence to 'the realisation that here was I living a lifestyle which was in fact still illegal. That was quite a shock. And it was beginning to dawn what gay oppression really was, and that change was going to be a political struggle.' [108]

That struggle was taken up by an unlikely figure – a moderately well-known lord with a weekly column in the London *Evening News* and the curious nickname of 'Boofy'. Arthur Strange Kattendyke David Archibald Gore, eighth Earl of Arran, never really explained why he adopted the cause of homosexual law reform. In 1972 he told *Encounter*, 'I honestly don't know. Most probably my "liberation" of the male homosexual derives from my unhappiness at the time over a purely domestic matter (nothing to do with homosexuality!).' This may have been a reference to his elder brother, Arthur Paul Gore, the seventh Earl of Arran, who was rumoured to be gay and died in obscure circumstances in 1958 aged 55. In 1933 he published a novel (republished in 1956) called *William, or More Loved than Loving*. Arthur Strange, who inherited his brother's title, liked to refer to the Sexual Offences Bill he later introduced in the House of Lords as 'William' – a pun on 'bill', but also a possible reminder of his dead brother's novel. Whatever his motives, Arran first broached the subject of homosexual law reform in a letter to the prime minister Alec Douglas-Home in January 1964. [109]

I feel that public opinion is now ready for this step forward. The changed attitude of the more serious newspapers, and the forthright views expressed on television and the radio which go unchallenged seem to indicate that the violent 'antis' are now a minority, though admittedly a vocal minority. Moreover, the attitude of the schoolmasters and schoolmistresses seems much more tolerant than in the past. And this, of course, reflects itself in the attitude of the younger generation. Finally, and most pragmatically of all, those peers who feel most deeply about, and spoke most strongly against, Wolfenden have now been removed from their Lordships' House, either through divine intervention or through other causes, and I think we stand a reasonable chance of getting a majority vote. Many people tend to regard the Labour and Liberal parties as the parties of compassion, and it would be useful, I feel, if the Tories were to give their blessing to this major piece of social legislation. [110]

Douglas-Home took five weeks to reply.

I don't really share your confidence that the balance of parliamentary and public opinion is now in favour of amending the law. I have no reason to think that there has been a significant change in the balance of opinion since that time, and I know the home secretary,* who has been keeping the matter under review, agrees with me. [111]

With a tight general election looming, Douglas-Home's reluctance to address homosexual law reform was understandable. But he was mistaken in thinking that public opinion had not changed. In a survey conducted by Michael Schofield for *Sociological Aspects of Homosexuality* (which was partly funded by a grant from the Home Office), 35 out of 50 heterosexual men (70%) thought that homosexual acts between consenting adult men in private should no longer be a criminal offence. Just ten (20%) were opposed to changing the law. Of the 35 in favour of reform, 11 (31%) thought that the age of consent should be 18. Fifteen (43%) thought it should be 21. Their comments showed an acceptance of gay men, and a corresponding disapproval of the law.

I wouldn't lock them up. What good does that do? It's a defect, you see. The best thing is to tell them: 'We'll leave you alone providing

---

*   Henry Brooke, home secretary from July 1962

you behave yourself, keep out of public sight, and don't go making a nuisance of yourself.'

We should have moved out of the times of Oscar Wilde by now.

I can't see anything against it if they do it in private. We've all got kinks of some sort. Live and let live, I say.

They're built that way. It's no good telling them to stop. I mean, if someone told me to stop going for women, well, I couldn't, could I?

I think they are badly treated. They are fairly harmless, you know. I don't see why they should be kicked around. And as for using policemen as bait, I think that's quite immoral. [112]

Possibly encouraged by Schofield's findings, Arran introduced a motion in the House of Lords on 12 May 1965 calling attention to homosexual law reform. He won the backing of eight Church of England bishops, who sent a letter to *The Times* the day before stressing 'the necessity for this reform' and the need to implement the Wolfenden recommendations. Interest in Arran's motion was also piqued by the arrest of Patrick Lord Moynihan on 20 April for importuning in Piccadilly Circus. The 58-year-old stockbroker and former chairman of the Liberal Party executive had intended to speak on Arran's motion in the Lords but was arrested while 'collecting information and equipping himself for the forthcoming debate'. Three days before his case was due to be heard at Bow Street magistrates' court, Moynihan suffered a cerebral haemorrhage and died. In the event, Arran received enough support to encourage him to return to the Lords on 24 May with a Sexual Offences Bill, which passed by 94 votes to 49. Two days later, MP Leo Abse asked the House of Commons to consider a similar bill under the Ten Minute Rule. His motion failed, but only by 19 votes. [113, 114]

Outside parliament, the British public was increasingly favourable towards homosexual law reform. A cartoon by Osbert Lancaster in the

Daily Express in June 1965 captured both the prevailing mood and the generational divide on the issue. In it, an older man reads a newspaper report headlined 'Population Explosion', while his daughter jeers, 'Go on, you old square! Let's hear you blame THAT on the homosexuals!' In October the *Daily Mail* published a National Opinion Poll in which 63% of respondents thought that homosexual acts between consenting adults should no longer be a criminal offence. Favourable responses were highest among women. Sixty-six per cent of them supported law reform, compared to 59% of men. Fifty-one per cent of respondents thought that it was wrong to send people to prison for a homosexual offence, while 93% saw no reason for the legal distinction between male and female homosexuality. The poll strengthened the hand of law reformers and weakened their opponents' long-standing argument that public opinion was against decriminalisation. As Michael Schofield pointed out on BBC Radio's *Ten O'Clock* news programme the day the poll came out, 'In the past politicians have been wont to say that though they may be personally in favour of reform of the law, they feel it's ahead of public opinion. Well now this argument won't wash any longer.' [115, 116, 117]

Over on BBC 1's *Twenty-Four Hours* a less reasoned discussion took place between the Conservative MP Cyril Osborne and Lord Arran, whose Sexual Offences Bill had just passed its third reading in the House of Lords by 96 votes to 31. When presenter Cliff Michelmore asked if the passing of the bill meant that Britain was becoming 'more tolerant and civilised or more lax and corrupted', Arran responded, 'I think it's because we are becoming more compassionate. I think it's because we're deciding that we don't like persecution of minorities.' Osborne vehemently disagreed: [118]

> I believe the vast majority of the people of this country are against the bill. I think it's the duty of government to protect virtue and to punish vice, and I regard homosexuality as filthy, disagreeable, unnatural and against all moral laws. There is a danger if you give this bill a passage in law. Then it will encourage homosexual practices between consenting males. And it will tend to bring temptation to younger men and boys.

I say it's wrong. I make no bones about it. It's a filthy, evil, dirty habit and I want it stopping. The majority of the people, in my opinion, are against this filthy, dirty habit that you want to increase.

Arran: And send the rest to prison and shoot them. Would that satisfy you?

Osborne: I'm not saying that. Don't be so stupid. I'm not an expert on it like Lord Arran. He knows a lot more about it; a lot more than people who do it. Like General Booth of the old Salvation Army I'm against sin and I believe this to be a wicked thing that ought to be stamped out if we can possibly so do.

Arran: And the bishops said…

Osborne: Oh, bishops be damned. The bishops in turn will soon be making excuses for Judas and putting stained glass windows in the cathedrals in his honour. [119]

The *Daily Mail* opinion poll found that 75% of respondents would not vote against their sitting MP in an election if they introduced a bill to decriminalise homosexual acts. Four per cent even said that they would be more likely to vote for an MP if they made such a move. This may have been a factor in prompting the Conservative member for Lancaster Humphrey Berkeley to introduce a private member's Sexual Offences Bill in December 1965. It closely followed Arran's bill and passed its second reading in the House of Commons in February 1966 by 164 votes to 107. Along with Arran's bill, however, it lapsed following the dissolution of parliament on 10 March ahead of the general election on 31 March. Berkeley lost his seat at the election, which he later blamed on negative reaction to his bill. But fellow Conservative MP William Shepherd, who was a vociferous opponent of homosexual law reform, was also ousted from his Cheadle constituency.

As the tide of opinion in favour of legal change continued to turn, C.H. Rolph, the new chairman of the HLRS,* told *The New Statesman* in February 1966: 'What was once the special knowledge of a sophisticated minority has in the past ten years become commonly known and accepted; namely that homosexual tendencies are present

---

*   Kenneth Walker died in January 1966.

in varying degrees in many different kinds of people, social classes and levels of intelligence.' In April BBC Radio reporter Barbara McDonald wandered the streets of Manchester after dark in search of *The Night People* – those who 'hover in the shadows; people we normally avoid'. As well as 'the prostitute', 'the drug addict' and 'the layabout', she encountered 'the homosexual' – two, in fact. Both told her that they were relaxed about their sexuality and the fact that other people knew about it. One of them – a young man 'with dyed blonde hair and make-up' – told McDonald, 'I'm lucky where I work because they don't mind. If I tried to hide it, then it'd mean I'm ashamed of it, and I'm not. I don't mind letting other people know what I am. It's them that are ignorant, not me. That's how I was born. The normal way for me to act is the way I do.' The other man, a plastics welder, said that the law did not greatly concern him: 'I keep my practice private, and what the law doesn't know, well!' [120, 121]

Britain's legal position on homosexuality was also beginning to look ridiculous in the eyes of the rest of the world. The day after *The Night People* was broadcast both *The Times* and the *Daily Express* reported the story of 29 Swedish female students who had been ejected from a hearing at the Royal Courts of Justice during an educational visit. The girls, aged 17 and 18, had walked in on the court martial appeal of Alan Jones, a former chaplain on the Ark Royal aircraft carrier, who had been convicted of indecent behaviour with a rating. The girls' teacher, Gunhild Kyle, could not understand what all the fuss was about: 'We just wanted to see your English courts at work. We knew nothing about that particular case. I do not think, having received sex instruction at school, they were likely to be shocked by anything they heard there.' Jones eventually lost his appeal. [122, 123]

Another foreign observer, German-born social activist Judith Piepe, spoke up for gay men on BBC 1's *Meeting Point* in November 1966. She described them as 'a despised and outcast minority' and 'probably the only minority in this country which is not yet equal before the law'. She praised young people who spoke up for 'the damaged ones' in society. Young musicians in particular, she said, were the 'troubadours of the

1960s', singing ballads to 'win your love of the unloved, the despised, the rejected'. One such troubadour was 21-year-old Al Stewart, who appeared on the programme singing *Pretty Golden Hair* at Les Cousins folk and blues club in London's Soho. The song featured on Stewart's 1967 debut album *Bed-Sitter Images* and is a Hogarthian tale of a young man's descent into prostitution and suicide. [124]

> Ah, the days soon grew thin
> And boredom fast set in.
> His job was thrown away without a care,
> For a man who softly said
> You'll earn twice as much instead
> With those blue eyes and pretty golden hair.
>
> Well London town possessed
> Of many a tempter's nest,
> And thus he fell with scarce another care
> As so easily he slipped
> Into prostitution's grip,
> Foundationed by his pretty golden hair.
>
> Ah, but the years quickly flew
> And his mind slowly grew
> From early freedom into deep despair.
> As the money ceased to roll
> A tired and lonely soul
> Poured curses on his pretty golden hair.
>
> Ah, the years stole their time.
> Now the living's hard to find,
> And early friends have vanished in the air.
> And the gay parties' ease
> Changed to public lavatories
> Have turned to grey his pretty golden hair.

Oh his life was only used
And his body just abused
By those who never think and never care.
But though his file said suicide,
No that wasn't why he died.
It was murder by his pretty golden hair. [125]

Pop group The Kinks hinted at close male relationships in their single *See My Friends*, released in July 1965. In an interview with music journalist Maureen Cleave, lead singer and guitarist Ray Davies explained: 'The song is about homosexuality. I know a person in this business who is quite normal and good-looking, but girls have given him such a rotten deal that he becomes a sort of queer. He has always got his friends. I mean it's like football teams and the way they're always kissing each other. Same sort of thing.' Davies later claimed that the song was about 'a youth who is not sure of his sexuality'. His brother, The Kinks' lead guitarist Dave Davies, experienced a same-sex relationship with Michael Aldred, a presenter on ITV's Friday evening pop show *Ready Steady Go!*. Davies later remembered: 'Me and Michael had a really great time because he had a wonderful sense of humour and he looked a bit like a young Dirk Bogarde. But I found after a while Michael was taking the relationship quite seriously, and that's when I saw the other side of it, and thought, I can't take advantage of his feelings like this. I can't tell him I'm just exploring and having a bit of fun. The guy loved me.' [126, 127]

Record producer Joe Meek also released a gay-themed song – *Do You Come Here Often?*, the B-side of The Tornadoes' final single *Is That A Ship I Hear?*. Released in August 1966 (six months before Meek shot dead his landlady Violet Shenton and then himself), it includes a waspish conversation between two gay men.

'Do you come here often?'
'Only when the pirate ships go off air.'
'Me too.' (giggles)
'Well, I see pyjama styled shirts are in, then.'

'Well, pyjamas are out, as far as I'm concerned anyway.'

'Who cares?'

'Well, I know of a few people who do.'

'Yes, you would.'

'Wow! Here's two coming now. What do you think?'

'Mmm. Mine's all right, but I don't like the look of yours.'

'Well, I must be off.'

'Yes, you're not looking so good.'

'Cheerio. I'll see you down the 'Dilly.'

'Not if I see you first, you won't.' [128]

Donovan's *To Try For The Sun*, which he included on his October 1966 album *Fairytale*, suggested a physical as well as an emotional relationship between a singer and 'the gypsy boy'.

> We huddled in a derelict building,
> And when he thought I was asleep
> He laid his poor coat round my shoulder
> And shivered there beside me in a heap.
> And who's going to be the one
> To say it was no good what we done?
> I dare a man to say I'm too young,
> For I'm going to try for the sun. [129]

By the time the new parliament sat in April 1966 the implementation of the Wolfenden Report seemed inevitable. On 26 April Arran reintroduced his lapsed bill in the House of Lords. It passed its second reading on 10 May by 70 votes to 29, and its third reading on 16 June by 70 votes to 60. On 5 July Leo Abse (who retained his seat at the election with a large and slightly increased majority) again used the Ten Minute Rule to introduce another Sexual Offences Bill. This time his motion passed by 244 votes to 100. The government then took the decision to back Abse's bill by giving him Home Office help to draft it, and by guaranteeing it parliamentary time. Key support came from the home secretary Roy

Jenkins. Home Office minister Dick Taverne remembered the importance of Jenkins' personal influence: 'There were certain bills he wanted to try and get onto the statute book, and abortion law reform and homosexual law reform were two of them.' Not all of Jenkins' cabinet colleagues were supportive of homosexual law reform. According to transport minister Barbara Castle, the secretary of state for economic affairs George Brown 'set off on a remarkable diatribe against homosexuality' during a cabinet meeting in February 1966: 'This is how Rome came down. Don't think teenagers are able to evaluate your liberal ideas. You will have a totally disorganised, indecent and unpleasant society. You must have rules! We've gone too damned far on sex already. I don't regard any sex as pleasant. It's pretty undignified and I've always thought so.' In October the leader of the House of Commons (and HLRS executive committee member) Richard Crossman noted in his diary that Brown, prime minister Harold Wilson and chancellor of the exchequer James Callaghan were nervous about government support for Abse's bill. They wanted to know 'why any time should be given to such a bill and why we should abandon the neutrality which the Labour cabinet had always shown to such controversial issues as homosexuality, abortion, divorce and Sunday opening of cinemas.' Crossman skilfully argued that 'we couldn't really be completely neutral in this case because both Houses had already expressed a clear will for legislation. In that case it was clearly better to let the House of Commons debate the matter freely now and to provide time for this rather than let the subject drag on until nearer the election.' With that, Wilson was persuaded 'to drag the rest of his colleagues with him.' [130, 131, 132]

By the end of 1966 the near certainty of legal change was raising expectations of a freer, more open society. 'We are beginning to unlace our Victorian corsets and emerge into queasy freedom,' declared Irma Kurtz in *Nova* in February 1967. 'We are changing; our laws are changing, and we shall have to stop condemning a large section of the community according to a concept which is nearly a century old.' In Martin Goff's *Indecent Assault* (1967) David's girlfriend Karen tells his father, government minister Mark Coulsden, why she thinks the decriminalisation of male homosexuality must come. [133]

'There's no better way of judging a society than by the way it treats a minority. Wouldn't this country be a better place if we weren't so frightened to discuss this sort of thing? For a Jew, queer or coloured person, his difference is the central factor of his life. He's got all the other problems like earning a living, keeping healthy, voting for a party or making a number of viable relationships, but first on his list is his particular difference. And if we were big enough, we'd regard helping him to adjust to himself as one of our top priorities. Desegregation and legal amendments are only a start.' [134]

Some in the Church of England were also moving in a radical new direction. In an article in *New Christian* in March 1967 Norman Pittenger wrote: 'I cannot see that the fact that one loves a person of the same sex, and wishes to act upon that love, is in and of itself sinful; nor can I see that acting upon that desire, when there is the true intention of love with the mutuality, fidelity, respect and tenderness I have urged, is in and of itself sinful.' In a later pamphlet Pittenger held out the prospect of gay unions taking place in church: 'Is there not the possibility of some kind of blessing which might be given to two men – or two women – who are entirely ready to state their intention in the presence of some agent of the religious community to which they belong or would like to belong? I know of some clergymen who have been willing to do just this.' [135, 136]

In June – just three weeks before the third and final reading of Abse's bill in the House of Commons – the writer Maureen Duffy told BBC 2's *Late Night Line-Up*: 'Since it seems likely that the bill will go through, many male homosexuals have said to me that for the first time they have declared themselves to their friends, workmates, parents; and they felt a tremendous liberation of spirit because of this feeling that at last they are not criminals when they are in bed.' Out of four guests on the programme – Duffy, Michael Schofield, the Conservative MP for Totnes Ray Mawby and an unnamed female doctor – only Mawby argued against homosexual law reform. He thought that the issue was 'a twilight area of abnormal people, and I don't think it's something that is out for public discussion.' He repeated the argument that gay men were 'more liable to blackmail, as we've seen in many of the security cases in the past'. Ironically, after his death in 1990 it was revealed that Mawby spied for the Czech communist authorities during the 1960s. Under the codename 'Laval', he passed information about parliamentary committees, fellow Conservative MPs and the floor plans of the prime minister's office in the House of Commons. [137, 138]

By 1967 views such as Mawby's were seen as eccentric and extreme. They corresponded to the kind of far-right opinions voiced by the Greater Britain Movement, which was trying to extend its influence following the Tories' defeat at the 1966 election. In July 1966 the movement's *Spearhead* magazine described homosexual law reform as 'pansies' emancipation' and part of a 'revolting cult of degeneration in our national life' practised by 'the political left and its liberal fellow travellers. The fanatical zeal with which these people campaign for their aims might make one believe that Britain stood on the threshold of everlasting darkness and damnation but for the national acceptance of legalised pouffery. It is just one of the hundredfold ways in which subversion casts its slimy hand on the fabric of British life.' [139]

Amid the general excitement surrounding homosexual law reform, some voices counselled caution. In August 1966 the writer Giles Playfair penned an article for *The Sunday Telegraph* in which he questioned whether the Wolfenden Report was still 'a satisfactory blueprint for legislation'. He pointed out that while the decade-old report 'took it for granted that homosexuality was socially undesirable and morally reprehensible', current advocates of law reform argued that 'because homosexual inclinations are no more to be helped than heterosexual inclinations, freedom to pursue the one is as basic a human right as freedom to pursue the other'. By rallying round the Wolfenden Report, reform campaigners did not fully appreciate 'the implications of what they are asking for'. Playfair warned that the report's recommendations would not satisfy them, and that sooner or later there would be 'a further outcry for reform'. He also thought that fixing the age of consent at 21 would 'give the law far greater scope for interference in male homosexual behaviour than in other sexual activities'. Playfair predicted that 'the demand for the social acceptance of homosexuality will gather momentum after the Wolfenden proposals have become law', and that 'we shall have a society in which homosexual relationships are considered no less "natural" or more shameful than heterosexual relationships. Homosexual couples will be free to embrace in public without risk of causing offence; homosexual love stories will be fittingly told on the stage. It may be that the theme of homosexual literature, which at the moment is "pity us" will change to "envy us".' [140]

That was not the sort of vision advocated by Arran and Abse. Their speeches and comments in parliament and the media focused on the overdue necessity of homosexual law reform rather than its liberalising nature. At almost every opportunity they stressed the unpleasantness of their task and their personal disapproval of homosexuality. During his spat with Cyril Osborne on *Twenty-Four Hours* Arran told viewers, 'Nobody is suggesting that we should make homosexuality into something which is good'. At the third reading of his bill in the Lords on 16 June 1966 he noted: 'In all the discussions we have had and in all the speeches, no single noble lord or noble lady has ever said that homosexuality is right or a good thing. It has been universally condemned from start to finish, and by every single member of the House.' During the second (unopposed) reading of his own bill in the Commons on 19 December Abse stated: 'All in this House, on both sides, and all sections of opinion, wish to see a diminution in the incidence of homosexuality. No one except those who are wilfully blind to the nature of our proceedings can possibly spell out of the bill any condonation whatever of homosexual conduct.' The following day on BBC Radio's *Today* programme Abse repeated his point that MPs did 'not approve of homosexuality. What the House of Commons has decided is that the homosexual has enough troubles without in addition having the fear and insecurity and the blackmail that arises from the existing law. The bill gives immunity to discreet homosexuals who live out their unfortunate condition in private.' [141, 142, 143, 144]

Abse's bill eventually passed its third reading in the Commons on 4 July 1967 by 99 votes to 14 after an exhaustive all-night sitting.

'Opposition conked out,' noted Richard Crossman in his diary. 'Neither Cyril Osborne nor Cyril Black, the leaders, could get there. The chief [whip John Silkin] and I spent the night going round the lobbies and encouraging the troops.' A tired Barbara Castle stayed in the Commons all night to give her support: 'Trailing through the lobby at 4 a.m. I ran into Lena Jeger [Labour MP for Holborn and St Pancras South], who put her arm round me and said in a piercing voice, "Aren't we good, doing our bit for the boys!"' [145, 146]

The politicians and campaigners who had pushed the bill through parliament were relieved rather than jubilant. Roy Jenkins told the House of Commons that it was 'an important piece of social legislation', but that it was 'not a vote of confidence in or congratulation for homosexuality. Those who suffer from this disability carry a great weight of loneliness, guilt, shame and other difficulties.' Richard Crossman wrote in his diary that the 'Buggers' bill' was 'extremely unpleasant'. He added: 'It may well be twenty years ahead of public opinion; certainly working-class people in the north jeer at their members at the weekend and ask them why they're looking after the buggers at Westminster instead of looking after the unemployed at home. It has gone down very badly that the Labour Party should be associated with such a bill.' Leo Abse felt 'too emotionally drained to react to praise or blame'. After the vote he drove home to his wife, who 'took me into her arms. I needed her comfort. For nothing fails like success.' Antony Grey felt 'at once triumphant and empty because what had been the driving force of our life over four or five years had suddenly happened and we were left with a sense of accomplishment and also a sense that there was a lot more to be done.' John, an HLRS volunteer, also attended the debate and felt that he had witnessed 'something very important in the British way of life'. Another volunteer, John Alcock, recalled: 'I came out with Antony Grey and all the crowd, and we all said good night to one another. I walked down the Embankment on the side of the Thames. I stood and lit a cigarette and was looking down into the water, and I was very aware that in my small way I'd been a part in making history.' [147, 148, 149, 150, 151, 152]

The Sexual Offences Bill quickly passed through the House of Lords. At its third and final reading there on 21 July Arran expressed the hope that it might ease the lives of gay men. But he also warned that it did not grant them any new rights or freedoms.

Because of the bill now to be enacted, perhaps a million human beings will be able to live in greater peace. I find this an awesome and a marvellous thing. The late Oscar Wilde, on his release from Reading Gaol, wrote to a friend, 'Yes, we shall win in the end, but the road will be long and red with monstrous martyrdoms.' Mr Wilde was right. The road has been long, and the martyrdoms many, monstrous and bloody. Today, please God, sees the end of that road. I ask those who have, as it were, been in bondage and for whom the prison doors are now open to show their thanks by comporting themselves quietly and with dignity. This is no occasion for jubilation; certainly not for celebration. Any form of ostentatious behaviour now or in the future, any form of public flaunting, would be utterly distasteful and would, I believe, make the sponsors of the bill regret that they have done what they have done. Homosexuals must continue to remember that while there may be nothing bad in being a homosexual, there is certainly nothing good. Lest the opponents of the bill think that a new freedom, a new privileged class, has been created, let me remind them that no amount of legislation will prevent homosexuals from being the subject of dislike and derision or at best of pity. We shall always, I fear, resent the odd man out. That is their burden for all time, and they must shoulder it like men – for men they are. [153, 154]

But it was Lord Boothby, the man who had first called for an enquiry to investigate homosexual offences, who summed up most people's feelings on the issue. During the second reading of the bill on 13 July he told the House of Lords, 'I cannot help hoping that when this bill and the abortion bill are both out of the light we shall not hear of sex in this House again for a very long time. Because the plain truth is that, after a while, sex can be very boring.'[155]

Chapter 6 references

1. Axle Publications
2. Pocket Cartoon, *Daily Express*, 1 July 1960
3. Gordon Westwood, *A Minority: A Report on the Life of the Male Homosexual in Great Britain*, Longmans, 1960
4. Readers' Report, 15 August 1960, Lord Chamberlain Plays Correspondence Files, British Library
5. Maurice Richardson, 'Television Clowns', *Twentieth Century*, July 1961
6. Martyn Goff, *The Youngest Director*, Putnam, 1961
7. Ibid.
8. Angus Wilson, *Late Call*, Secker & Warburg, 1964
9. Ibid.
10. Ibid.
11. Ibid.
12. Anthony Burgess, *The Wanting Seed*, Heinemann, 1962
13. *Victim*, Allied Film Makers, 1961
14. John Lahr, *Prick Up Your Ears: The Biography of Joe Orton*, Allen Lane, 1978
15. Martyn Goff, *The Youngest Director*, op. cit.
16. Angus Wilson, *Late Call*, op. cit.
17. Julian Mitchell, *Imaginary Toys*, Hutchinson, 1961
18. Ibid.
19. Ibid.
20. *Victim*, op. cit.
21. Leonard James Harper, *Teddy Boy Ahoy*, Thames-Side Publications, 1963
22. Ibid.
23. Meg Elizabeth Atkins, *The Gemini*, Peter Owen, 1964
24. Richard Hauser, *The Homosexual Society*, The Bodley Head, 1962

25. Alkarim Jivani, *It's Not Unusual: A History of Lesbian and Gay Britain in the Twentieth Century*, Michael O'Mara Books, 1997

26. J.R. Ackerley, *We Think the World of You*, The Bodley Head, 1960

27. John Pearson, *Notorious: The Immortal Legend of the Kray Twins*, Century, 2010

28. Eliot George, *The Leather Boys*, Anthony Blond, 1961

29. Gordon Westwood, *A Minority*, op. cit.

30. Antony Grey, *Speaking Out: Writings on Sex, Law, Politics and Society, 1954-95*, Cassell, 1997

31. Martyn Goff, *The Youngest Director*, op. cit.

32. Philip King, *How Are You Johnnie?*, Samuel French, 1963

33. George Moor, *The Pole and the Whistle*, Four Square, 1966

34. Michael Schofield, *Sociological Aspects of Homosexuality: A Comparative Study of Three Types of Homosexuals*, Longmans, 1965

35. Richard Hauser, *The Homosexual Society*, op. cit.

36. Martyn Goff, *The Youngest Director*, op. cit.

37. '10 Accused Of Sex Offences', *Bolton Evening News*, 25 June 1963

38. '"Tempter" Is Gaoled For 18 Months', *Bolton Evening News*, 9 July 1963

39. 'Blackmail Made Easy?', *The Observer*, 1 September 1963

40. *Male Homosexual*, BBC Home Service, 5 January 1965

41. *The BBC and the Closet*, BBC Radio 4, 29 January 2008

42. Memo from Graham Miller to J.A. Camacho, 9 September 1963, op. cit.

43. Memo from J.A. Camacho to Graham Miller, 13 September 1963, op. cit.

44. Memo from Graham Miller to J.A. Camacho 24 September 1963, op. cit.

45. Anthony Rowley, 'Another Kind of Loving: What is it like to be a homoscxual?', *Axle Spokes*, 4, 1963

46. Antony Grey, recorded interview, February 1990, Hall-Carpenter Oral History archive, British Library

47. Dirk Bogarde, *By Myself*, Channel 4, 18 January 1992

48. Lynne Reid Banks, *The L-Shaped Room*, Chatto & Windus, 1960

49. *A Taste of Honey*, Woodfall Film Productions, 1961

50. Andrew Salkey, *Escape to an Autumn Pavement*, Hutchinson, 1960

51. Desmond Donelly, 'Blackmailer's Charter', *The Spectator*, 23 February 1962

52. Alkarim Jivani, *It's Not Unusual*, op. cit.

53. 'Sir Ian Says No to Life Peerage', *Daily Express*, 14 April 1962

54. Terence Stamp, *Stamp Album*, Bloomsbury, 1987

55. Ibid.

56. 'Charges of Indecency Against Sir Ian Horobin', *The Times*, 6 June 1962

57. 'Great Career of Sir Ian Ends in Jail', *Daily Mirror*, 18 July 1962

58. 'Sir Ian Jailed for Four Years', *Daily Express*, 18 July 1962

59. 'Sir Ian Horobin Sentenced to Four Years' Imprisonment', *The Times*, 18 July 1962

60. 'Boy "Was More Sinned Against"', *The Times*, 20 July 1962

61. 'Boy Driver of MP's Car is Charged', *Daily Express*, 5 March 1963

62 '9-Month Sentence on Guardsman', *The Times*, 21 May 1963

63. '"Scandals Discovered" by Bell', *The Guardian*, 9 October 1963

64. 'Man Accuses a Minister', *The Daily Telegraph*, 11 October 1963

65. Ibid.

66. Michael Bloch, *Jeremy Thorpe*, Little, Brown, 2014

67. 'Salesman is Cleared of 9 Charges', *The Times*, 17 October 1963

68. 'The Army "Sacks" Bell Case Witness', *Evening Standard*, 24 October 1963

69. Anthony Rowley, 'Another Kind of Loving:', op. cit.

70. Alastair Heron (ed.), *Towards a Quaker View of Sex*, Friends Home Service Committee, 1963

71. *The Brian Epstein Story, Part 1: The Sun Will Shine Tomorrow*, BBC 2, 25 December 1998

72. Philip King, *How Are You Johnnie?*, op. cit.

73. Bill Naughton, *All in Good Time*, Samuel French, 1965

74. 'Greek to Me', *The Sunday Times*, 3 February 1963

75. 'How BBC Pronounces the Word', *The Sunday Telegraph*, 3 February 1963

76. Angus Wilson, *Late Call*, op. cit.

77. Jack Bell, 'BBC Shelves Film on Club', *Daily Mirror*, 21 May 1963

78. 'BBC-TV Scraps Film on Holland Homosexuals', *Variety*, 29 May 1963

79. *That Was The Week That Was*, BBC Television, 1963

80. 'Confession', op. cit.

81. *Panorama*, BBC Television, 5 August 1963

82. Julian Mitchell, *Imaginary Toys*, op. cit.

83. Gordon Westwood, *A Minority*, op. cit.

84. *Victim*, op. cit.

85. Eustace Chesser, 'The Hidden Problem', *Family Doctor*, October 1961

86. Bill Naughton, *All in Good Time*, op. cit.

87. Colin MacInnes, 'Dark Angel: The Writings of James Baldwin', *Encounter*, August 1963

88. James Margach, 'Henry Brooke and the Unpublished Picture', *The Sunday Times*, 19 July 1964

89. Norman Lucas, 'Peer and a Gangster: Yard Inquiry', *Sunday Mirror*, 12 July 1964

90. 'The Picture We Must Not Print', *Sunday Mirror*, 19 July 1964

91. 'Lord Boothby: An Unqualified Apology', *Sunday Mirror*, 9 August 1964

92. *This Week: Homosexuals*, ITV, 22 October 1964

93. Ibid.

94. Policy – Sexual Offences (1963-1964) file, BBC Written Archives

95. *Male Homosexual*, BBC Home Service, 12 January 1965, BBC Written Archives

96. *Male Homosexual*, BBC Home Service, 5 January 1965

97. Ibid.

98. *The BBC and the Closet*, op. cit.

99. *Woman's Hour*, BBC Light Programme, 9 March 1965, BBC Written Archives

100. Ibid.

101. *Woman's Hour*, BBC Light Programme, 11 March 1965, BBC Written Archives

102. Monica Furlong, 'Can Such a Sentence on This Boy Be Justified?', *Daily Mail*, 30 November 1965

103. Recorded Crime Statistics 1898-2001/2, Home Office Statistics

104. Bob Cant, Susan Hemmings (ed.s), *Radical Records: Thirty Years of Lesbian and Gay History*, Routledge, 1988

105. Philip Rescorla, recorded interview, November 1985, Hall-Carpenter Oral History archive, op. cit.

106. Alison Pressley, *Changing Times: Being Young in Britain in the 60s*, Michael O'Mara books, 2000

107. Christopher Spence, recorded interview, September 1990, Hall-Carpenter Oral History archive, op. cit.

108. Ibid.

109. Lord Arran, 'The Sexual Offences Act: A Personal Memoir', *Encounter*, March 1972

110. Harford Montgomery Hyde, *The Other Love: An Historical and Contemporary Survey of Homosexuality in Britain*, Heinemann, 1970

111. Ibid.

112. Michael Schofield, *Sociological Aspects of Homosexuality*, op. cit.

113. Letters, *The Times*, 11 May 1965

114 Obituaries, *The Times*, 5 May 1965

115. Pocket Cartoon, *Daily Express*, 2 June 1965

116. Gordon Greig, 'Homosexuality: Alter the Law', *Daily Mail*, 28 October 1965

117. *Ten O'Clock*, BBC Home Service, 28 October 1965, Albany Trust files, London School of Economics.

118. *Twenty-Four Hours*, BBC 1, 28 October 1965, BBC Written Archives

119. Ibid.

120. C.H. Rolph, 'Homosexuality: Reform At Last?', *The New Statesman*, 4 February 1966

121. *The Night People*, BBC Home Service, 4 April 1966

122. 'Schoolgirls Leave Court', *The Times*, 5 April 1966

123. Frank Goldsworthy, '29 Blondes Get Marching Orders from "Sex" Case', *Daily Express*, 5 April 1966

124. *Meeting Point: Outcasts and Outsiders,* BBC 1, 20 November 1966

125. Al Stewart, *Pretty Golden Hair, Bed-Sitter Images*, CBS, 6 October 1967

126. Jon Savage, *The Kinks: The Official Biography*, Faber and Faber, 1984

127. *Dave Davies: Kinkdom Come*, BBC Four, 15 July 2011

128. Joe Meek, *Do You Come Here Often?*, Colombia, 12 August 1966

129. Donovan, *To Try for the Sun, Fairytale*, Pye Records, 22 October 1966

130. *Measure of Conscience: Consenting Party*, BBC 2, 26 April 1972

131. Barbara Castle, *The Castle Diaries, 1964-70*, Friday 11 February 1966, Weidenfeld & Nicolson, 1984

132. Richard Crossman, *The Diaries of a Cabinet Minister: Volume 2: Lord President of the Council and Leader of the House of Commons, 1966-68*, Thursday 27 October 1966, Hamish Hamilton, 1976

133. Irma Kurtz, 'Homosexuality: The Unlocking of a Law', *Nova*, February 1967.

134. Martyn Goff, *Indecent Assault*, André Deutsch, 1967

135. Norman Pittenger, 'Time For Consent', *New Christian*, 9 March 1967

136. Norman Pittenger, *Time for Consent? A Christian's Approach to Homosexuality*, SCM Press, 1967

137. *Late Night Line-Up*, BBC 2, 14 June 1967

138. Richard Alleyne, 'Tory Minister Spied for Communists in the House of Commons', *The Daily Telegraph*, 28 June 2012

139. 'Pansies' Emancipation', *Spearhead*, July 1966

140. Giles Playfair, 'Time to Forget Wolfenden', *The Sunday Telegraph*, 14 August 1966

141. *Twenty-Four Hours*, op. cit.

142. Antony Grey, *Quest for Justice*, op. cit.

143. Patrick Higgins, *Heterosexual Dictatorship: Male Homosexuality in Post-War Britain*, Fourth Estate, 1996

144. *Today*, BBC Home Service, 20 December 1966

145. Richard Crossman, *The Diaries of a Cabinet Minister*, Monday 3 July 1967, op. cit.

146. Barbara Castle, *The Castle Diaries*, Monday 3 July 1967, op. cit.

147. 'At 5.50 BST After a Night of Dubious Jokes and Personal Clashes a Social Revolution Begins', *Daily Mirror*, 5 July 1967

148. Richard Crossman, *The Diaries of a Cabinet Minister*, Monday 3 July 1967, op. cit.

149. Leo Abse, *Private Member*, Macdonald & Co., 1973

150. Antony Grey, recorded interview, February 1990, Hall-Carpenter Oral History archive, op. cit.

151. 'John', recorded interview, 1996, Tony Dean Gay Commercial Scene interviews, British Library

152. John Alcock, recorded interview, July 1985, Hall-Carpenter Oral History archive, op. cit.

153. *Gay Times: The Sex Lives of Us*, BBC Radio 4, 13 September 2007

154. Michael McManus, *Tory Pride and Prejudice: The Conservative Party and Homosexual Law Reform*, Biteback Publishing, 2011

155. Ibid.

Chapter 7

IT'S LEGAL NOW

Queers mostly lead normal lives; never in trouble. Reform has made
little difference to them. Some don't know it has happened.

Ray Gosling, *New Society*, 29 August 1968 [1]

On 13 July 1967 Kenneth Williams recorded in his diary the passing
of the Sexual Offences Bill at its second reading in House of Lords: 'It's
all right between consenting adults in private, except the services and in
Scotland. So it won't do any good for the queens of Dundee and the like.'
Ten days later Williams went to see Joe Orton and Kenneth Halliwell.
'We chatted about homosexuality and the effect the new clause would
have. We agreed it would accomplish little.' [2, 3]

Such indifference to the new law was widespread. 'My generation
was not going to be tied down by laws and constraints, whether the law
changed in 1967 or whether it had to wait until 1977,' recalled Peter
Burton. Fashion designer Richard Cawley did not even know that the
Sexual Offences Act had happened: 'I can honestly say that all through
the 60s I was totally unaware of anything to do with homosexual law
reform. It might have been in certain newspapers, but I didn't read
newspapers.' Trevor Thomas from South Wales was similarly 'unaware
of the political agitation, the campaign to change the [law]. It didn't
seem to register much in my mind. I thought, oh well, it's legal now.'
Bill Thorneycroft from London was also unimpressed. When Leo Abse's

bill was passed by the House of Commons early in the morning on 4 July he and his partner Fred were in bed together: 'We said, "We don't feel any different."' [4, 5]

NWHLRC secretary Allan Horsfall was disappointed with the outcome of ten years of campaigning: 'I don't think boredom quite expresses the way we felt. Tedium perhaps. I don't remember cracking any bottles of champagne or going on any carnival marches.' Two days after royal assent on 27 July Antony Grey confessed to Horsfall, 'I am experiencing a feeling of anti-climax at the moment, but I hope that this will pass.' Other reformers, like Patrick Trevor-Roper, wanted gay men to heed Lord Arran's advice to behave discreetly: 'I think everybody was feeling, well, we mustn't let it be visible to the public because the image would be bad if we start[ed] rioting.' Tony Dyson hoped that the Sexual Offences Act would mark 'the beginning of a period when the discussion would die down and homosexuals would be allowed to lead their own lives'. C.H. Rolph felt that his objective of implementing the Wolfenden Report had been achieved and that it was time to step down from campaigning: 'I did feel that having got the Act through, one could regard that as a kind of winning post. So I bowed out. There was nothing left for me to do.' [6, 7, 8, 9, 10]

Others were more positive. Watching events from prison, John Vassall recalled being 'on tenterhooks when at last the Wolfenden proposals were finally passed, and I gave an enormous sigh of relief that never again could one be blackmailed or fear being persecuted, as had been the case in the past.' John Fraser thought that the Sexual Offences Act 'opened the doors to a future inconceivable in my youth – life free from fear'. Colin Spencer remembered 'a feeling that at last, I'm legal, that something was lifted'. The photographer Cecil Beaton wrote in his diary: 'When one realizes what damage, what tragedy has been brought on by this lack of sympathy to a very delicate and difficult subject, this should be a great time of celebration.' [11, 12, 13, 14]

Many people misunderstood the purpose of the Act. Joe Orton recounted how, after returning from a trip to Morocco, he chatted to his agent Peggy Ramsay about his liking for north African boys: '"Well, you're legal now," she said, showing her ignorance. "It's only legal over twenty-one," I said. Kenneth Williams encountered similar ignorance on 14 July during his visit to the Bridge Tavern in Canning Town: 'All these young chaps were crowding round. One of them said to me, "Kaw! Ken, it's legal now, you know." And he started to pull his trousers down.' Yorkshire miner Fred Dyson heard about the passing of Abse's bill while travelling on a bus with a friend: 'I got hold of him and I gave him a great big kiss. And everybody on the bus was looking, but I wasn't bothered. I said, "You can all look. It's legal now."' But his behaviour was not legal. And neither was Ernie's at the Bridge Tavern. [15, 16, 17]

Under the terms of the Sexual Offences Act homosexual behaviour was only permitted within certain Wolfenden-approved limits. A 'homosexual act' was no longer a criminal offence, but only if it took place 'in private', and if 'the parties consent thereto and have attained the age of twenty-one years'. The 'in private' provision did not include a situation in which more than two people were present, and the Act specifically outlawed sexual activity in public lavatories. Unlike the Wolfenden Report, which had advocated no change, the Sexual Offences Act increased the penalty for 'procuring or attempting to procure' gross indecency with an under-21-year-old, from a maximum of two years' imprisonment to five. The crime of 'soliciting by men and importuning for immoral purposes' – which carried a maximum penalty of two years' imprisonment – remained unchanged, although the Act did impose a 12 month time limit on proceedings for that offence, and also for gross indecency and buggery. The Wolfenden recommendation that the maximum sentence for consensual buggery by a man aged over 21 with a partner aged between 16 and 21 should be reduced from life imprisonment to five years was adopted, while the maximum penalty for consensual buggery by a youth aged 16 to 20 was also reduced from life to two years in prison. Another Wolfenden-inspired clause dealing with the protection of young people raised the maximum punishment for over-21-year-olds who committed gross indecency with youths aged 16 to 20 from two years to five. In addition, it was ruled that no proceedings should be taken against under-21-year-olds 'except by or with the consent of the director of public prosecutions'. Homosexual acts by members of the army, air force and navy remained illegal, as did sex between crewmen on United Kingdom merchant ships.* The Act applied to England and Wales only. In Scotland and Northern Ireland, which were specifically excluded from its provisions, all homosexual acts remained illegal. [18]

Discontent with the Sexual Offences Act was voiced even before it became law. In April 1967 Antony Grey told a meeting of Young Conservatives in Surrey that 'the present bill going through parliament did not go far enough'. Less than six months after it was passed, Leo Abse told the *British Journal of Criminology* that his bill 'reflected the appeasement required to assuage the irrational fears which otherwise could have overspilled and totally engulfed the bill. The penalties attached to some public displays of homosexuality are too harsh. The provisions concerning servicemen and seamen aboard merchant navy ships are unrealistic and could, if harshly administered, cause grave anomalies. More important, the interpretation of privacy within the Act, if too narrowly applied, could thwart the legislature's intentions.' He added that 'vigilance will be required amongst reformers in the early years of the Act'. [19, 20]

Further reform did at first seem possible. On 27 July 1967 – the day the Sexual Offences Act received royal assent – the home secretary Roy Jenkins told parliament that he would ask the Criminal Law Revision Committee to review the law on sexual offences, including male soliciting. 'This,' wrote Antony Grey, 'gives the HLRS both a new task and an opportunity to start working immediately for the elimination of some of the more undesirable features of the new law.' In the event, however, the committee decided not to review the laws on homosexual behaviour. [21]

---

* Speaking about this part of the Sexual Offences Act at a conference in 1970, Antony Grey remembered: 'We had never even heard of this great apprehension on the part of the merchant navy, and at this very late stage of the bill I rather suspect that it was manipulated by two elderly Roman Catholic trade unionsists, the members, I believe, for Bootle and Preston, the Mahon brothers, who did a very nifty bit of lobbying with the shipping industry and the Seamen's Union.' He was referring to Simon Mahon, the Labour MP for Bootle, and Peter Mahon, the Labour MP for Preston South. [21]

Comparison of Homosexual Offences in England and Wales, 1956-1967

Sexual Offences Act 1956		Wolfenden recommendations, 1957		Sexual Offences Act 1967	
Offence	*Maximum penalty*	*Proposed offence*	*Suggested maximum penalty*	*Offence*	*Maximum penalty*
Buggery	Life imprisonment	Buggery by a man aged 21+ with a partner aged 16-20	Five years' imprisonment	Buggery by a man aged 21+ with a partner aged 16-20	Five years' imprisonment
		Buggery by a youth under 21 with a consenting partner over 16	Two years' imprisonment	Buggery by a youth aged 16-20	Two years' imprisonment
				Procuring a man to commit buggery with another man	Two years' imprisonment
Gross indecency between males	Two years' imprisonment	Gross indecency by a man aged 21+ with a partner aged 16-20	Five years' imprisonment	Gross indecency by a man aged 21+ with a partner aged 16-20	Five years' imprisonment
Procuring acts of gross indecency between males	Two years' imprisonment	No change	No change	Procuring acts of gross indecency with males under 21	Five years' imprisonment
Attempting to procure acts of gross indecency between males	Two years' imprisonment	No change	No change	Attempting to procure acts of gross indecency with males under 21	Five years' imprisonment

Hopes for change were also raised by the publication of the Latey Report in July 1967, which recommended lowering the age of majority from 21 to 18. This, it was thought, would result in a corresponding lowering of the age of homosexual consent. Most Wolfenden Committee members had been in favour of eighteen, as was Lord Arran. In November 1967 he wrote to the Lord Chancellor, Lord Gardiner: 'If it is going to be legal for a boy and a girl to marry at 18 without parental consent, then it is surely illogical that it should be illegal for two boys of over 18 and under 21 – or for that matter a man and a boy over 18 – who indulge in intercourse in private to be treated as criminals. If legislation is introduced to implement Latey on marriage at 18, I think it likely that some peer will seek at that time to amend the Sexual Offences bill so that the age of consent for homosexual practices is lowered to 18.'* While privately agreeing with Arran, Gardiner thought that the time was not yet right for another parliamentary battle over homosexual law reform. He wrote to 'Dear Boofy' a few days later: 'It is a question of what one can get through parliament at any particular time, and although I think that it ought to be eighteen all round, I am sure that it would be a great mistake to try to alter your Act so soon.'** [23, 24]

Efforts to clear the convictions of men prosecuted for offences which after 1967 were no longer crimes also failed. Antony Grey referred the issue to Leo Abse in October 1967 after receiving enquiries from three HLRS supporters. One of them complained of 'difficulties involved in emigration and visa formalities for the USA and elsewhere; job applications abroad, etc.'. In November Home Office minister Dick Taverne told Abse that although Roy Jenkins had ordered two men to be released from prison 'because he was satisfied that it would not be right to continue to detain them' under the Sexual Offences Act, it would not be possible to expunge the criminal records of men who had previously had 'a valid conviction' at the time. [25, 26]

---

* Arran reiterated his point a decade later. He told *Gay News* in 1976, 'I mean, if a man can get married at eighteen, then the same thing ought to apply to homosexuals. Marriage after all is a much more important step than two men tucking up in bed together.' [27]
** The age of consent for homosexual acts was finally lowered to 18 in 1994, and to 16 in 2000.

The definition of homosexual acts 'in private' was never fully clarified – even after the case of Regina v. Marshall and Oswald in 1968. This involved two men arrested for committing an indecent act in a van parked in a field near a country lane. No one else was in the vicinity at the time, except for the arresting police officers, who did not actually see the act taking place. In court the men's defending barrister, W. Fitch, argued that a homosexual act could be in private even if it did not take place behind closed doors. Conversely, an act inside someone's home might not be in private if, for example, someone else was present in the building at the same time. After considering whether consenting adults should first make 'absolutely sure that it was not possible under any circumstances for others to become aware of their activities', the judge at Essex assizes, Eric Blain, told the jury that it was up to them to decide whether or not Marshall's and Oswald's actions had been committed in private, because 'parliament had left it to them to decide what test they might apply'. He also urged the jury 'to use their ordinary common sense in coming to their decision'. The two men were found not guilty. [28]

The Sexual Offences Act did at least help to free up some gay men's lives. For George and Steve from Hove, the Act brought 'a great sense of relief [that] we were now not against the law. That made a great deal of difference.' After the Act was passed, the pair decided to buy a home together, and they went to see the manager of a building society in Brighton to ask for a loan. 'I remember it was the Abbey National in the Western Road, and I'd got Steve in tow,' recalled George. 'And I said, "I want a mortgage for myself and my friend here." So he started to look at the form and it gave our two names. So he said, "Mm, it's unusual to sign two men. What's going to happen if one of you decides not to pay the mortgage? How can I guarantee that there's a firm relationship there?" So I leaned across the desk [and] I said, "Look, all the money we've got in the world is in my bank account. If he goes, it stays with me." And he was good; he gave it to us. It must have been quite a thing to do then.' [29]

Rex Batten and his partner John had already lived together in East Dulwich, south London for ten years before they decided to buy a double bed and have it delivered to their home. 'That was a hell of a statement to make,' remembered Rex, 'because everybody would know what came in. We never had any comment about it. We just wanted to fit in with the street, and we were accepted.' [30]

But for most consenting adult couples the Sexual Offences Act made little or no difference. Seven weeks after it became law, *The Guardian*'s Geoffrey Moorhouse interviewed John and Eric, who had been together for 20 years. They agreed that the Act meant that they did not have to worry about visits from the police; but this had never been a problem anyway, 'with cops among their heterosexual friends attending poker parties in their council flat'. For them, the legal changes did not make 'a ha'porth of difference'. Moorhouse also spoke to Neville, a 'homosexual and living alone', who thought that 'some small sense of shame [had] been lifted'. But he remained 'worried by his self-consciousness at being homosexual'. At his workplace he was still aware of 'a tension in every conversation; waiting for it to turn to sex, when his choice is between keeping quiet – and therefore risking identification – and talking in a way that is unnatural to him'. Legal adjustments alone, Moorhouse concluded, would not 'remove the stigma from being a homosexual.' [31]

The legalisation of adult homosexual behaviour did not lessen the threat of blackmail either. The total number of reported incidences in England and Wales rose to 427 in 1967 – more than three-and-half times the number reported a decade earlier. What proportion of these had a homosexual element is unknown, but as Quentin Crisp observed in 1968, 'The argument that the repeal of the laws against private indecency will lessen opportunities for blackmail is founded on a misunderstanding. Blackmail operates by the threat to reveal facts of which a man is ashamed to those whose good opinion he prizes. It may easily be the victim's mother or wife or employer. To rob blackmail of its potency, it would be necessary to remove the homosexual's feeling of shame.' Writing in *The Observer* two years later, Joanna Slaughter pointed out that 'many men, even if they have done nothing illegal, are so anxious to conceal their homosexual state from relatives and colleagues that they are as vulnerable as if they had actually broken the law'. Slaughter spoke to a Samaritans worker who told her, 'It is just not true to say that because a man can't be sent to prison, he can't be blackmailed. There has been a decrease in the most vicious kind of blackmail since the passing of the Act, but that is all.' [32, 33, 34]

Many gay men also thought that the Sexual Offences Act gave the police and the judiciary more control over their lives. John from Tyneside thought that the Act made men 'more wary about going to bed with younger people. At one time it didn't matter how old you were if you went to bed with somebody, you were still in trouble.' But after 1967 'you [were] told that you mustn't have anybody unless they [were] 21'. Bill Thorneycroft thought that 'sex was easier before 1967. After, it gave a blueprint to the police for arrests.' Tony Papard also believed that the Act was 'used by the police to persecute gay men. Before that, since all male homosexuality was underground, illegal and invisible to the general public, they often turned a blind eye to what went on in toilets, cruising grounds and gay clubs. However, as soon as the 1967 Act was passed the police and courts had a blueprint for what was legal and what was illegal, and they used it to hound gay men.' [35, 36, 37]

There was certainly no reduction in police action against gay men in the years following the passing of the Sexual Offences Act. As early as June 1967 Antony Grey told Allan Horsfall: 'I very much doubt whether [the] attitude on the part of the authorities is going to be altered by the passage into law of Abse's bill. The naïve belief on his behalf and that of other MPs that the mere passage of the bill into law is going to indicate to the police that they should be generally lenient, when such draconian provisions and penalties have been written into it, is in my view a pathetic fallacy.' [38]

Incidences of recorded homosexual crime in England and Wales peaked at 5,027 in 1967 – their highest since 1963. Over the next few years they fell back slightly to 4,712 in 1968, 4,662 in 1969 and 4,781 in 1970. But because post-1967 incidences no longer included consenting adults in private, these figures may have represented an overall increase. In Scotland, which was not covered by the Sexual Offences Act, prosecutions were lower. This was explained, as it had been to the Wolfenden Committee, as being due to the different legal and police systems there. Even so, 149 men were prosecuted for sodomy and indecency in 1968, and 148 in 1969. [39, 40]

A decade later, criminologist Roy Walmsley investigated the England and Wales figures and noted that incidences of gross indecency rose from 840 in 1967 to 1,069 in 1972 – a 27% increase. He attributed this to greater activity by London's Metropolitan Police and two other (unnamed) forces. Walmsley also found that the prosecution rate for this offence rose from 31% in 1967 to 60% in 1971. Between 1967 and 1973 convictions increased by 73%. Walmsley concluded that in some regions the police were 'more ready to prosecute homosexual offences than they were before 1967'. He also confirmed the suspicions of Bill Thorneycroft, Tony Papard and others that the Sexual Offences Act was used by the police as a 'blueprint' to target gay men. [41]

> The 1967 Act brought to an end a period, lasting at least since the publication of the Wolfenden Report some ten years earlier, when the law prohibiting all homosexual acts between males had been called into question. The way in which the 1967 Act resolved this uncertainty was to distinguish homosexual acts in private from those committed in public places. This was not however merely a decision that certain acts in private, previously illegal, should cease to be so, but also meant or implied that parliament had decided that homosexual acts in public should continue to be unlawful. Thus it may well be that the 1967 Act, by re-affirming this aspect of the law, provided the police with an up-to-date basis on which action could more confidently be taken against those involved in homosexual acts in public. [42]

Walmsley added that because the Sexual Offences Act ordered summary trials for cases of gross indecency, prosecutions for this offence could be brought more easily. 'As a result,' he noted, 'offenders can be apprehended one afternoon, be brought before the magistrates' court the following morning, plead guilty, be fined and leave the court very much in the way in which drunks are often handled by police and courts – it being unnecessary for the police to produce members of the public who were offended.' [43]

Walmsley's findings were borne out by a string of court cases which demonstrated the increased zealotry of the police in pursuing homosexual offences and drew attention to the inconsistent administration of the new law. In Staffordshire a police swoop on young gay men led to the convictions of four youths and the suicide of a fifth. The case, which caused some consternation in the press, began in autumn 1967 when William Quick from Newcastle-under-Lyme went into hospital, leaving David Bourne, a 19-year-old public baths attendant, in charge of his house. The following week, Bourne started hosting parties at the house. The parties drew between 30 and 50 young men at a time. According to guests, these gatherings were 'not grossly indecent: youths danced together and occasionally kissed. From time to time some of them went in pairs to bedrooms and made love in private, behind locked doors.' One evening a group of five partygoers who were on their way to the house from Stoke-on-Trent removed lightbulbs from the bus they were travelling on. They were arrested for the alleged theft and, in the course of questioning by the police, 'other matters came to light concerning their sexual habits'. A 25-year-old was tried and acquitted of stealing the light bulbs, but the other four – William Ansell, 19, Clifford Fitzgerald, 17, Stephen Cheetham, 17 and an unnamed 16-year-old – were briefly sent to a remand home before being released on bail. Ansell was subsequently re-arrested on an unrelated larceny charge and sent to a remand centre at Risley, near Warrington. It was there that he hanged himself. Meanwhile, according to *The Sunday Times*'s Tony Geraghty, 'energetic police investigations continued among the Potteries' active and unblushing homosexual society, and the DPP brooded over the boys' statements'. The three youths and party host Bourne were eventually charged with gross indecency and sentenced at Stafford assizes to indeterminate periods of borstal training. [44]

What disturbed many about the case was not just Ansell's suicide and the severity of the sentences against the others (despite probation officers' recommendations that probation would be the best way of dealing with them), but the fact that the youths were prosecuted at all. Geraghty thought that the case seemed to 'mock the purpose of last summer's legal reform', because the intention of fixing the age of consent at 21 was 'not to imprison adolescents but to protect them from the advances of older men'. Had the youths been 21, their private acts, which were 'admitted by all concerned to be within the scope of the recent Sexual Offences Act', would have been legal. 'They were prosecuted,' Geraghty said, 'because they were consenting adolescents and not consenting adults.' He also detected in 'the case of the Gay Boys of Staffordshire' the same underhand police practices which had troubled the Wolfenden Committee a decade earlier: 'A series of voluntary statements admitting homosexual behaviour were made while the boys were in custody, being questioned about petty larceny. One youth was convicted of gross indecency almost exclusively on the basis of his own statement of admission to the police.' Geraghty also asked why the director of public prosecutions, Norman Skelhorn, had allowed the case to proceed when the purpose of his decision-making powers under section eight of the Sexual Offences Act was to protect rather than punish gay youths. [45]

It was no surprise when the four Stoke youths' appeals against their convictions failed. At their appeal trial in April 1968 Lord Justice Winn said that they had 'entirely misconceived the intentions of parliament' in thinking that the 1967 Act was there to protect them from older men and that they would not be prosecuted for consensual homosexual acts in private between themselves. The court did, however, set aside the sentences of borstal training for Clifford Fitzgerald and the 16-year-old youth because they had 'developed some strength of character and had prospects of establishing normal relationships with young women'. David Bourne and Stephen Cheetham, on the other hand, were ordered to remain in borstal because, according to Winn, they needed guidance and protection against 'the misery which life will have in store for them if they fail to develop natural sexual impulses and desires'. [46]

The plight of under-21-year-olds troubled many. While the four Stoke youths were awaiting their unsuccessful appeal, HLRS supporter

Brian Clow wrote to Antony Grey in March 1968 about the case of Graham Spencer, a 20-year-old from St Osyth in Essex, who had been charged with 'serious offences with another man'. Clow thought that Spencer's case showed that 'the 18-21 age group seem now to be victims of an injustice even more isolated in its harshness than before the change of law'. *The Observer's* Roy Perrott also pointed out that the Sexual Offences Act 'encouraged a more relaxed attitude among homosexuals, particularly younger ones' which did not 'find a matching response in police practice'. He thought that 'the battle for tolerance for the homosexual is now going through a difficult phase'. A year later, Antony Grey and Donald West told *New Society* that despite the provisions for the protection of youths under 21 written into the 1967 Act, 'minors are still sometimes sentenced for such activities with each other'. Citing the Stoke case, they added that 'the holding of homosexual parties involves another legal risk that heterosexuals do not face'. [47, 48, 49, 50]

Ignorance and misunderstanding about the 1967 Act was certainly widespread among gay youths. In Andrew McCall's 1968 novel *The Au Pair Boy* 'chubby fair-haired' Gavin has to explain to a friend why it is a problem that their older acquaintance Michael Musgrave has been 'carrying on with some chicken'. [51]

'I thought they didn't prosecute any more.
'He's 19.'
'So what?'
'He's a minor, you fool.' [52]

The Stoke and Essex police forces were not the only ones actively enforcing the Sexual Offences Act. During the late 1960s new constabularies were created from the merger of smaller forces, and many of these deliberately targeted gay men as a way of proving their effectiveness in detecting crime. As Quentin Crisp noted, the 'scramble to gain promotion by securing a large number of arrests is an unpleasant part of the police system'. Leo Abse acknowledged that in some parts of the country there was 'an excess of zeal on the part of the police'. Tony Smyth, general secretary of the National Council for Civil Liberties, also thought that 'the degree of police activity against homosexuals depends very largely on the chief constable of the area'. One police officer even told Joanna Slaughter in 1970 that he was 'frankly relieved' when his chief constable left the area: 'All we seemed to do was go about pinching pooves.' [53, 54]

The Hampshire Constabulary – a new force formed in April 1967 from the amalgamation of the Hampshire and Isle of Wight Constabulary and the Portsmouth and Southampton city forces – gained a particularly notorious reputation in this respect. In February 1968 the HLRS received the first of many complaints about police activity in and around Portsmouth's public toilets.

Since the new laws on homosexuality came in, Portsmouth has had a purge worse than anything in the old days, but only an occasional case is reported in the local paper, and then only because of the changes in penalties. In this purge the police employ three men full time! One of these acts as 'bait' to get men to approach him. The three engaged in this purge are:-

• Det. Sgt Herbert
• Det. Con. Russell
• PC Gunter (the bait).

Apparently PC Gunter waits about in public conveniences, masturbating his person, and smiling at any man whom he suspects of being homosexual. When the case is heard, the framing of the charges is frequently the same – 'Importuning (or behaving indecently with) another man not in custody (or another man unknown)'. It is difficult to understand how a man can be convicted under such circumstances, but detectives Hubert and Russell give evidence to the effect that they observed the indecent behaviour, and that the other man ran away.

As I am not personally concerned in this matter, I am unable to sign this letter, but have the strongest reasons for believing the allegations to be true. [55]

The following June 35-year-old college lecturer Tudor Rawkins was arrested by plain clothes officers near the public toilets on Western Parade in Southsea, Portsmouth. One of the officers, Alan Russell, was the same constable Russell cited in the anonymous letter to the HLRS four months earlier. The other, Cyril Hubert Walker, may possibly have been the sergeant 'Herbert' also cited in the letter. Rawkins – the head of geography at Portsmouth College of Technology, and an examiner for the University of London – explained that on the night of 7 June, after attending a charity reception and a party, felt 'a little groggy' with an upset stomach. He drove to the toilets on Western Parade to be sick and there saw Russell, Walker and another officer in civilian dress. Rawkins left the toilets, but then stopped in a nearby alleyway to be sick. 'As I did this,' he recounted, 'I realised that there beside me was a body. He was in the shadow of the wall. He grabbed me, saying, "Got you – I've been watching you all night."'[56]

The policemen's version of events was rather different. Walker told magistrates that he and Russell had seen Rawkins masturbating and smiling at them in the toilets. Rawkins then followed Walker out of the toilets and down the alleyway, where he said 'hello' and, 'without further comment, touched the sergeant's genitals'. Rawkins was subsequently charged with importuning for an immoral purpose, indecent assault and attempting to procure an act of gross indecency. He was also suspended from his job after Hampshire police told Portsmouth College about his arrest. In the event, Rawkins was found not guilty by an all-male jury at Portsmouth quarter sessions on 30 July. But his college continued to bar him from doing field work with students. This, Rawkins claimed, was proof that he was 'still being punished for undefined behaviour which did not conform to the norm'. [57]

Rawkins' case was taken up by the HLRS after it was sent copies of Russell's and Walker's witness statements, which revealed details of Hampshire south-east area vice squad's operations against gay men. Russell reported on the 'usual observations' that evening of the toilets on Western Parade, St George's Road and The Circle in Southsea, while Walker recounted 'dealing with another person for a similar offence' at St George's Road. [58]

I was acting as an *agent provocateur*, which was part of my duty. I was waiting to see the actions of the accused. I was waiting to see if his actions were those of a homosexual. I was not acting in such a way that anybody would think I would welcome a homosexual advance. This is what is commonly done in this city, and has been so for many years. [59]

Walker's admission to being an '*agent provocateur*' caused deep embarrassment to Hampshire Constabulary after Antony Grey sent copies of Russell's and Walker's statements to the minister of state at the Home Office, Lord Stonham. Although chief constable Douglas Osmond claimed he was 'satisfied that no improper techniques were being used', he did make arrangements 'for police constable Russell's relief from duty'. Stonham also told Grey that although 'no-one pretends that these duties of the police are other than unpleasant and difficult, there is no disagreement that it would be wrong for an officer to perform them in the manner of an "*agent provocateur*".' [60]

Nevertheless, such police tactics continued. The Bournemouth and Dorset Constabulary – formed in October 1967 from the merger of Dorset County Constabulary and Bournemouth Borough Police – was also the subject of an anonymous letter to Antony Grey in early 1968.

The Bournemouth and Dorset police force, a new creation, has continued the town's strict attitude to homosexuals and at the Poole midsummer quarter sessions there were 23 cases of gross indecency in the list – all at the same lavatory. The plain clothes police hid in a broom cupboard and observed everyone entering. There have since been many more, in other lavatories in the town – in one of which a priest was involved. In March a young schoolmaster committed suicide by throwing himself over a suspension bridge. Naturally I do not approve of indecency in public places, but I think some inquiry is due into the methods, offensive to say the least, of the local police since the law was changed. It is said that in a case involving boys and the manager of W.H. Smith, Westbourne, in the last month or two, the youths and schoolboys were questioned for hours with a persistence that was quite irregular. Sergeants Rose and Baldwin are the ones called 'the Hammers of the Homos', and I have heard they are not above strong-arm methods. [61]

In July the National Council on Civil Liberties also received an unsigned letter (which it forwarded to the HLRS) about police action at the same public lavatory.

> My son, aged sixteen, still at school, went into a lavatory in Meyrick Park. Whilst using the toilet, he sensed he was being watched when he saw movement behind the wire netting in a broom cupboard. He saw a man's face or figure there. I need not tell you how embarrassing and rather frightening the sensation was to him. I mentioned this to a constable I know and he admitted that [the] vice squad do this regularly to arrest homosexuals. Sometimes they act as *agents provocateurs*. Sergeant Baldwin is the one usually, but I was advised to drop the idea of complaint to the Dorset and Bournemouth Constabulary. [62]

Sussex Constabulary (another new amalgamation, formed in January 1968 from the East Sussex, West Sussex, Brighton, Eastbourne and Hastings forces) was also busy in and around the toilets of Eastbourne, Brighton and Hastings. In March 1969 Audrey Wickens, the head and owner of a music school in Eastbourne, wrote to Antony Grey to protest about 'a great many convictions of homosexual offences reported in the local papers lately', including that of a violin teacher working at her school. Wickens was worried about bad publicity for the school, but she also had 'misgivings as to the genuineness of the charge' and felt that the teacher had been 'treated unfairly'. The following month P.V. Syrett from Sutton in Surrey also wrote to the HLRS to vented his anger against the Sussex police. [63]

> I was spending a weekend at Eastbourne. On the Saturday evening I met several of my host's friends in a local bar, including two who had driven over from Hastings. Apparently the town has one particular

convenience which, to put it politely, is popular with the boys. Quite by accident they discovered that it was being watched by two plain clothes policemen. Since this discovery they have sat in their car on a number of occasions and have watched these same two men at work. Quite often one or other of them will come out of the convenience and stroll into some nearby bushes, blatantly trying to entice some unsuspecting chap to follow. Reports in the local press, I gathered, showed that any arrests for importuning around Hastings invariably led to a £50 fine, and any claim by the accused that he had been led on by a plain clothes man was automatically disregarded. I am not for one moment suggesting that 'goings on' in public places should be encouraged or even allowed to continue unabated, but this sort of thing really makes my blood boil. It is a pity somebody cannot report the two policemen for importuning. [64]

In September an anonymous 'Oxford MA' from Brighton wrote to Grey to ask if 'nothing can be done to stop this frightful sort of prosecution, where the lives of those prosecuted, or perhaps one should say persecuted, are virtually destroyed – a result out of all proportion to the gravity of the offence. One has the impression also that there are those in the police force who obtain their own sexual satisfaction from taking part in these unpleasant cases.' [65]

In an address to parliament's civil liberties group the previous July, Antony Grey told MPs that there was 'a deliberate campaign' by the police to 'tighten things up'. [66]

Our case files show no diminution in the type of public lavatory case where the sole prosecuting evidence is that of plain clothes vice squad men who in certain towns appear to be most assiduous in frequenting places of relief, and whose evidence, although most invariably accepted by the courts, is frequently completely at odds with the defendant's version of events. Plain clothes police also seem to have been deployed in considerable numbers late at night in parks and open spaces recently – and in the daytime too. When one hears stories of special sub-stations being set up in park potting sheds, and bevvies of special duty officers in mufti arresting strolling men, one does begin to wonder what is going on. [67]

Jurists were also uncomfortable with the way the Sexual Offences Act was being policed. In October 1969 a jury at Bedford quarter sessions found Edward Cerrino, a 49-year-old chemist from Potton, guilty of committing gross indecency with another man in the public toilets at St Mary's Embankment in Bedford.* But the judge, recorder Denis Kelly, let Cerrinio off with a conditional discharge after telling the court that PC John Gemmel, the plain clothes officer who had found Cerrino 'standing in a corner committing an indecent act' with the other man, had only entered the toilet 'by accident' during a search for drug users and dealers. 'This offence took place at 10:30 at night,' Kelly noted. 'The only people present were the two offenders and a police officer.' The lavatory was unlit and there was no one else present. 'It might be worth considering in a case like this,' he added, 'if it couldn't be dealt with in some other way than a formal prosecution. Nowadays one sees couples behaving far more indecently in cars, in public places, and one doesn't see them prosecuted.' Kelly asked the police to 'consider whether cases like this should be handled in a different way, in a similar way that kissing-in-car cases are now handled.' [68]

Kelly's comments carried some influence. In November 1969 the *Justice of the Peace and Local Government Review* reported on Cerrino's case and told readers that the section of the Sexual Offences Act which excluded public lavatories from the 'in private' provision was only 'inserted during the passage of the bill through the House and was not in the original text'. While the *Review* acknowledged that members of the public should be able to use toilets 'without being confronted with offensive sights', it did not think that this justified 'retaining the grave offence of gross indecency otherwise than in public merely to secure this end.' [69]

Written communications between gay men also came under closer police scrutiny in the early years following the passing of the 1967

---

* The other man had earlier pleaded guilty at a magistrates' court and was fined £20.

Act. In August 1968 Grey expressed concern about chain prosecutions resulting from letters written by members of a private correspondence club. 'I am somewhat disturbed,' he told Allan Horsfall, 'because we have had about half a dozen cases within the last two months of people who have been prosecuted or questioned by the police in connection with their membership of the "Gayplume Pen Pals Club". The police seem to be going to quite extraordinary lengths in questioning people – some of them elderly – about letters which they wrote to other members of this organisation as long as eighteen months ago.' [70]

In April 1969 police officers raided the *International Times* in London, two months after it began accepting gay contact advertisements. The 'Males' column was discreet and inoffensive, although the intentions behind the ads were fairly obvious.

> TWO young bachelors with no limit to interests seek young partners and can offer overnight accommodation. Photo appreciated.

> SLIM gay male, 5 ft. 11 ins. Tall, good equipment, educated, requires physical culturist or similar to build up slight physique by weight training etc. Genuine and sincere friendship offered but coaching fees considered. Fully detailed letters and photo appreciated.

> GAY London bachelor (36) offers free overnight or weekend accommodation to young males. No 'hippies' please. All letters answered promptly. Photo helps. [71]

Using an Obscene Publications Act search warrant, the police removed files and questioned men who had used the column. When *IT* went to trial in November 1970 its directors were found guilty of conspiring to corrupt public morals and outrage public decency, and they were given suspended prison sentences. John Hutton from Hull wrote to Antony Grey in May 1969: 'Having used *IT*'s small ads facilities myself, I don't particularly care whether or not the police know I am homosexual; but the possibility of having my private life pried into by these gentlemen is something rather different.' Grey raised the issue at his meeting with parliament's civil liberties group in July. He pointed out that 'section four of the Sexual Offences Act 1967 specifically provides that it is no longer an offence for a man to procure a homosexual act with himself, if that act is itself not an offence. So I cannot see why the "Males" column of *International Times* is interesting to the police quite so much. *IT* of course carried similar advertisements of a heterosexual nature.' [72, 73]

In an effort to reach out to an emerging but disparate gay community, some enterprising individuals produced their own publications. *Camp*, published by Cottage Productions, appeared in 1968, calling itself 'a publication for the consenting adult'. Writer and NWHLRC member Ray Gosling described it as 'eight duplicated pages of small ads costing 10s 6d' which carried 'licentious' contact advertisements, for example: [74]

London area. Well educated young man, 34, car owner, wishes to meet riding master who is strict. Interested in leather and domestic correction. [75]

In May 1968 Antony Grey told the Albany Trust about a 'prospectus' produced by a 'friendship society' which had existed for four or five years. It listed adverts for mail order services, holiday travel, theatre visits, parties, box number correspondences and personal introductions. The society claimed that rather than 'promote homosexual activities', it wanted to 'keep a lot of homosexuality in its own circle.' [76]

TIMM (*The International Male Magazine*) was a more serious attempt at what Harford Montgomery Hyde called the 'poove and perve' type of magazine. It was launched in early 1968 by John Stamford, who ran it from his guest house in Brighton. Later renamed *Spartacus*, it was primarily a commercial vehicle for Stamford's mail order business. Peter Burton was employed as a writer, and it included news, fashion features, entertainment reviews, celebrity profiles, comment pieces, short stories, fun poems, competitions, a problem page and 'pin ups' of young men. It also promoted a gay social and political agenda. [77]

Public attitudes towards us are slowly, very slowly, becoming more lenient, and we are now legal. We still have a long way to go to become accepted. And furthermore, we will never become accepted as normal rather than queer unless those of us who are indistinguishable from heterosexuals in appearance and manner are prepared to be honest about our leanings rather than live a double life. If every gay doctor, lawyer, accountant, MP, factory worker was to be as honest about being gay as his married colleagues are about being heterosexual, sociey would have to accept us. [78]

A competitor of sorts emerged in 1969 with *Jeremy*. More self-consciously trendy than its rival, the magazine was published by 25-year-old photographer Peter Marriott and edited by 21-year-old Christopher Jones from offices in London's Carnaby Street. It was launched with some fanfare in August 1969 with an article in the *Daily Mirror*. Jones claimed that *Jeremy* was 'designed to appeal to gay people and bisexuals. It will not be at all crude, but very sophisticated and camp.' He added that the magazine had 5,000 subscribers, but he acknowledged distribution problems – retailer W.H. Smith had refused to handle it. With a prescient eye to the potential power of pink pounds, shillings and pence, Jones 'optimistically' reckoned that one in six men were homosexual and that hundreds of thousands of them had 'no mortgages, no kids, and plenty of surplus money to spend'. Questioned about the need for a magazine specifically for gay men, he responded, 'Smaller minority groups have their own papers. I mean, the coin collectors are well catered for, aren't they?' [79]

In its first issue *Jeremy* described itself as 'for people who simply don't care about sex – one way or the other; who have got their values straight'. The front cover showed a naked young man and woman ('Alan' and 'Barbara'), and contents included a news story about artist Peter Blake's exhibition at the Robert Fraser Gallery in London, an article about Judy Garland, a fashion feature on Barry Gibb's wardrobe, a review of the film *Midnight Cowboy* and short pieces about Ken Russell, Steve McQueen and Christopher Lee. Later issues carried advertising for boutiques, hair and grooming salons, books and travel. The magazine eschewed 'seedy classified advertisements for liaisons', but it did advertise gay venues. [80]

Commercial sex remained largely unaffected by the Sexual Offences Act – although South African writer Mervyn Harris did encounter two young male prostitutes who told him that since the passing of the Act 'you have to approach people – hunt for prey. Before that, they came up to you. Now you have to hustle.' In 1969 Harris began researching the lives of rent boys working in London. He found a pattern of casual prostitution similar to that described by Simon Raven in *Encounter* in 1960. [81]

> Male prostitutes have regular jobs and separate lives and only indulge in prostitution occasionally as a means of earning extra money, and can be grouped in two main categories. Traditionally they are the men in the armed services stationed in or near London, and the boys and young men in jobs of a respectable or refined nature, such as cosmetics, hairdressing and decorating. The latter may also find many opportunities for sex from people they meet in the course of their work. There is also a cross-section of boys and young men who may accept payment from the occasional partner. During the summer, a sprinkling of young, largely continental, tourists may finance their trip by offering their sexual services in Piccadilly. [82]

Male prostitutes continued to gather around Piccadilly Circus – at a pub with 'a reputation as a haunt for homosexuals', in the toilets at the underground station and by the arches of the County Fire Office. The latter location, where 'boys stand or lean against the railings', was known as 'the Meat Rack'. The Playland amusement arcade also served as 'a meeting ground for male and female prostitutes and other nefarious activities'. Harris noted that young rent boys were often migrants or runaways from other parts of the country. Many of them were already well informed about the opportunities available for prostitution in the capital before they arrived, and some had already engaged in it in their home towns 'on a part time or casual basis as a means of earning extra pocket money'. Sixteen-year-old Jimmy from the north-east of England was typical. He ran away from home and hitched a ride on a lorry. Once there, he teamed up with an older boy called Stan and began hanging around Piccadilly Circus. But Jimmy's career as a 'male hustler' was short-lived. He was spotted in an amusement arcade by two women police officers, who took him to a police station. His parents, who had already notified the police of his disappearance, were contacted and came to take him back home.' [83]

Sex with guardsmen was still common – though rendered riskier by the 1967 Act's specific ban on homosexual behaviour by members of the armed forces. The extent of soldier sex and the determination of the authorities to root it out was revealed in a series of court trials in spring 1968 involving at least ten guardsmen. The scandal originated with Laurence Bell, the newspaper stringer who had helped bring down the ministerial careers of Charles Fletcher-Cook and Denzil Freeth in 1963. By 1966 Bell was living in Berkshire and was a regular visitor to a pub in Sunningdale frequented by soldiers stationed at the nearby Windsor barracks. Bell became friendly with David Williams, a trooper in the life guards, who encouraged other soldiers to meet Bell. This network of contacts extended to soldiers from the Wellington and Knightsbridge barracks in London. They included Jeffrey Sheffield and Barry Brooks, who were introduced to interior designer Oliver Ford at Tattersalls Tavern in Knightsbridge. Ford subsequently hosted the pair at his house in Sparsholt Manor, Wantage and asked them to bring or send down other soldiers they knew. Sheffield did this quite regularly and was paid for his trouble.

Ford and his soldier friends were arrested in September 1967 and put on trial at the Old Bailey in May 1968. Speaking for the prosecution, detective inspector John Minors told the court that the police investigation into the sex ring covered a third of the troopers in the Life Guards, and that an additional 'thirty to forty other men were involved in these practices'. Prosecution barrister John Matthew explained that 'all the troopers voluntarily associated with Ford with their eyes wide open, and for the most part were not homosexuals. They were doing this simply for the money.' Indeed, Barry Brooks earlier told police: 'I heard in the barrack room that if you wanted to make a few bob you went to Tattersalls Tavern opposite the barracks and met the queers.' Jeffrey Sheffield also explained: 'Troopers boast how much they get out of homosexuals. I myself have only ever done it for money.' The trial judge, Graham Rogers, described both Brooks and Sheffield as 'male prostitutes', adding, 'A more contemptible way for any young man to earn his money is hard to imagine'. But he accepted that 'no one was seduced or corrupted'. [84, 85, 86, 87]

Brooks and Sheffield were given two year conditional discharges for contravening both the Sexual Offences Act and army law. Forty-two-year-old Ford was fined £700. Unlike the guardsmen, his conviction did his career no harm. He continued to attract high profile clients for his interior design business, including the queen mother. A year after his trial, Ford's mother wrote to him: 'How lucky we are to have such good children. We all have [faith in you] and thank god you spoke the truth right along my dearest.' David Williams, the guardsman who had first associated with Laurence Bell, was tried for procuring soldiers to commit indecent acts but was found not guilty after Judge Rogers told the jury that there was no admissible evidence against him. Bell avoided prosecution by moving abroad. John Matthew told the court that, otherwise, there was 'little doubt that he would be standing in the dock – where he ought to be. There is not the slightest doubt that a far more serious part in this matter was played by Bell.' [88, 89, 90]

Outdoor cruising for sex was as popular as ever. But even this form of sexual searching became the subject of increased press intrusion. In September 1968 London's Hampstead Heath received widespread publicity after *The People* ran an exposé of gay men's activities there. Journalist Peter Forbes and 'a squad of *People* reporters' discovered 'nightly sex orgies' in the park, 'some of them involving as many as 100 men'. 'Squad No.5' of the investigative team met one young man who asked them, 'Are you writing a book? *Last Exit to Hampstead*

Heath?[*] I come here for sex darling, sex. The same reason people go to gay clubs, to pick up somebody for sex.' The man formed part of an extensive and well-organised protection system which Forbes described as 'terrifying': 'They wear white polo-necked sweaters as a uniform. They have a network of look-outs and sentries. If some unsuspecting stroller or courting couple should venture into their enclave they have a complicated system of warning signals – sharp handclaps, whistles or arabesques traced in the darkness with lighted cigarettes. Once the signals are given, the "intruders" are shadowed. White-sweatered men follow them down the paths, dim figures in the bushes keep pace.' Gay cruisers, Forbes complained, made 'a mockery of recent social legislation which was designed only to help them. With the Sexual Offences Act 1967 the law finally came to recognise that homosexuality is an affliction that must be tolerated within bounds. This reform, long overdue, was bitterly attacked by many as a "queers' charter". The excesses now being practised on Hampstead Heath provide further ammunition for the reactionaries.' [91]

Press criticism of gay cruisers inevitably provoked hostility against them. The area around Queensmere Pond on Wimbledon Common in south London, for example, had long been a popular meeting place. *The New London Spy* described it in 1966 as 'quite a romantic setting', despite 'the occasional unpleasant beating-up of individuals by gangs'. By 1969 such attacks had become more frequent, and local police received calls from gay men complaining of harassment and assault. But the complaints were not followed up because men were unwilling to give their names and addresses in case the police took action against them. In September 1969 Michael De Gruchy, a 28-year-old solicitor's clerk, was murdered on the common by a gang of twelve youths, who battered him to death with their boots and sticks. With no other motive, the murder was Britain's first homophobic hate killing and part of a growing

---

[*] Hubert Selby Jr's *Last Exit to Brooklyn* (US, 1964) was published in the UK by Caldar and Boyars in 1966 and prosecuted under the Obscene Publications Act. The publishers were found guilty in November 1967 but the verdict was overturned on appeal in July 1968.

phenomenon of what the press dubbed 'queer bashing'. At their trial in January 1970, four of the killers were convicted of murder. The eldest, eighteen-year-old Geoffrey Hammond, was sentenced to life. Three others, aged sixteen and fifteen, were ordered to be detained indefinitely. The eight other boys were sent to borstal. [92]

The following year *The Sunday Times Magazine*'s Peter Gillman interviewed youths living on the Alton Estate in Roehampton where De Gruchy's killers had lived. He found that gang attacks on 'queers' were common. 'I remember the first time we beat up a pansy,' one youth told him. 'Some bloke hit him on the head with half a brick. You don't really think about getting nicked. It's just someone you can beat up and get away with. There was one. I had a big log and I smashed him and he fell down and yelled, "Help, help, help" and we all ran away. When I heard on that Friday that a queer had died I thought it was my one.' Another youth explained, 'When you're hitting a queer you don't think you're doing wrong. You think you're doing good. If you want money off a queer you can get it off him – there's nothing to be scared of from the law because you know they won't go to the law. A bloke walking down to the Queersmere [sic] with full-length leather gear on – you're a queer. What else was you doing over there? We beat up blokes and you know they're queer. I don't want some bloke screwing me. It's like the kids in West London and the Pakis. I hate them. I don't understand them. That's it.' [93]

Sexual encounters 'in private' could also be risky. 'Rolling the queers' through robbery and violence was as common after the 1967 Act as it had been before. In July 1968 university lecturer Harry Porter almost lost his life after taking unemployed labourer Gerald Hopewell back to his flat in London's Earl's Court. When Porter suggested sex, Hopewell refused and demanded money. Porter only had £2 and 10 shillings on him, so Hopewell 'hit him half a dozen times [with] a bottle and kicked him in the face'. At his trial at the Old Bailey two months later Hopewell described what happened next. [94]

I broke the bottle and slashed him across the face and kicked him. I kept hitting him but when I saw the state he was in I felt sorry for him. His face was looking like something from a horror film. I put him to bed. Every time he breathed, blood pumped out from him somewhere. I started crying. Then I grabbed a broken bottle and slashed him down the leg. I stuck the bottle in his face and all over his body. I looked over the flat, but could find no money and went back to the bedroom and tried to cut [his] throat. I thought he would die and, if he did not, he would be a key witness so I decided to kill him. I started hitting and kicking him and I thought he was dead. I meant to kill him as I don't like queers. [95]

Porter was found by his flatmates two days later. He spent two weeks in hospital and needed fifty stitches for cuts and wounds which left him permanently scarred. Detective Sergeant John Peel told the court that Hopewell 'lived by his wits and made no secret of the fact he got his living by "rolling queers"'. The judge, Justice Ashworth, described Hopewell as 'an absolute menace'. He told him: 'If that is the way you are going to live, by "rolling homos", I must send you away for a long time.' Hopewell pleaded guilty to attempted murder and robbery with violence and was sentenced to ten years' imprisonment. [96]

Being recognised as 'queer' could also lead to abuse. In her 1970 novel *A Fairly Honourable Defeat* Iris Murdoch describes an episode in which Simon Foster and his boyfriend Axel Nilsson are targeted by a gang of five youths at a Chinese restaurant in Fulham, south-west London. The gang enter the restaurant and begin beating up a black man.

'You stop,' said Simon, gasping for breath.

'Look who's here,' said another of them. 'A fucking queer. Listen to his squeaky little voice.'

'Want those pretty looks spoilt mister?' said the youth with the bicycle chain. 'We don't like pooves. Want to have this wrapped round your head, do you?' He swung the chain suggestively. [97]

Quentin Crisp, himself no stranger to queer bashing, noted that aggressive behaviour towards gay men was perpetrated even by the very young – a consequence of the increased awareness of homosexuality and the growing visibility of gay men since the passing of the 1967 Act. In 1968 he recounted how 'quite recently, I was asked for money and, when I feigned not to have heard, was kicked in the groin and threatened with worse by six children young enough to demand half fares when they scrambled on the bus that I had boarded to escape them. The leaders of the gang knew all the wounding words and were sufficiently worldly to threaten to tell the police that I had tampered with them in Trafalgar Square.' [98]

Gay bars, pubs and clubs offered only limited sanctuary from the unwanted attentions of queer bashers, the police and the press. In March 1968 *The People* turned its attention to the Hope and Anchor in 'the homely, respectable Yorkshire town' of Leeds. 'Last year,' wrote reporter Denis Cassidy, 'parliament passed a law legalising homosexual acts between consenting adults IN PRIVATE. Note the key words "in private". Acts must not be in a public place and must not involve more than two people. The new law makes it quite clear that acts offending public decency will not be tolerated. It allows stiff prison sentences for people who do not comply with it.' Cassidy was appalled by the behaviour he saw at the Hope and Anchor, which he thought 'went way beyond the bounds of decency', and which 'might well have an adverse effect on curious, impressionable youngsters'. [99]

DANCING CHEEK TO CHEEK to the music of a juke-box. KISSING PASSIONATELY on the dance floor and in secluded corners. HOLDING HANDS, PETTING and EMBRACING unashamedly in the packed room. There were men heavily made up and smelling strongly of perfume. Others were in women's clothing and wore charm bracelets and rings on their fingers. They giggled and talked among themselves in high-pitched voices. I watched effeminate-looking men disappear into the 'Ladies' to titivate their appearance and tidy their waved, dyed hair before going into the back room to dance and cuddle with their 'boyfriends'. One 19-year-old youth pulled down his trousers and began to roll down his underpants while dancing with another boy. [100]

Cassidy fumed: 'It's about time the authorities took some notice of the Hope and Anchor. It's about time, in fact, that the police put a stop to the odd goings-on here.' He agreed with Lord Arran's warning that '"any form of ostentatious behaviour, now or in the future, any form of public flaunting, would be utterly distasteful"', and he asked: 'Do we really want pubs like this? Even in this so-called enlightened and permissive society?' [101]

A month later police in Manchester began undercover surveillance of Club Rouge, a popular 'haunt of homosexuals', leading to the arrest of its manager Eduardo Verguillas for 'permitting dancing of a nature likely to cause a breach of the peace'. At Verguillas' trial at Manchester magistrates' court the following September, a police officer testified that he had observed 'a constant procession of men to the dance floor. They were seen to kiss and hold each other in passionate embraces.' He claimed that he had even been forced to dance with another man in order to continue his plain clothes observations without arousing suspicion. Verguillas pleaded guilty and was fined £30. [102]

The Flamingo Club in Wolverhampton was also raided in April 1968 – probably as the result of an article in the *Wolverhampton Express and Star* in January in which 19-year-old accounts clerk John Holland explained that he was trying to set up a national gay and lesbian network. He told the newspaper that Wolverhampton had 'the best social club in Europe, with 550 members drawn from all over the country'. Two weeks later the Flamingo was placed under police surveillance. Officers reported seeing 'orgies of a disgusting nature, comparable with the activities of Sodom and Gomorrah. Men were dancing together and engaging in improper behaviour. The behaviour in the dance room was depraved and there was also misconduct in the toilets.' On 12 April the club was raided by nearly forty policemen from the West Midlands Constabulary (another new force, formed in 1966), and charges were brought against its owner George Smith for breaches of licensing laws and for permitting 'obscene and indecent acts'. Police officers also took down the names of club members, several of whom were questioned in their own homes. At Wolverhampton quarter sessions the following July, Smith pleaded guilty to running a disorderly house and was ordered to pay £500 within three months or else face a nine month prison sentence. [103, 104]

But as clubs were raided and closed, new ones opened to meet a growing demand from gay men for places to meet, relax and socialise. 'We can't go into the normal pubs,' one former Flamingo Club member told BBC Radio 4's *The World This Weekend* in September 1968. 'They abuse us. They take the mickey out of us.' He told the programme that he and his friends went to the Flamingo to 'let ourselves go. We enjoyed ourselves. We enjoyed our own company.' [105]

It was around this time that Richard Scanes ('Tricky Dicky') began working as a DJ at the Union Tavern in Camberwell, south London. This became Britain's first gay disco, although it was never promoted as such. Dances were held on Monday and Tuesday evenings until the pub closed at 11:00 pm. Admission was free and anyone could come. 'Up until then I think gay people had been together only in a coffee club,' recalled Scanes. 'This was becoming more public. The law had been passed by then, but still it was a new concept to get gay people together in public. It was almost the only place to go of its kind.' [106]

The social needs of gay men greatly concerned law reformers. In 1969 the Albany Trust reported a steep rise in the number of men contacting them for advice and support – from about 150 in 1966 to more than 500 in 1968. But the two main campaigning organisations differed markedly in their approach to the issue. The Albany Trust and HLRS wanted to set up a string of small, discreet centres around the country that would offer counselling and legal advice. The NWHLRC, on the other hand, advocated a 'Dutch-style' network of social clubs modelled on the COC in Holland. Such clubs might host bars, dance floors and restaurants, as well as counselling services where gay men could 'bring problems to a panel of social experts, including lawyers and doctors'. In June 1967 the NWHLRC suggested to Antony Grey that the Albany Trust 'take on the sponsorship of some kind of club movement similar to the COC.' Grey's response was cautious: 'I do not believe that the time is yet right to contemplate the establishment of a club along "Dutch" lines. Premature action might bring about the "back-lash" which could destroy a great deal of our preparatory work and I therefore hope that your committee will not press this suggestion upon us at the present time.' He later told the NWHLRC's Colin Harvey, 'I do hope that the North-Western Committee will not get the bit between its teeth and go roaring off trying to set up the kind of homosexual club which might, at this stage, attract the unwelcome attention of the police.' [107, 108, 109, 110, 111]

The NWHLRC ignored Grey's advice and started its own club project. In summer 1967, ahead of the passing of the Sexual Offences Act, it sought the advice of the COC in Amsterdam, and by the end of July it had made an arrangement with Reg Kilduff, the owner of Manchester's Rockingham club, to form a business venture called Esquire Clubs. In December Wigan MP Alan Fitch went on behalf of the NWHLRC to the new home secretary, James Callaghan, to 'sound out his views about clubs'. Grey warned the NWHLRC that Callaghan, who had been uncomfortable about homosexual law reform whilst chancellor of the exchequer, was 'much less sympathetic to this whole subject than Roy Jenkins was, and I should not have thought that, with all the stuff currently in the papers about "vice" and the guards, this was quite the ideal moment for such an approach'. [112, 113]

By then, however, the press had got hold of the clubs story, unleashing the 'backlash' which Grey had feared. It began with John Holland, the 19-year-old who had told Wolverhampton's *Express and Star* about the Flamingo Club. In the same article, he talked about a new organisation, MANDFHAB – The Male and Female Homosexual Association of Great Britain. He told the newspaper that the Sexual Offences Act 'should have legalised the act in private for homosexuals under 21' and that he and his friend, 28-year-old Elizabeth Cooke, had set up MANDFHAB to create safe spaces for homosexual men and women across the country. 'It is no use trying to be close friends with heterosexuals,' he said. 'We are virtually a separate species, an underworld with our own language. I believe that by sticking together we are far happier than heterosexuals. We have happier times and are less serious. We want to live our own lives in our own way.' Holland explained that MANDFHAB wanted to raise money 'to buy a large house which we could convert into an office, clubroom, library, restaurant and bar'. Two weeks later, the *News of the World* picked up and embellished the story. It claimed that Holland and Cooke had started 'one of Britain's strangest organisations' and that MANDFHAB's 20 male and ten female members hoped to raise £6,000 to convert a building and set up activities that would, according to Holland, 'relieve loneliness and show the world what we can contribute'. [114, 115]

At the same time, the press learned about plans for a Church of England 'club' for gay men in Coventry. In reality, Coventry cathedral canon Stephen Verney and local social worker Tom Frost planned to start a counselling service in a meeting room near the cathedral. But their efforts to place advertisements for the service in the *Coventry Evening Telegraph* and the Coventry edition of the *Birmingham Evening Mail* had failed because both newspapers objected to the phrase 'homosexuality and other sexual difficulties'. Verney instead spoke to a *Coventry Evening Telegraph* reporter (who, according to Frost, had 'a reputation for being a bastard') in the hope that a news story might generate some publicity. The resulting article described the counselling service as 'Britain's first club for homosexuals'. It quoted Verney as saying, 'The number of homosexuals in Coventry could only be guessed at. But I am sure that under the surface, there are a lot of people waiting for a club like this.' The *Birmingham Evening Mail, Manchester Daily Express* and *Daily Mirror* all followed up the story. Frightened off by the furore and by complaints from churchgoers, Coventry's provost Harold Williams denied Verney and Frost use of the meeting room. In the end, the city's Council of Social Service provided an interview room, a telephone number and an answering service for what became Homosexuals Anonymous. Weekly group counselling sessions were held from October 1968, with attendance reaching a peak of 25 before dropping off. The service was wound up 1969. [116, 117, 118, 119, 120, 121, 122, 123]

MANDFHAB, meanwhile, was faring badly. Ten days after the *Wolverhampton Express and Star* article appeared, John Holland telephoned Antony Grey for advice about the letters and publicity he was receiving. He visited the HLRS in London at the end of January but, according to Grey, 'made very little headway': 'Although a sincere and well-meaning young man, [Holland] was very naïve, unsophisticated, and self-opinionated. He refused to contemplate a minimum age limit higher than sixteen for his club's membership and appeared adamant in his intention to proceed along these lines. We offered to assist with case referrals (he was receiving numerous requests for help from lonely and disturbed people), but we have had no direct communication with him since.' [124]

Shortly afterwards, Holland issued an ambitious and not altogether accurate press release from his home on the Parkfields council estate in Wolverhampton, where he lived with his parents and brother.

> MANDFHAB is a social organisation for homosexuals, the minimum age limit being sixteen years. We aim to end discrimination against homosexuals; to prevent loneliness; and to end the sordid activities which have given homosexuals a bad name. We can put members in touch, if required, with qualified psychiatric advice, and we work in close co-operation with The Albany Trust. We publish a monthly magazine, *Gay Today*, to keep members in touch. We organise social events (which must be self-sufficient), the precise nature of which depends on the members. We cannot make introductions for illegal purposes, and when we have premises, they may not be used for illegal purposes. Membership for one year is £2, 10s; for six months £1, 5s; or can be on a monthly basis at 5s per month. In addition, donations of any sort are welcome, and will bring nearer the day when we have our own premises in which to meet. [125]

In late 1968 Holland wrote to Allan Horsfall to tell him that Elizabeth Cooke had quit MANDFHAB, leaving him 'holding the baby': 'I was then swamped with literally hundreds of enquiries and about a dozen actual memberships. Postage alone exceeded the subscriptions and with other expenses involved I was put heavily in debt. At this point I decided to suspend the organisation as I was in trouble with my health.' Holland took a part-time job to clear his debts and repay the subscriptions. 'I have learned a lot by this misadventure,' he reflected, 'and I think I have been a help to some at least. I now have all I want – a husband and a future. Society's memory is short and I have sunk into anonymity, although I would still like to better the lot of the homosexual.' [126]

Plans by *TIMM (The International Male Magazine)* to open a hotel in London 'catering particularly for *TIMM* members' also came to nothing. In a letter to magazine subscribers in April 1968 it claimed that a building was being purchased to provide 'first class accommodation' at 'very reasonable prices'. Members would be able 'to stay overnight, weekends, or for longer periods. Facilities will also include a luxury sauna, and a members' lounge. It will be a place where one can be sure of meeting congenial companions, and will undoubtedly become the focal point of the London social scene. No member need ever spend a lonely evening either walking about London by himself, or be shut up in some miserable bed-sitter with only a gas ring for company.' *TIMM* promised an opening date of August 1968 and asked readers to pay a £5 annual membership fee, plus an £8 joining fee to cover the estimated £125,000 costs of the project. Esquire backer Ray Gosling was indignant. He told Radio 4's *The World This Weekend* in September 1968 that although there was a need for social clubs, 'I'd like to see it met by a responsible group rather than by a group of amateurs or a group of professional porn mongers – people running poove and perv magazines. There's a group in London wanting to set up an enormous hotel which would be like a vast brothel.' [127, 128]

Meanwhile, Esquire formed itself into a company and issued a leaflet outlining its aims in January 1968.

> We have agreed to take over the Rockingham Club in Manchester and negotiations are being completed.
>
> We have looked at premises, suitable and available; and we want to take options in several towns and cities in the Midlands.
>
> • If the demand does exist, and we are sure it does, we are capable of providing, and quickly, an ESQUIRE chain of clubs across this country.

- Much like existing clubs in Manchester, but with extended facilities, rather more like the COC.
- Each ESQUIRE club will exist to provide social intercourse: food, friendship, drink, dancing, entertainment.
- Each ESQUIRE club will in addition be able to offer a unique counselling service of lawyers/doctors, etc., to advise any member in personal difficulties.
- ESQUIRE Clubs Limited is a private limited liability company, the profits of which must by agreement be ploughed back into the company. The company offices are situated in Queen Street, Manchester, 2 – and the directors are Reg Kilduff, Allan Horsfall, Jack Jackson, Harold Pollard, Colin Harvey, Ray Gosling.
- Several prominent citizens in the North West, in London and elsewhere have already agreed to be our vice presidents. [129]

The NWHLRC and the Albany Trust and HLRS came into conflict the following month when Antony Grey accepted an invitation to become an Esquire vice president. When Leo Abse and Lord Arran were also invited to become vice presidents, in March and April respectively, the latter's reaction was to 'foam at the mouth', while Abse demanded an emergency meeting of the Albany Trust's executive committee. He confided to A.J. Ayer: 'I am certainly not at all happy about this new move. I feel that there should have been discussions with the Home Office and some explorations in this matter in order to know possible police reaction; and I am certainly more than apprehensive at the idea of clubs where men over the age of 21 are deliberately being brought into contact with young men under 21.' [130, 131]

At the meeting on 14 May – attended by C.H. Rolph, Leo Abse, J.B. Priestley, Michael Schofield, the bishop of Woolwich, Antony Grey and ten others – Abse complained that Esquire and its NWHLRC backers were 'rather ridiculous in aspiring to organise all the homosexuals of Britain. Whatever evolved socially would have to originate and grow organically – it could not be planned from the centre.' He added that 'heterosexuals did not go around looking for exclusive clubs before they felt they "belonged"', and that 'the whole idea of separation was wrong, and contrary to what the sponsors of the recent Act had set out to do'. Antony Grey was also ordered to immediately step down as an Esquire vice president. [132]

The NWHLRC's reaction was furious. Committee member John Martin Stafford wrote to Grey on 18 May: 'I would not have thought that your lot could be so out of touch with the situation as it is. The necessity for clubs is patently obvious to anyone of the meanest intelligence who is conversant with the facts. [The Albany Trust] will become an absolute laughing stock if it continues to abrogate its own aims and fail in its self-appointed task. If your lot think that all homosexuals are inherently wicked, then they are not worth helping, so why not pack up right away and close the office down.' NWHLRC anger was compounded by Lord Arran, who wrote in his *Evening News* column on 4 September that he would 'never' have introduced the Sexual Offences Bill if he had known that Esquire Clubs would be the result. 'In my final speech', he added, 'I begged homosexuals not to flaunt themselves because whether they liked it or not, the fact is that homosexual practices are ludicrous to most people and offensive to many. The setting up of these clubs is an open flaunting of the new and legal freedom of outlet. Moreover, the organisers of the proposed clubs would do well to remember the clause in William which makes a homosexual act in the presence of a third party a crime.' [133, 134]

Later in September Antony Grey, C.H. Rolph and Michael Schofield went to see Lord Stonham at the Home Office to clarify the legal status of gay clubs. Stonham told them that the government's attitude was one of 'neutrality towards any group of citizens who choose to form organisations so long as they keep within the requirements of the law'. But because of the 'controversial nature of this subject', he advised anyone who wanted to set up a club to 'consult beforehand the chief constable in any town where they propose to operate so as to be acquainted with his attitude and receive his advice, also keeping him fully informed of plans and activities as they develop.' Some were already doing that. In June 1968 the Albany Trust's case worker Doreen Cordell and office secretary Joy Blanchard held a meeting with a police sergeant, Terence Spencer, and a printer, I. Suckell, who lived together in Leeds. They discussed the 'urgent necessity in the Leeds area for a well-run club for homosexuals, where psychiatric, legal or perhaps spiritual help could be available to those members in need of counselling'. The pair had already spoken to the former chief constable of Leeds who had told them that 'everything was ok so long as they kept within the law'. It was unclear, however, if the Leeds club ever got off the ground. The HLRS never heard back from Spencer and Suckell. [135, 136]

Esquire Clubs, meanwhile, pressed on with its plans. On 9 September it told the Burnley *Evening Star* that it 'hoped to take an option on premises in Burnley for a nightclub', and that 'a large London brewery chain is believed to have offered to finance the clubs if sufficient membership can be guaranteed'. Esquire boasted that it already had 'nearly 1,000 members', and it announced that its first club would open in either Liverpool or Sheffield by the end of the year. Allan Horsfall explained that there would be strict controls, and 'no bedrooms, no gambling, and no indecency'. The clubs would be places where 'members will bring their sisters and heterosexual friends along'. But disagreements with Reg Kilduff, lack of funds, the failure to find suitable premises, local authority objections and bad publicity led to Esquire's eventual collapse. Plans for clubs in Blackpool, Bolton, Burnley, Eccles, Chester, Leeds, Liverpool, London, Nottingham, Sheffield and Swinton in Lancashire came to nothing, and by the end of 1969 the scheme was finished. [137]

The only gay men's club to survive the 1960s was the St Katherine's Group – a cross between the type of counselling service supported by the Albany Trust and the social club model advocated by the NWHLRC. It was formed following an Albany Trust conference in Wychcroft, Surrey in July 1968. Three delegates – Christopher Spence, his boyfriend Andrew Henderson and Malcolm Johnson (the chaplain of Queen Mary College, London) – suggested starting a group for gay men. Augustine Hoey, prior of the Royal Foundation of St Katherine's in Limehouse, east London, offered them the use of the foundation's common room, and in October 1968 they began hosting Saturday evening meetings. By 1969 St Katherine's had become a social club with a bar and dancing. 'For the first year we wondered if we would be raided by the police,' remembered one member. 'A deliberately boring social work-style handout was prepared, saying that we were helping lonely homosexuals who had come for counselling. We all wore smart clothes; someone played the piano, and there was an improving talk for about thirty minutes. The emphasis was on fostering sincere friendships and relationships.' Christopher Spence recalled how 'excruciating' early meetings were 'because the majority of the membership were people without any social skills at all because they'd been very, very isolated. It's hard really to describe how isolated people were. And they were terrified, absolutely frozen with terror at the prospect of coming to meet other gay men, although it was the thing they most wanted to do in the world. Slowly as the weeks went by one watched this amazing transformation in people as they began to make good connections with each other and build some safety. And then it [became] a very swinging scene, and people actually found friends and lovers and developed networks outside of that group.' [138, 139]

The dispute between the NWHLRC and the Albany Trust and HLRS over clubs led to a formal split in 1969. The NWHLRC formally disassociated from the HLRS and renamed itself the Committee for Homosexual Equality. In 1971 it became the Campaign for Homosexual Equality. The HLRS transformed itself into a broader campaigning organisation, and in 1970 it changed its name to the Sexual Law Reform Society.

The time and energy spent on the clubs issue arguably diverted the two organisations' attention from other matters and weakened their ability to campaign effectively on more pressing and achievable objectives. In September 1968 for example, Lord Arran wrote to the National Secular Society's president David Tribe, expressing his willingness to amend the Sexual Offences Act: 'The Act as it stands at present is in many respects unsatisfactory, and it is my hope that before I die I may be able to amend it on terms acceptable to public thinking in the future. Above all I am concerned with the age of consent. It is to me quite wrong that this should be 21 and not 18.' But by the time the new Conservative government came to power in June 1970 the moment had passed. In July Antony Grey told a conference in York, 'Whether the new Tory government, with their lip-service to individuality, minority rights and so forth will do anything, remains to be seen. I personally am a little bit gloomy about it because so much of the protest and the dissent comes from the left, regardless of the merits of the cause at issue, and so much of the natural urge to repress comes from the right and from people who think in an authoritarian sort of way.' [140, 141]

In Scotland law reform campaigners went their own way, setting up the Scottish Minorities Group in February 1969. Former NWHLRC member and Esquire director Colin Harvey became its first chairman. He and the SMG's other founding members understood that conditions in Scotland (including the fact that the Sexual Offences Act did not apply there) required a different approach. Harvey played down his earlier role in Esquire and instead focused on garnering the support of the Scottish churches. In 1970 he explained: 'The greatest fear of church reformers at that time was that attempts might be made to form clubs, or social meeting centres where isolated and lonely homosexuals could meet. This fear was expressed strongly at the early meetings of the group, largely because I myself had been closely connected with the promotion of a scheme to set up clubs in north-west England for several years.' The SMG successfully negotiated with the Church of Scotland to hold monthly meetings at church premises in Edinburgh and Glasgow, and in 1970 it started a telephone helpline. [142]

Whether or not public opinion in Britain was ready for further homosexual law reform was unclear. On the surface it seemed that most people in were favour – or at least were unopposed. In a 1968 Gallup poll only 31% of respondents thought that homosexuality was 'a very serious' social problem – down by 11% compared to a similar poll for the *News Chronicle* in 1957. In 1969 Geoffrey Gorer interviewed 1,987 people aged 16-45 for his book *Sex and Marriage in England Today* (1971). In answer to the question 'How do you feel about people who fall in love with members of their own sex?', just 24% responded 'revulsion' and 'disgust'. Twenty two per cent felt 'pity' or 'sorry for them'. Thirteen per cent thought that it was 'not understandable/odd'. Twelve per cent expressed 'tolerance'. Eight per cent disliked homosexuals. Three per cent thought homosexuals could not help what they were. Four per cent expressed moral disapproval. Three per cent thought that homosexuals were 'ridiculous'. Younger people were generally more sympathetic. 40% of those aged between 21 and 24 were 'tolerant' of homosexuals – in contrast to 43% of those aged 35-45, who felt 'hostile'. As in previous polls, there were marked social and regional differences. Gorer found that toleration decreased and hostility increased 'as one goes down the scale of social class'. Most hostility was in the north-west, followed by the midlands. Most tolerance was in the south-east, followed by the north-east. In another survey, conducted by National Opinion Poll in January 1970, 39% of people approved of the 'legalisation of male homosexuality'. That figure rose to 50% in the 16-34 age group and in the better-off 'ABC1' social classes. In the lower 'C2DE' classes approval dropped to 34%. [143, 144, 145]

Beyond the surveys and opinion polls there was evidence of a growing, if tacit, acceptance of homosexuality. Regular drinkers at the Hope and Anchor in Leeds, for example, watched the high jinks there 'without a murmur of protest'. Similarly, members of Wolverhampton's Flamingo Club – not all of whom were gay – rallied round the owner George Smith after it was raided by the police. School master Brian Carleton told Wolverhampton quarter sessions that the club 'served a useful and desirable purpose for homosexuals'. Another defence witness – a married woman – said that she 'knew the nature of the club, and that most of the members were homosexual. She had continued to visit the club and would not have done so, as the mother of two children, if she had considered anything to be improper.' When the Albany Trust published a survey of young gay men in 1970 it revealed that only one out of 17 under-18-year-olds thought that they might lose ther job if their homosexuality was revealed. Radio 4's *Parents and Children* programme even discussed the issue of 'homosexuality in schoolchildren' in December 1969. One mother explained why she was relaxed about the fact that her ten-year-old son might be gay. [146, 147, 148, 149]

I think it's perfectly natural and harmless. I think when he gets to 12 or 13 and he's in his puberty it will be necessary to discuss these things with him – about boys having very, very personal relationships with other boys, and why. He hasn't discussed it with me, but on the other hand, he hasn't ever said anything to make me feel that he doesn't know what is meant when you talk about a queer or a homosexual, and you say it's one man who fancies another man. He has not said, 'What's that?' or anything, so I presume he knows about it. [150]

By 1970 homosexuality featured much more frequently on radio and television, and in plays and films. Even before the Lord Chamberlain's powers of theatre censorship were abolished by the Theatres Act in September 1968, plays with gay themes and characters were routinely licenced – sometimes with only limited cuts. They included Peter Shaffer's *White Liars*, Lanford Wilson's *The Madness of Lady Bright* ('a strong sexual undertone'), Bertolt Brecht's version of Christopher Marlowe's *Edward II* ('made out to be patently homosexual'), Colin Spencer's *Spitting Image* ('the usual indecencies') and Christopher Hampton's *Total Eclipse* ('undeniably sordid and degrading'). In August 1968 the Royal Shakespeare Company's Stratford-upon-Avon production of William Shakespeare's *Troilus and Cressida* (which did not require a licence) featured an 'overtly homosexual' Achilles – 'a high camp posturer in tight golden braids who drapes himself in flimsy white veils to welcome Hector to his tent the night before their battle, in a kind of travesty marriage'. After the abolition of theatre censorship, three more plays with significant gay content were staged: Joe Orton's posthumously produced *What The Butler Saw* at the Queen's Theatre, London in March 1969, C.P. Taylor's *Lies About Vietnam* at the Traverse Theatre, Edinburgh in May 1969 and John Hopkins' *Find Your Way Home* at the Open Space Theatre, London in May 1970. [151, 152, 153, 154, 155]

The late 1960s also saw several gay-interest films pass through the BBFC with little or no fuss: *Portrait of Jason* (shown at London's New Cinema Club in January, February and March 1968), *The Lion in*

Winter (based on James Goldman's 1966 stage play), *The Detective* (in which William Windom plays a married, guilt-racked gay man), *The Fearless Vampire Killers* (with Ian Quarrier's comic portrayal of a gay vampire), *If...* (with scenes of homosexual love and desire at a boys' public school), *Theorem* (starring Terence Stamp as the mysterious seducer of a wealthy Italian family), *Inadmissable Evidence* (adapted from John Osborne's 1964 play), *Satyricon* (Federico Fellini's vision of decadent ancient Rome), *Midnight Cowboy* (the only 'X'-rated film ever to receive a best picture Oscar), *Staircase* (adapted from Charles Dyer's 1966 play), *Women in Love* (based on D.H. Lawrence's novel, and featuring a notorious nude male wrestling scene), *Entertaining Mr Sloane* (based on Joe Orton's 1964 play), *The Gay Deceivers* (a camp comedy about US army draft dodgers), *Performance* (Mick Jagger's 1968 movie vehicle, released in 1970), *Goodbye Gemini* (based on Jenni Hall's 1964 novel *Ask Agamemnon*), *Something for Everyone* (adapted from Harry Kissing's 1965 novel *The Cook*) and *The Boys in the Band* (a study of the lives of a group of gay men in New York, adapted from Mart Crowley's 1968 play).

British television continued to produce high quality plays which both stimulated debate and challenged traditional attitudes towards homosexuality. Simon Gray's *Spoiled*, a Wednesday Play broadcast on BBC 1 on 28 August 1968, explored the relationship between a young student and his maths teacher. Donald Clenham (Simon Ward) receives one-to-one tuition from Richard Howarth (Michael Craig) to help him pass his 'O' level exam. When Howarth invites Donald to spend a revision weekend at the home he shares with his pregnant wife, their relationship becomes intimate and complex. Audience reactions to *Spoiled* were mixed. Edward Johnson from Harrogate wrote to the BBC to complain that the play had 'little bearing on the facts of life.' He asked: 'Must homosexuals always be presented as mentally disturbed people? I get the impression that these authors have never met a homosexual, knowingly, and therefore have to invent them out of their imagination. Perhaps it is that most of us behave so naturally, that we go undetected. However I can assure you our emotional problems are no different from those of the heterosexuals, and the situations we get ourselves into at times are almost identical.' But Johnson also congratulated the BBC for 'putting on a play about homosexuality, a subject which up till now has been badly neglected, and I hope there will be many more forthcoming.' Clean Up TV campaigner Mary Whitehouse also praised the programme, but for rather different reasons. Writing on behalf of her National Viewers' and Listeners' Association, she called *Spoiled* a 'first class play' which 'dealt with homosexuality without wallowing in it, or normalising it, or justifying it; indeed, it was shown as the tragedy it is. It illuminated the kind of situation and relationship which can give rise to deviation.' [156, 157]

On 6 August 1970 BBC 2 broadcast British television's first on-the-lips gay kiss, in a recording of the Prospect Theatre Company's staging of Christopher Marlowe's *Edward II* at the Piccadilly Theatre in London. King Edward (Ian McKellen) and his lover Piers Gaveston (James Laurenson) kiss as they bid farewell in Act Two ('Therefore, with dumb embracement, let us part'). James Thomas of the *Daily Express* thought that 'the story of a king embracing his favourites, kissing them on the lips, is a little too much to take in the close-up confines of television'. Nevertheless, 'It was a considerable chance for TV to take'. [158]

On 19 December ITV broadcast a hard-hitting play about gay bullying at a Salford secondary modern school. *Roll on Four O'Clock* was scripted by Colin Welland and aired as part of Granada Television's Saturday Night Theatre series. It featured Clive Swift as art teacher Max Fielder, who defends a pupil, Peter Latimer (Frank Heaton), against bullying by other boys and teachers. In doing so, Fielder lays himself open to suspicions of homosexuality. Not everyone's attitudes are negative, however. When a new teacher, John Youngman, quizzes colleagues about Fielder's sexuality, he gets short shrift from fellow teacher Roy Gifford.

Youngman: I've just been talking to Alan about Max.
Gifford: Oh yeah.
Youngman: You don't reckon that he is, do you?
Gifford: Possibly. What if he is?

Youngman: Nothing. It's just coming across it here, you know.

Gifford: And you lived in London.

Youngman: Yeah, but there it's obvious, you know. Flamboyant.

Gifford: What do you expect him to do? Have a blue rinse? That's if he is, which I doubt. In any case, what if he is? It's his business isn't it? [159]

Eighteen months earlier, gay men in the US took a more defiant stand against bullying and harassment. In the early hours of Saturday 28 June 1969 New York police conducted a routine raid on the Stonewall Inn at 53 Christopher Street in the Greenwich Village area of the city – supposedly for an alleged infringement of the liquor licence. They evicted customers and arrested some of the staff. Unexpectedly, a crowd gathered outside and refused to leave. Violent and prolonged clashes with the police followed over the next few days, and within weeks activists had formed a Gay Liberation Front to organise further protests and to raise awareness of discrimination against gay men.

That summer British student Aubrey Walter, who had just finished a sociology degree at the London School of Economics, went to the US after reading about the GLF in *The Times*. While in New York he met Bob Mellors, another student at the LSE. When they returned to Britain, the pair decided to hold a meeting in a basement classroom at the LSE. Only nineteen people (18 men and one woman) attended what was the inauguration of the British Gay Liberation Front on 13 October 1970. But after activists distributed leaflets around London its membership began to grow, and within a month meetings were attracting around 200 people. On 27 November 80 members of the GLF held a torchlight parade in Highbury Fields to protest against the arrest of Liberal Party activist Louis Eakes, who had been accused of committing indecent acts there. At the end of the year the GLF drew up a manifesto which put forward a set of key demands:

- That all discrimination against gay people, male and female, by the law, by employers, and by society at large, should end

- That all people who feel attracted to a member of their own sex be taught that such feelings are perfectly valid
- That sex education in schools stop being exclusively heterosexual
- That psychiatrists stop treating homosexuality as though it were a sickness, thereby giving gay people senseless guilt complexes
- That gay people be as legally free to contact other gay people, through newspaper ads, on the streets and by any other means they may want, as are heterosexuals, and that police harassment should cease right now
- That employers should no longer be allowed to discriminate against anyone on account of their sexual preferences
- That the age of consent for gay males be reduced to the same as for straight
- That gay people be free to hold hands and kiss in public, as are heterosexuals. [160]

The media quickly took an interest, and in December 1970 the actor and GLF member John Breslin joined Albany Trust director Michael Delancy, London CHE organiser Roger Baker and *Sexual Deviation* author Anthony Storr for a BBC 2 *Late Night Line Up* discussion about homosexuality. In his opening remarks about the legal and social position of gay men, presenter Michael Dean pointed to 'the growing number of public figures who are prepared to admit their homosexuality, and evidence that some churchmen are ready to reform standard Christian teaching on morality.' [161]

Antony Grey was less optimistic about the future. In 1970 he wrote: 'In spite of all the progress in informing the public about these things, and despite law reform, there is still far too little real understanding of the true nature of homosexuality. Very many people, even today, still do not understand that in essence it is about love, and not simply some behaviour which immoral people indulge in for "kicks".' [162]

Harford Montgomery Hyde was more positive. In *The Other Love* (1970) he conceded that 'there is some considerable way yet to go before homosexuals become fully integrated in the community of Britain', but he believed that 'their complete social acceptance here is only a matter of time. There is no logical reason why they should continue to be regarded as inferior or second class citizens. Something of this attitude is already apparent among the younger generation.' [163]

But perhaps the biggest achievement of a decade-and-a-half of social, legal and cultural change was that gay men were at last beginning to live more open lives, and to regard themselves as 'normal' rather than 'odd'. For Simon in Iris Murdoch's *A Fairly Honourable Defeat* this is the great revelation of his love for Axel.

> Axel did something extremely important for Simon. He made Simon understand for the first time that it was perfectly ordinary to be homosexual. Simon had never exactly felt guilty about his preference. But he had felt it as a peculiarity, something rather nice and even perhaps a bit funny, something rather like a game, but definitely odd, to be concealed, giggled about and endlessly discussed and inspected in the private company of fellow oddities. He had never quite seen it as a fundamental and completely ordinary way of being a human being, which was how Axel saw it. [164]

Chapter 7 references

1. 'Homosexuals Now'
2. Russell Davies (ed.), *The Kenneth Williams Diaries*, Thursday 13 July 1967, Harper Collins, 1993
3. Ibid., Sunday 23 July 1967
4. Alkarim Jivani, *It's Not Unusual: A History of Lesbian and Gay Britain in the Twentieth Century*, Michael O'Mara Books, 1997
5. Bill Thorneycroft, personal interview with author, June 2009
6. Alkarim Jivani, *It's Not Unusual*, op. cit
7. Letter from Antony Grey to Allan Horsfall, 29 July 1967, Hall-Carpenter Antony Grey Files, London School of Economics
8. Patrick Trevor-Rooper, recorded interview, August 1990, Hall-Carpenter Oral History Archive, British Library
9. Tony Dyson, recorded interview, February 1990, op. cit.
10. C.H. Rolph, recorded interview, August 1990, op. cit.
11. John Vassall, *Vassall: The Autobiography of a Spy*, Sidgwick and Jackson, 1975
12. John Fraser, *Close Up: An Actor Telling Tales*, Oberon Books, 2004
13. Colin Spencer, personal interview with author, 30 October 2012
14. Hugo Vickers, *Cecil Beaton: The Authorised Biography*, Weidenfeld and Nicolson, 1985
15. John Lahr, *The Orton Diaries*, 4 July 1967, Da Capo Press, 1996
16. Ibid., 23 July 1967
17. Alkarim Jivani, *It's Not Unusual*, op. cit.
18. Sexual Offences Act 1967
19. 'Reform That Doesn't Go Far Enough', *The Surrey Comet*, 22 April 1967
20. Leo Abse, 'The Sexual Offences Act', *British Journal of Criminology*, January 1968

21. Letter from Antony Grey to Keith Wedmore, 16 August 1967, Hall-Carpenter Antony Grey Files, op. cit.

22. Conference on Social Needs, York University, 10-12 July 1970, transcript, Hall-Carpenter Albany Trust Files, London School of Economics

23. Letter from Lord Arran to the Lord Chancellor, 8 November 1967, op. cit.

24. Letter from the Lord Chancellor to Lord Arran, 13 November 1967, op. cit.

25. Letter from Antony Grey to Leo Abse, 19 October 1967, op. cit.

26. Letter from Dick Taverne to Leo Abse, 16 November 1967, op. cit.

27. Michael Mason, 'Arran's New Bill', *Gay News*, 23 September 1976

28. 'Homosexual Act "In Private"', *Justice of the Peace and Local Government Review*, 30 November 1968

29. Peter Dennis (ed.), *Daring Hearts: Lesbian and Gay Lives in 50s and 60s Brighton*, QueenSpark Books, 1992

30. Matt Cook, *Queer Domesticities: Homosexuality and Home Life in Twentieth-Century London*, Palgrave Macmillan, 2014

31. Geoffrey Moorhouse, 'Homosexual Says "Sense of Shame" Is Lifted, *The Guardian*, 16 September 1967

32. Recorded Crime Statistics 1898-2001/2, Home Office Statistics

33. Quentin Crisp, *The Naked Civil Servant*, Jonathan Cape, 1968

34. Joanna Slaughter, 'The Men Who Still Feel Hunted', *The Observer*, 1 February 1970

35. Jeffrey Weeks, Kevin Porter, *Between the Acts*: *Lives of Homosexual Men, 1885-1967,* Rivers Oram Press, 1998

36. Bill Thorneycroft, personal interview with author, op. cit.

37. Tony Papard, e-mail to author, 6 June 2009

38. Letter from Antony Grey to Allan Horsfall, 9 June 1967, Hall-Carpenter Antony Grey Files, op. cit.

39. Recorded Crime Statistics 1898-2001/2, op. cit.

40. Scottish Minorities Group, Chairman's Report 1969 1970, 30 June 1970, Hall-Carpenter Albany Trust Files, op. cit.

41. Roy Walmsley, 'Indecency Between Males and the Sexual Offences Act 1967', *Criminal Law Review*, July 1978

42. Ibid.

43. Ibid.

44. Tony Geraghty, 'The Disturbing Case of the Consenting Teenagers', *The Sunday Times*, 17 March 1968

45. Ibid.

46. 'City Youths "Misconceived" the Intention of the Act – Judge', *Evening Sentinel*, 9 April 1968

47. 'St Osyth Man For Trial', *Essex County Standard*

48. Letter from Brian Clow to Antony Grey, 16 March 1968, Hall-Carpenter Antony Grey Files, op. cit.

49. Roy Perrott, '"Getting Too Tough with Homosexuals"', *The Observer*, 31 March 1968

50. Antony Grey, Donald West, 'New Law But No New Deal', *New Society*, 27 March 1969

51. Andrew McCall, *The Au Pair Boy*, Anthony Blond, 1968

52. Ibid.

53. Quentin Crisp, *The Naked Civil Servant*, op. cit.

54. Joanna Slaughter, 'The Men Who Still Feel Hunted', op. cit.

55. Anonymous letter to the HLRS, February 1968, Hall-Carpenter Antony Grey Files, op. cit.

56. Tony Geraghty, 'The Night a College Lecturer and a Police Sergeant Met in a Dark Alleyway', *The Sunday Times*, 11 August 1968

57. Ibid.

58. Copies of witness statements, 8 July 1968, Hall-Carpenter Antony Grey Files, op. cit.

59. Ibid.

60. Letter from D.J. Brown, private secretary to Lord Stonham, to Antony Grey, 9 September 1968, Hall-Carpenter Antony Grey Files, op. cit.

61. Anonymous letter to Antony Grey, Hall-Carpenter Antony Grey Files, op. cit.

62. Copy of anonymous letter to National Council on Civil Liberties, July 1968, op. cit.

63. Letter from Audrey Wickens to Antony Grey, 4 March 1969, op. cit.

64. Letter from P. V. Syrett to Antony Grey, 10 April 1969, op. cit.

65. Anonymous letter to Antony Grey, 16 September 1969, op. cit.

66. Antony Grey, *Speaking Out: Writings on Sex, Law, Politics and Society, 1954-95*, Cassell, 1997

67. Ibid.

68. '"Don't Prosecute For This Type of Offence"', *Bedfordshire Times*, 17 October 1969

69. *Justice of the Peace and Local Government Review*, 15 November 1969

70. Letter from Antony Grey to Allan Horsfall, 19 August 1968, Hall-Carpenter Antony Grey Files, op. cit.

71. Ray Gosling, 'Homosexuals Now', *New Society*, 29 August 1968

72. Letter from John Hutton to Antony Grey, 10 May 1969, Hall-Carpenter Antony Grey Files, op. cit.

73. Antony Grey, *Speaking* Out, op. cit.

74. Ray Gosling, 'Homosexuals Now', op. cit.

75. Harford Montgomery Hyde, *The Other Love: An Historical and Contemporary Survey of Homosexuality in Britain*, Heinemann, 1970

76. Memorandum by Antony Grey to Albany Trust Executive and Development Committee, 2 May 1968, Hall-Carpenter Antony Grey Files, op. cit.

77. Harford Montgomery Hyde, *The Other Love*, op. cit.

78. *Spartacus*, Issue 14, 1970, Hall-Carpenter Archive, London School of Economics

79. 'Yes, There May Be Many Like Him: But Is Jeremy Really So Gay?', *Daily Mirror*, 5 August 1969

80. Ibid.

81. Mervyn Harris, *The Dilly Boys: Male Prostitution on Piccadilly*, Croom Helm, 1973

82. Ibid.

83. Ibid.

84. 'Director is Fined £700 in Guards Case', *Liverpool Echo*, 6 May 1968

85. 'Director Fined for Indecency with Guards', *The Guardian*, 7 May 1968

86. Arnold Latcham , 'Man in Vice Case with Guards is fined £700', *Daily Express*, 7 May 1968

87. 'Guardsmen Case Man Fined £700', *The Times*, 7 May 1968

88. Matt Cook, *Queer Domesticities*, op. cit.

89. 'Guardsman Cleared of Vice Charge', *The Daily Telegraph*, 8 May 1968

90. 'Interior Decorator Fined £700', *West Lancashire Evening Gazette*, 6 May 1968

91. Peter Forbes, 'The Sick Men of Hampstead Heath', *The People*, 1 September 1968

92. Hunter Davies (ed.), *The New London Spy: A Discreet Guide to the City's Pleasures*, Anthony Blond, 1966

93. Peter Gillman, 'The Queer-Bash Killers', *The Sunday Times Magazine*, 7 February 1971

94. '10 Years for Attempt to Kill Homosexual', *Yorkshire Post*, 28 September 1968

95. Ibid.

96. Ibid.

97. Iris Murdoch, *A Fairly Honourable Defeat*, Chatto & Windus, 1970

98. Quentin Crisp, *The Naked Civil Servant*, op. cit.

99. Denis Cassidy, 'Even in These Permissive Times Do We Want Pubs Like This?', *The People*, 24 March 1968

100. Ibid.

101. Ibid.

102. 'Why a Policeman Had to Dance', *Manchester Evening News*, 9 September 1968

103. Ray Seaton, '"There's Nothing Queer About Us"', *Wolverhampton Express and Star*, 8 January 1968

104. Memorandum by Antony Grey to Albany Trust Executive and Development Committee members, op. cit.

105. *The World This Weekend*, BBC Radio 4, 1 September 1968, Albany Trust Files, op. cit.

106. Richard Scanes, Tony Dean, Gay Commercial Scene interviews, British Library

107. Albany Trust, *Homosexuality: Some Questions and Answers*, 1969

108. 'Burnley May Get Club for Homosexuals', [Burnley] *Evening Star*, 9 September 1968

109. Letter from Allan Horsfall to Antony Grey, 18 June 1967, Hall-Carpenter Antony Grey Files, op. cit.

110. Letter from Antony Grey to Allan Horsfall, 19 June 1967, op. cit.

111. Letter from Antony Grey to T. Colin Harvey, 13 October 1967, op. cit.

112. Letter from Allan Horsfall to Antony Grey, 29 December 1967, op. cit.

113. Letter from Antony Grey to Allan Horsfall, 4 January 1968, op. cit.

114. Ray Seaton, '"There's Nothing Queer About Us"', op. cit.

115. Ron Mount, 'A Very Strange Club', *News of the World*, 21 January 1968

116. Telephone note from Doreen Cordell to Antony Grey, 12 October 1967, Hall-Carpenter Albany Trust Files, op. cit.

117. Letter from Tom Frost to Doreen Cordell, 27 October 1967, op. cit.

118. Letter from Tom Frost to Antony Grey, 12 January 1968, op. cit.

119. Letter from Tom Frost to Antony Grey, 20 January 1968, op. cit.

120. 'Canon Forms Club For "Lonely Men"', *Coventry Evening Telegraph*, 10 January 1968

121. 'Provost Defends Sex Clinic Plan', *Birmingham Evening Mail*, 12 January 1968

122. 'Cathedral to Open Clinic for the "Lonely Ones"', *Manchester Daily Express*, 12 January 1968

123. Paul Connew, 'Special "Clinic" for Homosexuals at a Cathedral', *Daily Mirror*, 12 January 1968

124. Memorandum by Antony Grey to Albany Trust Executive and Development Committee members, op. cit.

125. Press release by John Holland, 1968, Hall-Carpenter Albany Trust Files, op. cit.

126. Peter Scott-Presland, *Amiable Warriors: The Official History of the Campaign for Homosexual Equality and Its Times, Volume One: Space to Breathe*, Paradise Press, 2015

127. Letter from *TIMM* to subscribers, April 1968, Hall-Carpenter Albany Trust Files, op. cit.

128. *The World This Weekend*, BBC Radio 4, 1 September 1968, op. cit.

129. Esquire Clubs leaflet, Hall-Carpenter Antony Grey files, op. cit.

130. Letter from Antony Grey to Allan Horsfall, 28 March 1968, op. cit.

131. Letter from Leo Abse to A.J. Ayer, 11 April 1968, op. cit.

132. Minutes of a Joint Meeting of the Executive Committee of the Homosexual Law Reform Society and the Trustees and Development Committee of the Albany Trust, 14 May 1968, op. cit.

133. Letter from John Martin Stafford to Antony Grey, 18 May 1968, op. cit.

134. The Arran Column, *The Evening News*, 4 September 1968

135. Letter from C.H. Rolph, to Allan Horsfall, 12 September 1968, Hall-Carpenter Antony Grey files, op. cit.

136. Notes, 24 June 1968, Hall-Carpenter Albany Trust Files, op. cit.

137. 'Burnley May Get Club for Homosexuals' *Evening Star*, op. cit.

138. Tony Walton (ed.), *Out of the Shadows: A History of the Pioneering London Gay Groups and Organisations, 1967-2000*, Bona Street Press, 2010

139. Christopher Spence, recorded interview, September 1990, Hall-Carpenter Oral History archive, op. cit.

140. Letter from Lord Arran to David Tribe, 13 September 1968, Hall-Carpenter Antony Grey files, op. cit.

141. Conference on Social Needs, York University, 10-12 July 1970, Hall-Carpenter Albany Trust Files, op. cit.

142. Scottish Minorities Group, Chairman's Report 1969-1970, op. cit.

143. George H. Gallup, *The Gallup International Public Opinion Polls: Great Britain, 1937-1975, Volume One*, 1976

144. Geoffrey Gorer, *Sex and Marriage in England Today: A Study of the Views and Experience of the Under-45s*, Nelson, 1971

145. Marcus Collins (ed.), *The Permissive Society and Its Enemies*, Rivers Oram, 2007

146. Denis Cassidy, 'Even in These Permissive Times Do We Want Pubs Like This?', op. cit.

147. Wolverhampton Quarter Sessions, 24 July 1968, Hall-Carpenter Antony Grey Files, op. cit.

148. Social Needs Survey, 1970, op. cit.

149. *Parents and Children*, BBC Radio 4, 17 December 1969, BBC Written Archives

150. Ibid.

151. 'The Madness of Lady Bright', Lord Chamberlain Plays Correspondence Files, British Library

152. 'Edward II', op. cit.

153. 'Spitting Image', op. cit.

154. 'Total Eclipse', op. cit.

155. Ronald Bryden, 'Stratford's House Style', *The Observer*, 11 August 1968

156. Letter from Edward Johnson to Graeme McDonald, 29 August 1968, *Spoiled*, The Wednesday Play, programme file, BBC Written Archives

157. Letter from Mary Whitehouse, National Viewers' and Listeners' Association, op. cit.

158. James Thomas, 'A King in Close Up', *Daily Express*, 7 August 1970

159. *Roll on Four O'Clock*, Saturday Night Theatre, ITV, 19 December 1970

160. Gay Liberation Front, *Manifesto*, 1971, http://legacy.fordham.edu/halsall/pwh/glf-london.asp

161. *Late Night Line Up*, BBC 2, 4 December 1970, BBC Written Archives

162. 'Sex, Morality and Happiness', *Man and Society*, No. 11, 1969-70

163. Harford Montgomery Hyde, *The Other Love*, op. cit.

164. Iris Murdoch, *A Fairly Honourable Defeat*, op. cit.

BIBLIOGRAPHY

BOOKS

Leo Abse, *Private Member*, Macdonald & Co., 1973

Miriam Akhtar, Steve Humphries, *The Fifties and Sixties: A Lifestyle Revolution*, Pan Macmillan, 2001

Anthony Aldgate, *Censorship and the Permissive Society: British Cinema and the Theatre, 1955-1965*, Clarendon Press, 1995

Anthony Aldgate, James C. Robertson, *Censorship in Theatre and Cinema*, Edinburgh University Press, 2005

Robert Aldrich (ed.), *Gay Life and Culture: A World History*, Thames & Hudson, 2006

Clifford Allen, *A Textbook of Psychosexual Disorders*, Oxford University Press, 1962

Clifford Allen, *Homosexuality: Its Nature, Causation and Treatment*, Staples Press, 1958

Paul Anderson, *Mods: The New Religion, The Style and Music of the 1960s Mods*, Omnibus Press, 2013

Noel Annan, *Our Age: Portrait of a Generation*, Weidenfeld & Nicolson, 1990

Robert B. Asprey, *The Panther's Feast*, Jonathan Cape, 1959

Geoffrey Aquilina Ross, *The Day of the Peacock: Style for Men 1963-1973*, V&A Publishing, 2011

Paul Baker, *Polari: The Lost Language of Gay Men*, Routledge, 2002

Paul Baker, Jo Stanley, *Hello Sailor! The Hidden History of Gay Life at Sea*, Longman, 2003

John Bancroft, 'A Comparative Study of Aversion and Desensitisation in the Treatment of Homosexuality', in Laurence E. Burns, James L. Worsley (ed.s), *Behaviour Therapy in the 1970s: A Collection of Original Papers*, John Wright & Sons, 1970

Michael Banton, *The Coloured Quarter: Negro Immigrants in an English City*, Jonathan Cape, 1955

J.C. Barker, Mabel E. Miller, 'Some Clinical Applications of Aversion Therapy', in Hugh Freeman (ed.), *Progress in Behaviour Therapy: Proceedings of a Symposium Held at the Postgraduate Medical Institute, University of Salford*, John Wright & Sons, 1968

Richard Barnes, *Mods!*, Plexus Publishing, 1991

R.H. Beech, *Changing Man's Behaviour*, Pelican Books, 1969

Justin Bengry, 'Queer Profits: Homosexual Scandal and the Origins of Legal Reform in Britain', in Heike Bauer, Matt Cook (ed.s), *Queer 1950s: Rethinking Sexuality in the Postwar Years*, Palgrave Macmillan, 2012

Charles Berg, *Fear, Punishment, Anxiety and the Wolfenden Report*, Allen & Unwin, 1959

Michael Bloch, *Closet Queens*, Little, Brown, 2015

Michael Bloch, *Jeremy Thorpe*, Little, Brown, 2014

Dirk Bogarde, *Snakes and Ladders*, Chatto & Windus, 1978

Tony Booth, *Stroll On: An Autobiography*, Sidgwick & Jackson, 1989

Robert Boothby, *Recollections of a Rebel*, Hutchinson, 1978

Stephen Bourne, *Black in the British Frame: The Black Experience in British Film and Television*, Continuum, 2001

Stephen Bourne, *Brief Encounters: Lesbians and Gays in British Cinema, 1930-1971*, Cassell, 1996

Michael Bronski, *A Queer History of the United States*, Beacon Press, 2011

Charlotte Brunsdon, *London in the Cinema: The Cinematic City Since 1945*, British Film Institute, 2007

Richard Buckle (ed.), *Self-Portrait With Friends: The Selected Diaries of Cecil Beaton, 1926-1974*, Weidenfeld and Nicolson, 1979

Michael J. Buckley, *Morality and the Homosexual: A Catholic Approach to a Moral Problem*, Sands & Co., 1959

Katherine Bucknell (ed.), *Christopher Isherwood, The Sixties: Diaries, Volume Two: 1960-1969*, Chatto & Windus, 2010

Peter Burton, *Parallel Lives*, GMP Publishers, 1985

Bob Cant, *Footsteps and Witnesses: Lesbian and Gay Lifestories from Scotland*, Word Power Books, 2008

Bob Cant, Susan Hemmings (ed.), *Radical Records: Thirty Years of Lesbian and Gay History*, Routledge, 1988

Barbara Castle, *The Castle Diaries, 1964-70*, Weidenfeld & Nicolson, 1984

Peter Catterall (ed.), *The Macmillan Diaries, Volume I: The Cabinet Years, 1950-1957*, Macmillan, 2003

Peter Catterall (ed.), *The Macmillan Diaries, Volume II: Prime Minister and After, 1957-1966*, Macmillan, 2011

Eustace Chesser, *An Outline of Human Relationships*, Heinemann, 1959

Eustace Chesser, *Live and Let Live: The Moral of the Wolfenden Report*, Heinemann, 1958

Eustace Chesser, *Odd Man Out: Homosexuality in Men and Women*, Gollancz, 1959

Deborah Cohen, *Family Secrets: Living with Shame from the Victorians to the Present Day*, Penguin Viking, 2013

John Coldstream, *Dirk Bogarde: The Authorised Biography*, Phoenix, 2005

John Coldstream, *Victim*, Palgrave Macmillan/British Film Institute, 2011

Sean Cole, *Don We Now Our Gay Apparel: Gay Men's Dress in the Twentieth Century*, Berg, 2000

Sean Cole, 'Invisible Men: Gay Men's Dress in Britain, 1950-1970', in Elizabeth Wilson, Amy de la Haye (ed.s), *Defining Dress: Dress as Object, Meaning and Identity*, Manchester University Press, 1999

Ray Coleman, *Brian Epstein: The Man Who Made the Beatles*, Viking, 1989

Ilsa Colsell, *Malicious Damage: The Defaced Library Books of Kenneth Halliwell and Joe Orton*, Donlon, 2013

Alex Comfort, *The Anxiety Makers: Some Curious Preoccupations of the Medical Profession*, Nelson, 1967

Matt Cook (ed.), *A Gay History of Britain: Love and Sex Between Men Since the Middle Ages*, Greenwood Publishing, 2007

Matt Cook, *Queer Domesticities: Homosexuality and Home Life in Twentieth-Century London*, Palgrave Macmillan, 2014

Matt Cook (ed.), *Queer 1950s: Rethinking Sexuality in the Postwar Years*, Palgrave Macmillan, 2012

Francesca Coppa, 'A Perfectly Developed Playwright: Joe Orton and Homosexual Reform', in Patricia Juliana Smith (ed.), *The Queer Sixties*, Routledge, 1999

Quentin Crisp, *The Naked Civil Servant*, Jonathan Cape, 1968

Rupert Croft-Cooke, *The Verdict of You All*, Secker & Warburg, 1955

Richard Crossman, *The Diaries of a Cabinet Minister, Volume 2: Lord President of the Council and Leader of the House of Commons, 1966-68*, Hamish Hamilton, 1976

Michael Darlow, *Terence Rattigan: The Man and His Work*, Quartet Books, 2000

Richard Davenport-Hines, *An English Affair: Sex, Class and Power in the Age of Profumo*, Harper Press, 2013

Richard Davenport-Hines, *Sex Death and Punishment: Attitudes to Sex and Sexuality in Britain since the Renaissance*, Fontana, 1990

Hugh David, *On Queer Street: A Social History of British Homosexuality, 1895-1995*, Harper Collins, 1997

Michael Davidson, *Some Boys: A Homosexual Odyssey*, David Bruce & Watson, 1970

Michael Davidson, *The World, the Flesh and Myself*, Arthur Barker, 1962

Roger Davidson, 'Law, Medicine and the Treatment of Homosexual Offenders in Scotland, 1950-1980, in Imogen Goold, Catherine Kelly (ed.s), *Lawyers' Medicine: The Legislature, the Courts and Medical Practice, 1760-2000*, Hart Publishing, 2009

Roger Davidson, Gayle Davis, *The Sexual State: Sexuality and Scottish Governance, 1950-1980*, Edinburgh University Press, 2012

Hunter Davies, *The Beatles*, Ebury Press, 2009

Hunter Davies (ed.), *The New London Spy: A Discreet Guide to the City's Pleasures*, Anthony Blond, 1966

Russell Davies (ed.), *The Kenneth Williams Diaries*, Harper Collins, 1993

Peter Dennis (ed.), *Daring Hearts: Lesbian and Gay Lives in 50s and 60s Brighton*, QueenSpark Books, 1992

Tom Dewe Mathews, *Censored: What They Didn't Allow You to See And Why – The Story of Film Censorship in Britain*, Chatto & Windus, 1994

Tommy Dickinson, *Curing Queers: Mental Nurses and Their Patients, 1935-74*, Manchester University Press, 2015

Jonathan Dollimore, 'The Challenge of Sexuality', in Alan Sinfield (ed.), *Society and Literature, 1945-70*, Methuen & Co., 1983

Tom Driberg, *Ruling Passions: The Autobiography of Tom Driberg*, Jonathan Cape, 1977

Harold Evans, *Downing Street Diary: The Macmillan Years, 1957-1963*, Hodder & Stoughton, 1981

H.J. Eysenck, *Crime and Personality*, Routledge & Kegan Paul, 1964

Robert Fabian, *The Anatomy of Crime*, Pelham Books, 1970

Sebastian Faulks, *The Fatal Englishman*, Vintage, 1997

M.P. Feldman, 'The Treatment of Homosexuality by Aversion Therapy', in Hugh Freeman (ed.), *Progress in Behaviour Therapy: Proceedings of a Symposium Held at the Postgraduate Medical Institute*, University of Salford, John Wright & Sons, 1968

M.P. Feldman, M.J. MacCulloch, *Homosexual Behaviour: Therapy and Assessment*, Pergamon Press, 1971

Paul Ferris, *Sex and the British: A Twentieth Century History*, Michael Joseph, 1993

Richard Findlater, *Banned! A Review of Theatrical Censorship in Britain*, MacGibbon & Kee, 1967

Donald Ford, *The Delinquent Child and the Community*, Constable, 1957

John Fraser, *Close Up: An Actor Telling Tales*, Oberon Books, 2004

Hugh Freeman (ed.), *Progress in Behaviour Therapy: Proceedings of a Symposium Held at the Postgraduate Medical Institute, University of Salford*, John Wright & Sons, 1968

Kurt Freund, 'Some Problems in the Treatment of Homosexuality', in H.J. Eysenck (ed.), in *Behaviour Therapy and the Neuroses: Readings in Modern Methods of Treatment Derived from Learning Theory*, Pergamon Press, 1960

P.N. Furbank, *E.M. Forster: A Life, Volume Two, Polycrates' Ring, 1914-1970*, Secker & Warburg, 1978

John Furnell, *The Stringed Lute: An Evocation in Dialogue of Oscar Wilde*, Rider & Company, 1955

Bruce Galloway (ed.), *Prejudice and Pride: Discrimination Against Gay People in Modern Britain*, Routledge & Kegan Paul, 1983

George H. Gallup, *The Gallup International Public Opinion Polls: Great Britain, 1937-1975, Volume One*, 1976

James Gardiner, *Who's a Pretty Boy Then? One Hundred and Fifty Years of Gay Life in Pictures*, Serpent's Tale, 1997

William Gaskill, *A Sense of Direction: Life at the Royal Court*, Faber & Faber, 1988

Geoffrey Gorer, *Sex and Marriage in England Today: A Study of the Views and Experience of the Under-45s*, Nelson, 1971

Tony Gould, *Inside Outsider: The Life and Times of Colin MacInnes*, Allison and Busby, 1993

Jonathan Green, *All Dressed Up: The Sixties and the Counter-Culture*, Pimlico, 1999

Antony Grey, 'Homosexual Law Reform', in Brian Frost (ed.), *The Tactics of Pressure: A Critical Review of Six British Pressure Groups*, Galliard, 1975

Antony Grey, *Quest for Justice: Towards Homosexual Emancipation*, Sinclair-Stevenson, 1992

Antony Grey, *Speaking Out: Writings on Sex, Law, Politics and Society, 1954-95*, Cassell, 1997

Robin Griffiths, *British Queer Cinema*, Routledge, 2006

Lesley Hall, *Sex, Gender and Social Change in Britain Since 1880*, Palgrave, 2002

Hall-Carpenter Archives Gay Men's Oral History Group, *Walking After Midnight, Gay Men's Life Stories*, Routledge, 1989

Mervyn Harris, *The Dilly Boys: Male Prostitution on Piccadilly*, Croom Helm, 1973

Ian Harvey, *To Fall Like Lucifer*, Sidgwick & Jackson, 1971

Cate Haste, *Rules of Desire: Sex in Britain, World War I to the Present*, Pimlico, 1992

Nick Hasted, *The Story of the Kinks: You Really Got Me*, Omnibus Press, 2013

Richard Hauser, *The Homosexual Society*, The Bodley Head, 1962

Mark Hertsgaard, *A Day in the Life: The Music and Artistry of the Beatles*, Pan Books, 1996

Patrick Higgins, *Heterosexual Dictatorship: Male Homosexuality in Post-War*

Britain, Fourth Estate, 1996

John Hill, *Sex, Class and Realism: British Cinema 1956-1963*, BFI Publishing, 1986

Philip Hoare, *Noel Coward: A Biography*, Sinclair Stevenson, 1995

Richard Hornsey, *The Spiv and the Architect: Unruly Life in Postwar London*, University of Minnesota Press, 2010

Matt Houlbrook, 'Daring to Speak Whose Name? Queer Cultural Politics, 1920-1967', in Marcus Collins (ed.), *The Permissive Society and Its Enemies*, Rivers Oram, 2007

Matt Houlbrook, 'For Whose Convenience? Gay Guides, Cognitive Maps and the Construction of Homosexual London, 1917-1967', in Simon Gunn, R.J. Morris (ed.s), *Identities in Space: Contested Terrains in the Western City Since 1850*, Ashgate, 2001

Matt Houlbrook, *Queer London, Perils and Pleasures of the Sexual Metropolis, 1918-1957*, Chicago University Press, 2005

Richard Huggett, *Binkie Beaumont: Eminence Grise of the West End Theatre, 1933-1973*, Hodder & Stoughton, 1989

Steve Humphries, Pamela Gordon, *A Man's World: From Boyhood to Manhood, 1900-1960*, BBC Books, 1996

Robert Hutton, *Of Those Alone: An Autobiography*, Sidgwick & Jackson, 1958

Julian Jackson, 'Homosexuality, Permissiveness and Morality in France and Britain, 1954-1982', in Marcus Collins (ed.), *The Permissive Society and Its Enemies*, Rivers Oram, 2007

Derek Jarman, *At Your Own Risk: A Saint's Testament*, Hutchinson, 1992

Derek Jarman, *Kicking the Pricks*, University of Minnesota Press, 2010

Stephen Jeffery-Poulter, *Peers, Queers and Commons: The Struggle for Gay Law Reform from 1950 to the Present*, Routledge, 1991

Roy Jenkins, *A Life at the Centre*, Macmillan, 1991

Alkarim Jivani, *It's Not Unusual: A History of Lesbian and Gay Britain in the Twentieth Century*, Michael O'Mara Books, 1997

John Johnston, *The Lord Chamberlain's Blue Pencil*, Hodder & Stoughton, 1990

Nicholas de Jongh, *Not in Front of the Audience: Homosexuality on Stage*, Routledge, 1992

Nicholas de Jongh, *Politics, Prudery and Perversions: The Censoring of the English*

Stage, 1901-1968, Methuen, 2000

Charles Kaiser, *The Gay Metropolis, 1940-1996*, Weidenfeld & Nicolson, 1998

Christine Keeler, *Scandal!*, Xanadu Publications, 1989

Ludovic Kennedy, *The Trial of Stephen Ward*, Victor Gollancz, 1964

Alfred C. Kinsey, Wardell B. Pomeroy, Clyde E. Martin, *Sexual Behavior in the Human Male*, W.B. Saunders, 1948

David Kynaston, *Family Britain, 1951-57*, Bloomsbury, 2010

David Kynaston, *Modernity Britain: A Shake of the Dice, 1959-62*, Bloomsbury, 2014

David Kynaston, *Modernity Britain: Opening the Box, 1957-59*, Bloomsbury, 2013

John Lahr, *Prick Up Your Ears: The Biography of Joe Orton*, Allen Lane, 1978

John Lahr, *The Orton Diaries*, Da Capo Press, 1996

Edward Lamberti (ed.), *Behind the Scenes at the BBFC: Film Classification from the Silver Screen to the Digital Age*, Palgrave Macmillan/British Film Institute, 2012

Yoti Lane, *The Psychology of the Actor*, Secker & Warburg, 1959

Brian Lewis, *Wolfenden's Witnesses: Homosexuality in Postwar Britain*, Palgrave Macmillan, 2016

Ken Livingstone: *You Can't Say That: Memoirs*, Faber & Faber, 2011

Bryan Magee, *One in Twenty*, Secker & Warburg, 1966

Jessica Mann, *The Fifties Mystique*, Quartet Books, 2012

John Marshall, 'Pansies, Perverts and Macho Men: Changing Conceptions of Male Homosexuality', in Ken Plummer (ed.), *The Making of the Modern Homosexual*, Hutchinson, 1981

Brian Masters, *The Swinging Sixties*, Constable, 1985

Angus McLaren, *Sexual Blackmail: A Modern History*, Harvard University Press, 2002

Michael McManus, *Tory Pride and Prejudice: The Conservative Party and Homosexual Law Reform*, Biteback Publishing, 2011

Neil Miller, *Out of the Past: Gay and Lesbian History From 1869 to the Present*, Vintage, 1995

Harford Montgomery Hyde, *The Other Love: An Historical and Contemporary Survey of Homosexuality in Britain*, Heinemann, 1970

Sheridan Morely, *Dirk Bogarde: Rank Outsider*, Bloomsbury, 1999

John Morris, *Hired To Kill*, Rupert Hart-Davis/The Crosset Press, 1960

Frank Mort, *Capital Affairs: London and the Making of the Permissive Society*, Yale University Press, 2010

Simon Napier-Bell, *Black Vinyl, White Powder*, Ebury Press, 2002

Tim Newburn, *Permission and Regulation: Law and Morals in Postwar Britain*, Routledge, 1992

Philip Norman, *Shout! The True Story of the Beatles*, Pan Books, 2004

Margaret O'Brien, Allen Eyles (ed.s), *Enter the Dream House: Memories of Cinemas in South London from the Twenties to the Sixties*, British Film Institute, 1993

Joe Orton, *Up Against It: A Screenplay for the Beatles*, Eyre Methuen, 1979

Tony Parker, *The Twisting Lane: Some Sex Offenders*, Hutchinson, 1969

Frank Parkin, *Middle Class Radicalism: The Social Bases of the British Campaign for Nuclear Disarmament*, Manchester University Press, 1968

Matthew Parris, *Great Parliamentary Scandals*, Robson Books, 1997

W. Patterson Brown, 'The Homosexual Male: Treatment in an Out-Patient Clinic', in Ismond Rosen (ed.), *The Pathology and Treatment of Sexual Deviation: A Methodological Approach*, Oxford University Press, 1964

John Pearson, *Notorious: The Immortal Legend of the Kray Twins*, Century, 2010

John Pearson, *The Profession of Violence: The Rise and Fall of the Kray Twins*, Granada Publishing, 1973

Barry Penrose, Simon Freeman, *Conspiracy of Silence: The Secret Life of Anthony Blunt*, Grafton Books, 1987

Norman Pittenger, *Time for Consent? A Christian's Approach to Homosexuality*, SCM Press, 1967

Douglas Plummer, *Queer People: The Truth About Homosexuals*, W.H. Allen, 1963

Kenneth Plummer, *Sexual Stigma: An Interactionist Account*, Routledge & Kegan Paul, 1975

Mel Porter, 'Gender Identity and Sexual Orientation', in Pat Thane (ed.), *Unequal Britain: Equalities in Britain since 1945*, Continuum, 2010

Alison Pressley, *Changing Times: Being Young in Britain in the 60s*, Michael O'Mara books, 2000

Pete Price, *Namedropper*, Trinity Mirror North West & North Wales, 2007

S. Rachman, J. Teasdale, *Aversion Therapy and Behaviour Disorders: An Analysis*, Routledge & Kegan Paul, 1968

Peter Rawlinson, *A Price Too High: An Autobiography*, Weidenfeld & Nicolson, 1989

Geoffrey Rayner, Richard Chamberlain, Annamarie Stapleton, *Pop! Design, Culture, Fashion, 1956-1976*, ACC Editions, 2012

Dan Rebellato, *1956 and All That: The Making of Modern British Drama*, Routledge, 1999

Jeremy Reed, *The King of Carnaby Street: The Life of John Stephen*, Haus Publishing, 2010

John Repsch, *The Legendary Joe Meek: The Telstar Man*, Cherry Red Books, 2000

Robert Rhodes James, *Bob Boothby: A Portrait*, Hodder & Stoughton, 1991

Peter G. Richards, *Parliament and Conscience*, Allen & Unwin, 1970

Vito Russo, *The Celluloid Clo*set, Harper & Rowe, 1981

Dominic Sandbrook, *Never Had It So Good: A History of Britain from Suez to the Beatles*, Abacus, 2006

Dominic Sandbrook, *Seasons in the Sun: The Battle for Britain, 1974-1979*, Penguin Books, 2012

Dominic Sandbrook, *White Heat: A History of Britain in the Swinging Sixties*, Abacus, 2006

Jon Savage, 'Tainted Love: The Influence of Male Homosexuality and Sexual Divergence on Pop Music and Culture Since the War', in Alan Tomlinson (ed.), *Consumption, Identity and Style: Marketing, Meanings and the Packaging of Pleasure*, Routledge, 1990

Jon Savage, *The Kinks: The Official Biography*, Faber and Faber, 1984

Eugene de Savitsch, *Homosexuality, Transvestism and Change of Sex*, Heinemann, 1958

Michael Schofield, *The Sexual Behaviour of Young People*, Longmans, 1965

Michael Schofield, *Sociological Aspects of Homosexuality: A Comparative Study of Three Types of Homosexuals*, Longmans, 1965

Peter Scott, 'Definition, Classification, Prognosis and Treatment', in Ismond Rosen (ed.), *The Pathology and Treatment of Sexual Deviation: A Methodological Approach*, Oxford University Press, 1964

Peter Scott-Presland, *Amiable Warriors: The Official History of the Campaign for Homosexual Equality and Its Times, Volume One: Space to Breathe*, Paradise Press, 2015

Brian Sewell, *Outsider: Always Almost; Never Quite*, Quartet Books, 2011

Brian Sewell, *Outsider II: Always Almost; Never Quite*, Quartet Books, 2012

David Sheff, G. Barry Golson, *Last Interview: All We Are Saying – John Lennon and Yoko Ono*, Sidgwick & Jackson, 2000

Dominic Shellard, *Kenneth Tynan: A Life*, Yale University Press, 2003

Dominic Shellard, Steve Nicholson, Miriam Handley, *The Lord Chamberlain Regrets…: A History of British Theatre Censorship*, The British Library, 2004

Simon Shepherd, *Because We're Queers*, Gay Men's Press, 1989

Antony Sher, *Beside Myself: An Autobiography*, Hutchinson, 2001

Ann Shillinglaw, '"Give Us A Kiss": Queer Codes, Male Partnering, and the Beatles', in Patricia Juliana Smith (ed.), *The Queer Sixties*, Routledge, 1999

Pete Shotton, Nicholas Schaffner, *John Lennon In My Life*, Coronet Books, 1984

Alan Sinfield, 'Is There a Queer Tradition and Is Orton in It?', in Francesca Coppa (ed.), *Joe Orton: A Casebook*, Routledge, 2003

Alan Sinfield, *Out on Stage, Lesbian and Gay Theatre in the Twentieth Century*, Yale University Press, 1999

Helen Smith, *Masculinity, Class and Same-Sex Desire in Industrial England, 1895-1957*, Palgrave Macmillan, 2015

Colin Spencer, *Backing into Light: My Father's Son*, Quartet Books, 2013

Colin Spencer, *Homosexuality: A History*, Fourth Estate, 1995

Colin Spencer, *Which of Us Two? The Story of a Love Affair*, Penguin Books, 1991

Norman St John-Stevas, *Life, Death and the Law: A Study of the Relationship Between Law and Christian Morals in the English and American Legal Systems*, Eyre & Spottiswoode, 1961

Terence Stamp, *Stamp Album*, Bloomsbury, 1987

Liz Stanley, *Sex Surveyed, 1949 to 1994: From Mass-Observation's 'Little Kinsey' to the National Survey and the Hite Reports*, Taylor & Francis, 1995

Anthony Storr, *Sexual Deviation*, Penguin Books, 1964

John Sutherland, *Offensive Literature: Decensorship in Britain, 1960-1982*, Junction Books, 1982

Christopher Simon Sykes, *Hockney: The Biography, Volume One, 1937-1975*, Century, 2011

John Russell Taylor, *The Second Wave: British Drama of the Sixties*, Methuen & Co., 1971

John Trevelyan, *What the Censor Saw*, Michael Joseph, 1993

Wendy Trewin, J.C. Trewin, *The Arts Theatre, London, 1927-1981*, The Society for Theatre Research, 1986

J. Tudor Rees, Harley V. Usill (ed.s), *They Stand Apart*, Heinemann, 1955

Lars Ullerstam, *The Erotic Minorities: A Swedish View*, Calder & Boyars, 1967

John Vassall, *Vassall: The Autobiography of a Spy*, Sidgwick and Jackson, 1975

Hugo Vickers, *Cecil Beaton: The Authorised Biography*, Weidenfeld and Nicolson, 1985

Kenneth Walker, *Sexual Behaviour, Creative and Destructive*, William Kimber, 1966

Tony Walton (ed.), *Out of the Shadows: A History of the Pioneering London Gay Groups and Organisations, 1967-2000*, Bona Street Press, 2010

Jeffrey Weeks, *Coming Out: Homosexual Politics in Britain from the Nineteenth Century to the Present*, Quartet Books, 1977

Jeffrey Weeks, *Sex, Politics and Society: The Regulation of Sexuality Since 1800*, Longman, 1981

Jeffrey Weeks, Kevin Porter, *Between the Acts: Lives of Homosexual Men, 1885-1967*, Rivers Oram Press, 1998

Richard Weight, *Mod! A Very British Style*, The Bodley Head, 2013

Donald West, *Gay Life, Straight Work*, Paradise Press, 2012

Donald West, *Homosexuality*, Duckworth, 1955; Pelican Books, 1960

Rebecca West, *The Meaning of Treason*, Penguin Books, 1965

Rebecca West, *The Vassall Affair*, Sunday Telegraph, 1963

Gordon Westwood, *A Minority: A Report on the Life of the Male Homosexual in Great Britain*, Longmans, 1960

Gordon Westwood, *Society and the Homosexual*, Gollancz, 1952

Francis Wheen, *The Soul of Indiscretion: Tom Driberg*, Fourth Estate, 2001

Stephen Whittle, 'Consuming Differences: The Collaboration of the Gay Body with the Cultural State', in Stephen Whittle (ed.), *The Margins of the City: Gay Men's Urban Lives*, Arena, 1994

Peter Wildeblood, *A Way of Life*, Weidenfeld & Nicolson, 1956

Peter Wildeblood, *Against the Law*, Weidenfeld & Nicolson, 1955

John Wilson, *Logic and Sexual Morality*, Pelican Books, 1965

John Wolfenden, *Turning Points: The Memoirs of Lord Wolfenden*, The Bodley Head, 1976

Ian Young, *The Male Homosexual in Literature: A Bibliography*, The Scarecrow Press, 1982

Wayland Young, *Eros Denied: Studies in Exclusion*, Weidenfeld and Nicolson, 1965

JOURNALS

Leo Abse, 'The Sexual Offences Act', *British Journal of Criminology*, January 1968

Lord Arran, 'The Sexual Offences Act: A Personal Memoir', *Encounter*, March 1972

John Bancroft, 'Abnormal Sexual Behaviour: Homosexuality in the Male', *British Journal of Hospital Medicine*, February 1970

John Bancroft, 'Aversion Therapy of Homosexuality: A Pilot Study of 10 cases', *The British Journal of Psychiatry*, December 1969

J.H.J. Bancroft, H. Gwynne Jones, B.R. Pullan, 'A Simple Transducer for Measuring Penile Erection, with Comments on its Use in the Treatment of Sexual Disorders', *Behaviour Research and Therapy*, August 1966

John Bancroft, Isaac Marks, 'Electric Aversion Therapy of Sexual Deviations', *Proceedings of the Royal Society of Medicine*, August 1968

Eva Bene, 'On the Genesis of Male Homosexuality: An Attempt at Clarifying the Role of the Parents', *The British Journal of Psychiatry*, September 1965

Christopher Chavasse, 'The Church and Sex', *The Practitioner*, April 1954

Eustace Chesser, 'The Hidden Problem', *Family Doctor*, October 1961

Stephen Coates, 'Homosexuality and the Rorschach Test', *British Journal of Medical Psychology*, 1962

Desmond Curran, Denis Parr, 'Homosexuality: An Analysis of 100 Male Cases Seen in Private Practice', *British Medical Journal*, 6 April 1957

Roger Davidson, 'Psychiatry and Homosexuality in Mid-Twentieth Century Edinburgh: The View From Jordanburn Nerve Hospital', *History of Psychiatry*, December 2009

Roger Davidson, Gayle Davis, '"A Field for Private Members": The Wolfenden Committee and Scottish Homosexual Law Reform, 1950-67', *Twentieth Century British History*, Vol. 15, No. 2, 2004

Tommy Dickinson, Matt Cook, John Playle, Christine Hallett, '"Queer"

Treatments: Giving a Voice to Former Patients Who Received Treatments for their "Sexual Deviations"', *Journal of Clinical Nursing*, May 2012

M.P. Feldman, M.J. MacCulloch, 'The Application of Anticipatory Avoidance Learning to the Treatment of Homosexuality – I. Theory, Technique and Preliminary Results', *Behaviour Research and Therapy*, January 1965

M.P. Feldman, M.J. MacCulloch, Valerie Mellor, J.M. Pinschof, 'The Application of Anticipatory Avoidance Learning to the Treatment of Homosexuality – III. The Sexual Orientation Method', *Behaviour Research and Therapy*, November 1966

B.H. Fookes, 'Some Experiences in the Use of Aversion Therapy in Male Homosexuality, Exhibitionism and Fetishism-Transvestism', *British Journal of Psychiatry*, March 1969

Kurt Freund, 'A Laboratory Method for Diagnosing predominance of Homo- or Hetero-erotic Interest in the Male', *Behaviour Research and Therapy*, May 1963

Martin Gayford, 'Not Grim At All', *Art Quarterly*, Autumn 2015

Roger Gellert, 'A Survey of the Treatment of the Homosexual in Some Plays', *Encore*, January/February 1961

T.C.N. Gibbens, 'The Sexual Behaviour of Young Criminals', *The Journal of Mental Science*, July 1957

S. Gold, I.L. Neufeld, 'A Learning Approach to the Treatment of Homosexuality', *Behaviour and Research Therapy*, January 1965

Geoffrey Gorer, 'Man to Man', *Encounter*, May 1961

Antony Grey, 'Homosexuality: Time For Action Now', *Views*, Summer 1963

Matthew Grimley, 'Law, Morality and Secularisation: The Church of England and the Wolfenden Report', *The Journal of Ecclesiastical History*, October 2009

T.G. Grygier, 'Psychometric Aspects of Homosexuality', *The Journal of Mental Science*, July 1957

J.A. Hadfield, 'The Cure of Homosexuality', *British Medical Journal*, 7 June 1958

R.E. Hemphill, A. Leitch, J.R. Stuart, 'A Factual Study of Male Homosexuality', *British Medical Journal*, 7 June 1958

Derek Hill, 'The Habit of Censorship', *Encounter*, July 1960

Basil James, 'Case of Homosexuality Treated by Aversion Therapy', *British Medical Journal*, 17 March 1962

Michael King, Glenn Smith, Annie Bartlett, 'Treatments of Homosexuality in Britain since the 1950s – An Oral History, The Experience of Professionals', *British Medical Journal*, 21 February 2004

François Laffite, 'Homosexuality and the Law: The Wolfenden Report in Historical Perspective', *British Journal of Delinquency*, July 1958

C.G. Learoyd, 'The Problem of Homosexuality', *The Practitioner*, April 1954

A. Leitch, 'Male Homosexuality as a Medico-Legal and Sociological Problem in the United Kingdom', *International Journal of Social Psychiatry*, Autumn 1959

M.J. MacCulloch, M.P. Feldman, 'Aversion Therapy in Management of 43 Homosexuals', *British Medical Journal*, 3 June 1967

M.J. MacCulloch, M.P. Feldman, J.M. Pinshoff, 'The Application of Anticipatory Avoidance Learning to the Treatment of Homosexuality – II. Avoidance Response Latencies and Pulse Rate Changes', *Behaviour Research and Therapy*, August 1965

Colin MacInnes, 'Dark Angel: The Writings of James Baldwin', *Encounter*, August 1963

Colin MacInnes, 'A Taste of Reality', *Encounter*, April 1959

John Maude, 'Homosexuality and the Criminal Law', *The Practitioner*, April 1954

Louis William Max, 'Breaking Up a Homosexual Fixation by the Conditioned Reaction Technique: A Case Study', *The Psychological Bulletin*, November 1935

R.J. McGuire, M. Vallance, 'Aversion Therapy by Electric Shock, A Simple Technique', *British Medical Journal*, 18 January 1964

Frank Mort, 'Mapping Sexual London: The Wolfenden Committee on Homosexual Offences and Prostitution, 1954-57', *New Formations*, Spring 1999

W. Lindesay Neustatter, 'Homosexuality: The Medical Aspect', *The Practitioner*, April 1954

W. Lindesay Neustatter, 'Sexual Abnormalities and the Sexual Offender', *The Medico-Legal Journal*, 1961

W. Lindesay Neustatter, 'The Wolfenden Report. I. – Homosexuality', *The Howard Journal*, Vol. 10, No. 1, 1958

P.J. O'Connor, 'Aetiological Factors in Homosexuality as Seen in Royal Air Force Psychiatric Practice', *British Journal of Psychiatry*, September 1964

Isaac Oswald, 'Induction of Illusory and Hallucinatory Voices with Considerations of Behaviour Therapy', *The Journal of Mental Science*, March 1962

Denis Parr, 'Homosexuality in Clinical Practice', *Proceedings of the Royal Society of Medicine*, September 1957

Denis Parr, 'Psychiatric Aspects of the Wolfenden Report', *British Journal of Delinquency*, July 1958

Stanley Rachman, 'Aversion Therapy, Chemical or Electrical?', *Behaviour Research and Therapy*, April 1965

Simon Raven, 'Boys Will be Boys, The Male Prostitute in London', *Encounter*, November 1960

Anthony Rowley, 'Another Kind of Loving: What Is It Like To Be A Homosexual?', *Axle Spokes,* 4, 1963

L. H. Rubenstein, 'Psychotherapeutic Aspects of Male Homosexuality', *British Journal of Medical Psychology*, 1958

Elsa Schmidt, David Castell, Paul Brown, 'A Retrospective Study of 42 Cases of Behaviour Therapy', *Behaviour Research and Therapy*, August 1965

Michael Schofield, 'Social Aspects of Homosexuality', *British Journal of Venereal Diseases*, June 1964

P.D. Scott, 'Homosexuality with Special Reference to Classification', *Proceedings of the Royal Society of Medicine*, September 1957

Peter Scott, 'Psychiatric Aspects of the Wolfenden Report', *British Journal of Delinquency*, July 1958

C. P. Seager, 'Aversion Therapy in Psychiatry', *Nursing Times*, 26 March 1965

Alan Sinfield, 'Closet Dramas: Homosexual Representation and Class in Postwar British Theatre, *Genders*, November 1990

Eliot Slater, 'Birth Order and Maternal Age of Homosexuals', *The Lancet*, 13 January 1962

Glenn Smith, Annie Bartlett, Michael King, 'Treatments of Homosexuality in Britain since the 1950s – An Oral History: The Experience of Patients', *British Medical Journal*, 21 February 2004

S.J.C. Spencer, 'Homosexuality Among Oxford Undergraduates', *The Journal of Mental Science*, April 1959

G.I.M. Swyer, 'Homosexuality: The Endocrinological Aspects', *The Practitioner*, April 1954

J.G. Thorpe, E. Schmidt, 'Therapeutic Failure in a Case of Aversion Therapy', *Behaviour Research and Therapy*, March 1964

J.G. Thorpe, E. Schmidt, P.T. Brown, D. Castell, 'Aversion-Relief Therapy: A New Method for General Application', *Behaviour Research and Therapy*, May 1964

J.G. Thorpe, E. Schmidt, D. Castell, 'A Comparison of Positive and Negative (Aversive) Conditioning in the Treatment of Homosexuality', *Behaviour Research and Therapy*, March 1964

Northage J. de Ville Mather, 'The Treatment of Homosexuality by Aversion Therapy', *Medicine, Science and the Law*, October 1966

Roy Walmsley, 'Indecency Between Males and the Sexual Offences Act 1967', *Criminal Law Review*, July 1978

Chris Waters, '"Dark Strangers" in Our Midst: Discourses of Race and Nation in Britain, 1947-1963,' *Journal of British Studies*, April 1997

Peter Wildeblood, 'The Boys Who Cried Wolfenden', *Encounter*, February 1959

Angus Wilson, 'Problems and Plays. The Theatre Faces the World: Morality', *International Theatre Annual*, No. 4, John Calder, 1959

Mary Woodward, 'The Diagnosis and Treatment of Homosexual Offenders', *British Journal of Delinquency*, July 1958

Barbara Wootton, 'Sickness or Sin?', *The Twentieth Century*, May 1956

PRESS

'Law and Hypocrisy', *The Sunday Times*, 28 March 1954

Robert Fabian, 'No Mercy – That Was The Rule Of This Rogue', *Empire News*, 10 July 1955

Robert Fabian, 'Downfall of a Mastermind', *Empire News*, 17 July 1955

'It Was a Big Price for the Victim to Pay', *News of the World*, 20 January 1957

'One Million Need This New Clinic', *Daily Express*, 23 August 1957

'Vice: Official', *Daily Mirror*, 5 September 1957

'Views on the Report'; 'Discussion by TV Panel'; 'Keeping Vice Off the Street', *The Daily Telegraph*, 5 September 1957

'What They Say About the Vice Report', *The Evening News*, 5 September 1957

'Vice Report Starts Off a Sharp Controversy'; 'The Legal Solution'; '"Homosexuality Should Be Legalised"'; 'New Law Would Licence Licentiousness'; 'Nation Morally in the Gutter', *The Scotsman*, 5 September 1957

'A Doctor Tells on TV', *Daily Mail*, 6 September 1957

'"I Am a Homosexual" Says a Doctor on TV', *Daily Mirror*, 6 September 1957

George Gulley, 'The Skipping Technique for Thin Ice', *Tatler and Bystander*, 11 September 1957

Francis Williams, Fleet Street Notebook, *New Statesman*, 14 September 1957

'Dr Ramsey Supports Report on Vice'; 'Law's Concern with Morals', *The Times*, 27 September 1957

C. H. Rolph, 'Wolfenden Revisited', *New Statesman*, 28 September 1957

News in Brief, *The Times*, 7 October 1957

'Homosexuality Law "Grave Injustice"', *The Times*, 14 October 1957

'Company Director Went to Soho', *News of the World*, 10 November 1957

J.B. Priestley, 'Outlaws We Should Bring Within the Law', *Reynolds News*, 10 November 1957

'Church Assembly Approve Report on Homosexuality', *The Times*, 15 November 1957

'Government Caution on Wolfenden Reforms', *The Times*, 5 December 1957

'Dangers of the Crush', *The Times Educational Supplement*, 6 December 1957

'The Wolfenden Report', *The Tablet*, 7 December 1957

Richard Wollheim, 'The Road to Toleration', *The Spectator*, 4 April 1958

'The Repentant Photographer', *News of the World*, 13 April 1958

Denis Duperley, Geoff Donaldson, 'Will Britain See These Films?', *Films and Filming*, May 1958

'The PC Turned to Blackmail', *News of the World*, 3 August 1958

Cecil Wilson, 'Lord Blue Pencil Lifts Stage Ban', *Daily Mail*, 7 November 1958

'Brought Shame on His Family', *News of the World*, 23 November 1958

Kenneth Allsop, 'Suddenly… SEX Without a Snigger', *Daily Mail*, 26 November 1958

'£5 Fine on Ian Harvey. He Will Pay to End of Life', *The Times*, 11 December 1958

'Men Die After "Suicide Pact"', *The Daily Telegraph*, 16 December 1958

'Blackmailer "Bled" Mr X in Terror of the Phone', *Evening Standard*, 9 January 1959

'£8,800 by "Slow Torture"', *The Times*, 10 January 1959

London Diary, *New Statesman*, 31 January 1959

John Deane Potter, 'Isn't It About Time Someone Said This Plainly and Frankly?', *Daily Express*, 9 April 1959

'Menaces Charge: Man Remanded', *The Times*, 26 May 1959

'Alleged Demands to "Mr. X"', *The Times*, 3 June 1959

Graham Turner, 'Growing Problem of the Homosexual', *The Scotsman*, 5 June 1959

Graham Turner, 'Control Must Come Before Cure', *The Scotsman*, 6 June 1959

Graham Turner, 'Church Has a Major Part to Play', *The Scotsman*, 8 June 1959

'Threatening Letters After 30 Years', *The Times*, 3 July 1959

'Clergyman Says He Paid £1,500', *The Times*, 22 August 1959

'Clergyman's Ex-Valet Gaoled', *News of the World*, 20 September 1959

'Minister's Reply on Homosexuality', *The Guardian*, 10 May 1960

Edrward Hyams, 'The Spurious Problem'; Kenneth Robinson, 'The Time for Decision'; 'The Homosexual and the Law', *New Statesman*, 25 June 1960,

R.A. Cline, 'Letter of the Law: Further Outlook – Bleak?', *The Spectator*, 18 November 1960

Ronald Maxwell, 'Twilight Men – Now They Can Be Cured', *Sunday Pictorial*, 5 February 1961

George Martin, 'Admiralty Man in Secrets Case', *The Daily Telegraph*, 14 February 1962

'Dirk Bogarde Takes His Most Daring Role', *Evening Standard*, 17 February 1961

Peter Warren, 'Rank's "Victim" May End Up a 'Martyr', *Films and Filming*, April 1961

J.W.W. Thompson, 'They Walk in the Shadow of Fear', *Evening Standard*, 22 February 1962

Desmond Donelly, 'Blackmailer's Charter', *The Spectator*, 23 February 1962

Jack Miller, 'Murders in a Half World', *News of the World*, 25 February 1962

Abraham Marcus, 'How Doctor Cured a Homosexual', *The Observer*, 18 March 1962

'Sir Ian Says No to Life Peerage', *Daily Express*, 14 April 1962

'Gaol for "Frustrated Actors"', *The Times*, 16 May 1962

'Sir Ian Gave Me Trip in His Rolls', *Daily Mirror*, 6 June 1962

'Charges of Indecency Against Sir Ian Horobin', *The Times*, 6 June 1962

'Sir Ian Spoke of "Us Poor Devils" – Vicar', *Daily Mirror*, 19 June 1962

'Sir Ian Jailed for Four Years', *Daily Express*, 18 July 1962

Great Career of Sir Ian Ends in Jail', *Daily Mirror*, 18 July 1962

'Sir Ian Horobin Sentenced to Four Years' Imprisonment', *The Times*, 18 July 1962

'Boy "Was More Sinned Against"', *The Times*, 20 July 1962

Peter Barnsley, 'Faces Without Shadows', *Town*, September 1962

John Owen, 'Admiralty Man in Secrets Case', *The Daily Telegraph*,
      14 September 1962

'Goings on at The Kandy Lounge', *News of the World*, 16 September 1962

'How They Caught Him After 6 Years', *Daily Sketch*, 23 October 1962

'Premier Sets Up Three-Man Spy Inquiry'; '18 Years' Gaol for "Traitorous Tool
      of Russians"'; 'Weaknesses That Led to Vassall's Fall', *The Daily Telegraph*,
      23 October 1962

Ron Mount, 'Spies – Vice Probe'; John Deane Potter, 'Twilight Traitors', *News
      of the World*, 28 October 1962

Norman Lucas, 'Spy Catchers Name "Sex Risk" Men – in Whitehall'; '42
      Faces of the Spy Who Bares His Soul', *Sunday Pictorial*, 28 October 1962

Norman Lucas, Bill Hamilton, 'The Letters in Vassall's Flat'; 'How the Russian
      Spy Masters Broke Me Down', *Sunday Pictorial*, 4 November 1962

Roy East, 'New Spy Sensation', *The People*, 11 November 1962

'Vassall: the Scandal Grows', *The People*, 4 November, 1962

'Secret of Red Spy School', *News of the World*, 11 November 1962

'The Men Who Came to See Me – and the Women? They Gave Me Mother
      Love', *Sunday Pictorial*, 11 November 1962

Donald Maclachlan, 'Who's to Blame for Vassall?', *Sunday Telegraph*,
      11 November 1962

'Vassall and the The Pictorial', *Sunday Pictorial*, 18 November 1962

Roy Perrott, 'A Club for Homosexuals', *The Observer Weekend Review*,
      13 January 1963

George Martin, 'Secrets of the Scented Flat'; 'The Cuddly-Toy Spy', *Daily
      Sketch*, 24 January 1963

'The Night I Killed George Brinham', *News of the World*, 27 January 1963

Clifford Davis, 'TV Looks in at a Strange Club', *Daily Mirror*, 1 February 1963

'How BBC Pronounces the Word', *The Sunday Telegraph*, 3 February 1963

'Greek to Me', *The Sunday Times*, 3 February 1963

'Boy Driver of MP's Car is Charged', *Daily Express*, 5 March 1963

'MP Says Charges Against Staff Officer "Hushed Up"', *Birmingham Post*, 9 March 1963

Michael Dove, 'Admiralty Man Quits After Scouts Sack Him', *Sunday Express*, 10 March 1963

Lionel Crane, 'How to Spot a Possible Homo', *Sunday Mirror*, 28 April 1963

'9-Month Sentence on Guardsman', *The Times*, 21 May 1963

Jack Bell, 'BBC Shelves Film on Club', *Daily Mirror*, 21 May 1963

'BBC-TV Scraps Film on Holland Homosexuals', *Variety*, 29 May 1963

'The Nightmare World of the Homosexual', *Peace News*, 21 June 1963

'10 Accused of Sex Offences', *Bolton Evening News*, 25 June 1963

'"Tempter" Is Gaoled for 18 Months'; 'Ten Plead Guilty to Sex Charges', *Bolton Evening News*, 9 July 1963

'Blackmail Made Easy?', *The Observer*, 1 September 1963

'Famous Names in Guardsman's Book', *Yorkshire Post*, 4 October 1963

'"Scandals Discovered" by Bell', *The Guardian*, 9 October 1963

'Man Accuses a Minister', *The Daily Telegraph*, 11 October 1963

'Unwarranted Inferences, Says MP', *The Guardian*, 13 October 1963

'Salesman is Cleared of 9 Charges', *The Times*, 17 October 1963

'Army Puts Pub Ban on Guards', *Daily Mirror*, 18 October 1963

'The Army "Sacks" Bell Case Witness', *Evening Standard*, 24 October 1963

'The Man Who Wrote "Telstar"', *The Evening News*, 12 November 1963

'Concern at Heavier Sentences on Homosexuals', *Daily Worker*, 13 March 1964

John Hopkins, 'Z Cars: a Man Outside the Law', *Radio Times*, 28 May 1964

Norman Lucas, 'Peer and a Gangster: Yard Inquiry', *Sunday Mirror*, 12 July 1964

James Margach, 'Henry Brooke and the Unpublished Picture', *The Sunday Times*, 19 July 1964

'The Picture We Must Not Print'; Leo Abse, 'Homosexuals: What Has Made the Government Change Its Mind About Them?', *Sunday Mirror*, 19 July 1964

'The Law and the Homosexual', *Sheffield Telegraph*, 20 July 1964

'Policy on Homosexuals "Has Not Changed"'; 'Crime and Punishment', *The Daily Telegraph*, 20 July 1964

Anne Sharpley, 'London's Hidden Problem', *Evening Standard*, 20, 21, 22, 23 July 1964

Noyes Thomas, 'Into the Twilight World', *News of the World*, 26 July 1964

Noyes Thomas, 'The Men Behind the Mask', *News of the World*, 2 August 1964

'Lord Boothby: An Unqualified Apology', *Sunday Mirror*, 9 August 1964

Monica Furlong, 'The Law and the Homosexual', *Daily Mail*, 21 October 1964

'Hospital Projects to Help Mentally Ill', *The Guardian*, 25 November 1964

Robert Traini, 'Murder Squad Ask: Did You See Him?', *Sun*, 7 December 1964

'Surely Someone Somewhere Could Give Me a Chance', [Brighton] *Evening Argus*, 13 March 1965

Quentin Crewe, 'Will My Son Be a Homosexual?' *Daily Mirror*, 14 April 1965

Quentin Crewe, 'The Boy Who Sat by Me in the Cinema', *Daily Mirror*, 15 April 1965

'Homosexuals Still Blackmailers' Prey', *The Guardian*, 22 April 1965

'Ld. Moynihan Accused of Importuning', *The Times*, 22 April 1965

'Lord Moynihan: Case Brought Forward', *The Times*, 28 April 1965

'Lord Moynihan "Critically Ill"', *The Times*, 30 April 1965

'No Inquest on Lord Moynihan', *The Times*, 1 May 1965

'Lord Moynihan Court Plea Fails', *The Times*, 4 May 1965

Anne Simpson, 'What Every Man Must Know', *Yorkshire Post*, 19 May 1965

'Million are Homosexuals' Says Society, *Evening Standard*, 7 July 1965

Ronald Brydon, 'Osborne at the Ball', *New Statesman*, 9 July 1965

'"Powdered and Painted Men 'Infested' Pub"', *Stratford Express*, 13 August 1965

'Street Where 'Mod' Look Was Born', *Business Week*, 28 August 1965

Roy Smith, 'The Men Apart', *Newcastle Evening Chronicle*, 7, 8, 9 September 1965

Gordon Greig, 'Homosexuality: Alter the Law', *Daily Mail*, 28 October 1965

Nicholas Tomalin, 'Homosexuals: Three Cases for Reform', *The Sunday Times*, 28 November 1965

Monica Furlong, 'Can Such a Sentence on This Boy Be Justified?', *Daily Mail*, 30 November 1965

Personality Page, *Boyfriend*, 8 January 1966

C.H. Rolph, 'Homosexuality: Reform at Last?', *The New Statesman*, 4 February 1966

'Cordle Slams Bill on Homosexuals', *Bournemouth Evening Echo*, 14 February 1966

'Mr Berkeley's Bill', *The Scotsman*, 11 February 1966

'Oppose This Bill, Dorset Asked', *Bournemouth Evening Echo*, 19 February 1966

Frank Goldsworthy, '29 Blondes Get Marching Orders from 'Sex' Case', *Daily Express*, 5 April 1966

'Schoolgirls Leave Court', *The Times*, 5 April 1966

'Pansies' Emancipation', *Spearhead*, July 1966

Giles Playfair, 'Time to Forget Wolfenden', *The Sunday Telegraph*, 14 August 1966

J.B. Priestley, 'Dandy Days', *New Statesman*, 4 November 1966

James Margach, 'Red Duster Lobby Blow to Abse's Bill', *The Sunday Times*, 27 November 1966

Jane Gaskell, 'Joe Has a Colourful Way with Words', *Daily Sketch*, 30 November 1966

'"Sink of Filth": Coffee Bar Man Jailed', *Chelsea News*, 2 December 1966

'Suitcase Killer Hunt in Soho', *The Evening News*, 20 January 1967

'Killer Hunt in Vice Haunts', *The Evening News*, 21 January 1967

Irma Kurtz, 'Homosexuality: The Unlocking of a Law', *Nova*, February 1967

Norman Pittenger, 'Time for Consent', *New Christian*, 9 March 1967

'Reform That Doesn't Go Far Enough', *The Surrey Comet*, 22 April 1967

'At 5.50 BST After a Night of Dubious Jokes and Personal Clashes a Social Revolution Begins', *Daily Mirror*, 5 July 1967

Brian Silk, Peter Burdon, 'Jealousy Theory In Playwright's Murder'; Jane Gaskell, 'How Success Didn't Change Joe Orton', *Daily Sketch*, 10 August 1967

Nik Cohn, 'Ready Steady Gone', *The Observer* magazine, 27 August 1967

Geoffrey Moorhouse, 'Homosexual Says "Sense of Shame" Is Lifted,

The Guardian, 16 September 1967

'Indecency Court Martial A Nullity', *The Times*, 21 November 1967

Ray Seaton, '"There's Nothing Queer About Us"', *Wolverhampton Express and Star*, 8 January 1968

'Canon Forms Club For "Lonely Men"', *Coventry Evening Telegraph*, 10 January 1968

'Provost Defends Sex Clinic Plan', *Birmingham Evening Mail*, 12 January 1968

Paul Connew, 'Special "Clinic" for Homosexuals at a Cathedral', *Daily Mirror*, 12 January 1968

'Cathedral to Open a Clinic for the "Lonely Ones"', *Manchester Daily Express*, 12 January 1968

'Provost's "No" to "Club"', *Coventry Evening Telegraph*, 17 January 1968

Ron Mount, 'A Very Strange Club', *News of the World*, 21 January 1968

Tony Geraghty, 'The Disturbing Case of the Consenting Teenagers', *The Sunday Times*, 17 March 1968

Denis Cassidy, 'Even in These Permissive Times Do We Want Pubs Like This?', *The People*, 24 March 1968

Roy Perrott, '" Getting Too Tough with Homosexuals"', *The Observer*, 31 March 1968

'City Youths "Misconceived" the Intention of the Act – Judge', [Stoke] *Evening Sentinel*, 9 April 1968

'Director is Fined £700 in Guards Case', *Liverpool Echo*, 6 May 1968

'Interior Decorator Fined £700', *West Lancashire* [Blackpool] *Evening Gazette*, 6 May 1968

Arnold Latcham, 'Man in Vice Case with Guards is Fined £700', *Daily Express*, 7 May 1968

'Director Fined £700 in Guardsmen Case', [Nottingham] *Guardian Journal*, 7 May 1968

'Director Fined for Indecency with Guards', *The Guardian*, 7 May 1968

'Guardsmen Case Man Fined £700', *The Times*, 7 May 1968

'Guardsman Cleared of Vice Charge', *The Daily Telegraph*, 8 May 1968

'Guardsman Was Led Astray by Luxury', *Evening News*, 10 May 1968

Norman Pittenger, 'Christian Morality and the Homosexual', *The Times*, 1 June 1968

'Cleared by Jury', *Portsmouth Evening News*, 31 July 1968

Tony Geraghty, 'The Night a College Lecturer and a Police Sergeant Met in a Dark Alleyway', *The Sunday Times*, 11 August 1968

Ray Gosling, 'Homosexuals Now', *New Society*, 29 August 1968

Peter Forbes, 'The Sick Men of Hampstead Heath', *The People*, 1 September 1968

The Arran Column, *The Evening News*, 4 September 1968

'Burnley May Get Club for Homosexuals', [Burnley] *Evening Star*, 9 September 1968

'Why a Policeman Had to Dance', *Manchester Evening News*, 9 September 1968

'10 Years for Attempt to Kill Homosexual', *Yorkshire Post*, 28 September 1968

'Which Ad Has the Family Touch?', *Campaign*, 10 January 1969

'Homosexual's Court-Martial "Test Case"', *Eastern Daily Press*, 2 February 1969

Antony Grey, Donald J. West, 'New Law But No New Deal', *New Society*, 27 March 1969

'Yes, There May Be Many Like Him: But Is Jeremy Really So Gay?', *Daily Mirror*, 5 August 1969

'Leos' Plan Help for Drug Addicts and Homosexuals', *Leyton Express*, 29 August 1969

'"Don't Prosecute For This Type of Offence"', *Bedfordshire Times*, 17 October 1969

Paul Barker, John Harvey, 'Facing Two Ways: Between the 60s and 70s, *New Society*, 27 November 1969

Joanna Slaughter, 'The Men Who Still Feel Hunted', *The Observer*, 1 February 1970

Claire Rayner, 'Should Shame Be the Cure?', *Daily Mail*, 10 September 1970

Peter Gillman, 'The Queer-Bash Killers', *The Sunday Times Magazine*, 7 February 1971

Peter Pringle, 'Fears Over Aversion Therapy Grow: Using Shock Tactics to Bend the Mind', *The Sunday Times*, 9 May 1971

Peter Tatchell, 'Aversion Therapy "Is Like a Visit to the Dentist"', *Gay News*, No. 11, November 1972

RADIO

Behind the News, BBC Home Service, 11 November 1953 [

Woman's Hour, BBC Light Programme, 28 November 1955

The Homosexual Condition, BBC Home Service, 25 July 1957

Any Questions?, BBC Home Service, 15 November 1957

Woman's Hour, BBC Light Programme, 10 July 1958

Henry de Montherlant, *The Land Where the King is a Child* (*La Ville Dont le Prince est un Enfant*), BBC Third Programme, 10 March, 10 April 1959; 5 April 1960

The Brains Trust, BBC Home Service, 26 June 1960

Woman's Hour, BBC Light Programme, 8 July 1964

Gear Street, South East Special, BBC, 22 August 1964

The Ruffian on the Stair, BBC Third Programme, 31 August 1964

Male Homosexual, BBC Home Service, 5 January 1965

Male Homosexual, BBC Home Service, 12 January 1965

Woman's Hour, BBC Light Programme, 9 March 1965

Woman's Hour, BBC Light Programme, 11 March 1965

Ten O'Clock, BBC Home Service, 28 October 1965

The Night People, BBC Home Service, 4 April 1966

Today, BBC Home Service, 20 December 1966

Round The Horne, BBC Light Programme, 19 February 1967; 2 April 1967

Subject for Sunday, BBC Radio 4, 12 May 1968

The World This Weekend, BBC Radio 4, 1 September 1968

Parents and Children, BBC Radio 4, 17 December 1969

TELEVISION

Is This Your Problem? BBC Television, 14 February 1957

Press Conference: Sir John Wolfenden, BBC Television, 6 September 1957

Lifeline, BBC Television, 26 November 1957

South, Play of the Week, ITV, 24 November 1959

The Brains Trust, BBC Television, 23 June 1960

On Trial: Sir Roger Casement, ITV, 8 July 1960

On Trial: Oscar Wilde, ITV, 5 August 1960

Honeymoon Postponed, Armchair Theatre, ITV, 29 January 1961

In the News, ITV, 10 March 1961

The Collection, Television Playhouse, ITV, 11 May 1961

Adventure Story, Sunday Night Theatre, BBC, 12 June 1961

Afternoon of a Nymph, Armchair Theatre, ITV, 30 September 1962

That Was The Week That Was, BBC Television, 1963

Dangerous Corner, Play of the Week, ITV, 19 March 1963

Panorama, BBC Television, 5 August 1963

'Somebody… Help', *Z Cars,* BBC 1, 3 June 1964

This Week: Homosexuals, ITV, 22 October 1964

A Quick Look Round: The Success Story of John Stephen, BBC 1 (Scotland),
    9 February 1965

Horror of Darkness, The Wednesday Play, BBC 1, 10 March 1965

Twenty-Four Hours, BBC 1, 28 October 1965

A Whole Scene Going, BBC 1, 26 January 1966

The Connoisseur, The Wednesday Play, BBC 1, 4 May 1966

Meeting Point: Outcasts and Outsiders, BBC 1, 20 November 1966

'Murder Reported', *Softly, Softly,* BBC 1, 23 November 1966

The Division, ITV, 25 May 1967

Man Alive: Consenting Adults 1. The Men, BBC 2, 7 June 1967

Late Night Line-Up, BBC 2, 14 June 1967

Friends, Half-Hour Story, ITV, 6 September 1967

Late Night Line Up, BBC 2, 4 February 1968

Entertaining Mr Sloane, Playhouse, ITV, 15 July 1968

Spoiled, The Wednesday Play, BBC 1, 28 August 1968

The Last Train Through The Harecastle Tunnel, The Wednesday Play, BBC 1,
    1 October 1969

World in Action: Seven Men, ITV, 6 July 1970

Edward II, BBC 2, 6 August 1970

Late Night Line Up, BBC 2, 4 December 1970

Roll on Four O'Clock, Saturday Night Theatre, ITV, 19 December 1970

Measure of Conscience: Consenting Party, BBC 2, 26 April 1972

FILMS

I Am a Camera, Romulus Films, 1955

Tea and Sympathy, Metro-Goldwyn-Mayer, 1956

Anders als du und ich/Das dritte Geschlecht (*Different From You and Me/The Third Sex*), Arca-Filmproduktion, 1957

The Strange One/End as a Man, Columbia Pictures, 1957

Look Back in Anger, Woodfall Film Productions, 1959

Serious Charge, Ava Films, 1959

Suddenly Last Summer, Columbia Pictures 1959

The Savage Eye, City Film Corporation, 1959

Carry On Constable, Peter Rogers Productions, 1960

Oscar Wilde, Twentieth Century Fox, 1960

The League of Gentlemen, Allied Film Makers, 1960

The Long and the Short and the Tall, Michael Balcon Productions, 1960

The Trials of Oscar Wilde, Warwick Film Productions, 1960

A Taste of Honey, British Lion Film Corporation, 1961

The L-Shaped Room, British Lion Film Corporation, 1961

Victim, Allied Film Makers, 1961

A View from the Bridge (*Vu du Pont*), Transcontinental Films, 1962

Advise and Consent, Otto Preminger Films, 1962

Five Finger Exercise, Columbia Pictures, 1962

Il Mare, Buffardi, 1962

Scorpio Rising, Puck Film Productions, 1963

This Sporting Life, Independent Artists, 1963

The Leather Boys, Raymond Stross Productions, 1964

Darling, Vic Films, 1965

Dream A40, Reckord Productions, 1965

The Knack …and How to Get It, Woodfall Film Productions, 1965

The Pleasure Girls, Compton Films, 1965

The Family Way, Boulting Brothers, 1966

Portrait of Jason, Shirley Clarke, 1967

The Fearless Vampire Killers/Dance of the Vampires, Cadre Films, 1967

If…, Memorial Enterprises, 1968

Inadmissible Evidence, Woodfall Film Productions, 1968

Performance, Goodtimes Enterprises, 1968 (released 1970)

Teorema, Aetos Produzioni Cinematografiche, 1968

The Detective, Arcola Pictures, 1968

The Lion in Winter, Haworth Productions, 1968

Satyricon, Produzioni Europee Associati, 1969

Staircase, Twentieth Century Fox, 1969

The Gay Deceivers, Fanfare Films, 1969

The Italian Job, Oakhurst Productions, 1969

Women in Love, Brandywine Productions, 1969

Come Dancing, Bill Douglas, 1970

Entertaining Mr Sloane, Canterbury Film Productions, 1970

Goodbye Gemini, Joseph Shaftel Productions, 1970

Something for Everyone/Black Flowers for the Bride, Cinema Center Films, 1970

The Boys in the Band, Cinema Center Films, 1970

Fortune and Men's Eyes, Metro-Goldwyn-Mayer, 1971

Villain, Anglo-EMI, 1971

PLAYS

Philip King, *Serious Charge* (1953), Samuel French, 1955

Ruth Goetz, Augustus Goetz, *The Immoralist* (1954), Dramatists Play Service, 1982

John Van Druten, *I Am a Camera* (1954), Dramatists Play Service, 1983

Julien Green, *South* (1955), Marion Boyars Publishers, 1991

Arthur Miller, *A View from the Bridge* (1956), Penguin Modern Classics, 2010

John Osborne, *Look Back in Anger* (1956), Faber & Faber, 1957

Robert Anderson, *Tea and Sympathy* (1957), Heinemann, 1957

Ronald Duncan, *The Catalyst* (1957), The Rebel Press, 1964

Philip King, Robin Maugham, *The Lonesome Road* (1957), Samuel French, 1959

Brendan Behan, *The Hostage* (1958), Methuen & Co., 1958

Shelagh Delaney, *A Taste of Honey* (1958), Methuen Drama, 2009

Roger Gellert, *Quaint Honour* (1958), Secker & Warburg, 1958

Willis Hall, *The Long and the Short and the Tall* (1958), Heinemann, 1994

Jeremy Kingston, *No Concern of Mine* (1958), Samuel French, 1959

Terence Rattigan, *Variation on a Theme* (1958), *The Collected Plays of Terence Rattigan*, *Volume Three*, Hamish Hamilton, 1964

Peter Shaffer, *Five Finger Exercise* (1958), Samuel French, 1958

Tennessee Williams, *Cat on a Hot Tin Roof* (1958), Penguin Modern Classics, 2009

Tennessee Williams, *Suddenly Last Summer* (1958), Penguin Modern Classics, 2009

Sandy Wilson, *Valmouth* (1958), Samuel French, 1958

Beverley Cross, *One More River* (1959), Samuel French, 1960

Frank Norman, *Fings Ain't Wot They Used T' Be* (1959), Secker & Warburg, 1960

Arnold Wesker, *Roots* (1959), *The Wesker Trilogy*, Jonathan Cape, 1960

Terence Rattigan, *Ross* (1960), *The Collected Plays of Terence Rattigan, Volume Three*, Hamish Hamilton, 1964

Alan Bennett, Peter Cook, Jonathan Miller, Dudley Moore, *Beyond the Fringe* (1960-61), Methuen 2003

Ann Jellicoe, *The Knack* (1961), Encore Publishing, 1962

Harold Pinter, *The Collection* (1961), Eyre Methuen, 1963

Arnold Wesker, *Chips With Everything* (1962), Jonathan Cape, 1962

Philip King, *How Are You Johnnie?* (1963), Samuel French, 1963

Bill Naughton, *All in Good Time* (1963), Samuel French, 1965

Terence Rattigan, *Man and Boy* (1963), *The Collected Plays of Terence Rattigan, Volume Four*, Hamish Hamilton, 1978

Frank Wedekind, *Spring Awakening* (1963), Caldar & Boyars, 1969

Pauline Macaulay, *The Creeper* (1964), *Plays of the Year, Vol. 29, 1964-1965*, Elek Books, 1965

Joe Orton, *Entertaining Mr Sloane* (1964), *Orton: Complete Plays*, Methuen Drama, 1998

Joe Orton, *The Ruffian on the Stair* (1964), *Orton: Complete Plays*, Methuen Drama, 1998

John Osborne, *Inadmissible Evidence* (1964), *John Osborne Plays 3*, Faber & Faber 1998

Peter Shaffer, *The Royal Hunt of the Sun* (1964), Hamish Hamilton, 1964

Edward Bond, *Saved* (1965), Methuen Drama, 2000

John Osborne, *A Patriot for Me* (1965), *John Osborne Plays 3*, Faber & Faber, 1998

Peter Shaffer, *Black Comedy* (1965), Hamish Hamilton, 1968

Noël Coward, *A Song at Twilight* (1966), Methuen, 1999

Charles Dyer, *Staircase* (1966), Samuel French, 1966

James Goldman, *The Lion in Winter* (1966), Samuel French, 1966

Christopher Hampton, *When Did You Last See My Mother?* (1966), Samuel French, 1967

Joe Orton, *Loot* (1966), *Orton: Complete Plays*, Methuen Drama, 1998

Colin Spencer, *The Ballad of the False Barman* (1966), unpublished manuscript, courtesy of Colin Spencer

Simon Gray, *Wise Child* (1967), Faber & Faber, 1968

Joe Orton, *What the Butler Saw* (1967; performed 1969), *Orton: Complete Plays*, Methuen Drama, 1998

Christopher Hampton, *Total Eclipse* (1968), *Christopher Hampton: Plays 1*, Faber & Faber, 1991

John Herbert, *Fortune and Men's Eyes* (1968), Grove Press, 1967

Peter Shaffer, *The White Liars* (1968), Hamish Hamilton, 1968

Colin Spencer, *Spitting Image* (1968), unpublished manuscript, Lord Chamberlain's Plays, British Library

Lanford Wilson, *The Madness of Lady Bright* (1968), Methuen & Co., 1968

Mart Crowley, *The Boys in the Band* (1969), Penguin Books, 1970

Cecil P. Taylor, *Lies About Vietnam* (1969), *Gay Plays, Volume Two*, Methuen, 1985

John Hopkins, *Find Your Way Home* (1970), Penguin Books, 1971

NOVELS

Gore Vidal, *The City and the Pillar*, John Lehmann, 1949

Fritz Peters, *Finistère*, Gollancz, 1951

G.F. Green, *In the Making*, Peter Davies, 1952

Angus Wilson, *Hemlock and After*, Secker & Warburg, 1952

James Barr, *Quatrefoil*, Vision Press, 1953

Rodney Garland, *The Heart in Exile*, W.H. Allen, 1953

Audrey Erskine Lindop, *Details of Jeremy Stretton*, Heinemann, 1955

Gillian Freeman, *The Liberty Man*, Longmans, 1955

Compton Mackenzie, *Thin Ice*, Chatto & Windus, 1956

Mary Renault, *The Last of the Wine*, Longmans, Green & Co., 1956

Angus Wilson, *Anglo-Saxon Attitudes*, Secker & Warburg, 1956

James Baldwin, *Giovanni's Room*, Michael Joseph, 1957

John Braine, *Room at the Top*, Eyre & Spottiswoode, 1957

Martyn Goff, *The Plaster Fabric*, Putnam, 1957

John Boland, *The League of Gentlemen*, T.V. Boardman & Company, 1958

Robin Maugham, *The Man With Two Shadows*, Four Square, 1958

Michael Nelson, *A Room in Chelsea Square*, Jonathan Cape, 1958

John Wiles, *The Asphalt Playground*, Gollancz, 1958

Angus Wilson, *The Middle Age of Mrs Eliot*, Secker & Warburg, 1958

Paul Buckland, *Chorus of Witches*, W.H. Allen, 1959

James Courage, *A Way of Love*, Jonathan Cape, 1959

Colin MacInnes, *Absolute Beginners*, MacGibbon & Kee, 1959

Simon Raven, *The Feathers of Death*, Anthony Blond, 1959

Mary Renault, *The Charioteer*, Pantheon Books, 1959

J.R. Ackerley, *We Think the World of You*, The Bodley Head, 1960

Lynne Reid Banks, *The L-Shaped Room*, Chatto & Windus, 1960

Allen Drury, *Advise and Consent*, Collins, 1960

Alfred Duggan, *Family Favourites: A Roman Scandal*, Peter Davies, 1960

Colin MacInnes, *Mr Love and Justice*, MacGibbon & Kee, 1960

Andrew Salkey, *Escape to an Autumn Pavement*, Hutchinson, 1960

David Storey, *This Sporting Life*, Longmans, Green & Co., 1960

Maxence Van der Meersch, *Mask of Flesh*, William Kimber, 1960

Eliot George, *The Leather Boys*, Anthony Blond, 1961

Martyn Goff, *The Youngest Director*, Putnam, 1961

Julian Mitchell, *Imaginary Toys*, Hutchinson, 1961

Anthony Burgess, *A Clockwork Orange*, Heinemann, 1962

Anthony Burgess, *The Wanting Seed*, Heinemann, 1962

Stuart Lauder, *Winger's Landfall*, Eyre & Spottiswoode, 1962

Jay Gilbert, *The Goose Girl*, Hutchinson, 1963

Leonard James Harper, *Teddy Boy Ahoy*, Thames-Side Publications, 1963

David Stuart Leslie, *Two Gentlemen Sharing*, Secker & Warburg, 1963

Colin Spencer, *Anarchists in Love*, Eyre & Spottiswoode, 1963

Meg Elizabeth Atkins, *The Gemini*, Peter Owen, 1964

Jenni Hall, *Ask Agamemnon*, Cassell, 1964

Montague Haltrecht, *Jonah and his Mother*, André Deutsch, 1964

Christopher Short, *The Black Room*, Jonathan Cape, 1964

Angus Wilson, *Late Call*, Secker & Warburg, 1964

James Leo Herlihy, *Midnight Cowboy*, Simon & Schuster, 1965

Neville Jackson, *No End to the Way*, Barrie & Rockiff, 1965

George Moor, *The Pole and the Whistle*, Four Square, 1966

Kyle Onstott, Lance Horner, *Child of the Sun*, W.H. Allen & Co., 1966

Hubert Selby Jr, *Last Exit to Brooklyn*, Calder and Boyars, 1966

Michael Campbell, *Lord Dismiss Us*, Heinemann, 1967

Martyn Goff, *Indecent Assault*, André Deutsch, 1967

Simon Raven, *Fielding Gray*, Anthony Blond, 1967

Angus Wilson, *No Laughing Matter*, Secker & Warburg, 1967

James Barlow, *The Burden of Proof*, Hamish Hamilton, 1968

Robin Maugham, *The Second Window*, Heinemann, 1968

Andrew McCall, *The Au Pair Boy*, Antony Blond, 1968

Angus Stewart, *Sandel*, Hutchinson, 1968

Robin Maugham, *The Link*, Heinemann, 1969

Robin Maugham, *The Wrong People*, Heinemann, 1970

Iris Murdoch, *A Fairly Honourable Defeat*, Chatto & Windus, 1970

Ursula Zilinsky, *Middle Ground*, Longman, 1970

OTHER

Homosexuality and Prostitution, A Memorandum of Evidence Prepared by a Special Committee of the Council of the British Medical Association for Submission to the Departmental Committee on Homosexuality and Prostitution, British Medical Association, 1955

Homosexuality: Some Questions and Answers, Albany Trust, 1969

Homosexuals and the Law: An Examination of this Human Problem, Homosexual Law Reform Society, 1959

Lambert and Stamp, Motocinema Harms/Cooper, 2014

Minutes of Evidence Taken at Public Hearings Before the Tribunal Appointed to Inquire into the Vassall Case and Related Matters, Her Majesty's Stationery Office, 1963

Report of the Committee on Homosexual Offences and Prostitution, Her Majesty's Stationery Office, 1957

Report of the Tribunal Appointed to Inquire into the Vassall Case and Related Matters, Her Majesty's Stationery Office, 1963

Sexual Offences: A Report of the Cambridge Department of Criminal Science, MacMillan, 1957

What is Unlawful? Does Innocence Begin Where Crime Ends? Afterthoughts on the Wolfenden Report, Church Information Office, 1959

Sexual Offences: A Report of the Cambridge Department of Criminal Science, Macmillan, 1957

Sexual Offences Act 1956

Sexual Offences Act 1967

Sexual Offences, Consent and Sentencing, Home Office Research Study, No. 54, 1979

Sexual Offenders and Social Punishment: Being the Evidence Submitted on Behalf of the Church of England Moral Welfare Council to the Departmental Committee on Homosexual Offences and Prostitution, with Other Material Relating Thereto, Church Information Board, 1956

The Celluloid Closet, Drakes Avenue Pictures Ltd, 1995

The Problem of Homosexuality: A Memorandum Presented to the Departmental Committee on Homosexual Offences and Prostitution by a Joint Committee Representing The Institute for the Study and Treatment of Delinquency and the Portman Clinic, ISTD, 1957

Towards a Quaker view of Sex, Friends Home Service Committee, 1963

What is Unlawful? Does Innocence Begin Where Crime Ends? Afterthoughts on the Wolfenden Report, Church Information Office, 1959